THE FENCE
AND THE
NEIGHBOR

SUNY series in Jewish Philosophy
Kenneth Seeskin, editor

and

SUNY series in Contemporary Jewish Thought
Richard A. Cohen, editor

THE FENCE AND THE NEIGHBOR

Emmanuel Levinas,
Yeshayahu Leibowitz, and
Israel Among the Nations

ADAM ZACHARY NEWTON

State University
of New York
Press

A University Cooperative Society Subvention Grant was awarded by the University of Texas at Austin to help in the preparation of this book.

Cover photograph: Kadesh Naphtali. American Colony Studio, © 1900. Courtesy Silver Print Collection, Ein Hod, Israel.

Published by
State University of New York Press, Albany

© 2001 State University of New York

Production by Susan Geraghty
Marketing by Anne M. Valentine

Printed in the United States of America

For information, address State University of New York Press,
90 State Street, Suite 700, Albany, NY 12207

Library of Congress Cataloging-in-Publication Data

Newton, Adam Zachary.
   The fence and the neighbor : Emmanuel Levinas, Yeshayahu Leibowitz, and Israel among the nations / Adam Zachary Newton.
      p. cm. — (SUNY series in Jewish philosophy) (SUNY series in contemporary Jewish thought)
   Includes bibliographical references and index.
   ISBN 0-7914-4783-9 (alk. paper) — ISBN 0-7914-4784-7 (pbk. : alk. paper)
      1. Philosophy, Jewish. 2. Philosophy, Modern—20th century. 3. Levinas, Emmanuel. 4.
Leibowitz, Yeshayahu, 1903– 5. Jews—Identity. 6. Jews—Politics and government—1948–
I. Title. II. Series. III. Series: SUNY series in contemporary Jewish thought

   B5800 .N39 2000
   181'.06—dc21

                                                                           00-022597

10 9 8 7 6 5 4 3 2 1

CONTENTS

For Lisa

The caress of love, always the same, in the last accounting . . . is always different and overflows with exorbitance the songs, poems, and admissions in which it is said in so many different ways.

La sagesse de l'amour à le service de l'amour.

—Emmanuel Levinas

Au repoussoir

Time and again, at the end of a working day, I marveled to see that Ferber, with the few lines and shadows that had escaped annihilation, had created a portrait of great vividness. And all the more did I marvel when, the following morning, the moment the model had sat down and he had taken a look at him or her, he would erase the portrait again, and once more set about excavating the features of his model, who by now was distinctly wearied by this manner of working, from a surface already badly damaged by the continual destruction. The facial features and eyes, said Ferber, remained ultimately unknowable for him. He might reject as many as forty variants, or smudge them back into the paper and overdraw new attempts upon them; and if he then decided that the portrait was done, not so much because he was convinced that it was finished as through sheer exhaustion, an onlooker might well feel that it had evolved from a long lineage of gray, ancestral faces, rendered unto ash but still there, as ghostly presence, on the harried paper.

—W. G. Sebald

PREFACE

Fences and Neighbors

Something there is that doesn't love a wall,
That sends the frozen-ground-swell under it,
And spills the upper boulders in the sun,
And makes gaps even two can pass abreast.
The work of hunters is another thing:
I have come after them and made repair
Where they have left not one stone on a stone,
But they would have the rabbit out of hiding,
To please the yelping dogs. The gaps I mean,
No one has seen them made or heard them made,
But at spring mending-time we find them there.
I let my neighbor know beyond the hill;
And on a day we meet to walk the line
And set the wall between us once again.
We keep the wall between us as we go.
To each the boulders that have fallen to each.
And some are loaves and some so nearly balls
We have to use a spell to make them balance:
"Stay where you are until our backs are turned!"
We wear our fingers rough with handling them.
Oh, just another kind of out-door game,
One on a side. It comes to little more:
There where it is we do not need the wall:
He is all pine and I am apple orchard.
My apple trees will never get across
And eat the cones under his pines, I tell him.
He only says, "Good fences make good neighbors."
Spring is the mischief in me, and I wonder
If I could put a notion in his head:
"Why do they make good neighbors? Isn't it
Where there are cows? But here there are no cows.
Before I built a wall I'd ask to know
What I was walling in or walling out,
And to whom I was like to give offense.
Something there is that doesn't love a wall,
That wants it down." I could say "Elves" to him,
But it's not elves exactly, and I'd rather
He said it for himself. I see him there

Bringing a stone grasped firmly by the top
In each hand, like an old-stone savage armed.
He moves in darkness as it seems to me—
Not of woods only and the shade of trees.
He will not go behind his father's saying,
And he likes having thought of it so well
He says again, "Good fences make good neighbors."

—"Mending Wall," by Robert Frost

This is a book about peoplehood and religious self-understanding. But it is also about the reach, the portage, of place. Boundaries, landmarks, homelands, the native and the foreign, are some of its points of reference; "fence" and "neighbor," in multiple senses, are its orienting terms. As an apt place to begin, I am put in mind of the poem by Robert Frost in which such terms figure as both topic and refrain—not least because my own environs, professionally speaking, are fenced by literary studies (there are as many poets mentioned in this preface as philosophers). "He will not go behind his father's saying," says the narrator of Frost's poem at its end, referring to his neighbor. "And he likes having thought of it so well/ He says again, 'Good fences make good neighbors'." "His father's saying," just like his father's fence, is something that gets made, both transversely in space by adjoining neighbors and sequentially in time by fathers and forefathers. Fences make good neighbors, but epigrams do, as well. The saying does the work of fences—as in turn does the poem containing them both.

And so Frost's poem does what much good poetry does: it talks about an object and in so doing talks about itself *as* object, *as* activity. Walls or fences differentiate territory, contain and exclude, delimit and mark boundaries. Poems do this. Homes do this. Consciousness, and the various shapes it assumes through language and other kinds of symbolic action, performs perhaps the most intricate mending/walling of all. In this particular poem about fences and neighbors, natural forces over-write human interventions for form and division; the one mimics the other. But even across the putative division between human and natural expression—"the work of hunters is another thing"—a common act gets recapitulated: invention, making, fashioning. On the one hand, "Something there is that doesn't love a wall . . . *makes* gaps even two can pass abreast. . . . No one has seen them *made* or heard them *made*" (l.10). On the other, "Good fences *make* good neighbors" (ll. 27, 43).

And it is the precise nature of such making that lies at the poem's heart. *Do* fences make neighbors? Or is it the making of fences that permits, serves as the pretext for, other more subtle kinds of making—like speech or "saying?" And there—in language—do fences make good neighbors too? And there—in language—what exactly does setting the wall and keeping the wall between us *do*? What gets walled in, walled out? And what, finally—still on the plane of language—is the relationship, not between pine and apple tree but rather between them both and the wall, its loaves, its balls, and its gaps? "Mending Wall" entertains a twofold task about eventfulness or motion that in the process of describing, it enacts: 1) how to move between the given (or sown or planted—a making that sends or spills) and the fashioned (or manipulated or built—a making that sets or keeps); 2) how to move, one neighbor relative to another: an outdoor game or ritual that makes a "we" of "he" and "I."[1]

And because the poem makes us notice them as more and more objects come into view, the wall not only articulates neighbors, joining while dividing them in space as well as in sound, but it also *presents the occasion for* hunters, rabbits, yelping dogs, imagined cows, elves, fathers, and of course the literary artifact itself. "Mending wall" is the poem's title because it orients everything in it. A fence is what imposes itself upon the landscape and what the landscape in turn unsettles, it gives rabbits a brief edge over hunters and their dogs, it sanctions maxims and even more fanciful uses of language, it makes neighbors neighbors. The poem's speaker says, "I could say 'Elves' to him" (l. 36) as he imagines conversing with his fellow about the "thing" that wants a wall down. "But it's not elves exactly, and I'd rather/He said it for himself." It may be that the poem finally, is about getting (or wanting) someone to speak. As "mending wall" can signify both an activity—*mending the wall*—and a description—*a wall that mends*—so saying refers to both a task or process—*I could say*—and a finished fact or thing—*his father's saying*. In other words, fences possess discursive force, just as neighbors are made by the practices of language, by rituals of articulation.

In the spirit of such practices and rituals, I invoke now another terrain besides literature in which I find myself fenced. It compels loyalties and allegiance of its own, wherein "fence" and "neighbor" promise a different set of significations, unknown to Frost certainly and perhaps to the average literary critic, but no less "poetic" in Frost's own sense of the profoundest poetry containing within itself its own literary criticism, its own theory.[2] The Rabbis of Judaism's Oral Tradition, Sages of the Talmud, *Chazal* in Hebrew, were logicians, rhetoricians, and if we follow the lead of the French-Jewish metaphysician Emmanuel Levinas, philosophers as well. But they were also craftsmen, artisans, and husbanders of the soil—artificers, exemplars of what the Israeli religious thinker Yeshayau Leibowitz calls "praxis." In both capacities the Sages were makers too, and thus not so far removed from the concerns of

Frost's poem as one might at first think. For "mending walls," "fences," and "neighbors" all appear in the Talmud not only as their own concrete points of reference, but also in more figurative, metaphoric connotations still anchored by the sense of simple triconsonantal roots and stems:

1. Two words for "fence" in biblical and rabbinic Hebrew, גדר *geder* and סיג *s'yag*, commonly denote a protective partition. Etymologically, *geder* means "cutting," therefore "setting off" (e.g., *Tos. Sh'biit* III:13); the root meaning of *s'yag* is "to mark off, erect a boundary" (e.g., Deut. 19:14, *lo tasig g'vul re'akha, do not remove your neighbor's landmark*). *Geder* registers the sense of *exclusion*, with connotations of controlling and warding off (the past participle, *gadur*, for instance, means "abstinent"). *S'yag* (or *sug*), on the other hand, suggests a more inward-turning sense, closer to the idea of *enclosure*, of fencing something *in*. In both cases the idea of "fencing" develops much the same way as it does in Frost's poem—as metaphor—using the conditions of agrarian life to talk about human relations. A well-known example: "The *Massorah* [textual tradition] is a fence [*s'yag*] to the Torah; tithes form a fence to wealth; vows are a fence to self-restraint; a fence to wisdom is silence" [*Pirke Avot* 3:17).

2. ריע *re'ah* ("fellow," "neighbor," from a root meaning "to join") in both Scripture and the Oral Law can designate Jews or non-Jews, depending on the context, but typically signifies the former for the purpose of legal enactments, as does the term "person." It belongs to a cluster of similar denotative concepts such as *ger* (stranger), *akher* (other), and *karev* (a root that underpins the words for drawing near, offering, mediation, and consanguineous relationship).[3] But for the purposes of this inquiry, like the wall or the mending of it, the word itself introduces the question of particularity in human relationship: just who will count—by being differentiated as such—as my neighbor?

It is this move from exclusion and enclosure—*walling in and walling out*—to human interposition—*setting and keeping the wall between us*—that compactly describes the thematic arc of this book. In other words, from within a rabbinic framework, when adjusted to the dimensions of nation and peoplehood, "Mending Wall"'s abutment of persons discloses another, intrinsically Jewish sense of fence-and-neighbor. Frost's poem, then, provides me with a lexical point of departure, a thematic orientation, for exploring this other terrain. And I do so here by juxtaposing the work of the two contemporary Jewish thinkers already mentioned, born within three years of one another and recently deceased within two: Emmanuel Levinas and Yeshayahu Leibowitz. They are themselves neighbors of a sort, at once joined and divided by the fences of philosophy, cultural/religious heritage, and nationality.

As "fence" and "neighbor" thus provide the figurative terms for my inquiry, its substantive terms are similarly linked. As with Levinas's and Leibowitz's own work, they are drawn from two not always congruent intellectual traditions: (1) rabbinic—*halakhah* (law) and *aggadah* (lore) as the principal forms of Talmudic discourse; and (2) Western philosophical—*politics* and *ethics* as the principal domains at issue in a consideration of Levinas's and Leibowitz's essays on Judaism. Within each discursive tradition, the terms themselves become linguistic or conceptual neighbors articulated by a fence that differentiates as well as joins. The two pairings—*halakhah/aggadah* and *ethics/politics*—serve this book as a whole in the identical way that the title of "Mending Wall" reflexively serves the meaning of Frost's poem; and as in the poem, figure and substance in this book become coefficient.

As I have hinted, Levinas and Leibowitz will themselves be correlated in the following pages as *geographic and cultural* neighbors divided and joined by a *Judaically anchored* fence. Neighbors, because of where each has come from in Jewish Eastern Europe. Divided and joined by a Judaically anchored fence, in the sense of the enclosures and exclusions signifying the margins of philosophical and Jewish practice, as exposed by the places each has ended up, where each has made his home. Very like the concrete plane of reference in Frost's poem, "fence-and-neighbor" can also signify origins and destinations, *aliyah* or going up and *yeridah* or going down—what the poem calls "sending and spilling"/"setting and keeping." In Leibowitz's and Levinas's cases, this means intellectual itineraries and Jewish identities that, as Levinas piquantly phrases it, cannot help but walk a tightrope.

Intentionally then, I have chosen fence-and-neighbor as a thematic trope flexible enough to let me thread together several interrelated concerns. I use it primarily as a device to bridge two figures each of whom espouses transcendental categories or possibilities for a legitimate Judaism in the modern world—to couple them as philosophers of Judaism. Accordingly, after an introduction that locates them both, philosophically and Jewishly, a chapter is devoted respectively to Levinas as ethicist and Leibowitz as halakhist. Implicit in these chapters and linking them, however, is also an awareness of the specific cultural and political contexts that impinge upon Levinas's and Leibowitz's intellectual itineraries—the *places* the men have been and carry with them. The final chapter, consequently, returns to more concrete ramifications of place and its impingements for two thinkers on whom modern Jewish, modern European, and modern Middle-Eastern history weigh heavily, and for whom the Holocaust and the establishment of a modern Jewish state represent the most compelling fence-linked neighbors in twentieth-century Jewish life.

As a final turn of the screw, I conclude this preface and inflect the trope of fence-and-neighbor one last time by affirming a certain authorial stake in these matters myself: as regards intellectual itinerary, Jewish identity, and a certain tightrope of my own. I will speak to the first two elements now, and let the third take shape across the pages that follow. *The Fence and the Neighbor* forms the third part of a critical trilogy that began with my first book, *Narrative Ethics*, and continued with *Facing Black and Jew: Literature as Public Space*. I did not plan these books in a ternary structure. But it became obvious to me as the idea germinated for this book while I was completing the second, that all three formed not only a distinct group but a sequence, moving ever more intimately from intellectual predilections to cultural and finally to religious ones. As archaeology, the three books work through the strata of a self sedimented in the inverse direction.

Each book has applied some dimension of Emmanuel Levinas's thought to critical practice, and in so doing, consciously echoed Levinas's sense of ethics itself *as practice*, as the *undertaking or undergoing of answerabilities*. Each, moreover, as a kind of fugue, has exposed Levinas's voice to other voices sounding contrapuntally against his—sometimes at the same pitch and at other times differently accented or colored: first Mikhail Bakhtin and Stanley Cavell, subsequently Walter Benjamin, and now Yeshayahu Leibowitz. In the words of the poet Adam Zagajewski (a demi-namesake), "Only others save us, even though solitude tastes like opium/ . . . in return someone else's poem offers the fidelity of a sober dialogue" (60). For me, this principle does double duty: it operates at the core of my religious beliefs and practice, and it explains my critical temperament.

In each book I have conducted my own dialogue with Levinas's thought as I have sought, or needed, to place that thought in call-and-response with that of Others. Here too, I would like to think that my methodology proceeds in the spirit of Levinas's fundamental principle that the self is always in a state of *turning* to Others and listening for what Robert Frost calls counterspeech: strophe and antistrophe, word and answer-word. Acoustically, I have amplified the volume of my own Jewishness and its centrality in my life a notch or two louder each time—from the *sotto voce* of *Narrative Ethics* to the double-voiced call-and-response of *Facing Black and Jew* to the sustained declamations of *The Fence and the Neighbor*. If, as Osip Mandelstam wrote, "It is enough for [one] to tell of the books he has read, and his biography is done" (110), in my case, it is the books and the writers I have chosen, or needed, to write about that perhaps say as much about me as they say about themselves.[4] And though like many an author perhaps, no doubt I would unsay or resay parts of them if I could, with each book I have conducted an ever-more public voicing of private self in the midst of critical inquiry.

Each book, finally, has sought like Frost's poem to enact what it describes—each in dynamic form as well as content aspiring to an ethics of criticism. When I first thought to carve out an intellectual and professional niche in literary studies, ethics as such was a somewhat moribund affair, far from the hum and buzz of frontier criticism. A decade later, the word itself now appears prominently in book titles, calls for papers, a focal point for special issues of professional journals and conferences. When I first thought of applying certain Levinasian themes to literary criticism, like the sporadic rainfall in the Land of Israel, only a few studies of Levinas had been written or published and not all of his work translated. A decade later, with each successive year, a Nile of titles regularly irrigates the critical landscape. The metaphor puts me in mind again of Mandelstam, who wrote that the acquisition of a public voice depends on listening to "the swelling noise of the age . . . bleached by the foam on the crest of its wave." Thus, the poet says, does one "track down the age, the noise and the germination of time" (110). But far from such deliberate pursuit, the tidal pull toward ethics in my own writing has only gradually revealed itself to me as a personal validation of a related idea that we *arrogate* a certain critical or philosophical voice and theme in order to gave shape to the place of story in our lives—as Stanley Cavell has put it, "that each one here has a story, to begin with, the story of his or her path here, as if to make credible to oneself the sheer fact that one is here" (*A Pitch of Philosophy*, 12). And indeed, to show how that is true for Emmanuel Levinas and Yeshayahu Leibowitz is the story of this book—borrowing a page from Levinas, to model one way in which to read their stories and trace their *signature*.[5]

But I would be less than scrupulously accountable to the fence—or tightrope—that makes my own books each other's neighbors, that anchors their common story and gives them a common voice, if I did not lay personal claim at the outset and thus in my own capacity *sign the world*.[6] As expressed Judaically, "Rabbi Zusya said, 'In the other world I will not be asked, Why were you not Moses? I will be asked, Why were you not Zusya?'" Although the conversation this book initiates must necessarily "overflow the admissions" embodying it here, let me therefore put my signature to it as the most recent installment of my story too, in memory of my father *zt"l*, who passed from this life on the 23rd of Tevet, 5759, and in the name of my mother, *ir tsu lange yor.*

ACKNOWLEDGMENTS

In a letter to Levinas, Martin Buber notes that the Hebrew verb form הודות first means *to come in support of someone* and only later *to thank*, in contrast to Germanic and Romance languages where "to thank" means *having in one's thoughts or remembering someone*. "He who thanks rallies in support of the one thanked," Buber says. "He will now—and from now on—be his ally. This includes, to be sure, the idea of memory, but implies more. The fact occurs not only within the soul: it proceeds from there toward the world, to become act and event. Now to come in support of someone in this way is to confirm him in his existence." For turning the face, then, as trusted friends and readers, I thank—*I come in support of, I confirm*—Craig Ackermann, Rabbi Michael Balinsky, Shamir Caplan, Evan Carton, Adam Cohen, Itzik Gottesman, Harold Liebowitz, Jo Keroes, Esther Raizen, Shawn Ruby, Shaindy Rudoff, Andew Sekel, Charles Selengut, and for his matchless sonority, David Suchoff. All, in knowing me, know the bifold between not just fence-and-neighbor but fox-and-hedgehog, too. A subvention grant from the University Cooperative Society at the University of Texas at Austin partially underwrote production costs. Production itself was expertly facilitated by my editor James Peltz, copyeditor Susan Geraghty, and typesetter Skip Baker. Finally, I am profoundly indebted to the *Rabbeim* of Yeshivat Har Etzion whose *shiurim* on the Israel Koschitzky Virtual Beit Midrash have offered me a *makom Torah*.

ABBREVIATIONS

David Hartman:

CV	*Conflicting Visions*
LC	*A Living Covenant*

Emmanuel Levinas:

BPW	*Basic Philosophical Writings*
BV	*Beyond the Verse*
CPP	*Collected Philosophical Papers*
DF	*Difficult Freedom*
FTF	*Face to Face with Levinas*
ITN	*In the Time of Nations*
NTR	*Nine Talmudic Readings*
OS	*Outside the Subject*
PN	*Proper Names*
TI	*Totality and Infinity*

משה קבל תורה מסיני, ומסרה ליהושע, ויהושע לזקנים, וזקנים
לנביאים, ונביאים מסרוה לאנשי כנסת הגדולה. הם אמרו שלשה
דברים, הוו מתונים בדין, והעמידו תלמידים הרבה, ועשו סיג לתורה

אבות א,א

*Moses received the Torah at Sinai and handed it down to Joshua; Joshua
to the elders; The elders to the prophets; and the prophets handed it
down to the men of the Great Assembly. The latter said three things: Be
patient in the administration of justice; cause many students to stand;
and make a fence for the Torah.*

—Tractate *Pirke Avot* (Chapters of the Fathers) 1:1

דאמר ליה ההוא מינא ללב כהנא אמריתו נדה שרי לייחודי בהדי גברא
אפשר אש בנעורת ואינה מהבהבת אמר ליה התורה העידה עלינו סוגה
בשושנים שאפילו כסוגה בשושנים לא בהן יפרצו.

סנהדרין לז,א

*This is what was said by a certain heretic to R. Kahana: "Your law per-
mits a man to stay alone with his wife during the days of her menstrua-
tion. Is it possible that flax and fire should be together and should not
burn?" And he answered: "The Torah has testified for us, fenced about
with lilies (Song of Songs 7:3)—that is, even a fence of lilies is sufficient
for us—and it will never be broken."*

—Tractate *Sanhedrin* 37a

*To have an outside, to listen to what comes from outside—oh miracle of
exteriority! That is what is called knowledge or Torah.*

—Emmanuel Levinas

*The uniqueness of the Jewish people is not a fact; it is an endeavor. The
holiness of Israel is not a reality but a task. . . . The ultimate meaning of
the Day of Atonement is that man, as such, has no intrinsic value; he
acquires value only insofar as he stands before God. . . . Israel has no
intrinsic holiness and the Mitzvoth do not derive from its holiness.
Rather it is the Mitzvoth, when observed, that confer sanctity upon the
land.*

—Yeshayahu Leibowitz

The autobiographical dimension of philosophy is internal to the claim that philosophy speaks for the human, for all; that is its necessary arrogance. The philosophical dimension of autobiography is that the human is representative, say, imitative, that each life is exemplary of all, a parable of each; that is humanity's commonness, which is internal to its endless denials of commonness.

—Stanley Cavell

INTRODUCTION

Signing the World

ANECDOTES

Upon recently rereading Emil Fackenheim's *Encounters between Judaism and Modern Philosophy: A Preface to Future Jewish Thought—* a truly formative text for me—I was transfixed by a footnote that a first reading of the book many years ago had perfunctorily filtered. Indeed, there was no particular reason then that I should have remarked on it. It appears but one page from the end, and yet this time around minutes passed before I could actually leave off staring at it and finish the book; I felt like some lesser-Champollion at a more modest Rosetta, or maybe like anyone visited by the uncanny who has ever matched description to name, name to face, or a face, in this particular instance, to another face.

In the concluding chapter that corresponds to the note, Fackenheim discusses the cases of Sartre and Heidegger, two philosophers in our own century who, more culpably perhaps then Kant and Hegel before them (the book's principal examples), failed signally to open philosophy to the *lived specificities* of Jewish existence—at the very moment in Western history when, more urgently than ever before, Jewish history, Jewish experience, and Judaism *in its metaphysical integrity* needed to be given voice and be heard speaking in that voice. This is the footnote:

> In his essay, "Heidegger and God—and Professor Jonas," [William] Richardson reports the following anecdote:
>
> > Two years ago at a reception someone who had read my book made reference to the chapter on the Epilogue to *What is Metaphysics?* that begins (banally enough) by saying: "1943 was a prolific year." The gentleman said: "I remember 1943 well, Father. I was just talking with some of your friends about it, regaling them with amusing stories—they laughed and laughed. You know in 1943, I was in one of the concentration camps. It was a very prolific year indeed." [263]

That one-of-a-kind surge of recognition: I even checked the source to make sure that Fackenheim had not left anything out, or abbreviated it in some way.[1] But yes, there at the end of the article by William J. Richardson, S.J., in a thirty-year-old issue of *Thought*, was the same anecdote, its anonymity still safely preserved, its ring no less hollow in my ears.

For it was that very anecdote that formed the centerpiece of its author's presentation, "The Irresponsible Subject," some thirty years later at the *International Conference on the Thought of Emmanuel Levinas* at Loyola University in 1993. This time, however, as Levinas the Platonist might say, "speech attended manifestation," clandestinity gave way to disclosure, and anonymity ceded to a face in what, from my seat in the lecture hall, seemed an astounding piece of inadvertent theater. For as Professor Richardson now disclosed, the "someone who had read my book," the "gentleman" of the mordant and flinty wit interned in a concentration camp, was none other than Levinas himself. The "reception" mentioned in the footnote thirty years previous was in fact the congratulatory party following Richardson's successful Ph.D. defense at Louvain, in which Levinas participated as an examiner.[2] According to this now-detailed account, Levinas tapped the philosopher on the shoulder, made his remark, and, "spinning on his heels," departed. From interpellation to submerged allusion to charged revelation, the encounter, evidently, had haunted Richardson to this day. One could call it: *Portrait of the Philosopher as Inspector Javert.* Or, *The Case Against Levinas.* Or more simply, *The Uncanny.*

A *Festschrift* volume was published in Professor Richardson's honor two years later in 1995 entitled *From Phenomenology to Thought, Errancy, and Desire: Essays in the Honor of William S. Richardson, S.J.* In it, Charles Scott, a contributor who also presented at the Loyola conference, writes an informal "Letter to Bill Richardson" which argues for the free-standing quality of Heidegger's thought in relation to Christian belief. I let an excerpt from it now precede the record of my own response because it so ironically bears out—and compulsively repeats—the shadow cast by the word "errancy" in the book's title: a continuum encompassing Richardson, Heidegger before him, and the myriad pairs of twentieth-century ears misattuned to hear philosophically minded Jewish voices speaking at their own distinctive pitch of philosophy. (This is also, appropriately enough, the main import of Fackenheim's book.)

> You have been speaking indirectly and a lot recently about what I would call original sin. I thought you addressed the issue effectively in your paper at the International Conference on Levinas in Chicago last year. In your introduction to it, you described a complex situation in which Levinas acted in an apparently irresponsible way that violated his own values. It was a harmless enough, if startling and disconcerting occurrence of everyday psychopathology, and it was many-layered and complex. But it showed to you, I thought, the importance of hard, psychological investigation and judgment, and it showed, I thought

you also suggested, an *opening to something beyond* the limits of such judgment, *an opening to a fallenness from God* that cuts through all of our lives and gives them definitive division from the Source of life and redemption. This fallenness can be experienced as a kind of madness, a living despair that cannot recognize itself in its own enactment, particularly in its enactments that seem wise and good and responsible. I took you to be suggesting that no one, including Levinas, could eliminate the error that seams our lives and that we need reference to something beyond what Levinas can think to account for his and our lapse: his lapse *opened beyond what he could see and perhaps beyond what he was willing to know.* (229–230, my italics)

If the audience's response to Professor Richardson's paper at Loyola was any gauge, the imputation of "psychopathology" there was both startling and unseemly, and continues to be so here in Scott's recounting. Levinas's symbolic action, we were told, was the expression of a sedimented heritage welling up from the unconscious. With a few obligatory and hedged speculations about Levinas's family history, Richardson's ad hominem reproof mounted a facile, blunt Freudianism (through Lacan) whose clinician's veneer barely disguised the umbrage underneath—apposite enough, for an etiology of repression. Several audience members pointed out that the ethics of Levinas's jarring remark those many years ago could be seen as not only consistent with his philosophical commitment to the event of alterity but, perhaps more importantly, far closer in spirit to an ethical sense embodied by Torah—call it halakhic probity—than an enlightenment liberalism easily disposed to conflate ethics with etiquette, and to paper over ordeal with civility.[3]

That "The Irresponsible Subject," itself uncanny, generated a haunting afterlife in the form of the "Letter," leaves me disconsolate but unsurprised, for the latter picks up more or less where the former left off. Where Professor Richardson's *j'accuse* suggested that Levinas failed the test of his own stringencies, a disconnect between the man and his thought (and an accusation more commonly directed at Heidegger), the letter blithely *translates* Levinas's behavior into non-Jewish categories of sin and redemption, with Levinas again falling all too humanly short. Human error is "fallennesss," and fallenness answers to the corrective of divine dispensation. Now, the letter's principal concern—whether Heidegger should be understood as translating dimensions of Christian faith into philosophical categories (the position ascribed to Richardson) or whether he in fact resists such a move—animates me much less than this other, less innocent kind of translation. Levinas confronted Richardson in Louvain as Jew in the first person. Yet, the indifferent absorption of him into the universalizing substrate of non-Jewish theology displayed here is never questioned by either of his critics for a moment. As

Levinas has always been quite careful to distinguish the *formal* nature of his work from either religion or theology (whatever the tangencies), the unselfconscious un-Jewishness of the terms here, to my ears, sounds doubly egregious. Yet again, an errancy *ascribed* to Levinas more aptly *describes* the conditions motivating a judgment of him instead.

For "original sin" in this sense does not speak from within a Judaic vocabulary, and "including Levinas" assimilates him even where he might exclude himself.[4] The insinuation of "an opening to a fallenness from God" that risks forcing him outside of Jewish self-understanding, strands him there. Implied in this view, what consigns Levinas's "lapsed" condition to "madness" or "living despair," more than the psychopathology itself, must be an entrapment within its own insufficiently explanatory religious categories: "it cannot recognize itself in its own enactment." Levinas's lapse and perhaps even his ethics must therefore be referred to a more transcendent and encompassing judge than even he appears to know: the "Source of life and redemption," an infinite *more* infinite, an absolute *more* absolute, a beyond even *more* beyond than Levinas "can think to account." It is the *closure* in Levinas's thought that therefore marks an opening.[5]

And yet whatever it may have to say about Heidegger (or its addressee for that matter), to the degree that the letter ascribes its litany of "openings"—"an opening to something beyond"/ "an opening to a fallenness to God"/ "his lapse opened beyond what he could see and . . . know" to a failure enacted by Levinas's vision, it records a blindness and closure of its own. Blindness, because the "beyond" is such an essential category *within* Levinas's ethical philosophy—not only the place where God speaks and human others are manifest, but also the excluded middle named Judaism, or (as he himself phrases it in an essay on S. Y. Agnon), the resonance of the language called Hebrew on several registers (*PN* 10)—that to intimate a beyond that beyond would seem to find Levinas *religiously* wanting. Closure, because what precisely fails to find an opening, a hearing, a reckoning here, is the Jewish specificity of Levinas's person and experience. "Man must be able to listen and hear and reply," Levinas writes, in one of several pieces on Heidegger (*DF* 232). That an entire section of Levinas's book, *Difficult Freedom: Essays on Judaism*—about ecumenicism, no less—is entitled *Openings* and that one of the first essays in that book contains the italicized heading, "*How can we hear the voice of Israel*" [12][6] makes the irony here sufficiently glaring without my help. In short, which *errancy* should give us greater pause here?

To return full circle to Fackenheim:

> Philosophers keep on acting, as if, philosophically, there is no difference between the six million and one child dying of cancer, just as the-

ologians keep on acting as if, theologically, the "case" of Auschwitz were "covered" by Good Friday or the ninth of Av. So far as most philosophers and theologians are concerned there simply is no Holocaust. (*To Mend the World*, 11)[7]

From the letter to Professor Richardson, one would simply not know that Richardson was being held to account by Levinas in his capacity *as witness to National Socialist barbarism*. The exact reverse of the anecdote as quoted by Fackeneheim's book, what the letter does is to supply *merely* a name—third personally—minus any other pertinent information. And the reversal effected by that anecdote in all three of its "signed," "unsigned," and third-party versions is stunning: not the political impropriety of Heidegger's complicity with such barbarism, but rather the social impropriety of Levinas's pointing it out, is the censurable, errant (peccant?) thing.

"*Banally enough*" is how Professor Richardson describes his choice to begin a chapter on Heidegger that reads "1943 was a prolific year."[8] For contrast's sake, consider a sentence like the following, from Tomas Venclova's biography of Aleksander Wat, internee of the Gulag: "If the year 1940 was one of the most sinister in record history, it was particularly disastrous for the citizens of prewar Poland" (139). Such a sentence has moral *heft*—what Wat, elsewhere in the book, calls the "weight of words." Likewise, while speaking in 1957 at an Abbey in Morocco about the common monotheistic language shared by Christians and Jews, Levinas interrupted himself to testify, "In front of the representatives of so many nations, some of whom have no Jews in their numbers, *I should like to remind you* of what the years 1933 to 1945 were like for the Jews of Europe" (*DF* 11, my italics).[9] Such *reminder* is really what lies at the heart of his original rebuke to Richardson (from around the same time). "What was unique between 1940 and 1945 was the abandonment . . . the dropping away of all forms," Levinas writes in a more recent essay from *Proper Names* (119, 121). One can simply no longer speak lightly of the year 1943 in Europe; the date has acquired a density of its own: *numerical, atomic* weight.

"Judaism is an extreme consciousness"—independent of history as עבודה ומצוה, worship and service, but also seared into it as what (with conspicuous generosity and mindfulness), he often pointedly calls the experience of "Passion" (*DF* 12; *BV* 2, 6; *PN* 120). "To have an outside, to listen to what comes from outside—oh miracle of exteriority! That is what is called knowledge or Torah" (*DF* 29)—another reminder that Judaism, religiously understood, and the Jewish people, historically comprehended, signify for him preeminently a *vigilance* and exorbitant *care*, the difficult freedom of speaking and hearing as ethical, religious demands.

Nothing more dramatically opened up a crevasse between Jewish and non-Jewish scholars of Levinas for me as this improvident moment shortly before the Jewish Sabbath was to begin, at the St. Ignatius of Loyola University in Chicago.[10] (That Professor Richardson had misapplied an earlier comment of mine about "halakhic probity" to his own circumstances; and that my own Levinasian certainties were soon to bear the reticulum of what also indelibly "seams our lives"—the latticework on the heart left by Others—only magnifies retrospectively my personal stake in this particular "knot of correspondence," as Edmond Jabès might call it, "of things likely and unlikely.") It seems as manifestly clear to me now as then that the bicameral nature of Levinas's writing—two primary books of philosophy together with various monograph/essays, and a body of Talmudic readings and essays on Judaism—together with Levinas's own *personal* rapprochement between Athens and Jerusalem: this dual allegiance is something that his readers either feel themselves answerable to, or they do not. Few things are more distressing in this regard than to witness the cascade of philosophic treatments of Levinas that resist his own generous invitation to *encounter* philosophy from within the Judaic textual tradition he reads so closely.[11] When philosophy becomes autobiography in Cavell's sense, and autobiography, cultural inheritance, notice is placed on the vocation of academic philosophizing, that it begin *to listen to what comes from outside.*

On its face, the Jewish portion of the Levinasian bifold cannot be adequately understood independent of its rabbinic and biblical sources in concert with the philosophical critique to which Levinas subjects them.[12] But I would go further, to make the claim for Levinas as *Jewish philosopher* and *philosopher-Jew*: that is, despite his own professed distinction between the kinds of texts he writes,[13] someone whose stake in continental philosophy is webbed by Judaic tissues of meaning and the sinew of Jewish experience, who with exemplary care and modesty stages an encounter between Judaism and modern philosophy.[14] A glance at the essays collected in *Difficult Freedom, Beyond the Verse, In the Time of Nations* as well as the Talmudic readings themselves is sufficient to show how the substantive and figural terms of Levinas's philosophy are carried over into this other register and revoiced with a Jewish accent. As Jacob Meskin has put it, "to ignore this interconnection is to lose the full complexity of Levinas's work and its vital resistance to easy categorization" (*The Other in Jewish Thought and History*, 403). Steven S. Schwartzschild is even more pointed: "I would undertake to write a full Jewish, even Rabbinic, commentary (*perush*, with numerous cross-references) to any passage in Levinas' philosophical works, and I feel certain that he himself knows this is right" (105).[15] *Philosophy*, as Levinas understands the task, mirrors rabbinic

Judaism as "the ceaseless task of reinterpreting the text of reality so as to bring out the ethical relation dissimulated within it" (418). This is the arc from *perush* (commentary) to *hiddush* (insight). The text of Scripture encountered in religious study, in the midst of others who study alongside and across from me,

> beyond what it wants me to know, co-ordinates me with the other to whom I speak; it signifies in every discourse from the face of the other, hidden from sight yet unforgettable. . . . My co-ordination with the other in language is the expression of commandments received: writing is always prescriptive and ethical, the Word of God which commands and vows me to the other, a holy writing before being a sacred text. (*BV* xii)

The hard labor of reading and study and interpretation, textual analogues for ethical responsibility: these acquire meaning for Levinas from within the practice, millennia-old, of *talmud torah*—the study of Scripture and commentary as the prince of commandments and the quintessence of religiosity. The ethical subject as one summoned forth from autonomy to severe answerability, the facing Other who is the very event of ethics, the insomnia, ceaseless vigilance, and vulnerability suspending this Self and this Other in ethical equipoise: in Levinas's Talmudic readings and essays, these signify nothing more or less than *Jews* and *Judaism*, a stubborn presence that must haunt any reckoning with Levinas's philosophical work that conveniently elides it.

"This first inequality [of the Other's hunger] perhaps defines Judaism"; "the waiting for the Messiah marks the very duration of time"; "Jews wish not to be possessed but to be responsible"; "Judaism has discovered man in the nudity of his face"; "Judaism is an extreme consciousness. . . . Ethics is its primordial religious emotion"; "the knowledge of God comes to us like a commandment, like a *Mitzvah*—to know God is to know what must be done"; "Israel's unrepentant eschatology . . . the scandal of the Jews as a chosen people!": in such assertions and numerous others, Levinas reveals the work of philosophy—as undertaken by him—to be the practice of Jewish identity and the task, imposed by Judaism, of unsatisfiable *obligation*, of difficult freedom.

After Maimonides I can think of no other post–rabbinic Jewish thinker who has forced a comparable dialogue between "Greek" and "Hebrew." Or to be precise, "Greek" and "Hebrew/Aramaic," for Levinas, crucially and uniquely among modern European Jewish philosophers, turns not to the Bible but to *the Bible interpreted*—the Talmud, the privileged text of rabbinic Judaism. "The Judaism with a historic reality—Judaism, neither more nor less—is rabbinic" (*DF* 12).[16] Or as he says in another place, "The Jew of the Talmud must take precedence

over the Jew of the Psalms" (271). After Spinoza (and far more profoundly *than* Spinoza) I can think of no other philosopher-Jew who has
made a bolder bid for self-exposure to a Jewish past and a modern historical present, and to be encountered in just that dual capacity by readers.[17] Situating Levinas solely in the context of German postidealism,
French phenomenology, or postmodernism (Heidegger, Derrida, Lacan,
Jabès) risks a truncated Levinas; alternatively, linking him primarily to
what Fackenheim has called the "stateless Jewish philosophies" of the
twentieth century (Cohen, Buber, Rosenzwieg), risks scanting his philosophical investment in *Torah she'bal peh* (the Oral Tradition).[18] But in
the case of his aggrieved interlocutor and epistolary critic who risk effacing Levinas in their own acts of 'translating' him, much as Fackenheim
wrote of Heidegger, perhaps one must say, finally: "alas, the 'hearing'
Denker . . . to this day shows no signs of listening" (227).

The Levinas conference, then, was a moment even more formative
than my reading of Fackenheim some years before, and the convergence
of the two explains to a certain measure why I have come to write this
book: the uses of philosophy by post-Holocaust Jewish thinkers, and the
Jewish identity that conditions, even alters, the stakes of such philosophizing. But where Levinas appears in Fackenheim only peripherally,
muffled and veiled as it were by Richardson's anecdote,[19] he is placed in
full view and given a hearing in my own inquiry with the kind of seriousness that Fackenheim accords Kant and Hegel in his. As the latter
represent for Fackenheim stillborn opportunities for modern philosophy's encounter with Judaism and the Jewish role in modern history, so
the former may bear redemptory fruit here, and in that way take up the
challenge of Fackenheim's stated intent for his book—"a preface to
future Jewish thought"—in earnest.

It is in another of Fackenheim's writings, opportunely enough, that
I came upon a second anecdote shortly after I made the Levinas connection, that, while more frank in its naming of names, more galvanic
in its drama, and more Jewish in its accents—and thus altogether, more
Jewish—affords me the same advantage of ushering onto the stage the
other figure whose formidable presence will loom over this book.

At a Tel Aviv conference in the late 1980s—on the film *Shoah* yet!—
Yeshayahu Leibowitz asserted that what mattered was the survival of
Judaism, not that of Jews. Claude Lanzmann, the guest of honor, was
scandalized. He would ask just one question of the professor but
would have nothing more to say to him after that: "Where were you
during the Shoah?" Leibowitz replied that he had been in Palestine,
with Rommel at the gates, and that if the Shoah had also wiped out the
Yishuv he would think no differently. With Lanzmann not saying any-
more, it fell to me to answer and this, I felt, should be in behalf of

Judaism as much as of Jews. "If Professor Leibowitz says that Judaism would survive the murder of the last Jew he cannot be serious. He is joking about a desperately serious subject." I was booed by his supporters, and the two of us have not spoken to each other since. ("A Retrospective," 244)[20]

In this instance, of course, it is not Jewish singularity that strikes the dissonant chord, but rather discord and contestation among Jews themselves. Whereas in Richardson's presentation and the letter following it, "Jew" is the discreetly omitted third term, here it both defines the subject and describes the participants.

As a contemporary figure on the intellectual landscape Yeshayahu Leibowitz is no doubt much less familiar to readers than Emmanuel Levinas, and to illuminate each through the other's borrowed light is another reason that I have written this book. Leibowitz is probably most famous in his own right for just the kind of iconoclasm recounted above, and the personalized component to his thought that he lays claim to here—"in Palestine, with Rommel at the gates"—together with its counterpart in Levinas will be my special concern in the chapters that follow. But here let me simply point to what chiefly arrests my attention: the *anecdotal* or *offhand* as a certain kind of biographical fate. Fackenheim's essay is about himself, just as Professor Richardson's original piece in *Thought* was principally about Heidegger, but, as before, a visitation momentarily interrupts the discursive action only to haunt it thenceforward[21]— ghostly presences (W. G. Sebald's phrase), on the harried paper.

To clarify: it is not the anecdotal per se that I have in mind when I speak of a certain kind of biographical fate. Rather, it is how, in both these instances, intellectual figures—and the work for which they are known—get condensed into parables which serve either as ideological proof (Leibowitz) or moral reproof (Levinas), when it is a far more nuanced awareness of precisely the men's *biographies*, as Jews whose lives straddle the twelve year span in Europe from 1933 to 1945 and the declaration of the State of Israel in 1948, that might significantly inform a fresh reception of their thought. And while I do not think of commensurating the very different contexts for these two anecdotes, the stories themselves dovetail in being each a mini-morality play with its chosen protagonist as cameo object lesson. Levinas and Leibowitz are both noted only in passing.[22]

GENEALOGY

Let me then briefly reintroduce them here. Emmanuel Levinas, born in Kovno (1906), dies in France (1996); Yeshayahu Leibowitz, born in

Riga (1903), dies in Israel (1994).[23] Each is brought up in a household where Judaism and European culture intermingle and upon which education in philosophy supervenes—as a vocation for Levinas, and for Leibowitz, an adjunct to doctoral study in chemistry and medicine. Each bears witness to twentieth-century Jewish displacement and catastrophe. Each is an austere advocate of an austerely Jewish transcendentalism in uneasy relationship with both normative Jewish belief and the concrete reality of a Jewish State; in Levinas's case, this takes the form of an exorbitant metaphysic, in Leibowitz's, an astringent theory of praxis. Each often models a religious anthropology on the figure of Abraham—in Leibowitz's case, the Abraham of the *akedah* (the binding of Isaac, in Gen. 22:1) in Levinas's, of *lekh lekha* (God's command to Abraham to leave his land and his kindred, in Gen. 12:1).[24] Each is a commanding and uncompromising iconoclast. And each, finally, exhibits shades of both *maskil* (beneficiary of Enlightenment *Wissenschaft*) and *mitnagid* (the product of a sober intellectual Lithuanian Orthodox tradition associated most famously with R. Joseph Soloveitchik in our own time (1903–1993) and R. Eliahu ben Solomon, the Gaon of Vilna two centuries earlier).

Juxtaposing them in this way even preliminarily announces an intrinsically warranted relationship that makes its own strong case as an alternative to couplings of Levinas with the usual suspects of postmodern philosophizing on one side and of modern Jewish philosophizing on the other. It also corrects for the scant discussion of Leibowitz that tends to treat him as an entirely singular presence. But to go further and illuminate each thinker in the borrowed light of the other not only casts new light upon them both but discloses them in ways that each, independently, might not as transparently reflect. A set of common features—the specific biblical or rabbinic allusions each regularly and characteristically uses, or the particular philosophical countertext (or foil, in Leibowitz's case) each chooses—places them in peculiarly clarifying mutuality. That interchange, in turn, becomes all the more fruitful when seen against a background of modern Jewish philosophy from which the two already idiosyncratically stand out.

It would be misleading, however, if I did not just as swiftly assert a disparity between them. No, they are not commensurate as original philosophical minds. Where Levinas may well be this century's most important continental philosopher (certainly its greatest Jewish philosopher), Leibowitz I would characterize as a fascinating if comparatively marginalized religious thinker, even within Jewish circles. Coupling the two of them, however—with each performing the role of *eizer k'negdo*, a helpmate *against* the other (Gen. 2:18)—resonates for me far more compellingly than customary and overly repeated linkages of Levinas and Heidegger or Derrida, Levinas and Blanchot or Lacan, even Levinas and Buber or Rosenzweig.

What I would like to underscore in this book, through a counterpoint with Leibowitz's halakhism, is Levinas's self-positioning *ke-ilu kiblah me har-Sinai*—as a link in the unbroken chain of tradition. Associated exclusively with Rosenzweig, Buber, or Hermann Cohen, Levinas eludes a contextualization against the background of twentieth-century Jewish religious thought that would typically include figures like R. Abraham Isaac Kook, R. Joseph Soloveitchik, or more recently, Eliezer Berkovits, and David Hartman.[25] Classed as a continental philosopher in the company of other continental thinkers, his Judaism as much as his Jewishness become the stuff of phenomenological *epoché*—defeasible features, to be bracketed off. Leibowitz has fared little better, as a foil for Maimonides and R. Joseph Soloveitchik[26] (although propitiously enough for my purposes, he is mentioned in passing but respectfully in one of Levinas's own early essays).

The section that now follows elaborates this preliminary counterpoint by treating Levinas and Leibowitz each separately while making them converge around the shared questions of the place of politics, the meaning of Jewish peoplehood, and the Jewish stake in modern philosophy—more precisely, modern philosophy's stake in recognizing their Judaism. I hope thus to adumbrate the other ways in which they converge as well: (1) as parallel, dauntlessly idiosyncratic thinkers; (2) as a composite viewfinder—a stereopticon, if you will, of ethicism (ethics in its philosophical sense), and halakhism (the procedural apparatus of Jewish law and observance); and (3) as two figures whose cultural allegiances and personal fidelities intersect with the common pressures of nation, land, and state, and religious tradition. I begin with Leibowitz.

Yeshayahu Leibowitz

In an incisive essay, "Does Jewish Tradition Recognize an Ethic Independent of Halakha?" R. Aharon Lichtenstein mentions Leibowitz in passing as the example of a limit case:

> This point [that the Halakhah constitutes—or contains—an ethical system] has sometimes been challenged—most notably, in our own day, by Prof. Yeshayahu Leibowitz; but I do not think the challenge, albeit grounded in healthy radical monotheism, can be regarded seriously. (66)

("Healthy radical monotheism," R. Lichtenstein's phrase, turns out to be a very serviceable distillation of Levinas's philosophy as well, and I will come to that momentarily.) But what I find so telling here is that the essay pauses long enough to expel an irritant in the form of Leibowitz's uncompromising halakhic anthropology, and then proceeds digestively to the matter at hand. The essay concerns the respective characters of *din* and *lifnim mishurat hadin* (beyond the line of the law) toward establishing some provisional demarcations between the normative, codified practice of *halakhah* and a less particularist ethical complement to it. To this extent, the essay's terms are analogous to dialectical discussions about Torah as text and Torah as interpretation. But the mention of Leibowitz, as I think R. Lichtenstein realizes, points us in another direction. Indeed, speculations like R. Lichtenstein's remain at best academic for Leibowitz himself, whose essentialist reading of halakhic practice grounds it as *the* constitutive fact for Jewish identity. Where R. Lichtenstein is interested in defining terms, a relational enterprise, Leibowitz is concerned, rather, with foundational principles and absolute values.

Characteristically, as if to differentiate himself more rigorously than even Rav Lichtenstein would, Leibowitz once made the following reply to an encomium from Sir Isaiah Berlin, who had made the mistake of labeling him a humanist:

> As far as I understand, humanism, in the spirit of Kant, envisages the human person as the supreme value and end within any reality which man is capable of knowing. . . . From the standpoint of Judaism . . . man as a natural creature, like all of natural reality, is of neutral value. His existence can be meaningfully evaluated only in terms of his position before God as expressed in his mode of life. (vii)

Thus does one Isaiah admonish another (such forthrightness, as I have said, being Leibowitz's signature, a consistent arc between his person and his prose that made him a kind of latter-day *navi*, or prophet, in zeal and implacability). Humanism in Leibowitz's view, implies the very sort of transcendent human autonomy that he subordinates entirely to a *halakhic* imperative—the imprint of the Divine on an otherwise neutral identity.[27] If it means anything, to be Jewish consists prima facie in being *halakhically* obligated, just as being human can only have a positive value inasmuch as it is enacted through religious—in this sense, supraethical—practice. As command and duty, *halakhah* expresses man standing (and his standing) in the presence of his creator, not his signally neutral value as measured by and from within the interhuman.[28] The thrust here is anthropological, not characterological.

Transits of incommensurability define Leibowitz's position, and thereby delimit the Judaism it describes: between divinity and man, between duty and need, and between *mitzvot* and any other binding claim on Jewish identity. The fence of the Oral Torah, the fence of practice as obligation, the fence of worship as mandate, the fence between God and man: these define Jewish self-understanding for Leibowitz, just as biblical or rabbinic prohibitions fence around the commandments (the prohibition, for instance, of removing the poles attached to the Ark of Testimony (Ex. 25:13), lest the Ark be conveyed otherwise than upon the shoulders—a vivid embodiment of human submission to the Law's yoke). And thus it might be said for him that intra-Jewish fences *make Judaism*, irrespective of the impingement of any neighbors, or their identity. As Leibowitz explains in his essays and in his book on Maimoindes, the difference for him is not between faith and philosophy as different conceptual systems, but rather between *Torah* and *Torah lishmah* (for its own sake).[29] And Torah for its own sake, as study, as action, as prayer, means for Leibowitz a consistent and unyielding monism that has its parallel in his own insistent, relentlessly single-tracked thought.

But whether construed as "healthy radical monotheism," or, in his critics' view, barren legal positivism and Jewish puritanism, the interesting thing for me is that Leibowitz's idea of exceptionality, both here and in the context of the Lichtenstein essay, comes about, in part, *politically.* It follows upon, even as it anticipates, a *political* moment—the founding and subsequent administering of a Jewish state. For it is *as a citizen of the State of Israel* that Leibowitz insisted on defining Jewish identity and Jewish peoplehood as independent of and necessarily prior to the contingent realities of state and nation. Identity grounded in normative religious practice, self-understood in its commitment to the Halakhah is suprapolitical in the same way it is supraethical. Indeed, I would argue that it *begins* in Leibowitz's case as an awareness of the derived status that attaches to all political decisions, loyalties, actions, and so forth—Jewish life under the aspect of nationalism. Jewish identity that appeals to post-Enlightenment notions of moral will and post-Enlightenment notions of national will misconceives itself twice over. *Homo ethicus* and *homo politicus* alike describe an identity that faces toward the world and its matters, and away from divine commandment—an identity, so to speak, with dirty hands. Put in the terms spelled out by the Hebrew title of one of Leibowitz's essay collections, *Yahadut, 'Am Yehudi, u-Medinat Yisrael*, Judaism, the Jewish people, and the State of Israel are not necessarily at all coterminous, but rather neighboring regions divided by fences. Judaism is *halakhic* practice or it is nothing, in turn sanctioning a Jewish people and a Jewish state, which are epiphenomenal entities only. Put talmudically, Leibowitz intends the full spatial import of the Sages' famous statement in *Berakhot* 6b, "since the destruction of the Temple, God has in his world nothing but the four cubits of *halakhah*"—cubits that merely "make room" for national identity, cultural identity, and self-identity, and where Judaism has no greater meaning in Israel than any other place.

Emmanuel Levinas

To turn to that other strenuous exponent of healthy radical monotheism (and second of two hedgehogs, as Isaiah Berlin might have said), I quote from an essay by Levinas entitled "Means of Identification":

> Ideas, characters, and things can be identified in so far as they differ from other ideas, characters, and things. But people do not produce evidence in order to identify themselves. . . . Before he starts comparing himself to anyone else, he is just who he is. In the same way, one just is a Jew. (*DF* 50)

One should note that the slide from human identity to Jewish identity is a vexed and compressed one here, since one of the problems for the reader of Levinas, as I have suggested, is the exact relationship between a philosophical grounding for human subjectivity (a metaphysical condition), and collective Jewish particularity (as religiously sanctioned). Also, one should be aware of the seemingly contradictory remarks Levinas makes in an essay of the same vintage, "Ethics and Spirit," about Jewish identity as *practice* or conscious *labor*.[30]

Still, to reverse now the formulation I used in my brief introduction of Leibowitz, it is the impingement of the neighbor *generally speaking* for Levinas that provokes and undoes any fence around—or deriving from—the self. If I return to the vocabulary of Frost's poem, the "Something there is that doesn't love a wall/ That sends the frozen ground-swell under it/ And spills the upper boulders in the sun/ And makes gaps that even two can pass abreast" . . . is *Others*—concrete human persons who face me. Or, from another perspective, whatever mediates, circumscribes, or otherwise places a fence around the full autonomy and luxuriance of selfhood is the claim posed by otherness—*the neighbor*—in Levinas's philosophy.[31] Not, as in Leibowtiz, a halakhic anthropology but a "Jewish" or "biblical," *aggadic* humanism.

Inasmuch as that claim founds itself in the divine commandment לא תרצח, "do not murder," which parallels the first tablet's "I am the Lord," and for which the emblem and embodiment is the face of "the other man"—religious sanction oversees this condition of infinite obligation (as it does similarly for Leibowitz). But only to that extent. Reductively put for the purposes of this essay, Levinas answers Rav Lichtenstein's question, "Is there an ethic independent of Halakha?" with the answer, "Aggadically speaking, necessarily prior to": the transcendent demand of the other's humanity, a suprahalakhic, suprapolitical, exorbitantly ethical revelation of the divine precisely *within* and *through* the interhuman. Levinas calls this relation the "face-to-face."

For Levinas, God sanctions nothing more holy or commanding than another human being. And by extension, only a human being can endow the Torah with sanctity (a view that can be found in Maimonides). Ethics, thus, is not a Kantian explication of rules for conduct based on reason, as Leibowitz understands it; ethics just *is* the commanding fact of the other person, the face above and not simply in front of me. In Elias Canetti's apt formulation, "The misfortune of ethics: because it knows everything better, it *learns* nothing" (129). In Levinas's philosophy, this means that the interruption of the other into my complacence and my simultaneous exposure to him is always and necessarily a teaching and a discovery.

Far from being an outsized humanism predicated on an infinitely expanding set of symmetries between self and other (ethics in a Leibowitzian sense), the ethical relation of the face-to-face begins and ends in an asymmetry of height: like the divine, the Other approaches from on high—*mi-elyon*—or else in the form of an appeal from below, personified as the Torah's *ger, yatom, v'almanah*—the foreign, orphaned, and widowed. As Leibowitz subordinates humanism and everything anthropological to *halakhah*, so Levinas makes room for procedural morality or politics as what follows from the ethics of the face-to-face. The political moment in Levinas (when the other leads me to others) is akin to the ethical moment in Leibowitz, in that each is idiosyncratically defined and made accountable to a more transcendent imperative.

Nevertheless, for Levinas, "Judaism, the Jewish People, and the Jewish State" necessarily (if uneasily) align. Moreover, as adapted for Levinas, the four cubits specified by the Talmud cited earlier with respect to Leibowitz, delineate neither *halakhah* nor *prayer* (as the sixteenth-century R. Moses ibn Makhir troped on the talmudic dictum) but rather, the track of the Other's constant *approaching* but never coinciding with the ethical subject. In short, ethics—the event of the Other—founds politics—the claims of difference and multiple rights.

It is the boundary between the ethical and the political that brings me back to the internal dilemmas posed by Levinas's own essay, "Means of Identification" and his rapprochement between ethical identities and specifically Jewish ones, just as it did earlier in regard to Leibowitz's distinction between halakhic norm on the one hand, and wholly human constructs like nation and state on the other. If Leibowitz's halakhic astringency produces a healthy skepticism about the state and its allegiances, something materialized through a transplanted life in an *eretz Yisrael* transformed into a *medinat Yisrael*, Levinas's elevation of the face-to-face is, I believe, *materially* altered when it comes to a consideration of the State of Israel and specifically Jewish allegiances.

In respect to Israel, in other words, Levinas seems to allow for a special condition of national consciousness and loyalty to the State, or more precisely to the State and the "Holy History" it embodies as the spatial correlate of peoplehood that he grants nowhere else. Zionism for him expresses a wholly singular kind of nationalism and, as such, troubles a complacent accord between the rendering unto Caesar, which is political necessity, and the fear/love of God, which is ethical responsibility. "The Bible knows only a Holy Land, a fabulous land that spews forth the unjust, a land in which one does not put down roots without certain conditions" (*DF* 233). "The State of Israel . . . is not for us a State like any other. It has a density and depth that greatly surpass its scope and its political possibilities; it is like a protest against the world" (251). I look closely at such assertions and others like them in the following chapter.

For the moment, I will merely gesture in the direction a treatment of such complexities must take. And I do so by angling Levinas's own words, as it were, against their intended grain and in common application to Leibowitz: "Judaism has always been free with regard to place" (233).³² That is to say, where Jews emigrate from and where they migrate to profoundly determines how they think about both Judaism and place. I make this gesture as well by returning to American soil and my prefatory reconnaissance with Robert Frost's poetry. The coordinates in space and time for "Mending Wall" are those of the land and its seasonal connectivity to the humans who work it. The "*something* there is that doesn't love a wall" is the land itself. It is at "spring mending time" that the artifice and constructedness of humans walls is once more exposed: "*there* where it is we do not need the wall" is once again the land.

At the end of the poem, wall or fence—as *sense*—is itself semantically altered, just as it had been modified earlier as *reference*. The neighbor "moves in darkness, as it seems to me,/ Not of woods only and the shade of trees./ He will not go behind his father's saying." That is to say, human symbol-systems, like language—or saying—are a place unto themselves. They are so many fenced territories demarcating neighbor from neighbor, region from region, and indeed, neighbor from region.

On the same plane of topography and material reality—of physical here and there—Yeshayahu Leibowitz chose in 1934 to locate himself in a Palestine that became Israel, a Latvian Jew who made *aliyah*—"gone up" to the reconfigured status of Israeli citizen and resident. If we plot similar coordinates for Emmanuel Levinas, a Lithuanian Jew who, around the same time, emigrated south to France as a doctoral student,³³ from the perspective of the Judean Hills at least we descry a figure who has yet to move outside the *yeridah*—the "going down" of Exile. Still anchored in the Diaspora, Levinas espoused a transcendentalist relation to the Zionist dream and its vocation (as he called it) that Leibowitz, *because he lived there, in Israel,* could ill afford, given both the imme-

diacy of the state and his own contumacious, anti-humanist commitment to the Halakhah. "He overcame his materiality"—the fifteenth-
century commentator Don Isaac Abravanel's description of Abraham as
exemplary Knight of Faith, which Leibowitz is so fond of quoting in several essays—has to be reversed if we apply it to the cases of Leibowitz
and Levinas alike: for material reality resolutely *grounds* the two of
them. And consequently "in regard to place," Judaism leaves them
together with their fidelities both enrooted and complexly bound.

Might we thus speculate that it is the very emplacement and displacement of each philosopher and each Jew in his particular "here,"
that directly impinges on the tenor of his thought, whatever its claims to
transcendence? In that way, does an embodied Jewish identity lived out
in space and time, make itself *materially* present within the illimitable,
free-standing world-unto-itself that is critical reason? In that way, does
place serve as anchor and mooring—the quotidian ballast of land, terrain, hills (in the sense of Frost's poem) and their "beyond"? Perhaps it
is in no small way *because* Leibowitz lived in Israel that he could subordinate a generalized human identity so confidently. (Indeed, Leibowitz
makes a parallel biographical case for Maimonides's individualist
anthropology.) And, similarly, perhaps it is *because* Levinas left Eastern
Europe only to remain in the West, that he could introduce a certain
wrinkle into his otherwise seamless ethical philosophy: the valorized
place of Jewish particularity, where "one just is a Jew" as the sanction
for all universalism, all ecumenicism. Thus also does one philosopher's
emplacement, settlement, prismatically refract another's.

The issue here is not a small one, of course, but I express it now in
its plainest form before one final supplement at the level of the anecdotal. Jewish identity in the philosophies of Emmanuel Levinas and
Yeshayahu Leibowitz, the identity of individual Jews and of a Jewish
state, is also a shared topic between them, one fence that makes them
neighbors. But it is also the identity of the philosophers themselves—Jewishly specific, Jewishly self-understood, nationally circumscribed—that
marks out its own Jewish fences, locating sundry kinds of neighbors.

The chapter on Leibowitz that follows my discussion of Levinas is
confined to the essays collected in *Judaism, Human Values, and the Jewish State*, and his book on Maimonides. The Levinas chapter skirts
ground already covered by the many recent studies of his philosophy. I
do not systematically rehearse the characteristic themes of his philosophy, nor do I programmatically interrelate the Judaic and philosophical
writings. I confine myself entirely to the essays in *Difficult Freedom*,
Beyond the Verse, and *In the Time of Nations* concerning Jewish identity, the place of politics, and nationalism, and selected Talmudic readings. The chapter begins with a discussion of R. Joseph Soloveitchik's

concept of halakhic man in contradistinction to what I will call Levinas's aggadic man. It concludes by speculating on the not-always-fully consistent tension between Jewish election and Jewish universalism in Levinas's thought. The hinge to the chapter on Leibowitz, then, consists of both the halakhic criterion posed at the beginning of my treatment of Levinas and the value(s) I attach to particularism at the end. I close this introductory chapter, however, by strategically emplacing Levinas and Leibowitz a third and last time—only now illuminated by *ma'or she-bah*, "the light within" a textual world profoundly familiar to them both.

AGGADOT

In his essay, "Reflections on Jewish Education," Levinas writes, "To raise Judaism into a science, to think Judaism, is to turn these texts back into teaching texts. Until now, no one in the West has taken Talmudic texts seriously" (*DF* 268).[34] I want to take up that gauntlet by thinking Judaism accordingly, extracting what Levinas elsewhere calls its "secret scent." As a portal of sorts, I come round almost to where I began. For the Talmud, appositely enough, is replete with its own distinctive brand of anecdote: lapidary episodes about the *Tanna'im* and *Amora'im*, the Rabbis from the third century B.C.E. to the sixth century C.E. whose conversations underpin the Oral Torah. Such apologues function as authoritative sanction, as homily, and even as allegory when the process of regulating a Torah that is לא בשמים היא, "not in Heaven" (*Bava Metzia* 59b) becomes itself the focus of narration. Together with *midrashim* about biblical personalities, these anecdotes are illustrative of the Aggadah—the narrative, allusive dimension—as opposed to the Halakhah—the strictly procedural elaboration of the Oral Law—of reconstituted Judaism during the rabbinic period. While distinctively compressed, such "incidents in the lives of the Rabbis" provide, in fact, much and in some cases all, of the biographical information about these men that has come down to us. That is, they are meant not to reduce but rather adduce, and thus I have selected two of my own, one Leibowitzian in spirit, the other Levinasian. That is, the following short narratives can be heard as it were to speak both about and to Levinas and Leibowitz in a register that they speak both to and about, themselves.

> R. Yehudah, R. Yose, and R. Shimon [bar Yochai] were sitting, and Judah, a son of proselytes, was sitting near them. R. Yehudah commenced [the discussion] by observing, "How fine are the works of this people [the Roman authorities]! They have made streets, they have built bridges, they have erected baths. R. Yose was silent. R. Shimon bar Yochai answered, "All that they made they made for themselves;

they built market-places to set harlots in them; baths, to rejuvenate themselves; bridges, to levy taxes for them." Now, Yehudah the son of proselytes went and related their talk, which reached the government. They decreed: Yehudah, who exalted [us] shall be exalted; Yose, who was silent, shall be exiled to Tzipori [Sepphoris]; Shimon, who censured, let him be executed. . . . So he and his son went and hid in a cave. A miracle occurred, and a carob tree and a spring were created for them. They would strip their garments and sit up to their necks in sand. The whole day they studied; when it was time for prayers they robed, covered themselves, prayed, and then put off their garments again, so they should not wear out. Thus they stayed twelve years in the cave. Then Eliyahu came and stood at the opening of the cave, and said "Who will let Bar Yochai know that the Caesar has died and decrees are nullified?" So they emerged. Seeing a man plowing and sowing, they exclaimed, "These people are neglecting life and occupying themselves with transient life!" Whatever they cast their eyes upon was immediately burned up. A *bat kol* [heavenly voice] declared to them, "Did you go out to destroy my World?! Go back to your cave!" They went back in and lingered twelve months, saying "The wicked are judged in *Gehinnom* [purgatory] for twelve months." Then a *bat kol* came forth, declaring, "Go forth from your cave." (*Shabbat* 33b)

A folded deed was once brought before Rabbi, who remarked, "There is no date on the deed." [Thereupon] R. Shimon son of Rabbi said to Rabbi, "It might be hidden between its folds." [On] ripping [the seams] he saw it. Rabbi turned around and looked at him with displeasure. "I did not write it," [said the other]. "R Yehudah the tailor wrote it." "Keep away from talebearing," [Rabbi] called to him. Once he was sitting in his presence when he finished reading a section of the Book of Psalms. "How correct the writing is!' said Rabbi. "I did not write it," replied the other. "Yehudah the tailor wrote it." "Keep away from talebearing," [Rabbi] called to him. In the first case one can well understand [Rabbi's exhortation] since there was slander. Which talebearing, however, was there here? Owing to [the teaching] of R. Dimi: a man should never speak in praise of his friend, because by praise he brings about his blame. (*Bava Batra* 164b)[35]

Not coincidentally, both tales involve the weight of words and their concomitant waywardness. As I have implied, they might also be understood as teaching a lesson in aural acuity, the characteristic grain of a voice and how best to hear it. It is this pitch of particularist speech that makes them such a sonorous countertext to the two anecdotes with which I began. Thus, the thrust of the anecdote about Yehudah Hayatta (the tailor), in its movement from writing to speech, from parchment to persons, is the exorbitant *care* diction warrants rather than a carelessness that is . . . "banal enough." It poses the same dilemma Zagajewski captured as the problem of pronouns: "That is why I wonder what word should be used, 'he' or 'you,'/ For every 'he' is a betrayal of a certain 'you.'" Rabbi's exhortation to "keep away from talebearing" has the weight of a *mitzvah*, a commandment, which Levinas defines as knowing what is to be done. To that degree it is not so very far removed from Levinas's ascription of the commandment not to murder to the Face of the Other, for it signifies an interdict against the ethical homicide wielded by words and even looks, or, *pari passu*, by silence and looks away.[36]

The story about R. Shimon Bar Yochai, on the other hand, narrates a cautionary lesson about zeal, about Torah-for-its-own-sake, which, in rabbinic Judaism, is the greatest of *mitzvot*. In the *gemara*, however, Shimon bar Yochai is rebuked.[37] Plowing and sowing have their place; not all Jews can be sufficiently rarified to devote their lives to single-minded pursuit of *halakhah*. And yet the fire that surrounds R. Shimon's house after his death, and that prevents others from approaching it in a parallel account in the *Zohar* (the thirteenth-century book of Jewish mysticism ascribed to bar Yochai[38]), suggests that a delineation between the many and such few may in fact be necessary. I spoke of the spirit here as Leibowitzian, not only because the figure of R. Shimon in his cauterant zeal calls Leibowitz to mind, but also because such differentiation is one of Leibowitz's organizing philosophical principles in regard to the ground of Jewish identity, a tension between the wisdom of the feasible, the Sages' faith in היכא דאפשר אפשר, "where it is possible, it is possible" (*Chullin* 11b), and on the other side, the sheer force of divine commandment, the intrinsic value of halakhic norms. Here too, (though I neither gainsay Fackenheim's motivations for his judgment of Leibowitz nor equate the meaning of his object lesson with Richardson's psychoanalysis of Levinas), a different kind of talmudic anecdote clarifies a merely anecdotal pointillism. That is to say, one can compress a life or person into an illustrative story and thereby open a window on revelation, amplify voice as through a *shofar*. Or one can use that same narrative device to shade light and mute sound instead.

These two *aggadot*, then, tell me more about Levinas and Leibowitz than certain anecdotes could, because the voice is as it were pitched nearer to their own. But I have also turned to them at the end of my introduction because my counterpoint between Levinas and Leibowitz will inevitably rendezvous with rabbinic discourse in such a way as to emphasize its *use* by these philosophers over and above its meaning in textual context. Indeed, the principal way I distinguish but also relate them as neighbors-mediated-by-a-fence is as halakhist (or meta-halakhist) and ethicist (or meta-aggadist), respectively—*ba'al halakhah v'ba'al aggadah, Halakhic* and *Aggadic Man*. Levinas's autobiographical essay "Signature" at the end of *Difficult Freedom* (mentioned above) is in this respect a marvel of aggadic modesty: the first paragraph consists entirely of descriptive statements that scrupulously avoid the first person pronoun—as much as to say, "these texts, these places, these personages speak for themselves." The paragraph ends simply, "This disparate inventory is a biography" (291). One might see Leibowitz's implicit suppression of the autobiographic before the rigors of ideological consistency in a similar light: insofar as I assume the role of metahalakhic self-justification, I earn whatever meaning I would, personally considered, not otherwise merit.

Of the rich and cross-pollinating tension between the Halakhah and the Aggadah (and implicitly at least in part between the writings of Leibowitz and Levinas), I will defer finally to the artfully poised synthesis imaged by the twentieth-century poet of Hebrew and Yiddish, Chaim Nahman Bialik:

> They are related to each other as words are related to thought and impulse, or as a deed and its material form are to expression. *Halakhah* is the concretization, the necessary end product of *Aggadah*; *Aggadah* is *Halakhah* become fluid again. The vision moves forward to expression; the will becomes deed; the thought, word; the flower, fruit—and Aggadah becomes *Halakhah*. But concealed within the fruit lies the seed from which new fruit will grow. Out of *Halakhah*, raised to the status of a symbol . . . emerges in turn new *Aggadah*, either fashioned to its own image or of altogether different complexion. *Halakhah*, living and powerful, is *Aggadah* of the past and the future—and vice versa. And what are all the 613 commandments of the Torah but the end result, the synthesis upon synthesis of legendary words, of *Aggadah* and ancient custom, of a Torah of life, a Torah of the lips and heart which floated in space, as it were, for thousands of years since ages primeval, until the time came when it was concretized in the form of legal statutes chiseled in stone or inscribed on parchment? (64)

But what I have particularly wanted to suggest by my book-ending of *aggadot* with anecdote is that the fate endured by Levinas and Leibowitz in the latter is not so much misconceived as misapplied. The claim of biography, of genealogy, has not had its hearing. The philosophers' origins as mitnagdic Jews from Kouno and Riga, their maskilic odysseys that came to cultural maturity in Western Europe—where Levinas remained to witness the ascendance and defeat of the "Holocaust Kingdom," and which Leibowitz left for Palestine where he voted as a citizen for the new State of Israel—such *aliyot* and *yeridot*, landings and leavings, chime with not only the lateral reach and portage of place, but also—imagined longitudinally—the migrancy of words and practices, the chain and anchorage of tradition.

To cross-hatch these metaphors, yet again, if "fence-and-neighbor" connotes multiple topographic meanings, "Israel among the Nations" signifies similarly on the plane of sound—the audibility of Jewish philo-sophical voices; the enunciation of nationhood by and in those voices; and finally the voice of Israel itself. Accordingly, my wish is to make Levinas's and Leibowitz's philosophies speak to their biographies; to tune both philosophy and biography to a pitch at which Levinas and Leibowitz as Jews and post-Holocaust thinkers hear themselves speak-ing; and lastly, to listen acutely to the not-always harmonized treble of cultural and religious particularism: the place or condition assigned to "Israel" in their thought. Beyond the lives that get turned into story or the stories that get turned into lives, here I wish to speculate about the lives and stories that get turned into philosophy. And as one Jewish philosopher has put it, this "is not so much a matter of doing Jewish philosophy as of doing philosophy Jewishly."[39]

CHAPTER 1

Aggadic Man:
Levinas and the Neighbor
as (Br)Otherhood

1. *Ah, the scandal of the Jews as a chosen People!*
2. *How good it feels to be a Jew!*
3. *Judaism's original dissidence, a stiff-necked people with ulterior motives, resisting the pure force of things, and with the ability to disturb.*
4. *As if the history of Israel were the "divine comedy" or the "divine ontology" itself.*
5. *Israel would teach that the greatest intimacy of me to myself consists in being at every moment responsible for the others.*
6. *Judaism promises a recovery, the joy of self-possession within universal trembling, a glimpse of eternity in the midst of corruption.*
7. *In the cave that represents the resting-place of the patriarchs and the matriarchs, the Talmud also lays Adam and Eve to rest: it is for the whole of humanity that Judaism came into the world.*
8. *You see, this country is extraordinary. It is like heaven. It is a country that vomits up its inhabitants when they are not just. There is no other country like it; the resolution to accept a country under such conditions confers a right to that country.*

PRELIMINARY NOTE

In what follows, I peer through the lattice[1] of Levinas's Judaic writing with reference to two aligned but distinct polestars: R. Joseph Soloveitchik's exposition of *halakkah*, and an unapologetic politics of Jewish election. The common feature between these two is a friction between universality and particularity—the instantiation of general principles to specific cases as the very meaning of the Oral Law in the first instance, and the tension between a people's singularity and humanity in its widest sense in the second. As R. Soloveitchik's thought also informs my treatment of Leibowitz in chapter 2, I adduce it not merely as a modulating device but as a third and necessarily contrapuntal voice to Levinas's and Leibowitz's alike. This will become clear as the two chapters ultimately coalesce with each other after the model of talmudic *chavrutot*—partners in focused inquiry.

Dialogically speaking, it is also no accident that "universal" and "particular" pivot between the two purchases on Judaism I have provisionally laid out, which I have called the metahalakhic and the meta-aggadic. But let me interject a cautionary note, as much for myself as for my readers. The Judaism that shines through Levinas's prose, like the prose itself, is distinctive, inimitable, personally "signed." It is also at times less self-evident or unambiguous as Levinas may assume, such ambiguity, in my view, deriving precisely from the tension between universal and particular in the senses adumbrated above.

But this need not be seen as a matter of methodological imprecision, of "making strange" classical rabbinic texts for idiosyncratic philosophic purposes. Rather, I believe the friction here must rest with the fact that Levinas's essays expound extracts from talmudic texts in non-talmudic contexts, and that in such contexts he speaks as a culturally dedicated citizen of France while arguing for the singularity of the Jewish people embodied in our century by the State of Israel. In other words and he has formulated the phrase himself, Levinas manifestly walks a tightrope.

To be sure, Levinas recognizes the difference between *halakhah* and *aggadah*; that is, he is an insider knowingly addressing outsiders. Similarly, he is quite confident about just what kind of a Jew he is and where he lives. He cannot be tripped up so easily on the basis of an admittedly untraditional approach to the Oral Law and his acknowledged utopianism. What may appear, then, to be an overweening literalism in my own analyses to follow is, rather, a desire to delineate the boundaries—the fences—Levinas knowingly skews as philosopher-Jew.

As my goal here is to amplify the Hebraic (and Aramaic) accents of Levinas's distinctive French intellectual's voice, I take it for granted that other timbres in which he speaks passionately—post-Kantian, post-Hegelian, post-Nietzchean, post-Heideggerian, but also post-Sartrean, post-Célinean, and post-Malrauxian—have been ably captured in work that exceeds the boundaries of my own (the neighbors to my fences). I am speaking again of his purely philosophical stake in reforming the categories of Western thought in so aggressively *ethicizing* Cartesian ontology and Husserlian phenomenology. Differently put, that Levinas is a post-traditional and postHolocaust philosopher is to understand his Judaism as impinged upon by places other than Yavneh, Pumbedita, and

Sura, let alone by "a place in the Bible" (the title of one of his essays): by France, by postwar Europe, by the continental topography of contemporary philosophy—a tuition and training as personally and intellectually important as his education in what he calls Hebrew's "square letters." Surely, such impingement is absolutely central to his thought, just as surely as are such places themselves. In this book, however, their weight will have to stand as invoked from time to time rather than deliberately measured or hefted.

In his last essay in *Beyond the Verse*, "Assimilation and New Culture," Levinas weighs a necessary Jewish "provincialism"—that Jewish texts speak in Jewish accents—against an assimilationism that is the Jew's legacy from the West, signifying not "de-Judaization" but rather, in a pure sense, philosophy. What I hope to disclose in this chapter is how the seam between Greek and Hebrew, between Lithuanian-French and Latvian-Israeli, and finally between halakhic and aggadic perhaps not so simply *remains a seam*. I begin, then, with Levinas on one side and R. Joseph Soloveitchik on the other, keeping in mind the spirit of Moses's valedictory admonition on the plains of Moab *not to move a boundary of one's neighbor which the early ones have marked out*. For it is by fixing such boundaries or fences in the first place that neighbors come to be.

1. MEN HALAKHIC AND AGGADIC

In *Halakhic Man*, a book memorably summed up (by a Reform contemporary) as "a Mitnagged phenomenology of awesome proportions," R. Joseph Soloveitchik describes the perceptual orientation of the Torah-infused Jew this way:

> When halakhic man approaches reality, he comes with his Torah, given to him from Sinai, in hand. . . . His approach begins with an ideal creation and concludes with a real one. . . . There is no phenomenon, entity, or object in this concrete world which the a priori Halakha does not approach with its ideal standard. When halakhic man comes across a spring bubbling quietly, he already possesses a fixed, a priori relationship with this real phenomenon. The spring is fit for the immersion of a *zav* (a man with a discharge); it may serve as *mei chata* (waters of expiation); it purifies with flowing water; it does not require a fixed quantity of forty *se'ah*s. . . . Halakhic man is not overly curious, and he is not particularly concerned with cognizing the spring as it is in itself. Rather, he desires to coordinate the a priori concept with the a posteriori phenomenon. . . . When hahakhic man chances upon mighty mountains, he utilizes the measurements which determine a private domain (*reshut ha-yachid*): a sloping mound that attains a height of ten handbreaths within a distance of four cubits. . . . He approaches existential space with fixed laws and principles that were revealed to Moses on Mount Sinai: the imaginary bridging of a spatial gap less than three handbreaths; the imaginary vertical extension, upward or downward, of a partition; the imaginary vertical extension of the edge of a roof downward to the ground; the bent wall; the measurements of four square cubits, ten handbreaths, etc., etc. He perceives space by means of these laws just like the mathematician who gazes at existential space by means of the ideal geometric space. (19–22)

Although he sounds something like a Platonist counterbalancing the worlds of Being and Becoming, Forms and their material expression, or a Kantian weighing phenomena against noumena, or even a phenomenologist assaying the transcendental reduction, the secular intellectual R. Soloveitchik's man resembles most of all, the book tells us, is a *mathematician*. Notwithstanding the breadth of his author's familiarity with the logic of the West, halakhic man seems less philosopher than theoretical scientist.[2] He takes the measure of the world, and in the measuring he discovers all his duty.

> There never was an idolatrous city ['*ir hanidakhat*] and never will be. For what purpose, then, was its law written? Expound it and receive a reward! There never was a leprous house [*bayit negah*] and never will be. For what purpose, then, was its law written? Expound it and

receive a reward! There never was a rebellious son (*ben sorer u'moreh*, to be put to death] and never will be. For what purpose, then, was his law written? Expound it and receive a reward!

R. Soloveitchik quotes this passage from tractate *Sanhedrin* in the Talmud to emphasize the gap between the ideal world as textually constructed by Torah and the empirical world as halakhic man finds it, an incongruence that in no way diminishes the task assigned him: to realize the world *halakhically* until such time as it assumes its "full and complete realization . . . in the very nub of concrete reality." Until then, when the Temple is rebuilt and redemption is at hand, the "era when the Halakha will shine in all its majesty and beauty, in the midst of our empirical world," halakhic man measures, and he longs. (It is surely no accident that the most splendid biblical book of longing, The Song of Songs, is seen by the Rabbis as the ongoing dialogue—which is the very meaning of the Law—between God and Israel.) Like their spatial counterparts, temporal orientation and cognizance assume a very particular shape for halakhic man.

His time is measured by the standard of our Torah, which begins with the creation of the heaven and earth. Similarly halakhic man's future does not terminate with the end of his own individual future at the moment of his death but extends into the future of the people as a whole, the people who yearn for the coming of the Messiah and the kingdom of God. The splendor of antiquity and the brilliance of the eschaton envelop halakhic man's time consciousness. We have here a blurring of the boundaries dividing time from eternity, temporal life from everlasting life. (118)[3]

Halakhic man, in other words, experiences the passage of time from within a Hebrew calendar, where every seventh day, he steps into the rhythms of eternity, and where months draw the meanings from the holidays and memorials they embrace.

But halakhic man, as fleshed out by R. Soloveitchik, is at the same time something of a composite, partaking to different degrees of two counterfigures the author calls, respectively, "*homo religiosus*" (the transcendentalist religious personality), and "cognitive man" (the modern warrior of science). Where the first reads the world as an undecipherable text whose author has strategically hidden himself, the second instrumentalizes it and wrenches away its truths along with its uses. In contradistinction to both of these, halakhic man answers neither to holy bafflement nor expropriative problem-solving, but rather to the commandments he has received, with all Jews past and all Jews to come, at Sinai: "Better is one hour of Torah and *mitzvot* in this world than the whole life of the world to come," says the Mishna (*Avot* 4:17).

This, then, is the briefest of précis for *Halakhic Man*'s programmatic arc in its first part, "His World View and His Life." Part 2, "His Creative Capacity," concentrates on the paradoxical freedom of halakhic man's Torah-bound world that has the strength also of a commandment: "man is obliged to broaden the scope and strengthen the intensity of the individual providence that watches over him. . . . This is the man of God" (128). It is exactly this creative capacity (*chiddushei Torah*) that other metahalakhists—with the notable exception of Yeshayahu Leibowitz—make the centerpiece of their models of halakhic reasoning and practice, a creative labor pre-assigned by Holy Writ. For as Rashi (eleventh-century exegete) explains of the first part of Deut. 26:3, *If in My statutes you shall walk*, "walking," halakhically understood, means *ameilut ba'Torah—toiling* in the Torah.[4]

What I would like to highlight, however, in the Rav's writing—both here in *Halakhic Man* and in his other luminous though more intimate work of halakhic anthropology, *The Lonely Man of Faith*—is its distinctive, characteristic structure of *dramatis personae*. I mean that R. Soloveitchik did not so much expound his books, as *people* and *personify* them, with illustrative, monadic figures whom he backlights against an offset horizon, and differentiates according to a nomenclature that is almost anthropological (empirically speaking, this time), in its taxonomy: halakhic man, cognitive man, lonely man, majestic man, covenantal man; or, put collectively, *the metaphysical measure of man*—not an evolutionary timeline or teleology of species, but something, rather, on the order of a character grid, an inventory of players.

Such figures invite literary analogies too—classical, even modern-existential *mises-en-scène*, isolated men situated within, and against, a landscape alternately *zuhandlich* and refractory. (Not fortuitously does R. Soloveitchik title one of his essays "Catharsis."[5]) And significantly, there are no facing Others to speak of in this drama: only a single halakhic or covenantal or lonely man along with the world he faces, the texts he studies, and the *mitzvot* he undertakes—the Orthodox Jewish counterparts, if you will, to Camus's Sisyphus or Nietzsche's Zarathustra. (Philosophically speaking, Soloveitchik's analytic in *Halakhic Man* is mostly Kantian, however: halakhic man, according to David Hartman, "transforms an externally given norm into an autonomous product of his own creative intellect" [*LC* 81].)[6]

Over and above the "mitnagdic phenomenology" and existentialist vocabulary that are the hallmarks, the familiar identifying features, of R. Soloveitchik's model of the religious Jew's *Weltanshauung*,[7] one is continually struck by the *plottedness and figurality* of this rhetorical world, which both resembles but is also strangely unlike the biblical or rabbinic templates and "story-forms" that outline its ultimate narrative horizon. And struck also by its loneliness. For while halakhic man may be as creative as he is obligated, his ends correspond accordingly: creating or realizing himself in the act of serving God. *Lomed al menat la'asot*, study in order to fulfill, as the Sages put it.

True, in *The Lonely Man of Faith*, the Rav offers a paradigmatic reading of the double creation-story in Genesis 1 and Genesis 2 (*perek aleph* and *perek bet*, as they are known in the classical commentaries), fully infused by the spirit of *midrash*: one of those pressure points in the Torah that Rashi, prince of commentators, says, cry out *darshenu*, "interpret us." Having begun the book movingly in the first person, identifying himself as the lonely man, *ish haEmunah*, of its title (lonely exactly because he is a man of faith in a post-Kierkegaardian world), R. Soloveitchik proceeds to unpack the two Adams of Genesis 1 and 2 as typological categories: social, functionalist, "majestic" man on the one hand, and redemptive, lonely, "covenantal" man on the other,[8] in an exquisite melding of *peshat* (literal meaning) and *derash* (interpretive drawing-out).

Still, no matter how deeply it drinks from the wellsprings of Torah, R. Soloveitchik's twin narrative in *The Lonely Man of Faith* does not feel wholly Torah-like, for in contradistinction to the Kantianism of *Halakhic Man*, it sometimes seems as quasi-Kierkigaardian as midrashic (Kieerkegaard, not Hegel, is the Rav's dialectician of choice). "Let us portray these two men," Soloveitchik writes. In much the same prologomenal spirit, the author of *Fear and Trembling* says of himself in the prelude to his book, "he didn't know Hebrew, if he had known Hebrew, he perhaps would easily have understood the story and Abraham" (26), as the story and its existentialist *midrash* immediately follow. The footnotes in *The Lonely Man of Faith* invoke Maimonides and Nachmanides, yet the prose speaks in its own synthesis of modern philosophical accents and prose *t'amim* (cantillation marks that punctuate the vowel-less Torah).

Amidst all the philosophy and the learned exegesis ("a patchwork of scattered reflections . . . an incomplete sketch" [137] is the book's own summary judgment of itself), what R. Soloveitchik puts forth primarily, I think, are *allegories* that, while beginning in the concrete, constantly ascend to abstract and iconic levels. One feels constantly a kind of metaphysic of the *bet midrash*, a heroism confined to the study hall. The mythic, in the form of halakhic man's perfecting the world's imperfection, and the personal, in the form of his self-creativity, coalesce in an attenuated social world. The world through which halakhic man walks is populated by Soloveitchik's own typologies, not persons as such.[9]

Unsurprisingly, then, for a book ostensibly about *halakhah*, R. Soloveitchik makes liberal uses of talmudic apologue and homily. In the same way, from time to time he will introduce anecdotal family history about his eminently learned grandfathers and uncle, R. Hayyim of Brisk, R. Elijah of Pruzhan, and R. Meir Berlin, and his father, R. Moses Soloveitchik—character sketches that make for some of the book's most moving moments. The book's epigraph, from *Sotah* 36b, is thus so very telling: *"At that moment the image of his father came to him and appeared before him in the window."*[10] These are books, finally, about individual men, just as their titles announce—representative types but also embodied souls. For it is only through human deed, thought, and creative capacity that the Halakhah finds its legitimation and its sense. And in this way, the theoretical scientist meets another kind of technician: the philosopher-poet.

In one of his essays, Emmanuel Levinas also frames man within a certain kind of landscape, spatiotemporal coordinates that he will return to often. Yet such terrain makes for quite a different portrait from R. Soloveitchik's because of its own peculiar and distinctive sense of the *a priori.* And yet, I still want to say at the outset, it is no less mitnagdic.

> This, then is the eternal seductiveness of paganism, beyond the infantilism of idolatry, which long ago was surpassed: *The Sacred filtering into the world*—Judaism is perhaps no more than the negation of all that. To destroy the sacred groves—we understand now the purity of this apparent vandalism. The mystery of things is the source of all cruelty towards men. One implementation in a landscape, one's attachment to Place, without which the universe would become insignificant and would scarcely exist, is the very splitting of humanity into natives and strangers. And in this light, technology is less dangerous than the spirits [*génies*] of Place. . . . Socrates preferred the town, in which one meets people, to the countryside and trees. Judaism is the brother of the Socratic message: to perceive men outside the situation in which they are placed, and let the human face shine in all its nudity. (*DF* 232–233)[11]

Put more economically, from the very beginning of *Totality and Infinity* that quotes Rimbaud: "'The true life is absent'. But we are in the world."[12] Judaism frees Nature from a spell just as it liberates man from enrootedness.[13] The meaning of "place" for Levinas is *responsibility,* and it is fully portable. This is the sense of its *chosenness,* which "knows itself at the center of the world and for it the world is not homogeneous: for I am always alone in being able to answer the call, I am irreplaceable in my assumption of responsibility" (176–177).[14] Rooted to infinite demand, emplaced by infinite responsibility, at home in difficult freedom, אָן לדבר סוף: there is no end to my speaking.

One could say for this argument that nature is placed in one way, humanity in another; or more precisely, the former, in its pure desacralized givenness, teaches a lesson to the latter. On the one hand,

> What is an individual, a solitary individual, if not a tree that grows without regard for everything it suppresses and breaks, grabbing all the nourishment, air, and sun, a being that is fully justified in its nature and its being? What is an individual, if not a usurper?[15]

But then,

> Oh! Tamarisk planted by Abraham at Beer-Sheba! One of the rare "individual" trees planted in the Bible, which appears in all its freshness and color to charm the imagination in the midst of so much peregrination, across so much desert. But take care! The Talmud is perhaps afraid that we will let ourselves be carried by the song, in the southern breeze, and not look for meaning of Being. It wrests us from our dreams: Tamarisk is an acronym; the three letters needed to write the word in Hebrew are the initials used for Food, Drink, and Shelter, three things necessary to man *which man offers to man*. The earth is for that. Man is his own master, in order to serve man. Let us remain masters of the mystery that the earth breathes. (233)[16]

From man, to tree, to man again, to *other men*, all against the continuous horizon of landscapes, wildernesses, countries, and towns. The arc begins and ends with Torah and talmudic exegesis, sketching in habitable space in between—although Levinas's understanding of that duty and that practice departs significantly from the classical notion of תורה לשמה, Torah-for-its-own-sake, a point I take up at length below.[17]

"There is a prophetism and a Talmudism preceding theological considerations: its *a priori* (for it is doubtless also the very process of the coming of God to the mind) in the face of the other man" (*ITN* 112). This is Levinas's sense of the *a priori* in contradistinction to R. Soloveitchik's, an ethical precondition that underwrites the Halakhah, as opposed to a halakhic precondition that, Soloveitchik would say, necessarily encompasses what philosophy denominates as "ethics." In traditional Jewish education, the first verse of Torah a parent teaches the child is *The Torah that Moses handed down to us is the heritage of the community of Jacob* (Deut. 33:4).[18] Though he himself never cites it, I would imagine this *pasuk* affirms for Levinas an ethical responsibility to be lived out in history rather than a manifest sense of proprietary national unity.

Nevertheless, keeping pace with Soloveitchik's depiction of halakhic consciousness at its most boldly metaphysical, Levinas's "mitnagdic phenomenology" verges on the kabbalistic at times as well. In *kabbalah*, where the Torah is revealed in the last of its fourfold[19] interpretive possibilities—סוד ("secret" or "root")—the very text of the Torah precedes creation. Moreover, as Levinas quotes the interpretation of Gen. 2:7, "and man became a living being," from the *Nefesh Ha'Hayyim* by R. Hayyim of Volozhin, "But the verse, literally, does not say that the breath became a living soul in man; it says that man became a living soul for the countless worlds."

> And it is also in a literal sense that our author reads the ancient blessing pronounced . . . after reading the Torah, "Thou hast planted an eternal life within us" [as] "Thou hast planted the life of the world within us." . . . It is not through substantiality—through an in-itself and a for-itself—that man and his interiority are defined but through the "for-the-other": for that which is above self, for the worlds (but also, by interpreting "world" broadly, for spiritual collectivities, people, and structures. (*DF* 161)[20]

How might we, then, contrast R. Soloveitchik's fitting-out of man in halakhic garments, and emplacement of him in the world with Levinas's? For one thing, when Soloveitchik comes to the same verse in Genesis as above, he defers to Rashi's commentary on why the word for "formed," וייצר, has two of the letter *yod* instead of the expected one: it teaches us about the intrinsic duality of man.[21] Soloveitchik burrows inside the immanent self to discover transcendence like a secreted pearl; Levinas traces a ligature of clasped hands between one self and another.

The subtitle in Hebrew of R. Soloveitchik's *Ish haHalakhah* is *galui v'nistar*, revealed and hidden, which seems to suggest the poles between which halakhic consciousness is suspended; revelation for Levinas, conversely, takes place between persons. But *nistar* also connotes the grammatical notion of "speaking in the third person." By comparison, Levinas's counterbook to Soloveitchik's would have to be entitled *Ish ha Aggadah: m'daber v'nochach*, that is, "Aggadic Man: Speaking in the First and Second Person."

Moreover, Levinas neither speaks of nor depicts a figure analogous to R. Soloveitchik's that could, in the plain sense, be called *halakhic*. Ontic being-in-the-world for Levinas is being for, with, and, vexedly, in place of the other man. The phenomenological contours, thus, of human space and time—as inflected by the divine—follow from the primordiality of this ethical relation. And phenomenology, as Levinas defines it in relation to Torah in *Beyond the Verse*, is "the 'staging' in which the abstract is made concrete" (xiii) where "man and his interiority are defined—but through the 'for-the-other'." "I am trying to show," Levinas writes, "that man's ethical relation to the other is ultimately prior to his ontological relation to himself (egology) or to the totality of things we call the world (cosmology)" (*FTF* 21).

Biblical relationships, between not only God and Adam or Abraham, but also Judah and his brother Joseph, or Ruth and Naomi; the non-consanguineous, but just as authoritative, rabbinic bonds between teacher and student and among the "Doctors of the Talmud" generally; the lived allegiance to the verse; and finally, the illimitable affiliatedness that defines the privileged place Levinas assigns Jewish peoplehood vis-à-vis "the seventy nations" of the world: all of these are so many *versions* or *expressions* of this founding umbilicus between one and another.[22] In his philosophy, Levinas calls this affiliation the breach of totality, the rupture that is ethics; in Hebrew, he knows it as the linguistically grounded tie between אתר, *acher* ("other"), and אתרות, *achrayut* ("responsibility"). It is thus even, especially, a matter of syntax and lexis:

> It is by going back to the Hebrew text from the translations, venerable as they may be that the strange or mysterious ambiguity or polysemy authorized by the Hebrew syntax is revealed: words coexist rather than immediately being co-ordinated or subordinated with and to another, contrary to what is predominant in the languages which are said to be developed or functional. (*BV* 132)

As words, so persons. And as persons, so readers who "rub"[23] the text. "We shall find the modalities of the sacred," Levinas writes, "by teasing [*en sollicitant*] the texts of course, but these are texts which invite teasing [*sollicitent la sollicitation*]; without it they remain silent or incongruous" (*NTR* 143). Here, Levinas merely follows the lead of the interpretive tradition in religious Judaism, which (in Rashi) already glosses "face-to-face" as "words-to-words."

Four short examples in chronological order, taken from commentary on *Chumash* (the Pentateuch):

1. The Pentateuch's exact midpoint (Lev. 8:16) occurs between the words, דרש דרש, [*Moses*] *inquired insistently*, which an eighteenth-century commentary applies to the very reading of Torah itself—that is, an endlessly insistent inquiry.

2. In Gen. 2:1, *And the heaven and the earth were finished, and all their hosts*, the *Ohr Ha'Chaim* explains that the root for "were ended," כלה, also means "to yearn." Heaven and earth were "finished" by being imbued with a longing for the Divine that outlasts the act of creation.

3. S'forno, the great fifteenth-century exegete from Rome and Bologna, points out that in the verse, *And she called his name Moses, and she said "Because I drew him from water,"* not by coin-

cidence is the proper name מֹשֶׁה, signifying "one who draws forth others" as opposed to משוי, "one who is himself drawn out," for it prefigures Moses's role as rescuer to a whole people.

4. Finally and aptly, R. Soloveitchik reads the first two actions in the opening verses of *B'reishit*: "God saw" and "God said," as the look back and the look ahead, turning the face in retrospect, and turning it frontward.

But traditional *midrash*—in Levinas's beautiful phrase, "all the horizons that the flight [of] the folded-back wings of the Spirit can embrace" (*BV* 132)—on individual words, or even letters or cantillation marks *for* those letters, is anchored more or less in the same sort of halakhic phenomenology that R. Soloveitchik describes. One expounds בשם שמים, in the name of heaven, and לתורה לשמה, for Torah-for-Torah's-sake. For Levinas, however, the interpretive possibilities on lexical, grammatical, and syntactic levels, indeed in every way possible, teach lessons about the interhuman.

On the contrastive model of R. Soloveitchik, then, the figure of *aggadic man* captures for me not only the sort of humanity that traverses the Tamarisk-landscape of Levinas's idiosyncratic talmudic gloss, but also Levinas's own interpretive persona as well—where *aggadic* does not, strictly speaking, signify textual genre but rather a certain animating spirit of interpretation that finds what it already seeks. Perhaps one should also say then, *aggadic acts* or *aggadic faith*.[24] Consider the following:

> Obedience to prescriptions, in the material acts that they entail, is fervor. It is as if the ritual acts prolonged the states of mind expressing and incarnating their interior plenitude, and were to the piety of obedience what the smile is to benevolence, the handshake to friendship, and the caress to affection. (*BV* 7)

This vaguely resembles R. Soloveitchik at his most lyrical, but Soloveitchik's lyricism is still that of the Bible in Song of Songs as interpreted by the Sages: one, or rather Israel, is lovesick for *God*—whose look, handshake, and caress transcend bodily shape.

Certainly, Soloveitchik has himself partly in mind when he elaborates the figure of "halakhic man," for indeed he was a supreme halakhic authority in American Orthodoxy,[25] his books composing a kind of *apologia pro vita sua* for the halakhic life thoughtfully lived. But his delineation of that figure, as I have suggested, does not itself speak in a halakhic register. It is, rather, metahalakhic, a halakhic *poetics*, evoking, refracting, even rhapsodizing the structure and spirit of the Law, but as different from it in tonality as is the mixed mishnaic Hebrew/Aramaic

Oral Tradition from the biblical Hebrew Torah *it* expounds.[26]

R. Soloveitchik formulates a philosophy of the orthopraxis in *halakhah*, the *Geist* in its machine. Together with his published lectures on aggadic themes, the characteristic turn of mind that reveals itself is what Hebrew calls *hashkafah*, "the looking-down," or as the Rav might vocalize "outlook" in another timbre, *Weltanshauung*.

> "A law to Moses at Sinai"—not in the sense that in fact they originate from the time of Moses, but rather that their character is that of a law to Moses at Sinai: in other words, they were transmitted as a received tradition without explanation. It was simply said: See, this is what is done in Israel. (qtd. in Koppel, 93)[27]

Levinas's *hashkafah*, to sharpen the contrast now, conducts its arguments at an even more oblique angle to the lineaments of halakhic *form*, for it eschews a mimetic engagement with the Law's letter. That is because the philosophical implications of the rabbinic tradition are essentially meta-halakhic for Levinas but in a peculiarly aggadic sense, and it is the philosophical implications that animate him: not a philosophy-of-the-System, but rather the System-as-philosophy, what Levinas will call "the motivations of the Halakhah [which] remain under discussion, the whole order of thought . . . as present and living" (*BV* 127)—that is, *first philosophy*, or ethical revelation.

> This is very significant: the thought that issues from the prescriptive goes beyond the problem of the material gesture to be accomplished; although, right in the heart of the dialectic, it also enunciates what conduct is to be kept, what the *Halakha* is. A decision which is not, therefore, strictly speaking, a conclusion. It is as if it were based on a tradition of its own, although it would have been impossible without the discussion which in no way cancels it out. (140)

Levinas's consistent approach to the rabbinic tradition, in both his Talmudic readings and his essays is to see it as *a certain kind of philosophy*, and the Doctors of the Talmud as *certain kinds of philosophers* who practice *a characteristic philosophical method*, in the midst of their performance of *talmud torah* as *mitzvah*. And yet it is precisely *not* a conventionally Western sense of the philosophical task, but rather doing philosophy (enacting it)—the thinking-through of ethical wisdom to the point of its revelation—Jewishly.[28] As he will say, "Our great task is to express in Greek those principles about which Greece knows nothing. Jewish peculiarity awaits its philosophy" (200).

But to recall the preliminary note to this chapter, a blanket polarity between Levinas and R. Soloveitchik as respectively aggadic and halakhic in their predispositions remains heuristic at best. For in an important passage in one of his most breathtaking readings (of *Sotah*

37a–b), Levinas underscores the genius of halakhic particularism, borrowing from Genesis the image of Jacob's struggle with the Angel as the Torah's own: "to overcome the angelism of pure interiority" through "a special consent to the particularities which are all too easily regarded as transitory." I want to quote the paragraph that follows in its entirety because it needs to be borne in mind, I think, as a brake on a too-facile estimation of Levinas's understanding of Talmud even if his readings do not always or consistently accord with its doctrine.

> There is in the particular yet another reason for it to appear in the Law as an independent principle in relation to the universality reflected by all particular laws. It is precisely the concrete and particular aspect of the Law and the circumstances of its application which command Talmudic dialectics: the oral law is casuistic. It concerns itself with the transition from the general principle incarnated by the Law to its possible execution, its concretization. If this transition were purely deducible, the Law, as a particular law, would not have required a separate adherence. But it so happens—and this is the great wisdom the awareness of which animates the Talmud—that the general and generous principles can be inverted in their application. Every generous thought is threatened by its Stalinism. The great strength of the Talmud's casuistry is to be the special discipline which seeks in particular the precise moment at which the general principle runs the danger of becoming its own contrary, and watches over the general in light of the particular. This protects us from ideology. Ideology is the generosity and clarity of the principle which have not taken into account the inversion which keeps a watch on the general principle when it is applied; or—to pick up on the image used a while ago—the Talmud is the struggle with the Angel. That is why adherence to the particular law is an irreducible dimension of all allegiance, and you will see that R. Akiba thinks not only that it is as important as that of adherence to the Law in its general form, but also the place dedicated to its study—ultimately, the yeshivah—is one of the three places where the pact is made, and that dignity of this place equals that of Sinai, where the Torah is revealed, and that of the plains of Moab, where it is repeated by Moses. (78–79)[29]

Here Levinas is in perfect alignment with halakhic theory and praxis, which is to say, with R. Soloveitchik and his panegyric to halakhic man's worldview and creative capacity. And I will add only, in the spirit of the passage itself, that to the extent an aggadic spirit prevails over halakhic particularism in Levinas's Talmudic exegesis, or to the extent that exegesis becomes wholly and solely an ethics, the generosity of Levinas's thought is not a few times threatened by its own *Levinasism*. Levinas, in other words, is not his own or best casuist.

Another node of correspondence between Levinas and Soloveitchik is R. Hayyim b. Yitzchak of Volozhin (1749–1821), and the differential use to which he is put by Soloveitchik and Levinas. In *Halakhic Man*, by far the longest textual citation in the body of the text is given over to an excerpt from the commentary on *Pirke Avot* in the *Ruach Hayyim* (6:1). It is something of a peroration, concluding part 1 of R. Soloveitchik's book, and itself concluding, after a laudatory hymn to *Torah lishmah* and halakhic fervor, with the famous dictum from *Berakhot* about "the four cubits of the Halakhah"; R. Soloveitchik's comment after the citation runs as follows:

> The above is the declaration of R. Hayyim Volozhin, the outstanding student of the Gaon of Vilna and the founder of the Yeshivah of Volozhin; and it would appear to me that it needs no further comment. (89)

And indeed, Hayyim Volozhiner's phenomenology (which is mitnagdic in the original sense of the word) has as its core the study of Torah for its own sake elevated to supernal heights, as well as *iyyun yashar* (straight inquiry) into the Talmud in order to arrive at "practical halakhic conclusions." The latter, especially, typified the mitnagdic reaction to the Hasidic devaluation of Torah study as the central religious activity for religious Jews.[30]

The *Nefesh ha-Hayyim* is an interesting composite: like contemporaneous Hasidic discourses it uses Lurianic *Kabbalah* to sketch a mystical cosmogony that, however, places not God but his Torah at the cosmic-mystical pitch of creation. As such it makes a rejoinder to the Hasidic drive toward immanence that the Vilna Gaon and his school so bitterly deplored.[31] If mystical communion with God is to be had on the earth, according to R. Hayyim, it is through Torah study, and Torah study alone. When Levinas comes to discuss this work, he concerns himself entirely with its cosmology or general ontology, as he calls it, in order to bring out its distinct conceptualization of humanity's relation to the Infinite in the world. "Strictly speaking," he says in the essay in *Beyond the Verse*,

> that which is infinite and never-ending is not the absolute of God which nothing can determine, but the *act of thinking of the Absolute which never reaches the Absolute*, and this has its own way—which is quite something—of missing the Absolute[:] a beginning that does not move towards an end, but traces, as it were, a relation without a correlate. And yet it is from this remarkable possibility of the human psyche (or perhaps from the source of all psyche) that *Ein-Sof* [the endless] takes it meaning in order to appear in discourse, as if man were its very means of signifying. (164–165)

It will be seen from this essay, as well as "Judaism and Kenosis" from *In the Time of Nations* and his preface to the French translation of

Nefesh ha-Hayyim,[32] that Levinas, characteristically, offers a reading of the text as though it had been written by Levinas himself (and the *Nefesh haHayyim* is an esoteric text within the tradition as well). Interestingly, each of the two essays on R. Hayyim more or less corresponds to the philosophical concerns of either *Totality and Infinity* or *Otherwise Than Being*. Holiness in the world, the world itself, even the Absolute, all depend on man: the Levinasian *idée fixe par excellence* (as he might say). The horizon of creation (Being) is contracted into or ruptured by the human event of ethical responsibility. "In the Image of God" (the more *Totality and Infinity*–like of the two pieces) concludes as follows:

> The human finitude that [divine self-contraction] determines is not a simple psychological powerlesness, but a new possibility: the possibility of thinking of the Infinite and the Law together, the very possibility of their conjunction. Man would not simply be the admission of an antinomy of reason. Beyond the antinomy, he would signify a new image of the Absolute. (166–167)

In "Judaism and Kenosis" (the more *Otherwise Than Being*–like), the emphasis is on holiness in Jewish spirituality—prayer as an offering of oneself "for the others," and the "kenosis of a God who, though remaining the One to whom all prayer is addressed, is also the One *for whom* the prayer is said" (*ITN* 130). In one essay, a rigorous ethical humanism in the face of alterity: the fear of God as the fear of others, human deeds that count before God because they engage *other men*. In the other essay, a rigorous ethical humanism as substitution, the self held in hostage on behalf of God and the human other. The two essays together work as mortise and tenon for the totality of Levinas's philosophical thought.

And yet the word "Torah" is mentioned fewer than ten times in each essay and then only in passing; "Halakhah" occurs but twice. The closest Levinas comes to a traditional vocabulary for the text is the set of rhetorical questions he asks at the conclusion of "In the Image of God," the last of which reads, "Must we lay stress on the elevation above the Law and ethics from out of the Law, as on the very dynamism of the Torah?" As I say below, referring to a familiarity with the Oral Tradition gained only by those steeped in it through both upbringing and religious practice, readers whose access to the *Nefesh ha-Hayyim* depends solely on Levinas's highly idiosyncratic treatment of it, would never know that its raison d'être, the fundament (as Leibowitz might call it) by which it understands itself and by which it is known in the inner circle of tradition is, very simply, *Torah lishmah*, Torah for Torah's sake. It is a phrase, amazingly, that Levinas manages to skirt entirely, although it is essential to an understanding of not only the *Nefesh haHayyim*, but of the championing of Torah scholarship through the Volozhin *yeshivah* tradition that was R. Hayyim's most significant and lasting contribution.[33]

One has only to compare R. Soloveitchik's decision to let his excerpt from the *Nefesh ha-Hayyim* speak for itself, that is, to declare the beneficence of *Torah Lishmah*, with Levinas's ingenious and extended extrapolation of the same work to note how differently each relates to the same religious textual tradition. For Soloveitchik, R. Hayyim is a metaphysician of the Halakhah, exalting the practice of it which is study above even the sefirotic emanations of the Divine, in the realm of the *Ein Sof*; the kabbalistic innovations R. Hayyim introduced merely serve the mitnagdic ideology of *Talmud Torah*. For Levinas, on the other hand, R. Hayyim is the ontological counterpart to the phenomenologist "Doctors of the Talmud" whose glorified and glorifying schema of God, man, the cosmos, and Torah he decodes, after his exegetical fashion, *aggadically*, with the work's own emphasis on Torah study dwarfed by kabbalistic, that is, philosophical, mythopoesis.[34]

I express the difference in Levinas's and R. Soloveitchik's interpretive predilections in terms of *halakhah* and *aggadah* not because such a distinction is handy or conventional but because I think it best describes *how each of them reads Torah*. "Halakha is the way to behave," write Levinas; "Aggada is the philosophical meaning of this behavior" (NTR 194);[35] the Sages of the Oral tradition, more laconically, compared *halakhah* to meat and *aggadah* to wine [*Sifre*], their co-presence for a full repast being tacitly understood. And while R. Soloveitchik does approximate Levinas in certain aggadically tinged lectures,[36] the philosophical sensibilities of the two writers diverge, finally, in an unmistakable way. Where the Rav is dictated to by the Torah in its fullness, Levinas finds in that same amplitude trope after trope, parable after parable, that collectively reflect back to him his own abiding ethical concerns.

Or as the Sages themselves might put it, R. Soloveitchik harvests while Levinas plows. To recall one of my own two metaphors, Soloveitchik's interpretive fence around the Torah, aggadically speaking, is that of סיג *s'yag*—an inclusive net cast widely, and Levinas's that of גדר *gader*, a single-minded filtering out. (Obviously, such a distinction serves rhetorically at best.) My point, however, is that while R. Soloveitchik's aggadic essays are learned in a very traditional sense, and to that extent stay within the verse, Levinas's, by contrast, are sophisticatedly inventive, and are therefore always moving *beyond it*.

In the same way, R. Soloveitchik's sense of commandment is more or less normative.[37] *Mitzvot* are divisible into either *mishpatim*, ordinances that appeal to human reason, or *hukkim*, statutes that transcend such reason; in both cases, the commandments mediate between God and man through either rational commitment or passionate love. They form an apparatus of universal intelligibility, an optic through humanity and the Divine become visible to one another.[38] For Levinas, on the other hand, *ethics* is that optic, and the *mitzvah* takes on the form of an intermediation between man and the other man only through which can Divinity be glimpsed or felt. One is מצוה, commanded, in Levinas's aggadic sense, both by God through the other and by the other through God. "Ethics is not simply the corollary of the religious," Levinas writes in *Beyond the Verse*, "but is, of itself, the element in which religious transcendence receives its original meaning" (107).

In my introduction, I spoke of *aggadah* as everything in the rabbinic tradition that is not-*halakhah*; and as the Rabbis themselves tend to define *aggadah* aggadically—the surest clue to its reflexivity—it is perhaps best understood, in David Stern's useful account, as an extension of the biblical genre of wisdom literature, and as it has been most recently positioned relative to the *halakhah* as ideological coefficient in the work of Daniel Boyarin.[39] This is also how Levinas explains it, too: the living hermeneutics of the letter, biographical legend and parable in fruitful dialogue with legislative ruling. "The distinction between oral Law and written Law on the one hand, and *Aggada* and *Halakha* on the other, constitute, as it were, the four cardinal points of the Jewish revelation" (139).

> The pages of the Talmud, mischievous, laconic in their ironic or dry formulations, but in love with the possible, register an oral tradition and a teaching which came to be written down accidentally. It is important to bring them back to their life of dialogue or polemic in which multiple, though not arbitrary meanings arise and buzz in each saying. These Talmudic pages seek contradiction and expect of a reader freedom, invention, boldness. If this were not so, a reasoning rising to the summit of abstraction and rigor [*halakhah*] would not have been able to coexist with certain logical forms of exegesis which remain purely conventional. How could fanciful procedures [*aggadah*], even if codified—suppose to link the sayings of the sages to biblical verse—exist side by side with a masterly dialectic? Rather, we are in the presence of allusions made by hypercritical minds, thinking quickly and addressing themselves to their peers. (*NTF* 5)

(The traditional manner of such "address" consists of two students faced over the text, amidst the clamor of numerous other such pairs.[40] But one should also be aware that the tradition places limits on aggadic exegesis: *ein somekhin al ha-aggadah*, the Aggadah is not authoritative teaching, says the tenth-century Sa'adia Gaon, though Levinas would no doubt appeal to the other pole of the dialectic, *ein sof ve-lo tikhlah le-aggadot*, aggadists are free to improvise.)

But Levinas also calls *aggadah* Judaism's "philosophical anthropology," and exactly what he means by this, I think, is key to his idiosyncratic reading of and with the readers of Torah, the *talmidei hakhamim*. When he speaks of a "beyond" in relation to the scriptural verse, he means that the Infinite is contracted in Scripture in such a way as to overflow it at the same time, when it is pronounced, studied, shared by men. Yet that both is and is not a conventionally Orthodox position.

On the one hand Torah is understood by religious Jews as not only מן השמים, from heaven, and therefore imbued with Divine intent—hence the force of the commandments and indeed all *halakhah*—but also לא בשמים הוא, not *in* heaven (Deut. 30:12)—that is, humanly explicable, what R. Ishmael describes no less than eighteen times in the Talmud as *speaking the language of men.*[41] In *Midrash Rabbah* on the Book of Numbers, God is imagined saying, שגם עלי גזרין ואני מקים, *the rabbinic decrees are incumbent upon me also*. And in an ingenious explication of Deut. 17:11 (which seems to forbid changing or extending the law as given), the Rabbis derive the power to connect their law with the Torah's own so that Scripture in fact *warrants* rabbinic legislation.[42] (This is the principle underpinning rabbinic *takannot* [measures] like the institution of the festival of Hannukah and the rituals associated with it, or *gezerot* [decrees] like the device of *eruv* [interconnected abodes and spaces].) It is this dialectic between freedom and tablets of stone that Levinas will interpret as emblematic of the way ethics arcs between an always-beyond and an infinitely-here, a "continued revelation."[43]

> The reading processes that we have . . . seen at work suggest, first, that the statement commented on exceeds what it originally wants to say; that what it is capable of saying goes beyond what it wants to say; that it contains more than it contains. (*BV* 109)[44]

On the other hand (and this is R. Soloveitchik's understanding), *halakhah* does not originate as an *allegory* or *modality* of ethical responsibility; rather, it is a codification of laws and duties that define and sustain a nation dedicated to service to God, and thus undergirt by the constitutive principle of קדשים תהיו כי קדוש אני, "be holy for I am holy" (Lev. 19:2). To be holy is to be circumscribed by *halakhah*, and only therein does one find one's "creative capacity":

> Holiness, according to the outlook of halakha, denotes the appearance of a mysterious transcendence in the midst of the concrete world, the "descent" of God, whom no thought can grasp, onto Mount Sinai, the bending down of a hidden and concealed world, and lowering it onto the face of reality. [T]he halakhic conception of holiness: holy upon the

earth . . . the holiness of the concrete. An individual does not become holy through mystical adhesion to the absolute . . . but, rather, through his whole biological life, through his animal actions, and through actualizing the Halakha in the empirical world. (*Halakhic Man* 46)

As Soloveitchik conveniently formalizes it, the realization of the Halakhah correlates holiness with mundanity. And in the same way, despite its quasi-Levinasian implications, the title of Soloveitchik's essay, "Which Comes First, God or People," really means "which of these is of greater consequence to Jewish survival, the personal *mitzvah* commitment or the national commitment to peoplehood" (Besdin, 108). Holiness (a word in Hebrew whose root connotes separation due to a difference in kind), derives from a dual allegiance, practically speaking, to both שמרת המצוה, guarding the commandments, and כנסת ישראל, the assembly of Israel.

For Levinas, conversely, the sense of holiness is coextensive with Torah's philosophical anthropology, and means simply, *the face of the other*:

> But to follow the Most-High is also to know that nothing is greater than to approach one's neighbor, than the concern for the lot of the "widow and orphan, the stranger and poor" and that to approach with empty hands is not to approach at all. . . . My uniqueness lies in the responsibility for the other man; I could never pass it off on to another person, just as I could never have anyone take my place in death: obedience to the Most-High means precisely this impossibility of shying away; through it, my "self" is unique. To be free is to do only what no one else can do in my place. To obey the Most-High is to be free. But man is also the irruption of God into being, or the explosion of being towards God: man is the rupture of being which produces the act of giving, only giving with one's hands full rather than being struggle and plunder. (*BV* 142)

As I explain at greater length in this chapter, Levinas prizes the love of Torah over the love of God—because it is a Torah of and for men—but that Torah is something other than Torah-for-its-own-sake. It is, as he says, an "austere humanism, linked to a difficult adoration." And "it is an adoration," he goes on to add, "that coincides with the exaltation of man" (*DF* 145).[45] That strenuous emphasis on the intersubjective explains why he will typically interpret the Torah as follows, in one of his most beautiful *hiddushim*:

> I think of the last words of the verse from Genesis 30:30: "Now when shall I provide from my own household also?" In the biblical context they can mean neither that a self vowed, of itself, to others, is making a simple and sharp claim for its own interests, nor that the essential structure of the self is being denied. I think that in the responsibility for

others prescribed by non-archaic monotheism it reminds us that it should not be forgotten that my family and my people, despite the possessive pronouns, are my others, like strangers, and demand justice and protection. The love of the other—the love of one's neighbor. Those near to me are also my neighbors. (*BV* xvii)

(I return to this important passage below.) Or to take another example common to both Levinas and R. Soloveitchik, the latter would construe the talmudic parable of God's conversation with the moon (who, comparing herself with the sun, resents her state of monthly diminution), in terms of *tikkun*: "Man is obliged to perfect," he writes, "what his Creator 'impaired'" (107). R. Soloveitchik explains that such restitution takes place through actualizing the ideal of *halakhah* in the real world. And it is *halakhah* that "draws downward" the Divine Presence in order to fill the breach that It Itself has purposely left behind. Man heals creation for God's sake.

As David Hartman has pointed out, human creativity for Soloveitchik is not restricted to an *imitatio Dei*, within social and ethical categories as the Rabbis typically understood it. It is an expressive gesture, an existential *modus vivendi*. Thus it is that the Halakhah is mandated by God but at the same time freely chosen by man, or has Hartman puts it, "expresses humanity rather than compels it" (*LC* 69). The result is something of a paradox: halakhic man is at once a talmudic theoretician (personifying the rigorous intellectualism of the Lithuanian Brisker tradition Soloveitchik inherits), but also a talmudic activist whose "learning adventure" at least within the bounds of halakhic practice affects the world.[46]

Fortuitously enough, in the same essay in which he discusses the *Nefesh haHayyim*, Levinas reads the above *aggadah* (in its version in *Chullin* 60a), as also betokening God's *kenosis*, but the meaning he attaches to such contraction differs pointedly from Soloveitchik's. In the story, God tells the moon that because of her, "Israel will be able to reckon the days and nights," and thus be able to preside over biblical history and messianic history. She remains recalcitrant, however, and after repeated attempts at pacification, God resigns himself to the work of creation he has done; as the tractate concludes the parable, "The moon has since remained without any arguments. But Eternal God sees that she is not satisfied."

In an exquisite reading that needs to be appreciated in its entirety (as does the complete *aggadah* itself), Levinas writes of the moon's dissatisfaction and God's troubled awareness,

The residue of the stubborn convention of a nature persevering in its being, imperturbably affirming itself. To this there is no response, but for this, precisely Holiness takes on the responsibility. Here is the humility of God assuming responsibility for this ambiguity. The greatness of humility is also in the humiliation of greatness. It is the sublime kenosis of a God who accepts the questioning of his holiness in a world incapable of restricting itself to the light of his Revelation. (*ITN* 118)[47]

With even more drive to personification than R. Soloveitchik, Levinas will unpack the conversation itself as an ethical drama, and thus "ethicize" the story's cosmic *mise-en-scène*: "Perhaps it was necessary that among the categories of ontology—or despite these categories—the category 'Israel' should arise in order that the notion of smallness as great as—or greater than—should take on meaning" (118–119).

The implication throughout—from God to moon to Israel to the interhuman, and recalling the transit I delineated earlier from man to phenomenal reality to other men—is the insistent Levinasian axiom of being-for-the-other as ethical necessity: as he puts it later in the same essay, "Being *is* through ethics and man."

The world is justified in its being by human dis-interestment, which concretely signifies to the Torah, and therefore surely already study of the Torah. More important than God's omnipotence is the subordination of that power to man's ethical consent. And that, too, is one of the primordial meanings of kenosis. (126)

I will underscore only that where R. Soloveitchik sees halakhic duty, Levinas sees ethical necessity. Where Soloveitchik sees man healing creation through observance of the Law, Levinas sees the Law fully realized in man's duty, through the commandments, to the other man. And for R. Soloveitchik, as he refines his notion of *tzimtzum* (divine self-contraction) in *The Lonely Man of Faith*, Godly withdrawal models human recoiling, an ethics of abnegation; if there is an oscillation here between advance and retreat, it is between God and the individual man (and by implication, *Klal Yisrael*, all Jews), not self and other.[48]

But it is significant that Levinas does *not* typically dwell on ritual and *mitzvah* apart from the textual context of a talmudic homily or parable. Over the course of his Talmudic readings, he will speak, for instance, about the remembrance of the Exodus in Deuteronomy 16, '*arei miklat* (the cities of refuge) legislated in Deuteronomy 19, the ceremony of *ha-beracha v'kal'lalah*, (the blessing and curse) on Mounts Gezerim and Ebal detailed in Deuteronomy 27, the prohibition against the *m'chashefah* (the sorceress) in Exodus 22, the institution of *nazir* (the Nazirate) from Numbers 6, *Megillat Ester* (The Scroll of Esther), or even Mishnaic *halakhot* such as the structure of the Sanhedrin, *nezikin* (damages), or the treatment of hired workers.

He discuss neither matters of practical *halakhah*—the lived dimension of Jewish observance—nor any individual *mitzvot*: say, those singled out for *hidur* (beautification), the Four Species on Sukkot, for example, those tied to Sabbath and Festival observance, or any of the day-to-day rituals of practical worship, like the donning of *tefillin* or the *birkat hamazon* (blessing after a meal). The closest Levinas comes here, I think, is in a section of "The Youth of Israel" that (aggadically) discusses the saying of grace, and a footnote to "God and Philosophy" that mentions the ציצית, the fringes on the corner of the prayer shawl, again characteristically and aggadically linked (through the rabbinic commentary *Sifre* on Deuteronomy) to Song of Songs 2:9: מציץ מן החרכים, "[my beloved was] peering through the lattice" (*NTR* 131–132; *BPW* 190; *ITN* 79).

Nor does he make use of the classic commentaries on Mishna, Talmud, *Shulkhan Arukh* or *Arbah Turim* (Codes of Jewish Law) that are the daily bread of Torah study (the closest Levinas comes in this respect is the Maharsha [Moreinu HaRav Shlomo Eidels of Poland], whose seventeenth-century commentary on the Talmud is printed alongside it in most editions.[49]) Medieval philosophers such as Sa'adia Ga'on, Bahya ibn Pakuda, or Yosef Ibn Caspi, are never mentioned (Yehudah Halevi and Maimonides are discussed briefly in the essay "On Jewish Philosophy," from *In the Time of Nations*).

As Levinas's readings consist solely of talmudic *aggadah* extracted from its context within a given treatise, the classic Bible commentaries of Nachmanides, Abraham Ibn Ezra, Seforno, and the entire postmedieval tradition make no appearance; Maimonides does so briefly in two essays. After Moses Mendelssohn and except for R. Hayyim Volozhiner, the religious literature of the early modern period is similarly overlooked, whether maskilic (Solomon Rapoport), hasidic (*Kedushat Levi, Mei Hashiloach, Sefat Emet*), mitnagdic (R. Naftali Berlin), modern Orthodox (R. Samson R. Hirsch), or musar (the Lithuanian ethics movement associated with R. Israel Salanter). Finally, no mention is made of twentieth-century sources like R. Soloveitchik, R. Abraham Isaac Kook, or the popular *Iyunim b'Sifrei Torah* (*Studies in the Pentateuch*) by Nehama Leibowitz (sister of Yeshayahu).[50]

In sum, while Levinas approaches the Oral Law in no more or less inventive a way than traditionally anchored *mfarshim* and *mkubbalim* (interpreters and esotericists) before him, *he remains almost entirely and selectively within the ambit of the Gemara itself, ignoring most if not all of the aggregate medieval and modern commentary through which it is typically refracted.* To be sure, his own talmudic commentary adds to and is thus part of the sum of all previous commentary, and as such, is Torah in its maximalist sense. (Levinas elaborates on the double fence against merely subjective or amateur interpretation, "the historical con tinuity of the reading and the tradition of commentaries that cannot be ignored" in the crucial essay "Revelation in the Jewish Tradition," in *BV*). But as he modestly confesses, however deeply informed by the *spirit* of the religious study hall it may be, the act of soliciting text "on the fringe of purely philosophical studies," "equally attuned to life: the city, the street, other men" (*BV* 110), is not the approach liable to be encountered in even the most modern-orthodox of *yeshivot*.

Perhaps, then, Levinas is best described, in this context, as *aggadic* in his relation to the Halakhah, and idiosyncratic—Levinasian?—in his use of the Aggadah. "The *halakha*," he admits frequently, "requires a muscularity of spirit which is not given to all. I cannot pretend to it." As he says of his own definition of the verb לאמר (saying), "*lemor* would signify 'in order to say'" (*BV* 80), that is, to be sufficiently responsive to the discourse of the Law as to prompt response in others. Or (though in the same essay he says it require no explanations), we might voice his understanding of the command "to do" or "perform," לעשות, in the formulation given by the Netziv (R. Naftali Berlin), another eminent product of the same *yeshivah* as R. Hayyim of Volozhin: *to construct the meaning of the words.*[51] Indeed, in a footnote to another crucial essay on rabbinical hermeneutics, "On the Jewish Reading of Scripture," he compares commentary to the trope of "glowing coals" in tractate *Pirke Avot*, citing R. Chaim Volozhiner's interpretation: "the goals light up by being blown on, the glow of the flame that thus comes alive depends on the interpreter's length of breath" (*BV* 210).

I should also take this juncture to point out a relevant fact about the audiences for which Levinas fashioned his talmudic lectures and readings. They were addressed to the Colloquia of Jewish Intellectuals organized by the French section of the World Jewish Congress, a mostly secular, philosophical body; on occasion, Levinas also spoke to a mixed audience of Jews and non-Jews—"the city, the street, other men"—for whom, it is presumed, the classical Jewish textual tradition is an ember that needs to be brought to life. Hence, the choice of "extracts."[52] A synthesis of the teaching style of the enigmatic Mordechai Shushani (also Elie Wiesel's teacher)—"who made forever impossible a purely dogmatic or even theological approach to the Talmud"—and what he playfully refers to as the School of Paris—"Our mode of reading, although it has a style of its own, is common to a movement that arose within French Judaism after the Liberation" (*NTR* 8)[53]—Levinas's approach to rabbinic Judaism requires that the Rabbis be heard as philosophers. As he captures the distinction, "these are sages' thoughts, not prophetic visions . . . addressing themselves to reason" (14). In *yeshivot* and conventional Orthodox intellectual circles, by contrast, they are known as *Chazal*, Sages of Blessed Memory, and are heard, simply, as Rabbis.

Ze'ev Levy offers the equally relevant corollary about the state of
Levinas's cachet in Israel (that is, in Hebrew-speaking circles):

> I can also add, from personal experience, that [bringing Levinas to the
> attention of a wider intellectual audience] becomes much more difficult
> when one tries to teach Levinas's thoughts to students in Israeli uni-
> versities. Translations of almost all Levinas's principal books exist in
> English, German, Dutch, Spanish, and many other languages. . . . We
> have nothing of the kind in Hebrew. It is a shame that not one of his
> books has been translated into Hebrew until recently. Levinas, who for
> several years had been the chief editor of *Daath*, the Israeli periodical
> on Jewish philosophy and kabbalah, is practically unknown to the
> average Israeli student of philosophy and/or Jewish thought.
> (*Paradigms in Jewish Philosophy*, 244–245)

(On a personal note, Stéphane Mosès, Professor of Jewish Philosophy at
the Hebrew University, related to me that on one of the few occasions
Levinas came to speak in Jerusalem, only four people attended, two of
whom being his wife and son.) Similarly, while his books and books
about him do appear in Jewish bookstores in the United States that cater
to traditionalist needs, he yet remains a largely unfamiliar figure to most
observant communities and readerships, and this speaks to his standing
within a Jewish religious mainstream.

Given such qualifications and before I return to the more theoretical contrast between Levinas and R. Soloveitchik, an example of my
own version of Levinasian exegesis might be instructive at this point. It
will dramatize a difference not only between Levinas's aggadic predilections and Soloveitchik's halakhic ones, but more importantly, between
meaning on one hand and the *uses of aggadah* on the other.

For the following exercise in "interpreter's breath" (in the spirit of
Levinas's generally loose interpretation of the generic form and meaning
of *aggadah*), it will perhaps be useful to remember that the rules for scriptural exegesis Moses is said to have received along with Written and Oral
Torah were routinely applied by the Rabbis to the Aggadah as well the
Halakhah, and that certain *aggadot* themselves (especially those beginning with the phrase, "it is a *masoret* [tradition]" or "we have it by tradition") were considered Sinaitic in origin. Moreover, in addition to R.
Ishmael's thirteen principles of interpretation applying to *halakhah* and
aggadah alike, an exegetical apparatus consisting of thirty-two rules and
attributed to R. Eliezer b. R Jose the Galilean, was used solely to eluci-
date *aggadot*. Thus, however multiform were the Rabbis' own views
about where exactly the Aggadah fit within the total context of Torah, it
was understood too as bounded by its own restrictive fences. Finally, as
Joseph Heinemann appositely reminds us, *aggadah* (from a verb meaning
"to say or tell") is bound up intimately with the idea of speech.

2. EXCURSUS ON *AGGADAH* THROUGH LEVINAS

When the son of Rabban Yohanan ben Zakkai died, his disciples came to bring him comfort. R. Eliezer came in and took a seat before him [*l'fanav*] and said to him, "My lord, with your permission, may I say something before you [*lifanecha*]." He said to him, "Speak." He said to him, "The first Man had a son who died, and he accepted comfort in his regard. And how do we know that he accepted comfort in his regard? As it is said, 'And Adam knew his wife again' (Gen. 4:25). You too, be comforted." Said he to him. "Is it not enough for me that I am distressed on my own account, that you should mention to me the distress of the first Man?" R. Yehoshua came in and said to him, "My lord, with your permission, may I say something before you [*l'fanecha*]." He said to him, "Speak." He said to him, "Job had sons and daughters who died, and he accepted comfort in their regard. And how do we know that he accepted comfort in their regard? As it is said, 'The Lord gave and the Lord has taken away, blessed be the name of the Lord' (Job 1:21). You too, be comforted." Said he to him, "Is it not enough for me that I am distressed on my own account that you should mention to me the distress of Job?" R. Yosé came in and took a seat before him [*l'fanav*] and said to him, "My lord, with your permission, may I say something before you [*lifanecha*]. He said to him, "Speak." He said to him, "Aaron had two grown-up sons who died on the same day, and he accepted comfort in their regard. For it is said, 'And Aaron held his peace' (Lev. 10:3), and silence means only comfort. You too, be comforted." Said he to him, "Is it not enough for me that I am distressed on my own account, that you should mention to me the distress of Aaron?" R. Shimon came in and said to him, "My lord, with your permission, may I say something before you [*lifanecha*]. He said to him, "Speak." He said to him, "King David had a son who dies, and he accepted comfort in his regard. You too, be comforted. And how do we know that he accepted comfort in his regard? As it is said, 'And David comforted Batsheva his wife and went in and lay with her and she bore a son and called his name Solomon' (2 Sam. 12:24). You too, be comforted." Said he to him, "Is it not enough for me that I am distressed on my own account, that you mention to me the distress of King David?" R. Eleazar ben Arakh came in. When he saw him, he said to his servant, "Take from me [*l'fanai*] my clothes and follow me to the bathhouse [so that I can prepare to accept consolation], for he is a great man and I shall not be able to resist his arguments." He came in and took a seat before him [*lifanav*] and said to him, "I shall draw a parable for you. To what may the matter be compared? To the case of a man with whom the king entrusted a treasure. Every day he would weep and cry, saying, 'Woe is me, when shall I get complete and final relief from this treasure that has been entrusted to me.' You too, my lord, had a son, he recited from the Torah, Prophets, Writings, Mishnah, *halakhah*, *aggadah*, and has departed this world without sin. You have reason, therefore, to accept consolation for yourself that you have returned your treasure, entrusted to you, whole and complete." He said to him, "R. Eleazar b. Arakh, my son, you have given comfort to me in the right way in which people console each other." (*Avot d'Rabbi Natan*, B version, 14)

The story is taken from the Mishnaic work known as "The Fathers according to Rabbi Natan," a commentary on *Pirke Avot* and collection of legends and parables, and concerns the preeminent founder of the Torah academy at Yavneh after the Fall of Jerusalem in 70 C.E. I have highlighted the idioms that incorporate the root for "face" less for any overinterpretation I might make on their behalf than because it is plainly difficult to avoid them in the light of Levinas's favored trope for ethical relation.[54]

Following the concerns central to much of my work, what strikes me most about this tale is its implicit sense of face-to-face relation as an *expressive or narrative* answerability before another.[55] The various defective attempts at consolation that merely rehearse biblical proof texts, in a bold, almost antimidrashic moment, suggest to me that the very machinery of applying textual example to experience when the fabric of one's own life becomes rent at such a moment is insufficient. And what does R. Eleazar do differently? He uses what Levinas calls Saying as balm or unguent applied "beneath" the gauze or superficial dressing of formulaic quotation. It is not that the others mean to be sententious or indiscriminate. But when R. Yehoshua, for instance, invokes the Book of Job, he inadvertently calls to mind the uniform failure of Job's friends—memorably captured by Job himself in the compelling image of a desert caravan that looked for water and found none: בשו כי-בטח באו עדיה ויחפרו, *They were ashamed because they had hoped; they came there and were confounded* (6:20).[56] Rather, what Rabbi Yohanan's rebukes highlight, as I read the story, is a certain inappropriate and formulaic use of text that does duty for response. After all what Rabbis Eliezer, Yehoshua, Yose, and Shimon all fail to realize is that echoing R. Yohanan's distress with the distress of scriptural figures does him no service. For it is not words of consolation that he hears resounding in such analogies, but rather the word distress itself—*tza'aru*—which stings, and rings plangently in, his ears, compounding his grief instead of relieving it. (In *Ketubot* 104a, we are told that after his death, R. Judah HaNasi's disciples declared that whoever mentioned it should be pierced with a sword, so aggrieved was their own faculty of *hearing*.)

Jacob Neusner, in his gloss on the story, reads it as a lesson in the power that the Oral Torah has over even Scripture to "define the appropriate response" (Neusener, 100).[57] (And yet, halakhically speaking, there is a certain problem in the fact that instead of waiting for Rabbi

Yohanan to address them—as the Mishnah prescribes in its rules for אבלה, mourning—all his disciples speak first, albeit with his permission.[58]) Of course, this could be said to be the *aggadah*'s homiletic lesson. But I would want to read the story, in the spirit of Levinas, as intimating a self-consciousnessness about human response and address per se, as possible ways, rhetorically, *to turn the face*—the root meaning of the word for face in Hebrew. Thus, in the talmudic tractate *Eruvin* we are told that the best way to learn from a teacher is by being able to scrutinize his facial expressions up close.

I would point additionally to the imaginative capacity to fashion, or at least, contour Saying to the vicissitudes of a person's own lived story in the form of R. Eleazar's parable of the man and his treasure. R. Eleazar teaches a reflexive lesson about the uses of aggadah, as it were, intra-aggadically. In this case a text is rubbed (as Levinas expresses the metaphor in a Talmudic reading) for the life-blood it contains. The dramatic and unforeseen changes not only in the lot of human eventuality, but in its plot, and consequently, its narratability: these events that compel me to turn my life into a story communicate the best and most appropriate response, or as Levinas puts it in "Toward the Other," which treats of verbal hurt, the difference to be discerned between "pity" and "generous action."

Facing person and facing text alike demand a certain ethical propriety of answering, which—at its most sensitive—involves a kind of authorial boldness and finesse as well. "How could speech cause harm," writes Levinas, "if it were only *flatis vocis*, empty speech, 'mere word'?"

> This recourse to a quotation which seems totally unrelated to the topic, and to which only a seemingly forced reading brings us back from afar, teaches us that speech, in its original essence, is a commitment to a third party on behalf of our neighbor: the act *par excellence*, the institution of society. (*NTR* 20–21)[59]

Or, just as applicably, precisely the reverse in our *aggadah*: a turn back to the second party through a more generous proximity. But of course, the question *of* the tale's "normative aggadic thrust" is one that still remains open, and I would conclude this exercise/excursus by simply highlighting the *uses* to which I have put this *aggadah* alongside any contextual meaning it may possess within its talmudic tractate (a sanction I find in the biographical and anecdotal character of the *Avot d'Rabbi Natan* as a whole). That, it seems to me, describes Levinas's methodology of Talmudic reading as well in much less open-ended contexts. Whether or not the apologue of Rabbi Yohanan ben Zakai and R. Eleazar intends to teach a lesson in the ethics of Saying and Said, like Levinas before the texts he adduces, however, I have rubbed it sufficiently to leave my own mark on the sedimented layers that cover it, a process Levinas tells us that begins as soon as words appear in the open air of history.

"Not all Aggadah is Midrash and not all Midrash is Aggadah," Joseph Heinemann reminds us (41), the Aggadah (as here) often possessing only a peripheral relationship to scripture and scriptural interpretation. Likewise, its fundamentally oral character, unlike much *midrash*, incurs a loss when transposed to writing. And yet, I think Gerald Bruns's insight on the hermeneutics of midrash applies just as relevantly to my use of *aggadah*: "[I]nterpretation cannot mean simply giving uniform representations of a text that is sealed off from the heterogeneity of human situations; if a text is to have force it must remain open to more than the context of its composition" (192). Indeed, it resonates in the open air, attuned to the city, the street, other men.

3. FROM LEVINAS TO SOLOVEITCHIK TO MAIMONIDES

The extended juxtaposition with R. Soloveitchik has been necessary for two reasons: (1) to introduce religious Judaism's own self-under-stood interplay between Law and lore, the Halakhah and the Aggadah; (2) to contrast two different, albeit intermittently tangent, phenomenologies of the observant life, which, though they take their cue from halakhic and aggadic dimensions of Torah, will incline to either one side or the other. And to anticipate myself slightly, as R. Soloveitchik and Yeshayahu Leibowitz have themselves been dialecti-cally linked in recent accounts of contemporary Orthodox thought,[60] the hinge figure of Soloveitchik between Levinas and Leibowitz makes a certain methodological common sense. More immediately, however, as I modulate now to the main part of this chapter—the role of par-ticularism and the neighbor in Levinas—I want to have Levinas securely positioned not merely as one who "does philosophy Jewishly" but also as a certain kind of *meforesh* (expounder) in his own right, vis-à-vis a normative tradition of classical Jewish texts and religiously circumscribed behavior.

Halakhic man, we have learned, possesses an *a priori* orientation—talmudically expressed, לכתחילה, *l'chatchila*, versus בדיעבד, *b'diavad*, or *ex post facto*—which R. Soloveitchik grounds by beginning in physical space. He does so in order to drive home both the empirical principle that underwrites the *halakhah*, and its drive toward differentiation, or fencing. His world, therefore, is first the world that lies about him, a world, however, that is understood in its ultimacy as answering to God. (Leibowitz will return again and again to Psalm 16:8, "I have set the Lord always before me," as halakhic man's justification, first and last.) Psalm 19, which is recited every Sabbath morning, gives voice to the concomitant orientation to Torah:

> The Lord's Torah is perfect, refreshing the soul; the Lord's testimony is trustworthy, teaching the simple man wisdom. The Lord's precepts are right, gladdening the heart; the Lord's commandment is clear, enlightening the eyes. The Lord's faith is pure, enduring forever; the Lord's judgments are true, they are altogether just. They are more desirable than gold, than much rare gold; sweeter are they than honey, than honey from the honeycomb. The servant is indeed careful with them; in keeping them there is great reward.

And as we have seen, the world as recomposed and mapped by halakhic man, tinged by the twinned yellow of honey-amber and gold-vermillion, is at the same time feathered and striated by an extensive network of *s'yagim*, *g'derot*, *mechitzot*, and *havdalot*: fences, partitions, various kinds and degrees of differentiation, which give the world back to God and halakhic man alike, as inscribed by Torah.

Just as the created world in Genesis is keyed to a founding set of separated categories—night/day, land/water, weekday/Sabbath, humanity/creaturely existence—so halakic man understands Jewish law as proceeding in the identical spirit of מבדל, of distinguishing. Halakhic man thus more than measures. He divides and separates: dairy foods from meat, the menstrual cycle from the rest of the month, the "taking" of dough (challah) from the Sabbath and other loaves, the leftover gleanings from the field for the poor, the priests from a Nation of Priests, the Jewish calendrical year from Time as it passes otherwise. And such calculating and differentiating is no more than his appointed task, part ratiocinative, part pragmatic. In *The Lonely Man of Faith*, when he cites the verse in Genesis, *It is not good for man to be alone*, R. Soloveitchik interprets it, by supplementing the plain sense of the verse, לא טוב [עשות מלאכה לבדו], "It is not good *to work* (not to be) alone." "The words 'I shall make a him a helpmeet'," he writes, "would refer . . . to a functional partner to whom it would be assigned to collaborate with and assist . . . in his undertakings, schemes, and projects" (31). Perceptually speaking, halakhic man is thus something of a Crusoe figure (as Levinas will call the isolated ego), inasmuch as his orientation within his surroundings begins and always returns to the empirical, and the empirical always stays for him within a *halakhic* matrix.[61] He remains lonely in the fullness of his intellect and will, even as they halakhically preside over emotion and the senses.

This operative distinction between mere being-in-the-world and the stabilizing coefficient of *halakhah* is conveyed beautifully by the Torah itself in the third paragraph of the *Shema,* which contains the precept from the Book of Numbers to wear ציצת, garment-fringes as a daily reminder of the *mitzvot*. In the verse, *You shall not rove after your heart and your eyes after which you are wont to go astray* (15:39) the verb is תור, to rove or espy, not להלך, walk (the verb also used in reference to the *meraglim* who are sent to scout the land in the same Torah portion). The Malbim (R. Meir Levush), in his great nineteenth-century gloss on the Pentateuch, comments,

> Man's soul and capacities have been created in an upright manner. The heart is naturally attracted to good. Man spoils his nature and introduces into his heart evil thoughts. The text could not then say, "you shall not walk after your heart." For if man walked in the path mapped out form him by nature he would follow the good and upright path.

Halakhic man walks in the world purposefully; otherwise his progress through it would be the unbound and roving consequence of an existentially *fringeless* wardrobe—like Akaky Akakievich's overcoat in Gogol, if you will. This is the same meaning, I believe, of the *mishna* from *Pirke Avot* that must appear so foreign to modern eyes schooled in artistic looking: "R. Jacob said: He who travels on the road while reviewing what he has learnt, and interrupts his study and says, 'How fine is that tree, how fair is that field!' Scripture regards as if he committed a grave sin" (3:9). The world's naturalism and aesthetic have their place. Yet one *walks* through the world; one does not rove.[62]

For in nature and function, the Halakhah fundamentally makes the world available to the Jew and the Jew to the world, sub species aeternas. *Behold! To the Lord your God are the heaven and the highest heaven, the earth and everything that is in it* (Deut. 10:14). And from God to Abraham, a command, התהלך לפני והיה תמים, *Walk before me* [lit., *before my face] and be perfect* (Gen. 17:2), which is also a possessive phenomenology: כי לך אתננה קום התהלך בארץ לארכה ולרחבה, *Arise, walk about the land through its length and its breadth; for to you will I give it* (Gen. 13:17).

The theologian Eliezer Berkovits describes the *halakhah* in words that dovetail with this ambulatory ethos in Soloveitchik—for the word derives from a root meaning *to walk*—as "the bridge over which the Torah moves from the written word into the living deed" (1). And "since there is no such thing as life in general, since it is always a certain form of life at a specific time of history in a specific situation, Torah application means application to a specific time in a specific situation." *Halakhah* is also the bridge between the world as ideally conceived and the world as it must be *traversed*. To be in the world is to be fettered by God, the Rabbis say, for every Jew is bound *a priori* by the Revelation at Sinai, a bond which the fifteenth-century Sefardi commentator Don Isaac Abravanel expresses in the economic language of indemnification:

> For it was then that [Jews] were initiated into the service of God and all their issue shared that same obligation and subjection from which it can never be freed. . . . There is no doubt that if a man receives a loan from another that the duty of repayment falls on him and his descendants. Just as the children were not alive when the debt was incurred they are still liable to repay it.

The Torah as trust, the Promised Land as loan, metaphors well-known to the Sages themselves, as for instance: "Rabbi Tarfon said: You are not called upon to complete the work [of Torah study], yet you are not free to evade it—your Employer can be trusted to pay you for your work" (*Avot* 2:21).

For Levinas, on the other hand, the indebtedness to Torah reads out liability for the Other.

The Torah is a permanence because it is a debt that cannot be paid. The more you pay your debt, the more in debt you become; in other words, the better you see the extent of what remains to be discovered and done. A category that is to be transposed into the relation with the other man that the Torah teaches: the closer you get to the other, the greater your responsibility becomes. The infinite of duty—which is perhaps the modality of the relation to the infinite. Here again, there is a movement up. (*BV* 30)

Ab initio, the Jew is first in the world only and necessarily with relation to human others, an enjoined "liberty which is a also fraternity." The cultural heir to his adopted country's vinculum between *liberté* and *fraternité*, Levinas will write in *Difficult Freedom*, "the fundamental experience which objective experience itself presupposes is the experience of the Other. It is experience *par excellence* [for] external being is, *par excellence*, the Other" (293). To orient us halakhically, it is as though the commandments, indeed the entire apparatus of legislated Jewish life, *stand for the other man*, rather than, as Leibowitz would capture the dynamic, *man standing before God*, or R. Soloveitchik, *man abiding in the recesses of transcendental solitude*.

Thus Levinas will quote the famous passage in *Sotah* 24a that teaches: "The Torah begins and ends with acts of charity, since it is written at the beginning: *And the Eternal God made for Adam and for his wife garments of skins, and clothed them* (Gen. 3:21); and at the end it is written, *And he buried him [Moses] in the valley* (Deut. 34:6)." He pauses to exclaim, "The alpha and omega of the Divine, in the performance of the functions of clothier, tailor, and gravedigger" (*ITN* 115)! Or, to return to the contractual metaphor above, he will allude to the tractate *Bava Metzia* 10b that speaks of a day laborer who "as a servant of God retains with regard to his Employer" a certain inalienable freedom. He can "in certain circumstances leave his master right in the middle of the day's work," meaning a belonging that does not alienate, an independence that follows from being originally bound (*BV* 10).

But let me conclude this section, then, by quoting the tradition itself—as it were, from before and behind Soloveitchik and Leibowitz, and at an oblique angle to Levinas. I do not have in mind Levinas's favored textual point of departure for his own *a priori*, in all its "*par excellence*": Rashi's commentary on the very first verse of Torah, which (for Levinas) implies that the individual man is always potentially a usurper, but which more plainly justifies God's command for Israel to take possession of the Land.[63] Rather, I cite the opening and closing sentences of the Talmud, together with the first four *halakhot* in book 1, *Sefer ha-Mada*, from Maimonides's authoritative commentary on all of *halakhah*, the *Mishneh Torah*:

[Following the first *mishna* about the earliest time permissible to recite the evening *Shema*[64]]: On what does the Tanna base himself that he commences, "From what time?" Furthermore, why does he deal with the evening [*Shema*]? Let him begin with the morning [*Shema*]! The Tanna bases himself on scripture, where it is written (Deut. 6:7) *And thou shalt recite them]* . . . *when thou liest down and when thou risest up*, and he states [the Oral Law] thus: "When does the time of the recital of the *Shema* of lying down begin? When the priests enter to eat their *teruma* [tithe]. And if you like, I can answer: [He learns the precedence of the evening] from the account of the creation of the world, where it is written (Gen. 1:5) *And there was evening and there was morning, one day. (Berakhot* 1a)[65]

Sixty-three tractates later, in *Uktzin* ("Husks," which deals with the imparting of ritual impurity due to plants, roots, and stalks), the Talmud ends with this question and answer:

When do Honeycombs become susceptible to uncleanness on account of their being regarded as liquids? Bet Shammai say: From the moment he begins to smoke the bees out; but Bet Hillel say: From the time after [the honeycomb] has been broken.[66]

That is to say, the Talmud commences with man's duty to his creator (the *fifth* verse in Genesis), and ends with a *halakhah* involving his relationship with the natural world. *Taharot* (purity), from which this tractate comes, is the last and largest division in the Mishna, to which Yeshayahu Leibowitz puts his characteristically fine point by characterizing it as "deal[ing] with all the 'filthy' aspects of one's biological existence from which there is no escape" (Cohen and Mendes-Flor 69). According to Maimonides, as there is no source for this *halakhah* in the Written Law—being דרבנן (by rabbinic decree) rather than דאורייתא (according to Scripture)—it is rightly positioned at the Mishna's terminus. Which brings me, finally, to Maimonides himself and the opening of the *Mishneh Torah*:

Halakhah 1. The fundament of fundaments and the pillar of wisdom is to know that there is a first being and he gives being to all beings, and all beings in heaven and earth or between them have no being except the truth of his being.

Halakhah 2. And if it were to be conceivable that He is not, no other thing could be.

Halakhah 3. And if it were not to be conceived that all other beings except Him were not, only He would be, and He would not cease to be with their ceasing to be. For all beings require Him, and He, blessed be He, requires neither them nor any one of them; therefore His truth is not like the truth of any of them.

Halakhah 4. And this what the Prophet says [Jer. 10:10] *The Lord God is truth*. Only He is the truth, and no other has truth like His truth. And this is what the Scripture says [Deut. 4:35] *There is none else beside Him*—that is, there is no true being beside Him which is like Him. (*Hilchot Yesodei ha-Torah* 1)

The *mitzvot* themselves, as God's expression of Himself to man in the world, are their own end, because to observe them is to acknowledge, know, love, and fear God. Leibowitz supplements this idea in his book on Maimonides when he explains that the first commandment in the Decalogue is "I am the Lord God" because it teaches that knowledge of God's existence is not only a commandment unto itself but the one from which all other *mitzvot* devolve and assume their meaning.[67] *Mitzvah* after *Mitzvah* in verse after verse of the Torah end with the same three-word peroration: אני יי אלהיכם, *I am the Lord your God*.[68]

Commenting on this, Leibowitz will intone with the authoritative kerygma of a *shofar*, "Not the existence of man in itself but his standing before God," a position with which, when it comes to prayer, R. Soloveitchik completely concurs. For Levinas, conversely, each of these ontic conditions "stands for" the other in a complex and not always halakhically sanctioned metaphysic of *substitution*. But ultimately, the pressure point here, as well as the nexus between all three philosophers, is not theological but rather anthropological: God's nature may be apodictic, but who exactly is this "other," this neighbor and stranger?

How is he or she identified? Is mankind a class of differentiated parties like Self, Other, and other Others (or "the third"), as Levinas argues, a divisible fraternity for which, paradoxically, Jewish particularism shows the way to ethical universalism? Or, separately considered, is mankind, rather, a unity to the degree that *all men* (including Jews) share an innate valueless-ness, except insofar as they become conscious servants of God, doers of his will? The next section will explore such questions, and any conclusive answers they may yield.

I note here finally that the Sages explain that first word of God's self proclamation, and hence of the commandment to know Him, in Ex. 20:2 is an acrostic: אנכי stands for אנא נפשי כתיבה יהיב, *I put myself into writing*—as much as to say, His essence suffuses the letter of the text (*Shabbat* 105a). R. Soloveitchik will say that man's task, therefore, "is to fashion, engrave, attach, and create, and transform the emptiness in being into a perfect holy existence, bearing the imprint of the divine name" (101). And the "name" of God, according to the Sages, is God's *kedusha* (holiness) in the world, His presence in worshippers' mouths, which is, paradoxically, amplified in utterance: to sanctify, to bless God, is to strengthen His presence. Levinas, on the other hand, will say that in such words, "I hear my allegiance to the other. . . . Is this implication of ethical responsibility not in the original writing in which God has come to the idea, is named in the Said?" (*BV* xiii). The halakhic category of *devarim she-bikdusha*—prayers having to do with God's holiness, like *kaddish*, that can be said only in the presence of a quorum— he might therefore interpret as bodying forth this elemental tie between *kiddush haShem*, sanctifying God, and human community: that God's name is made great by a *plurality* of persons in proximity to one another—as neighbors. *I shall be sanctified in the midst of the children of Israel*, says Leviticus 32:22.

In the *kaddish* prayer said principally by sons in memory of their deceased parents, this condition of mutual obligatedness or *arvut* is pronounced through a doxology that is also a liturgical dialogue: God is hallowed through a call and response of persons. According to a nineteenth-century interpretation of that prayer by Simhah Bunim of Przysucha (made famous by S. Y. Agnon just before Israeli statehood in 1947, and recounted recently by Leon Wieseltier in *Kaddish*), God experiences a vacancy when a man dies, a lack that is rectified by "magnifying and sanctifying" His name, thus bringing together, as one writer has put it, not only mourners and the souls of the deceased but man and his neighbors. And yet, and again, who is the neighbor?

4. WHO IS THE THE NEIGHBOR?

If townspeople have a well [and it is a question] whether they or strangers [have first call on it], they come first, before the strangers.

[If it is a question] whether strangers or their own cattle come first, the lives of the strangers take precedence over their own cattle. Rabbi Yose says, their own cattle takes precedence over the lives of the strangers

[If it is a question] whether their own cattle or the cattle of strangers comes first, their own cattle takes precedence over the cattle of strangers.

[If it is a question] whether strangers or their own laundry comes first, the lives of the strangers take precedence over their own laundry. Rabbi Yose says, their own laundry takes precedence over the lives of the strangers [the *gemara* explains the reason as health hazards involved in doing one's own laundry].

[If it is a question] whether their own laundry or the laundry of strangers comes first, their own laundry takes precedence. (*Tosefta Bava Metzia* 11:33–36; *Nedarim* 80b)

Let us say neither reductively nor for expediency's sake that Levinas sees all the *mitzvot* as variations on the theme of אהבת רע, love of the neighbor. To be sure, the exact wording of the last half of Lev. 19:18, *you shall love your neighbor as yourself—I am the Lord* (and Leibowitz will remind us that the verse ends meaningfully with "I am the Lord") is not in strict accord with Levinasian ethics. For it seems to assign primacy to the Self as the metric of comparison rather than being accused or unsettled in its subjectivity. But as God loves the stranger (the only class of persons, said Martin Buber, with whom Scripture identifies God as lover), so the Jew is commanded likewise in relation to the neighbor, the *wisdom* of which love Levinas will hardly qualify. In his *Sefer ha-Mitzvot* Maimonides numbered this particular commandment as positive commandment 206 out of 248,[69] neither the crown nor the hub of religious observance. Other commentators, Nachmanides or Yehudah Halevi, for instance, assimilate it to the halakhic sense of national fraternity known as אהבת ישראל, the love of one's fellow Jews. The *Sefer Ha-Hinukh* by the thirteenth-century talmudist Aharon Halevi numbers it 219, and interprets its sense as the obligation "to love every Jew with devoted love."

Rabbi Akiva, often cited, makes it the fundamental principle of the Torah, as quoted in several parallel *midrashim*:

Rabbi Akiva said: The verse, *Love your neighbor as yourself* (Lev. 19:18) is a great principle in the Torah. Ben Azzai said: The verse, *This is the book of the history of mankind* (Gen. 5:1) is a greater principle still. That you should not say, since I am despised let my neighbor be similarly despised, since I am cursed, let my neighbor be similarly cursed. Said R. Tanhuma: If you act thus, know whom you are despising *in the likeness of God made He him.* (*Bereshit Rabbah* 24:6–7, *Sifra* on *Kedoshim* 4:12, and *Avot d'Rabbi Natan* [ed. Schecter], version B, 26)

And yet it is not at all clear that R. Akiva has non-Jews as well as Jews in mind, or that the Torah itself assigns the same metaphysic to the concept of neighbor here as Levinas typically will. For one thing, the command quoted above is only the second half of a verse whose first, *You shall not take vengeance or bear a grudge against the children of your people [your kin],* is demonstrably particularist.[70] Is the relationship between these two halves parallel or opposed? That is, is "neighbor" a member of the Jewish people, or rather every man, irrespective of origin and kinship? Such questions are exactly the stuff of halakhically grounded principles of scriptural hermeneutics, the order of generalization and specification in the biblical text, and how precisely instances of them will apply.

As Ernst Simon has shown in a valuable essay, "The Neighbor (*Re'a*) Whom We Shall Love," the referential outlines of *re'ah* in the Bible are multiple; sometimes the word designates Jews, sometimes non-Jews (even in relation to one another). Even when we turn to the analogous commandment in Deuteronomy to "love the stranger" (10:19) the problem becomes more ambiguous not less so, for the preceding verse says, *God loves the stranger, providing him with food and clothing,* whose final phrase can be understood both restrictively and absolutely. In Deuteronomy (15:2–3), we also find the distinction between *re'ah, ahiv* (kinsman) and *nokhri* (foreigner).[71] Moreover, the phrase "love thy neighbor as thyself" contains some crucial features in the Hebrew that directly bear on its translated meaning.

The *Biur* (nineteenth-century Bible commentary by Solomon Dubno and Moses Mendelssohn), points out that the word *kamocha* (as yourself) is not usually used adverbially but rather adjectivally, thus: "Love thy neighbor" *who is as thyself,* that is, created in the image of God. Furthermore, as Nachmanides argued centuries before, the verb complement, *l're'akha,* thy neighbor, is in the dative (*le*) not accusative (*et*)—not "Love thy-neighbor" but rather "Love/ for-thy-neighbor"—implying that as it would be unrealistic to love one's neighbor without limit, we should merely wish that he or she enjoy the same well-being as we ourselves. (In Deut. 10:19, however, the situation is reversed, with the suggestion, following Nachmanides's logic, that the stranger *is* to be loved illimitably; no other set of commandments, incidentally, is repeated as many times [36] in the Torah as those having to do with the stranger.) Simon notes that as ambiguous as the scriptural picture is, the general trend in rabbinic literature is, conversely, restrictive: "neighbor" and "stranger" assume in-group status, either as kinsman, convert, or resident alien. Maimonides, whom Levinas rarely invokes, justified the Mishnaic principle that Gentiles are liable for damages if their oxen gore Israelites, but not vice-versa, by invoking the general natural law that the lower in nature is ordained to serve the higher.[72] (Elsewhere in the *Mishneh Torah*, Maimonides will narrow the frame of reference even more restrictively to Jews who are *shomer mitzvot*, scrupulously observant. And in *Rozeah* 4:9, when he reviews Mishnaic and midrashic interpretations of Ex. 21:14 [the penalty for murdering one's neighbor], he again excludes Gentiles, and persistently sinful Jews, for "none of these is 'thy neighbor.'")[73]

One point to glean here, as Levinas takes such pains to emphasize, is that Scripture uninterpreted by the Oral Law simply does not suffice for Jewish tradition; the Torah may be God's word but it does not speak univocally in the "open air." Indeed, Levinas's sense of the need for interpretation is almost congruent with his understanding of the need or desire for the Other. *Sollicitation*, his word for a bold maneuvering of the text in direct response to its *demand* for interpretive proximity, is functionally analogous to the attunement of one-for-another that defines our relation to the neighbor and the stranger, each of whom *solicits* our regard. Indeed, it is in the essay, "On the Jewish Reading of Scriptures" that Levinas makes one of his most explicit links between a vigilance of text and of person. In the second section, "The Tribunal and the Love of One's Neighbor," he discusses a passage from the tractate *Makkot* that deals with judicial punishments like flogging, as sentenced by the Sanhedrin to compensate for the most serious theological punishment, כרת, excommunication. Levinas asks, "how can a human decision intervene in a domain which exceeds man" (*BV* 102).[74] The *sugya* (argument) is predicated on Deuteronomy 25:3 as invoked by R. Hananiah, *Forty shall he strike him, he shall not add; lest, he strike him an additional blow beyond these, and your brother be degraded in your sight*, and it is here that the Sages derive exegetically (למקל, in the direction of leniency), that the count should be one *fewer* than forty (*Makkot* 22b).[75] Levinas writes,

> In any case, R. Hananiah breaks with the dark mythological reality whose eventuality would indicate a religious tyranny, in order to proclaim that no sin exists in relation to heaven which cannot be expiated among men and in the light of day. The tribunal would thus be the place where the divine regenerative will is revealed. Admittedly, there is violence. But it is an act without a spirit of violence, contempt, or hatred. A fraternal act, without passion. It proceeds from a responsibility for others. To be the guardian of others, contrary to the vision of

the world according to Cain, defines fraternity. For the tribunal which reasons and weighs up, the love of one's neighbor would be possible. (104)[76]

Now, I would note first that the text here is even more restrictive that if it in fact deployed the word for "neighbor." The word it uses, in fact, is אח, *brother* (a scriptural parallel: Deut. 15:2, *he is not to oppress his neighbor or his brother*, by exegetical convention, distinguishes *both* categories from Jews proper). One can call the Sanhedrin's sentence of flogging a "fraternal act" (with or without passion) but the object of punishment here is by no means a generalized population of Others, "human beings expelled from the human," but a particularized group of Jews in a politically subjugated Israel. Levinas's reading here—though more condensed than usual—is exemplary in two ways: it implicitly correlates a hermeneutic of generosity with the fellow feeling that is the *text's* topic, and it uses the text's particulars to allegorize tenets of Levinas's own philosophy.

More than once, Levinas inflects Rashi's comment on Torah verses that they "cry out" for interpretation. Levinas's essays sometimes do the same: "The notion of Israel in the Talmud, as my master had taught me, must be separated from all particularism, except for that of election" (123). Along with this recurrent idea, I would recall the passage I cited earlier in reference to Gen. 30:31, this time calling attention to the fact that it follows a passionate defense of Zionism:

> it should not be forgotten that my family and my people, despite the possessive pronouns, are my others, like strangers, and demand justice and protection. The love of the other—the love of one's neighbor. Those near to me are also my neighbors.

And I would add one more, from a radio exchange with Shlomo Malkin and Alain Finkielkraut conducted after the Lebanese-run and Israeli-sanctioned incursion into the Sabra and Shatilah refugee camps in September 1982:

> E.L.: For me this is the essence of Zionism. It signifies a State in the fullest sense of the term, a state with an army and arms, and army which can have a deterrent, and if necessary, defensive significance. Its necessity is ethical— indeed it is an old ethical idea which commands us precisely to defend our neighbors. My people and my kin are still my neighbors. When you defend the Jewish people, you defend your neighbor; and every Jew in particular defends his neighbor, when he defends.

> S.M.: Emmanuel Levinas, you are the philosopher of the "other." Isn't history, isn't politics the very site of the encounter with the "other," and for the Israeli isn't the "other" above all the Palestinian?

E.L.: My definition of the other is completely different. The other is the neighbor, who is not necessarily kin but who may be. But if your neighbor attacks another neighbor, or treats him unjustly, what can you do? Then alterity takes on another character, in alterity we can find an enemy, or at least we are faced with the problem of knowing who is right and who is wrong, who is just and who is unjust. There are people who are wrong. (*Levinas Reader*, 293–294)

Admittedly, the topic varies here from passage to passage, but I block them out like this in order to underscore how Levinas himself moves more or less effortlessly back and forth between rabbinic exegesis, Levinasian philosophy, and political criticism. As I suggest in my introduction, the vocabularies he uses for each of these projects—if not homologous—are explicitly translatable into each other's terms. Philosophy is what the Oral Tradition *does*, according to Levinas, a *phronesis* that teaches the wisdom of love or ethical responsibility.

But to ask my own question again, are the Talmud's "neighbor" (and the Bible's for that matter), the "neighbor" in *Totality and Infinity* or *Otherwise Than Being*, and "the neighbor" in the essays on Zionism and Jewish identity all correspondent? Does the same Other make the same ethical claim in each case? Finally, does the *politics* of alterity transfer so seamlessly between the Mishnaic and Talmudic periods from 100 B.C.E. to 500 C.E., on the one hand,[77] and the exigencies of fully modern states and polities, on the other?

The last question is important because for Levinas, the latter alternative means effectively four things: the "Jewish Passion" of the Holocaust in mid-century Europe, the status of Jews (and Jewish intellectuals) in postwar France, the educational needs of Sefardic communities as served by the Alliance Israélite Universelle du Basin Méditerranéen, and finally the conflict between Arabs and Jews, Israelis and Palestinians, in the Middle East. Judaism and Jewish identity will be made to stand for many things in Levinas's writings, but chiefly a responsibility that models difficult freedom and entails persecution—but the extension to other others, other responsibilities, other freedoms, and other persecutions remains implicit at best. Who is the neighbor? How to reconcile the claims of ethical alterity with the claims of social, political, cultural difference? And how, finally, does one discriminate between *alterities*: between transcendence and proximity, between the Other (distant, abstract) and the neighbor or fellow human being (near, related)?

In the social world imagined by the tractate *Makkot*, *akh*, brother, and *re'ah*, neighbor, are not interchangeable concepts or entities. A fence divides them, the fence of halakhic differentiation. The Rabbis were hardly unaware of a non-Jewish presence around them, for in fact it surrounded them, as they were administered by it in both the Land of Israel and the diaspora. But their concerns in this tractate are nevertheless restrictive, for as R. Soloveitchik reminds us, the Halakhah imagines an ideal world within the real one. In that ideal/real world non-Jews would not be subject to judgments of the Sanhedrin that stipulate lashing. And in this case, Levinas's typical formulation, גרים יתום ואלמנה *strangers, the orphan, and widow* (as the Bible's own phraseology for alterity), or the shorter form of "the neighbor" deployed in both his philosophical and Judaic texts, cannot really be made to universalize what is so stubbornly particularized: the attributes (to paraphrase Alain Finkielkraut), differentiating neighbor from neighbor.

The most popular book in Jewish life is not the Bible or the Talmud, though it quotes from them both, but rather the Daily Prayerbook or *Siddur*, which was compiled and finalized after a long process of evolution by the Sages themselves. After he first dons *talit* and *tefillin* and recites some preliminary prayers, the male religious Jew utters the following triad of blessings at the beginning of each day: *Blessed art thou, Lord or God, King of the Universe, who has not made me a heathen; . . . not made me a slave; . . . not made me a woman.*

Taken from tractate *Menachot* 43b (a possible rejoinder to Paul's programmatic blurring of categories in *Galatians* 3:28 but also parallel perhaps to a saying ascribed to Thales or Socrates), these blessings are intended to express gratitude to God for the privilege of *mitzvot* incumbent upon the Male Israelite alone.[78] And yet there is no gainsaying the fact that the religious Jew begins his day—and that would include Levinas—by particularizing himself in the most dramatic of ways. This is also the sense (and taken so, paradigmatically, by Leibowitz) of the famous dictum by R. Haninah, "Greater is he who performs because he has been commanded than one performs without having been commanded" (*Bava Kamma* 87a; *Kiddushin* 31a).

About which, in what must be accounted one of his more spectacularly counterintuitive feats of apologetics, Levinas will exclaim:

> What have we made . . . of the theme of the six hundred and thirteen commandments constraining the children of Israel, whereas seven commandments sufficed for the children of Noah? To owe to the other more than one asks him for! Blinded by the brilliance of the sun of the West, a cursory glance distinguishes here only separation and arrogance. This is a fatal confusion. For one would have every right to ask if this apparent limitation of universalism is not what protects it from totalitarianism; if it does not arouse our attention to the murmurs of inner voices; if it does not open our eyes to the faces which illuminate and permit the control of social anonymity, and to the vanquished of humanity's rational history where it is not just the proud who succumb. (*BV* 200)

And yet when we track the Talmud's close-grained particularization of otherness, a whole class of "face and voice" appear at variance with Levinasian precepts of the ethical subject's indemnity and hostageship, freed from any markers of social, ethnic, or biological difference. One example would be the various gradations of non-Jew such as *ben Noach* (the Noahide), *ger* (the stranger), *kuti* (Samaritan), and *min* (the heathen).[79] *Baalei mumim* (the deformed), the *shoteh* (mad) and *cheresh* (deaf-mute), *mamzerim* (of uncertain issue), *eved* (slave), *zakein mamrei* (rebellious elder), *zar* (non-priest) and *mumar Yisra'el* (Jewish apostate) illustrate other modes of categorization.

Most dramatic is the case of women in general (to which one entire order of the Talmud is given over), and in particular: the *zonah* or *k'deshah* (prostitute), *sotah* (woman taken in adultery), *shifchah* (non-Jewish slave), *shivuyah* (captive) and *goya* (non-Jewess), the *moredet* (rebellious wife), *yoledet* (woman who has given birth), *nidah* (menstruant), and *agunah* (abandoned wife).[80] Finally, there is the host of persons made ritually impure (*tamei*) through contact—a deconsecration that can apply only to Jews, and that thus (in an interesting way) "neutralizes" the corresponding ritual status of Gentiles.[81] But all such differentiated assortments of otherness, whether ritual or civic, attest not to a localized "totalitarianism" but rather the "difficult particularity" of *halakhah*.

To take perhaps the most vexing for modern sensibilities, women's status within rabbinic (not to say biblical) culture had always been equivocal at best, against the horizon of a prevailing if still not entirely monolithic patriarchy:

> On the "positive" side of the ledger, sexuality was affirmed in rabbinic Judaism as an enduring aspect of the personality and as a God-given benefice to humanity both for their pleasure and well being and for the propagation of the species, itself understood as an unmitigated good. . . . But on the negative side, this construction defined sex roles absolutely and rigidly. Women were daughters, wives, and mothers, nearly exclusively. Although the activities of study of Torah and prayer were not opposed to procreation as spirit to flesh, and although, to the best of my knowledge, there were no representations of procreation in which the male contribution was spirit and the female, matter, there can be no doubt that the "upper body" was more valued than the "lower" in the culture, and upper-body activities were nearly entirely a male preserve. (Boyarin 236)[82]

Feminist critics of Levinas have pressed that no matter his avowed distinction between a crude biologism and categories intended more figurally, he is famously unreconstructed in his treatment of gender roles, a sensitivity to which fails to keep pace in his thought with the sophisticated critique of Western metaphysics and ontology. As a *mitnagid/maskil* with certain culturally inscribed prejudices about men and women and their respective *milieux*, it is not surprising to find Levinas recycle a conventional gender politics of male praxis and female "enablement."[83] "Difficult freedom," as both an ethical and intellectual good, tends to be the province of men alone in Levinas's thought.

To make a differently weighted political case, one might add to the list above a subgrouping of ethnic and cultural alterity: *apikorsim* (those who reject the truth of Torah[84]), *minim* (infidels), and the whole class of sectarian Jews considered by rabbinic authorities in varying degrees to be outside the fold: Karaites, Sadducees, or the Idumeans, who were forcibly converted under the Hasmonean king John Hyrcanus in the second century B.C.E. And if we fast-forward to present-day Israel, not only do the demographic divisions between Ashkenazim and Sefardim or secular and religious, or Ethiopian *olim* and an otherwise racialized majority trouble Levinas's sense of Jewish visual and aural acuity for faces and inner voices, but the minority of Arab citizens of the state and the Palestinians outside the Green Line offer powerful instances of otherhood amidst brotherhood.

In the case of Ethiopian immigrants one notes that while they have been incorporated as Jews in more or less good standing, they remain unassimilated fully into Israeli society, not only thus throwing into relief a certain fiction about national unity (by which I mean simply that heterogeneity is never fully "transcended" by the solidarity of nationalism or the state), but also opening a window onto the dynamics of othering—distancing or stigmatizing—from *within*.[85] No matter Levinas's egalitarian phenomenology, or indeed his privileging of the outcast and the proletarian, Judaism has always known caste in one form or another: priests, tribal captains, Sanhedrin, medieval Hasidei Askenaz and Kabbalists, Hofjuden and modern philanthropists on the one side; *zarim* (those barred from the Temple precincts) and the general mass of people on the other. Or still perhaps most dramatically in religious circles (where the texts Levinas reads are both studied and practiced): men set off from women.

This is simply to say that there have always been *other* Jews, from a separate class of *kohanim*, to Korach's insurgency, to the division between Northern and Southern kingdoms, to the general diasporic dissemination of Jews into East and West, and within that East and West further Easts and Wests.[86] It is also to point out there have always been *others* within the tribe who have not been "proximate" or perceived as "neighbors" in Levinas's sense, *kal vakhomer* (*a fortiori*) making the status of non-Jews all the more problematical. How exactly Jews realize the halakhic principle of *arvut* כל ישראל ערבים לזה זה—*all Israel is respon-*

sible, each for each—and *achdut* (unity) in the midst of internal sec-
tarianism, historical necessity, or straightforward halakhic particularization, has always been one of the great questions confronting it
at the level of peoplehood. And it is thus that Levinas's *own* text also
be rubbed. The grouping of persons into pure and impure classes, or
the differentiation among resident alien, Noahide, and heathen are
just the sort of intratalmudic inventories that lie at the very heart of
an analysis of halakhic man's duty, and pedagogically speaking, his
satisfaction (like R. Soloveitchik's). *Mutatis mutandis*, formulating
and discussing such distinctions also constitutes the halakhic praxis
that for Leibowitz justifies and existentially grounds Jews as practitioners of a Juda*ism* over and above their being Jews in an ethnocultural sense. Nevertheless, it is in that very sense that classical rabbinic Judaism was not at all shy about a Jewish chauvinism and
exclusivism relative to other peoples or other kinds of people: "A
non-Jew who observes *Shabbat* deserves death," we are told starkly
in *Sanhedrin* 58b.

Of course, how the Rabbis "talked about" persons in their argu-
mentations and anecdotes will not necessarily correlate with how those
persons were actually *faced* by them in daily encounter, though one
assumes a certain continuity of practice from textual study that has the
importance of a *mitzvah*, to quotidian life where the majority of other
mitzvot are concretized. And this is Levinas's own point if departure, it
is fair to say. Nevertheless, the actual tractate of *Makkot* that he analyzes in "On the Reading of the Jewish Scriptures" does not mention the
neighbor at all. Similarly, when the Oral Law makes reference to the
poor, as for instance, in the tractate *Peah*, which discusses the "poor
man's tithe," it is to the poor of Israel, and not a universalist expression
of the commonweal.[87]

The point that remains at issue is: how are we to understand Levinas's sense of the "other" in the text, when it is precisely in the text that
all "others" are not "brothers"? (It is worth recalling that *akher*, or
"Other," was the appellation given by the Rabbis to R. Elisha ben
Abuya after he ceased observing the *mitzvot*.) Because Levinas has interpreted the Halakhah generously? Or ההלכה לוז, *lezad ha-halakhah*—
because he has reached through the fence of normative categorization
and smuggled in an ethic (not to mention a secularization), *aside from
halakhah*? In the passage from *Makkot* quoted above, R. Hananiah is
speaking *halakhically*, and it is well to remember the principles[88] of
halakhic exegesis behind his interpretation of Scripture: דבר שהיה בכלל,
davar sh'haya b'khlal (something that was included in a generalization)
and כלל ופרט, *kelal uprat* (generalization and specific case). That is to
say, just as R. Hananiah is able to emend the scriptural command from

forty lashes to thirty-nine—remaining with the Torah's adjudicative ambit—so the brother "not to be degraded in your sight" is a fellow Jew, precisely *not* a neighbor in a general sense. Says Rava,

> How dull-witted are those people who stand up [in deference] to the scroll of the Torah, but do not stand up in deference to a great Sage, because while in the Torah forty lashes are stipulated, the Rabbis come and reduce them to one. (*Makkot* 22b)

Or as David Hartman has nicely framed it, one walks with God, like Noah, if one feels merely bound to the letter; one walks *before* God, like Abraham, if one creates the meaning of the words (*LC* 37).

In tractate *Makkot*, however, where an alteration in the punishment is made, other distinctions remain hard and fast. Indeed, taking such distinctions for a given is what Levinas himself in "Demanding Judaism" calls a religious subpoena as *liturgy*, the yoke of the Kingdom of Heaven (עול מלכות שמים) as a being seized by the lock of one's hair (from Ezekiel 8:3): "a belonging despite oneself, as if one were seized hold of" (*BV* 9). But of course, "belonging" in a somewhat different sense—the fence that separates parties—is exactly what we are inquiring after here.

> What is in fact the march towards universality of a political order? It consists in confronting multiple beliefs—a multiplicity of coherent discourses—and finding one coherent discourse that embraces them all, which is precisely the universal order. A coherent discourse is already open to the universal when the person holding it, who up until now has remained enclosed within his individual circumstances—though his discourse may have been coherent—concerns himself with the inner coherence of discourses other than his own, and so surpasses his individual state. This situation can also be described as the beginning of philosophy. (*DF* 94)

Levinas will equate such logic with a political condition, the Enlightenment that becomes part of state governance, its declarations and constitutions, the Hegelian "end of History that embraces all histories." Running counter to it, however, he offers the case of the Jews as a people outside peoples, "a people capable of diaspora, of remaining outside," which therefore has "a totally different vision of universality," one that does not traffic in totality, in the immorality—"the infernal cycle of violence"—that underpins the moral end of political conditions and decisions. "At the moment when the political temptations of the light 'of others' is overcome," he writes," "my responsibility becomes the more irreplaceable. At this point, the real universality, which is non-catholic, can affirm itself. It consists in serving the universe. It is called messianism" (*DF* 95).[89]

Israel does not measure its morality by politics, Levinas avers. In contradistinction to the *midrash* on the first man who was mammoth enough to stretch from East to West, Levinas imagines the upright man "who stands as tall as the gap between the heavens and the earth." This is *aggadic man*, as I have proposed the concept. But is it *halakkhic man*, the Jew circumscribed by Torah and *mitzvot* who thereby fences off the non-halakknic world? Time and again, Levinas will root Israel's particularism in its "demands" and "difficulties" that predicate a true, that is, ethical universalism, a universalism of "the other man." The religious relation is an ethical relation, and morality discovers the place of election that is made up not of privileges but of responsibilities (*DF* 21). Above its historical facticity, Israel is a moral category, and its "position outside nations" guarantees the "real universality" that its ethical particularity founds. In *Chagigah*, the tractate that deals with Festival offerings, the sages speak of the prohibition of work on the Sabbath as כהררים התלין בשערה, *like mountains hanging by a hair*, because a massive edifice of rabbinic restrictions rests on a scant scriptural basis. One might say that Levinas makes a similar claim about the particularism that underpins metaphysical fraternity—indeed it is just the sort of formulation he might select himself.

Thus, he will quote Rabbi Meir in the Talmud that a pagan who knows the Torah is the equal of the High Priest.[90] And yet that same Talmud prohibits the teaching of Torah to non-Jews. Similarly, Levinas returns again and again to Isaiah 57:19, שלום שלום לרחוק ולקרוב, *Peace, peace to him that is far off and to him that is near*, which for him "represents a spiritual event that transcends the anthropological" (*ITN* 172). But halakhically speaking, קרוב, "the one who is near," indicates a close familial relative of which there are seven degrees; רחוק, "the one who is far," can mean distance in the sense of keeping aloof from bad associates (*Berakhot* 60b), but it also signifies self-estrangement, keeping away from the Lord so as not to repent (*Midrash Yelamdenu* to Num. 10:29, qtd. in *Arukh*). The figure of proximity is understood in the Oral Law in terms of kin, while the figure of remoteness or withdrawal in any case connotes neither consanguinity nor relatedness.

When the Mishna and Talmud speak "meta-halakhically" about *zehirut* (care in the performance of *mitzvot*), the normative deftly shades into the axiological: (1) *One should not pass over a mitzvah when he meets it.* (2) *If an opportunity to perform a mitzvah presents itself to you do not be slow in performing it. Run to perform even a minor mitzvah.* (3) *When a mitzvah comes into your hands do not let it become chametz* (leaven). The Sages derive this last metaphor from the biblical verse, *guard the matzoh* (Ex. 12:17)—as much as to say, the *mitzvah* of *matzah* (the words are close in spelling) can also be understood as a reflexive sign for the performance of *mitzvot* generally, over and above the specific commandment regarding unleavened bread. Now, Levinas might point to the fact that in the second to last example, the *mishna* about *zerizut* (alacrity in performance) is sandwiched between two *mishnayot* in *Chapters of the Fathers* that speak of the necessity to learn from every man (מכל אדם), and not to despise any man (לכל אדם). And yet the thrust of *all* these statements is *Torah lishmah*, Torah-for-its-own-sake: the regenerative and circular machinery of *mitzvah* that supplies its own reward and reveals the concomitant loss incurred when the pure unleaven of *mitzvot* is left unattended, unperformed.

True, the Talmud is famous for holding even contradictory opinions in equipoise.[91] Self-understood, and according to Jewish religious tradition, this merely expresses the inexhaustibility of Torah, a work that cannot by definition be completed; for Levinas, however, it reads out the unfinalizability between persons that is proximity and justice. Also, as I have said, the Talmud balances *halakhot* and *aggadot* in complex and not always harmonious ways, often intertwining them at nodal points of argument (like the knots on the *tzitzit* that provoke remembrance).[92] The Rabbis are nothing if not peremptory and dogmatic when they need to be: "given to the usage of such expressions as, 'How long will you pile up such nonsense?,' or 'What do you know about aggada. Go study the minutiae of obscure halakhah'" (qtd. in Boyarin, 27).

True, conflicting interpretations sit side by side even in Torah commentaries, like those compiled in the *Mikraot Gedalot*. One of the more notable, for example, revolves around the identity of the Cushite woman Moses is said to have married (Num. 12:1). One *derash* sees her as Zipporah, Moses's original wife, either because she was dark-skinned or because the Torah wants to compliment her inversely; the other follows the legend that Moses served as king of Ethiopia after Egypt and before Midian, and there married an Ethiopian woman. Rashi, his grandson the Rashbam, Ibn Ezra, Onkelos, Targum Yerushalmi I and Targum Yerushalmi II all disagree on who is being described in the text. A consensual decision is never rendered (the norm for aggadic, as opposed to halakhic, gloss).

The Torah, in other words, is also contentedly composite, especially in its *sollicitation* for attentive eye and sensitive ear, and that is both its art and its science. But again, I emphasize that textual or interpretive call-and-response, if they are operating allegorically, reflect dialogues between God and Israel at the level of peoplehood, or man and the whole world in which he finds himself at the level of self-identity. The textual "other" does not always signify the human Other in the metaphysically ethical sense Levinas intends. *Torah* derives from a root meaning to shoot forth or permeate, and thus to point out, teach, and instruct. *Talmud* derives from a root meaning to be joined or affixed or accustomed, and thus to learn, study, argue. That is to say, in religious

Judaism even the narratives in the Pentateuch are scoured by commentators for their encoded *halakhic* meaning, and *halakhah* is by far the
more marked category here, both ideologically and pragmatically.

To *find* that meaning is already to be engaged in *mitzvah*, so completely is the Torah fenced by practice and observance. As Levinas himself takes such pains to emphasize, the Talmud is not simply a text that
is read or studied, but rather, continues to be enacted. What is notable
about Levinas's reading of the Talmud, however, is not only the selectivity of examples, all aggadic, but also the second step of midrashic
coup de maître that he permits himself. When he articulates a series, as
he often does, from "the neighbor" to "the first person to come along"
to "the stranger" (*ITN* 134, 172). he blurs certain clear-cut distinctions
that are nevertheless essential to talmudic reasoning, even if they do not
apply outside of the fence of *halakhah*.

> Genesis 24 relates the thankfulness of Abraham's servant. He gave
> Rebekah "two bracelets for her arms for two shekel weights of gold."
> Two bracelets weighing ten shekels, or two table of the Law? The
> Decalogue? The rabbinic doctors make the association. In their view,
> Abraham's servant recognized Sinai. It is a prefiguration on an enact-
> ment of the revelation in the responsibility for the first person to come
> our way . . . a responsibility exceeding the demand heard by myself in
> the face of the other. But "the first person to come along" for myself
> and the other person would also constitute the third party, who joins
> us or who always accompanies us. The third party is also my other,
> also my neighbor. Who would be the first to speak? Where does the
> priority lie? A decision must be made. The Bible requires justice and
> deliberation. (134)

Indeed. Thus, the "neighbor" is the one whose house may be next
to mine, and whose "proximity" to me I must therefore calculate of in
terms of cubits, adjoining partitions, ladders, the eventuality of damages, and the like. Or he may be the other in the desert in the famous
baraita from *Bava Metzia* 62a on Lev. 25:36, *that thy brother may live
with thee*), between whom and myself there is only enough water for
one. Who drinks? R. Akiva's opinion is upheld: "Your own life comes
before the life of your fellow man." *Pace* Levinas, Gen. 24 also relates
an initial confusion between servant and master that serves only to facil-
itate recognition; the crucial *disparity* in roles is then reaffirmed.[93]

The first person to come along may also very well be the Gentile
driver of a fallen ass owned by a Jew, in which case I need not *surely
unbind* (Ex. 23:5) or *surely lift up* (Deut. 22:4) with him, as the law
commands in regard to Jews. He may be a sinning friend or relative, and
thus my responsibility is excessive in another direction entirely: הוכח
תוכיח, to *surely rebuke* (Lev. 19:17).[94] If he is a *ger tzaddik* (convert), a

ger toshav (resident alien), or simply a *ger* (outsider), my dealings could differ accordingly. Such careful distinguishing—even between Levite gatekeepers and Levite singers (*Erkhin* 11a; *Hilkhot Kelei haMikdash* 3:10)—is the very stuff of halakhic life, normatively understood.

And yet in *Otherwise Than Being*, Levinas will say,

> Absolving himself from all essence, all genus, all resemblance, the neighbor, the first one on the scene, concerns me for the first time (even if he is an old acquaintance, an old friend, an old lover, long caught up in the fabric of my social relations) in a contingency that excludes the a priori. (86)

Not only halakhically speaking is the *a priori* untranscendable such that within its four cubits, God dwells and man walks. But "genus," "essence," "resemblance" are crucial to its workings, and thus absolute in themselves. Even at its seeming most ecumenical, when for instance in the discussion in *Gittin* 59–61 of "things done for the sake of peace," we are told, "The heathen poor are supported along with the Jewish, their sick visited along with the Jewish, their dead buried along with the Jewish," rabbinic law may simply be ruling cautiously, as a dependent minority instrumentally seeking peaceful relations for its own well-being.[94]

As Leviticus 18 and 20 demonstrate in the marking out of licit familial unions from illicit, and as the orders of *Taharot* (purity) and *Nashim* (women) in the Talmud underscore in minute detail, even within the kinship network, certain essential distinctions prevail. It is precisely such distinctions—between permitted and forbidden, pure and impure, mixed and unalloyed, this person and that person, this object and that object—that the classic Jewish legal texts seek endlessly to refine. And *that* is what makes so interesting, I think, a certain ambiguity between others and brothers in Levinas's thought.

In the passage I have quoted twice now where Levinas glosses Jacob's need to provide for his own family, the import, it seems, is that one makes one's brethren "alienable," in a paradoxical way, so that they become newly valuable as "others," and thus demanding of my responsibility. The immediately preceding context is the Arab world and Israel's place within it. (Levinas even cites himself from *Difficult Freedom*, amending his earlier use of "refugees" to "Palestinians."[95]) Conceptually at least, distance secures nearness. The neighbor models for me the ones who are already "mine"; I make them "other" in order to have them back again, ethically. And in defending them, I defend myself, for as Levinas says immediately prior to the verse he cites, "The great—the greatest—ethical idea of existence for one's neighbor applies unreservedly to me, to the individual and the person that I am" (*BV* xvii).

Now, the scriptural model for such ethical dispossession and repossession would seem to be Joseph reunited with his brethren. But Levinas chooses Jacob (whom the Sages call *bechir she ba-avot,* "the chosen of the Patriarchs") for his illustration of the dictum, *maase avot siman l'banim,* "the deeds of the fathers as a sign for the sons." Servant, toiler, slave (in Gen. 30–31), Jacob's hands are always busy, and hands, Levinas says elsewhere, are עסקנות, ever-grasping: "nothing is more mobile, more impertinent, more restless than the hand" (*ITN* 24).[96] According to Avivah Zornberg, this entire Torah scene plots the link between labor and a conscious possession of self and property:

> As Jacob speaks of knowledge in connection with labor, he comes progressively to appropriate for himself the right to his own labor. He knows himself and his own strength; he is intensely aware of "all his might," precisely because he has acquired it through long years of subjugation. . . . Jacob's success is conveyed in terms of material prosperity: *And the man became very prosperous [Vayifrotz]*—a clear fulfillment on the economic level, of God's promise, *And you shall spread out [U-faratzta]* [28:14]. Jacob's vitality is expressed in a thickening envelope of property: of things belonging to him, attached to him. (204)

Moreover, such acquisition actually *delays* Jacob's return to Israel from his mandatory sojourn in Charan; in the ensuing six years his "household" garners wealth from sheep, not new sons. Yet Levinas reads the verse as mediating between the claims of self-interest and of altruism; Jacob's assertion of his responsibilities to kin in the face of Laban teaches a lesson about synonymy between my family and "others," and between my people and "strangers" or "neighbors." "Those near to me are also my neighbors"—a relation also vividly embodied by the Bible in the Book of Ruth, the text from which the Rabbis derive most of the *halakhot* for conversion whereby גר (stranger) and אחר (other) become assimilated into משפחה (family) and עם (people).[97]

But Levinas does not cite Ruth, in which outsiders become insiders.[98] Rather, he quotes from Genesis, where insiders divide, partition, and fence off one another, where *berakhah* (blessing) is intimately tied to *bechirah* (intrafamilial choice), and where Jacob materially exploits his exile from Canaan. Levinas does not say that others and strangers are akin to family, but rather, "[kin] are my others, like strangers, and demand justice and protection." How are we to understand a moment like this, or its analogue in the radio interview quoted above, where Levinas explains that the other is the neighbor who "is not necessarily kin but who may be"? What distinguishes the alterity that confronts me in the form of an enemy, as opposed to the figure of alterity who approaches from height or destitution and to whom I give myself as hostage?

I believe this is one of those knots in Levinas where the two bodies of discourse, Greek and Hebrew, Western-philosophical and rabbinic-philosophical cross over and under each other. In order thus to get a feel for how Levinas understands "my household" here, we might pause for a moment and refer to the phenomenology of economy and family relations undertaken in *Totality and Infinity*, and the redefinition that Levinas assigns to stranger and neighbor in *Otherwise Than Being*. The latter text was Levinas's attempt to get beyond the ontological framework of his first book that stresses above all the incommensurable distance between self and Other. In *Otherwise Than Being*, the rupture no longer occurs from without in the form of the stranger's or neighbor's face, but rather from *within me*: my place and complacency are made strange to me by one who draws near. I am imprinted by the trace of an Other prior to any freedom I might exert, and am thus held hostage to a Responsibility-for-the-Other, "like the very act of substituting oneself for the other," as Levinas explains the recasting of terms from the first book to the second in his essay "Signature." Says one Levinas scholar, "It should not be overlooked that the language of *Totality and Infinity* remains the dominant language he employed for the exposition of his thought, even after he had completed *Otherwise Than Being*" (Peperzak, *Ethics*, 79).

In other words, while it is the second book that gives dimension and weight to the figure Levinas calls "the neighbor," it is in *Totality and Infinity* that the neighbor appears as one who approaches me against the horizon of my goods, my property, my household. In the section entitled "Interiority and Economy," Levinas treats "the envelope of property" and the self it encloses as follows:

> One lives one's life: to live is a sort of transitive verb, and the contents of life are its direct objects . . . which "occupy" it, which "entertain" it, of which it is enjoyment. . . . If enjoyment is the very eddy of the same, [subjectivity] it is not ignorance but exploitation of the other. (*TI* 111, 115)[99]

Or, translated into Hebrew proper names: Yaakov (Jacob) and Lavan (Laban).

The self is first an economic self, propertied and possessive, if only so that in turning to the other, it can offer those things it has aggrandized to those who approach it out of need. Both the demand of empty hands and the response of filling them transpire as economic conditions that are also ethical obligations within a dimension of distributive justice. Invoking Isaiah 58 as he often does and putting this into expressly theological terms, Levinas will say, those who "want to see the face of God and enjoy his proximity will only see his face once they have freed the slaves and fed the hungry" (*ITN* 162).[100]

Robert Gibbs explains how Levinas pursues this tie between economics and justice on two parallel courses: through love to fecundity and paternity, which Levinas calls religion, and through reason and the will to freedom as realized in the State, which he calls politics (237). They are distinct "solutions" but, interestingly enough, the former is assimilated by Levinas into the latter at the end of the book. That is, religion cedes to politics as the necessary institutional correlate for the ethical relation. While politics may "mistranslate" ethics (in Gibbs's phrase), the state cannot rest on familial, that is, religious structures for its sanction, and justice is still dispensed by and within the State.

But before God is made absent and invisible by Levinas, and before the political arena—the arena of the third party and distributive justice—receive its accounting (though of necessity, politics will defer to ethics for its critique), Levinas traces a line from the intimacy encountered in love to the sociality that follows intergenerationally—between parents and children, and between children and their siblings, each a model for sociality. This is the dimension I want to look at for a moment because I believe it provides a prism through which the concepts of neighbor and stranger are refracted or bent in Levinas's concept of Jewish identity and peoplehood. In *Totality and Infinity*, the treatment of eros and fecundity appears in the section "Beyond the Face," which as its title implies, makes the appeal to a temporal future where deferred justice receives its due. For Levinas, such a dimension opens up through the structure of family. Parents are responsible for their children, who are simultaneously like and unlike them, an extension but also a rupture. That meld of responsibility, discontinuity, and continuity means both generational procession and "religion" in a loose sociological sense—a responsibility for others' responsibilities.

Such responsibility is at once proleptic, as in *You are standing today, all of you before the Lord your God* (Deut. 29:9) and back-projected, as in, *In every generation a person should look upon himself as if he personally had come out of Egypt.*[101] To this degree, paternity (or maternity, as *Otherwise Than Being* shifts the reproductive trope), model an ethical relation that opens out onto the social world, familial structures being placed at the base and root of civic society. Philosophically speaking, this entails a return to Plato's communalization of the family in *The Republic* and a countermove to Hegel's delegitimation of it for the purposes of modeling societal structure in *The Philosophy of Right.*[102] Phenomenologically speaking, romantic love finds itself stranded midway between the condition of selfhood and the transcendent claims of the Other; temporally speaking, it can only promise indeterminacy. Its milieu, says Levinas, is clandestinity and self-mystification, where the body expresses itself voluptuously and the face shields itself or hides. To escape the impasse of a bond that is either pre-ethical or post-ethical but never fully ethical therefore, Levinas turns to the concept of fecundity. As an always "not yet," love is redeemed and fulfilled by the determinate future that opens up through procreation.[103]

The engendering that is fecundity, in turn (as perhaps most vividly concretized in Torah in the form of Jacob's twelve sons) begets what Levinas calls "Filiality and Fraternity," which is less a matter of biological succession than of investiture by one generation of another, what the Pentateuch calls נחלה inheritance, or מורשה, heritage. In a word that resonates throughout Levinas's essays on Judaism (but with perhaps a different sense), it also signifies *election*. I say "perhaps," because I am not sure that Levinas's allegiance to Judaism and Jewish peoplehood does not either underwrite or legitimate the analysis of kinship in *Totality and Infinity*.

"Fecundity" engenders "filiality," which in turn creates the conditions for "fraternity." Differently put, sonship, the uniqueness of each son, establishes the possibility of brotherhood, which is the solidarity of the social order.

> The father does not simply cause the son. . . . The son resumes the unicity of the father and yet remains exterior to the father: the son is a unique son. Not by number; each son of the father is the unique son, the chosen son. . . . And because the son owes his unicity to the parental election he can be brought up, be commanded, and can obey, and the strange conjuncture of the family is possible. (*TI* 179)[104]

Yet only partially does this describe the dominant pattern of generational succession (*toledot*) in Genesis. That fraternity for Levinas is a function of the solidarity among the sons of *many* fathers distinguishes it from both a simplistic generic and genetic unity between biological siblings. Accordingly, the pronounced move from *br'iyah* or universalism in Gen. 1–11 to *bechira* ("chosen," and thus necessarily *dechiya* "rejected") or particularism in Gen. 11–50, does not fit this schema from *Totality and Infinity* at all.

What it much more distinctly reflects and echoes, in fact, are the passages from Exodus and Deuteronomy (Ex. 13:8 and 13:14; Deut. 6:7 and 13:19; Ex. 12:26; Deut. 6:21) that command fathers to teach their sons, the first four of which are inscribed within the four compartments of the *shel rosh* (head piece of the *tefillin*) worn during morning prayer. Deut. 6:4–9 and 11:21, of course, comprise the first two paragraphs of the *Shema* recited by Jews twice daily, commanding that *you shall teach [these words] diligently to your children*.

That the ongoingness Levinas names "fecund,"—the Torah's very first *mitzvah* to increase and multiply—is not to be confined strictly to the biological here also becomes apparent when he speaks of it as a temporal accomplishment, "a discourse always addressing itself to another."

> The relation with the face in fraternity, where in his turn the Other appears in solidarity with all the others, constitutes the social order, the reference of every dialogue to the third part by which the We—or the parti—encompasses the face to face opposition, opens the erotic upon a social life, all signifyingness and decency, which encompasses the structure of the family itself. (280)

Adrian Peperzak remarks of this passage, "The teacher transcends his own life and death by being changed into his student, reader, successor, who after him, speaks in a new way to others" (To the Other, 196).

Thus, Rabbis in the Talmud and midrashim will habitually speak in the name of other Rabbis, and the first mishna in the tractate Pirke Avot, which appears as the first epigraph to this book, rehearses such a שלשלת קבלה (chain of transmission), which is also a מסרה (tradition), קשר (knot or tie), and מצוה (commandment, in the additional root sense of "join or connect"): Moses received the Torah [from God at] Sinai and gave it over to Joshua. Joshua [gave it over] to the Elders, the Elders to the Prophets, and the Prophets gave it over to the Men of the Great Assembly (1:1) Two mishnayot that follow enjoin their readers to develop many students, (literally, cause them to stand 1:3) and to assume a Master [for themselves] (1:6).

There is, then, the election that is God's choice of Abraham out from Ur-Kasdim and from the lineage of Terah his father, the choice of Isaac over Ishmael and Jacob over Essau and Joseph over his brothers— the sort of familial kinship called "looking to [one's] household" (that, ironically enough for Gen. 30–31, signifies enrichment in diaspora over homeland). Still, such heritage is genealogical in the plain sense. But there is also the election at the level of peoplehood that transpires between God and Israel as enabled first by Moses, then by Joshua and the Prophets, and forever mediated after them by the shalshelet kabbalah, the chain of tradition. That is the election Levinas calls "Talmudism," the strenuous ethical duty by which Judaism distinguishes itself in the way the epigraphs to this chapter so powerfully illustrate.

Passing over the genealogical patterns and inventories in Genesis, I would locate this second notion of election against the analysis of family structure in Totality and Infinity in the moment in the Book of Numbers (11:11–13) when Moses exclaims to God:

> Did I conceive this people? Did I give birth to them, that you should say to me, "Carry them in your bosom, as a nursing-father [omein] carries a sucking child" to the land that You have promised on oath to their fathers?

Here, even the grammar is uncanny, for Moses addresses God with the second-person pronoun in the feminine not masculine. And here, a pedagogy—*Moshe rabbenu*, Moses our teacher, as he is traditionally known to Jews—becomes a fecundity—*Moshe omeinu*, Moses our nurse, exactly in Levinas's sense of the necessary asymmetry and at the same time inalienable responsibility between selves and others, whereby teaching becomes natal care.[105]

And I do not think it overstated to regard Levinas himself as a kind of exegetical *omein*, a midwife or wetnurse to the text's (Levinasian) implications. Thus, of *Sanhedrin* 99b, in which Rabbi Yehoshua says, "Whoever learns the Torah and forgets it is like a woman who brings a child into the world only to bury it," Levinas writes, "The image suggests the idea that study is not just any activity but a giving birth—and that the result of study is another me, who answers me . . . and for whom I am answerable" (*ITN* 69). Or, again, from the lecture "Cities of Refuge":

> It is not out of keeping to underline the fecundity of the *mitzvah*: [Moses] would have said to himself: as soon as a divine commandment "comes within reach," it must be grasped and given effect. . . . The master teaching the multitude: the excellence of universal teaching, or of a teaching adapted to the many or of teaching capable, before a multitude of pupils, of responding to the uniqueness of every soul. And the excellence of the disciple capable of loving the master of the multitude; capable of a private conversation in a large crowd; or capable of a private conversation with the person of the master—capable of loving him—through the universality of the true. . . . According to Rashi, the fecundity of study "amidst a multitude" would mean study that is not done alone. . . . Again the pluralism is affirmed of the truth that is, however, *one*, of the truth from out of the personal: "be wary of the aberrations of the solitary who do not verify their 'inspired ideas' by calling to the other"! (*BV* 48–49)

But we are still left with a tie between natality and nation—a talmudism and prophetism that, even if the *kind* of election they identify means duties and responsibilities over theology or cultural origins, still seem to signify a *nativism*. It is not clear to me that Levinas ever satisfactorily resolves this confusion between two kinds of particularism that he distinguishes but perhaps never fully disentangles. At the end of his essay "Cities of Refuge," after a stunning refraction of the talmudic text through his own ethical-textual prism, Levinas wonders aloud, "Have we been right to do so?

> Have we been right to recognize in the ethical code on the level of the tribunal, understood as a council of the just, the actual place in which the spirit blows and the Other penetrates the Same? (113)

I do not have the audacity to answer the question directly but I will trace the rhetorical turns Levinas permits himself and thus after his own fashion rub them with vigilance and diligence. Predictably enough, Levinas lets the text answer for him, but angled so as to seem Levinasian. His rhetorical questions, it becomes clear, have nothing to do with the historical and cultural situatedness of the Jewish Doctors of the Talmud. Rather, he is openly contrasting modern and premodern notions of "inspiration, exegesis, and the moral message," the one being Kantian, the other, transcendent, religious, Judaic. In confirming the general argument of *Makkot* 23b, R. Eleazar—a figure for Levinas himself, we could very well say—"lifts out" the ends of verses, which he then "attributes to the echo of a heavenly voice" (*bat kol*).

Thus is demonstrated for Levinas an inspiration that "is said to be in the exercise of reason itself! The logos would already be prophetic!" Even the Talmud's preserving of the contrary opinion of Raba who sees "no need to have voices intervening in discourses where reason is sufficient" reads out for Levinas the necessity of the skeptical moment as man's best humanism, his self-expression in the face of transcendence. And the pull and push of the face of transcendence within the letter, within the tribunal that adjudicates it, within the tractate that records that adjudication: this is the place of the verse's "beyond" for him—"an alternation . . . from which stems the transcendence that does not impose itself with denials through its actual coming and which, in inspired Scripture, awaits a hermeneutic" (115).

What Levinas has not paused to wonder about, however, is his transcendentalizing of the specificities of a Jewish court of law, the Sanhedrin, dispensing halakhic justice to *Jews*. Whatever the philosophic implications of R. Eleazar's allegiance to the Infinite and Raba's to *s'bara* (common sense) in the context of Levinas's ethical schema, the move to transcendence outside the confines of *halakhah*, outside the fence of *Torah she'bal Peh* to *Torah she'bkhtav* (Oral to Written) that separates Jewish practice and custom from the practice and custom of other, even perhaps neighboring peoples, is not one made or suggested by the talmudic text. The *sugya* resides within its tractate as the tractate nestles comfortably in its order, one of six that form the breadth and extent comprising the Oral Tradition's *fence* around the Law. And here, necessarily, around Jewish peoplehood as well.

Levinas makes similar conceptual (though one could also say, ideological), moves in reading after reading, each one a marvel of fecund interpretation, of exegetical *omeinut*, or midwifery. In "Cities of Refuge" from *Beyond the Verse*, for example, (which discusses an earlier passage in *Makkot* about the scriptural provision for Cities of Refuge), Levinas begins with the conclusion of the *sugya*—with an idealized Jerusalem, "a city twinned with its model[, t]he awareness of a Judaism that is essential to the world"; and shows next how the device of the 'ir miklat (a refuge but also an exile for the accidental manslayer) highlights the murderousness that is latent in even the most liberal urbanism, the modern cities in which all of us dwell.

Following the contours of the Rabbis' discussion, he then relates the exile in such a city to the mandate nevertheless still in force to learn and teach Torah, which is "a complete justice which goes beyond the ambiguous situations of the cities of refuge . . . because in its expressions and contents, it is a call for absolute vigilance"; and finally, arriving at the end of the sugya where he began, situates Torah study and its justice in Jerusalem where we have an ultimate "footing." For unlike the purely political civilization of a city of refuge, Jerusalem—and the longing for Zion that is Zionism—"is the hope of a science of society, and of a society, which are wholly human." Toward the end of the reading, Levinas becomes almost ecstatic: "Ah the loftiness of these places, the unequaled light azure of this sky! The lighting. The science" (38, 52).

In "Who Plays Last?" from the same volume, which treats the שבד מלכויות, the oppression of great states like Rome, Persia, and Greece, the realpolitik of such structures is compared relative to preservation or destruction of the Temple in Jerusalem. "A symbol," says Levinas, "which signifies for the whole of humanity,"

> it is not simply a national institution. The biblical message and the history of a people of survivors, and the Passion of Israel through the history which they evoke, all belong to holy History. This latter does not immediately triumph over universal History, which inexorably unfurls: but it allows it to be judged. (63)[106]

"Transcendence becomes ethics," he writes two essays later in "The Name of God according to a Few Talmudic Texts." It is an assertion that he repeats obsessively, and could well be called his own philosophical Shema. But the question that gives this section its title—who is the neighbor?—as yet unanswered, runs perpendicular, it seems to me, to what we might call the vertical x-axis of height in Levinas's writing both Judaic and philosophical. It forms, by contrast, the y-axis of contiguity between peoples, the shared horizon of geography and demography as opposed to exalted line that stretches heavenward from earth upon which one meets God through the face of the human other.

A basic principle in the Talmud states, אמירתו לגבוה כמסירתו להדיוט, one declaration to the Most High is equal to transferring property to a common person. An aggadic-Levinasian interpretation might make the seemingly warranted connection between ethics and transcendence, the Most High relative to the position of a "common person." But halakhically understood—which is the only way the principle would be applied in the Talmud—it means simply that when one pledges verbally to sell an article to the Temple to be used in its rituals, it immediately becomes the legal property of the Temple, as opposed to the transfer of property between persons which can take place by a number of means. Only those versed in the halakhic minutae of *hekdesh* (consecrated property) and *kinyan* (conventional acquisition) would be able to make sense of the principle *as a principle, and not a metaphor*.

But then, to call attention finally to what has to stand as perhaps the most self-evident first principle of critique, only those thoroughly familiar with the Talmud and its many commentaries, religious Jews steeped in the study of the enormous corpus of classical Jewish texts, would know what to do with such a principle, which remains otherwise inaccessible to the non-initiate. As with his decidedly Levinasian reading of the *Nefesh haHayyim*, the secular intellectual contexts in which Levinas expounds the Oral Tradition in his Talmudic readings, are, on their face, alien to the conventional milieu in which that tradition is learned and practiced, and in which the meanings of those texts assume their full particularist import.

Indeed, such translatability becomes the very topic of Levinas's reading of *Megillah* 8b–9b in "The Translation of the Scripture" from *In the Time of Nations*, an essay that ends, tortuously but ingeniously, with the praise of "Greek" as a philosophical prose that is committed, like the Talmud, to patient commentray and self-critique, the language of deciphering, demystifying, and demetaphorizing. For as he writes, "One must always demetaphorize the very metaphors by which one has just demetaphorized the metaphors, and wring eloquence's neck" (54). It is thus only by universalizing the *sugyot* and *aggadot* that he selects *within the context in which they are offered* that Levinas can so boldly solicit their *sollicitation* "beyond the verse." That *beyond* will often exceed the bounds not only of the four cubits of *halakhah*, but also of the four walled fence, if I may, of the מדרש בית or house of learning. When, in "For a Place in the Bible," Levinas mounts an elaborate extension of the verb couplet, *kiymu v'kibelu* ([the Jews] fulfilled and the accepted) from the Scroll of Esther to "all men of goodwill [who] have already consented" (31);[107] or when, in "The Temptation of Temptation," he interprets the same couplet along with the Israelites' *na'aseh v'nishmah* from Ex. 24:7, (we will do and we will obey) as the "nonfreedom which, far from being slavery or childhood, is a beyond-freedom" (*NTR* 40)[108] for all of humanity; or finally when, in "The Pact," he construes the verb sequence from Deut. 5:1 and 11:19, *lilmod, lelamed, lishmor, la'asot* (to learn, to teach, to observe, to do) as an infinitely calculable regress of covenants through which "I always have, myself, one responsibility more than the other, for I am still responsible for his responsibility" (*BV* 85);[109] when deriving such meanings, Levinas has, hermeneutically speaking, come full circle, finding what he has originally set out to find.

Does that mean, then, that Levinas "misreads" the talmudic passages or kabbalistic philosophy he makes accessible to a wider than strictly Jewish or traditionalist audience? It is the kind of question that can be answered only equivocally, I think. On one hand, he makes good on his desire to "translate" classical rabbinic Judaism into a philosophical register through rabbinically sanctioned interpretation in the spirit of the most acute and inventive *midrash*. On the other hand, he "extracts that secret scent" apart from an ambient halakhic framework that is the fence through and by reference to which the texts' practical meanings are plainly manifest. For Levinas this is still to "turn away from idolatry by true reading or study" (*ITN* 59), but to recall R. Soloveitchik, it is the *halakhah* that nevertheless remains the very life of the text a "satisfying aroma to God" attesting to the performance of religious duty.

Above, I spoke of the very Jewish penchant, halakhically at least, for fencing in and fencing out, a move toward differentiation that begins with the creation of the world according to Jewish reckoning. Addressing the classical Jewish understanding of the universal and the particular, Gordon Lafer observes,

> Chaos is the lack of patterns, the lack of categories, the lack of boundaries; such a world, in Jewish thought, is both dangerously unpredictable and fundamentally unintelligible.—there is no way to take hold of, or operate within, such an undifferentiated world. In Jewish thought, then, the movement from opacity to intelligibility—from darkness to light—is a movement from aggregation to disaggregation and from the general to the particular. This ethic provides the prime rationale for the categories of membership into which Judaism divides the political world. For Jews, the differentiation of the earth's population into distinct regions is an integral step in making the political world intelligible. Even within the Jewish community, Jews are obligated to recognize differential obligations, to provide for family members ahead of nonrelatives, neighbors ahead of more distant townsmen, and even distant townsmen ahead of the Jewish poor of other jurisdictions. (193)

To do such is to make sense of the social and political world through the framework of *mitzvot* and *halakhah*, which, as Yeshayahu Leibowitz will argue in the next chapter, are the only means at Jews' disposal to make sense of themselves *as* practitioners of Judaism. But Levinas pointedly resists such particularism—the halakhic kind—in the name of a more modern, philosophic, aggadic counterpart.

In my introduction I suggested that the terms of Levinas's philosophy translate more or less fluidly into the slots opened up by his essays
on Judaism. That is to say, the ethical subject whose freedom and autonomy are called into question by being made difficult, is a "Jewish" subject: selected out to be holy, substitutive, even persecuted. Ethical transcendence is the Most High, Whose face cannot be seen and Who is
consequently known only by the trace He leaves. Saying, as the overflowing of the Said, applies to both the text and the interpretation of
Torah and Talmud. The Other goes by his biblical names, stranger and
neighbor, or the rabbinic title of Master. "Face"—*panim, lifanai, mifnei,*
"countenance, front, person, in the past, for the sake of"—is a common
Leitwort (leading word) in both Written and Oral Torah, for example:
in echo of the *keruvim* facing each other above the covering of the ark,
Maimonides describes the Ark's porters as carrying it "face to face, with
their backs facing outwards and their faces facing inwards" (*Hilkhot
Kelei ha-Mikdash* 2:12).

And although he does not flesh out the following translation of
terms himself, when Levinas speaks of the other as haunting our existence, keeping the psyche awake through ethical insomnia and bad conscience, the metaphor chimes with the prophetic books of the Hebrew
Bible and their call to vigilance, or the scenes of sleep cast by God upon
Adam and Abraham through which otherness and generational continuity are vouchsafed, or that of wrestling with the Angel, displacing
Jacob's slumber "until the break of dawn," or with the fatigue, finally,
that according to a *midrash* overcame the people of Israel the night
before the Torah was given on Sinai, a lapse that religious Jews com-
memorate, traditionally, by remaining awake all night on the festival of
Shavuot.

Concomitantly, while declaring himself an amateur in the talmudic
science whose style "distinguishes it from philosophical discourse," Levinas will repeatedly demonstrate how within the text, "a philosophical
option can be distinguished in the Talmudic positions" (*BV* 117). Thus
does he make Hellas into Zion. Other times, he will speak of the text
and his interpretation not philosophically but rather lyrically, musically.
In "Revelation in the Jewish Tradition," he calls attention to the verse's
"harmonics," and describes the text as being pulled tight over what tradition expands, like the strings on a violin's wood. In "The Name of
God according to a Few Talmudic Texts," he calls himself an amateur
practicing on a violin, and in the cases when that violin "is an orchestra,
or several orchestras," he offers, "To hold the conductor's baton as one
holds the bow is certainly to betray the work being interpreted" (116).

As a Jewish philosopher—or philosopher-Jew—like Maimonides,
Halevi, Spinoza, Cohen, Rosenzweig, and myriad others before him,

Levinas is entitled to distill from Jewish tradition the melodic figures and harmonies that appeal to him particularly. And they are certainly there to be found: the theme and variations of the face trope, the antiphonal chorus that places obedience before sense-impression— *na'aseh v'nishmah*, we will do and we will listen—the various *aggadot* like so many Bach chorales harmonically deepening and complicating the sense of "difficult freedom" or "beyond the verse."

And Levinas knows, conversely, when he is holding the baton as a bow or when he has tuned the violin "away" from its natural tuning, the interpretive cousin to a baroque musician's *scordatura*. Nevertheless, to highlight once again my own governing metaphor, the "neighbor" is not a free-standing entity in classical Jewish tradition perceived outside or independent of the fences that both circumscribe and set him off. What I have tried to suggest above in my own move from halakhic categories of otherness to the Genesis text about Jacob's household to the phenomenology of parentage in *Totality and Infinity* and back again to the rabbinic tradition through Moses's complaint in Numbers 11, is that as much as Levinas wants to transcendentalize the local and particular, these remain *at the level of an inherited tradition for him* a privilege of Jewish genealogy as well as Jewish intellectual legacy.

In the essay from *Reflections of the Rav*, "A Stranger and a Resident," R. Soloveitchik asks (in reference to Gen. 23:4), "Are not these terms mutually exclusive? One is either a stranger, an alien, *or* one is a resident, a citizen. How could Abraham claim both identities for himself" (169)? The rest of Soloveitchik's essay is spent mediating between this dual identity: belonging to the family of man on one hand, and to Jewish specificity on the other, what he will term, significantly, universal and *covenantal* (not particular). With the emphasis on how Judaism differs from other faiths, and Jews from other peoples, he ends by saying, "Our approach to the world has always been of an ambivalent character" (177).

Much the same, I think, could be said of Levinas's relationship to Jewish identity *tout court*. That seam between Jewish election, chosenness (*segula, bechira*), and secondly, talmudism, philosophy, an ethics-on-behalf-of-all, is most visible in the essays on Israel and Zionism and it is to those I now turn in the concluding section of this chapter. It is in those pieces that the difficult freedom required from Levinas's readers is most in demand. Accepting how a particularism becomes a universalism will have to be on their part—as it is on his—a matter of interpretive good faith.

DIFFICULT PARTICULARITY

Levinas begins his essay, "Jewish Thought Today," by asking, what, essentially, does Jewish thinking concern itself with. Amidst "a host of things we are not going to list," its basic message, he says,

> consists in bringing the meaning of each and every experience back to the relation between men, in appealing to man's personal responsibility—in which he feels chosen and irreplaceable—in order to bring about a human society in which men are treated as men. (*DF* 159)

Scriptural prooftexts for such a distillation could no doubt be drawn by Levinas from a "host" of sources, most likely prophetic passages like Isaiah 58, Zechariah 7–8, or Micah 6:8, *He has told you O man what is good and what the Lord seeks from you: the doing of justice, the love of kindness, and walking humbly with your God* (which is Emil Fackenheim's model of Judaic three-term morality). The Mishnaic tractate *Sayings of the Fathers* is a veritable fund of such summary statements, as is, to take another rabbinic example, *Makkot* 24a.

Still, résumés of being Jewish—or doing Jewish—are one of Judaism's distinctive hallmarks, are they not? The religion, through its texts, is forever reformulating and summarizing itself, whether through the Psalms, the Prophets, the Sages, the codes of Law and commentaries, or simply the Torah itself in which God dictates more than one précis to the Nation of Israel, perhaps the most powerful being קדשים תהיו כי אני קדוש , *You will be holy for I am holy.* Apologists from within and without, Halevi to Hans Küng, critics from without and within, the Church Fathers to Simone Weil, have persistently sought to capture Judaism's "secret scent" for a spectrum of different audiences.

To recall R. Soloveitchik as the most relevant example in this chapter besides Levinas, his short preface to *The Lonely Man of Faith* ends with the rhetorical flourish, "All I want is to follow the advice given by Elihu, the son of Berachel of old, who said, 'I will speak that I may find relief.'" It is thus not only in the Talmud that Jewish speakers speak in the name (or words) of other Jews when they come to speak about Judaism. Speaking thus in the name of others—as Eliezer does for his master Abraham, Joseph does for Egyptian baker and cupbearer in prison, Tamar does for Judah in Judah's own presence, or Moses does for the Lord God for most of Deuteronomy—is but one of many ways in Jewish tradition through which Saying overflows the Said.

Thus far in this chapter I have discussed Levinas in that capacity as "meta-aggadist," tracking his own tracking of Saying's overflow in talmudic *aggadah*. In this last section, I want to look to him in his capacity as Jewish apologist, polemicist, political philosopher, and Zionist, where the same dynamic of "overflow" he gives voice to in so many dimensions of his thought applies specifically to the plenitude Israel assumes as a nation unique in being for all the others. I begin with his introduction to *In the Time of Nations*, a volume that collects Talmudic readings given at the Colloquium of Jewish Intellectuals of the French Language and occasional pieces that together, in one way or another grapple, with Judaism's and Jews' singularity amidst a political aggregate Levinas calls, after its biblical and rabbinic name, "the Nations."

A theme rehearsed in that introduction, giving the volume its title, is Judaism as existing in some special *temporal* curvature vis-à-vis the rest of the world.

> In the "inner becoming" of the eternal people, there is an incessant reference to the time of the nations, an unfailing presence to their presence and their present, to the acme of their actuality, to their eventual modernity, their trials and hopes, despite the inextinguishable consciousness of the "time lag" between the clock of Universal History according to which Israel cannot be late, and the time of Holy History. (*ITN* 2)

It is well to remember how much of a philosophical debt Levinas acknowledges to Bergson, and how crucial a role time plays in all his philosophy, the complex lines of diachrony expressing otherness, history, and the divine. Principally, Levinas uses temporality to describe the self's relationship with the Other: a nonsimultaneous condition in which the other is always ahead of, beyond, or behind me. Part of Jewish singularity, not surprisingly therefore, is its own special diachrony, beginning with God's immemorial revelation, punctuated by the advent of Jewish peoplehood—what Levinas calls "Holy History"—and arcing finally into a Messianism, the time (echoing R. Soloveitchik), when the ideal and the real align through the Halakhah's perfection and fulfillment, and for Levinas meaning not an eschatology but rather an incessant wakefulness, a vigilance that refuses to slumber.

"Time," he writes, "is the most profound relationship a man can have with God, precisely as a going towards God," which he quickly tells us, "is meaningless unless seen in terms of my primary going towards the other person" (*FTF* 23).[110] Israel is called to God by going toward the Others, signifying its unique role as illuminator and hostage to the "seventy nations," its pedagogical and ethical mandate to be "an unfailing presence to their presence and their present." Judaism is a noncoincidence with its time, Levinas writes, an anachronism in the radical sense, a waiting for Messiah marking the very duration of time (*DF* 26, 222). It is as "as old as the world" but also impatient, attentive and thus eternally young. Judaism is synonymous with "human time, and hence beyond the limits of memory," just as Judaism is synonymous with "humanity as a whole."[111] And as temporal translatability, finally, so linguistic:

the privilege of a form of speech that succeeds in expressing everything that is human in the world . . . a success doubtless derived from a certain way the words have of fitting together, of ordering themselves into a discourse that questions in affirming, that affirms in denying—a manner that, beneath the vocables of the nations, was destined, across continents, to become academic, universal discourse. (2)[112]

Judaism, one could say, is the corrective to both Greenwich Meantime and Esperanto. Unrecognized or persistently misrecognized, it is fated to be the time the world will one day set its watch to, the discourse that makes final sense of language after Babel. It is a history overflowing memory, "as yet entirely novel, that has not yet happened to any particular nation" (ITN 82). And thus in the deepest sense, Israel means both a Jewish homeland for Levinas, and, metaphysically speaking, the world's future—the one country, nation, and land, on which all of it ultimately depends—and its raison d'etre: "It knows itself at the center of the world and for it the world is not homogeneous" (DF 176–177).

Hence the extension of Holy History universally, an extension that bad faith will see as a homeless wandering. Its very continuity will be misread as the primitive blindness of a memory closed to the future, and self-centered pride. A universal presence to the lights and shadows of being, including both the shadows cast by the illuminating paraphernalia of this enlightened world and, perhaps, the part of the "I" attentive to itself that remains unthought. Attention to the reflections of the light of the Torah itself, illuminating the seventy nations through Christianity and Islam. And in the suffering, disdain, and blood brought down upon the carrier of the Torah by so many triumphant bursts of its borrowed light, Israel has been able to see the traces of an approach heralding renewed violence—but perhaps also distant possibilities (which the Torah always taught) of a closer relationship than those derived from concepts. Israel, in its soul and conscience, i.e., Israel studying the Torah, is, from its own point of view, already in alliance with the whole universe of nations. A thought awakened, the sobered-up thought of the Talmud, i.e., an inspired thought, cocks its ear to hear, in the revealed word that seems constructed by the rigorous logic of the still impassible world, the premises of the human miracle. (ITN 3)[113]

This is Levinas at his most passionate . . . and, one must grant, most chauvinist. Or paternalistic, critics could just as reasonably say. Yet two points, I believe, call for reemphasis before continuing:

1. A passage such as the one above makes it unmistakable to me that Levinas's entire conceptual edifice is a *hinge* between post-Bergsonian, -Husserlian, and -Heidegerrian philosophy on the one side, and the body of Judaic texts and practices that are his cultural and religious inheritance on the other. At the risk of repeating my own caveats overmuch, scholars who simply parrot the distinction he himself makes between "philosophical and confessional texts" make the serious error of equating a line of demarcation, as he calls it—or a hinge, as I have called it—with a discontinuity or divergence when it functions as probably his most permeable discursive fence. When he writes, "[T]he ethical or biblical perspective" (20) (which is how he explains the innovation of his thought), the ethical/biblical "neighbors" on either side of the conjunction become for all intents and purposes conjoint. (Mortise-and-tenon was the metaphor I introduced previously.)

2. Hearkening back to my preliminary note to this chapter: to hold Levinas's idealized portrait of Israel to the political and social realities of the current *State* of Israel (and those underpinning a Jewish presence in the diaspora) is akin to calibrating his ethical philosophy against the vicissitudes of the world as it *really* is. Manifestly, Levinas is a utopian. He speaks of an Israel that has already happened historically (and textually) and will happen again through the perfection of ethical responsibility brought about by national fecundity. "This concern for the other," he has said, "remains utopian in the sense that it is always 'out of place' (*u-topos*) in the world, always other than the 'ways of the world'" (*FTF* 32).[114] But exposing the gap between ideal and real here does not teach us about some dead reckoning at the core of Levinas's thought to which he himself remains blind . . . or deaf.

That said, however, there is a difference to be sustained, I think, between the descriptive contours of Levinas's ethical philosophy, and an Israel or Jewish people (and Torah for that matter) that can only be understood as lived realities in time and history. In other words, the *dramatis personae* (as I have called it) of Levinas's philosophical landscape is fully utopian, like Soloveitchik's because, like halakhic man, aggadic man (be he Self, Other, Neighbor, Stranger) is a slot to be filled; he is, discursively speaking, abstract. But for "a place in the Bible," on the other hand, the Patriarchs and Prophets, and the Rabbis who have followed in their footsteps, have lived and died and studied Torah, all in the fullness of the concrete.

And there is a parallel distinction to be sustained as well between Levinas's Judeocentrism and a Judaism whose practical, quotidian concern remains the legalities, ritual observance, and ethical responsibilities of *Jews before others*. That is perhaps a Judaism less philosophical than Levinas would prefer, but it is a Judaism very difficult to pry apart from the thickness of all sorts of Jewish lives, past and present.

A critique of Levinas's difficult universality might thus invoke the enormous chunk of the world left out of Levinasian Judaism—a Judaism that is above all, prototypical and paradigmatic—because its religious systems are plainly non-monotheistic. A chunk more nonhomogeneous than Levinas may wish to grant. For Judeocentrism and monotheocentrism converge for Levinas around a set of privileged modalities that, irrespective of their utopian or messianic bent, manifestly fail to address an enormous number of the world's nations as either historically or presently constituted, which in no way would regard religious or political Zionism as a national, cultural *model*.[115]

Additionally (and I hint as much in the previous sections), the parenthesis Levinas smuggles in the passage above about the sort of utopian possibilities "which the Torah always taught" needs to placed in the context of all those other seemingly counterethical, tribalist, thoroughly particularist moments in Pentateuch, Prophets, Writings, and the Oral Law when Israel asserts either its hegemony or its antipathy in relation to other nations, in stark contrast to the relatedness or outsideness Levinas obsessively discloses as one of the Torah's ethical beacons.

This is what he means by "a propensity for the outside" in the Torah itself more intimate than a Jew's inner self: "a remarkable requirement to enter into relations with all the nations, all the families of humankind" (*ITN* 2) merging prophetic Judaism (Isaiah 53—Israel as suffering servant), rabbinic Judaism (Israel as Master teacher), and diasporic Judaism (Israel among the Nations). But David, Solomon, Hezekiah, Mattathias and his sons, and Bar Kochba were either warriors or kings, not servants; Akiva and Shimon Bar Yochai were famously insurgent; and Benjamin of Tudela (twelfth-century traveler of Jewish communities in the European continent and the Holy Land), finally, was not Marco Polo.

For, within the four cubits of *halakhah*, Judaism has always been deeply ambivalent about the Gentile world that abuts or surrounds it: in *Moed Katan* 14a, we are told that "to roam the world and see its sights, permission is not granted." And while Micah prophesied, *And the remnant of Jacob shall be in the midst of many peoples, like dew from the Lord* (5:6), and a *midrash* from the *Seder Eliahu Rabba* extols the Exile for saving the Nation of Israel from imminent destruction, and R. Oshaiah affirms in *Pesachim* 87b that "The Holy One, blessed be He, showed righteousness to Israel by scattering them among the nations": despite such expressions of providentiality, Jewish settling in the "far reaches" of the globe generally has reflected the turnabouts of migrancy, not an ethical humanism or existential being-for-others.

The Jewish "propensity for the outside" in practical affairs of state and community leadership has always been by and large and necessarily self-interested. For how could it not, in more or less an enduring state of peril and instability, as opposed to a self-declared State—governance, polity, republic—of its own, which it only re-accomplished finally at the midpoint of the twentieth century and the year 5708 of the Jewish calendar?

When Levinas elaborates on *ahavat Yisrael*, he calls it "the original tenderness for the other, the compassion and mercy in which lovingkindness arises," and further along, "Passion of Humanity bleeding through the wounds of Israel" (88). Such a position differs from each of the two polarities on Jewish election first elaborated by the medieval philosophers Maimonides and Judah Halevi and transposed in various ways ever since, positions Leibowitz calls the theocentric and androcentric, and David Hartman, the normative versus the ontological. (One could, of course, argue that Levinas dialectically resolves that very polarity inasmuch as he insists on the human choice that underwrites Judaism's difficult freedom [Maimonides], but also awards Jews as ethical subjects an originary "being chosen," prior to any freedom they might exert as rational subjects [Halevi]. But such a "synthesis" would be schematic at best since Levinas distrusts the free exercise of reason as much as he is repelled by a facile supernaturalism.) I turn briefly now to the Maimonidean/Halevian antinomy.

Levinas mentions Maimonides in only two essays, "On Jewish Philosophy" (treated in my epilogue), and another that I discuss in this section.[116] As an extended treatment of Maimonides properly belongs with the chapter on Leibowitz, suffice it to say here that Levinas the Aggadist has as little in common with Maimonides the halakhist (or Rambam, as he is known to students of the *Mishneh Torah*) as he does with Halevi the essentialist (or the Rihal). Neither legal systematicity nor a Jewish version of Natural Law quite harmonizes with his positionality as a modern (some would say, postmodern) philosopher on the other side of what Heidegger called ontotheology and Derrida, logocentricism.

As I outlined for Levinas and Leibowitz in their determinate shift to France and Palestine and the assumption of new cultural allegiances (French intellectual and organic intellectual respectively), I should note exactly where Maimonides and Halevi began and where they ended up before briefly discussing their views of Jewish election. Exiled by Spain, Maimonides (Moshe ben Maimon, 1135–1204) spent the rest of his years as *nagid* (community leader) in Egypt; by contrast, R. Yehudah Halevi (1085–1141) made a triumphant pilgrimage to the Holy Land in

the year of his death, convinced that only there could all the commandments be fully observed (a century later, Nachmanides, another mystically inclined philosopher, followed his example, leaving his native land
for Eretz Ysrael three years before his death in 1270).

Levinas twice alludes to R. Halevi, but his stature as Jewish philoso-
pher-ideologue in the religious tradition has been enduring, no less than
his status as one of Judaism's greatest poets. The philosophical work
with which he is most associated, the *Kuzari*, is a dialogue between religious faith and philosophy at the end of which the latter, as represented
by the King of the Khazars, more or less akin to Plato's philosopher-
king, concedes to the former, in the person of a philosopher-Jew named
chaver, or colleague.

Among the several topics it treats are: the concept of creation; the
doctrine of prophecy, and such relevant questions as the nature of God's
knowledge of man, the divinity of the Torah, and man's dialogue with
his Maker; the anticipation of individual and collective redemption; and
finally, Israel's special status and election by God. R. Halevi's aim is
both pedagogical and finally suasive, to instruct Jews themselves and
interested others in the essential uniqueness and superiority of Jewish
thought and peoplehood in relation to competing philosophies and religious systems.

On the topic of particularism, the Jewish people as סגולה (treasure or
acquisition), and מובכר[117] (chosen or selected out), Maimonides and
Halevi differ also along these specific lines: while Maimonides stresses
the prophetic gifts of the individual like Moses, contingent in part upon
rational choices, and only *a posteriori*, the elevation of a chosen few,
Judah Halevi believes that the entire nation is composed of prophets,
because the people itself is gifted with an innate and special power.
Halevi's quasimystical scheme places Jews at the acme of a scale of being
as God's prophetic elect.

If the Jewish people is chosen, according to the Rambam, it is
because of the obligation to keep the commandments and embody the
Torah. In other words, it is a privilege predicated on making the right
choices. As David Novak explains, "For this reason, one can appreciate
the prominent role Maimonides assigns to the convert, the person whose
Juda*ism* (as opposed to his or her Jewish*ness*) is initiated by his or her
choice [for] conversion" (*The Election of Israel*, 232). (Yeshayahu Leibowitz, as we will see, assumes the same distinction as an article of
faith.) In the case of the Rihal, by contrast, Jews are *segula*,[118] treasured
because special, a spiritual attribute existing prior to any given action
that thus justifies *bechirat Yisrael*, Israel's election.[119]

Levinas compacts such opposing ideas of peoplehood into a metaphysic about the quintessentially Jewish obsession with the other man,

as already shown by the linguistic kinship between *acher* ("the Other"), and *achrayut* ("responsibility"), and embodied in and by Torah study. Judaic particularity models universality by constituting "a *figure* in which a primordial mode of the human is produced," a particularism of election, of obligation as opposed to a "*particularism of the inert* . . . a particularism of the enrooted vegetable being . . . the persistence or insistence of beings in the guise of individuals jealous for their *part* (*ITN* 110). Or as he will paraphrase himself, a *difficult universality*.

True, the *Kuzari* can be said to anticipate Levinas when it suggests that the Jewish people's vulnerability—its "suffering, disdain, and blood"—awards it a privileged place among the nations. But if Israel sustains injury at the hand of other peoples, it is because those peoples are deficient *as others*, ontologically lesser when compared with Israel, much as a body member is to a vital organ. Halevi draws on his own experience as physician for such metaphors as these:

> We are not to be compared with the dead. We are like a sick patient of whom all the physicians have despaired but who yet hopes for a cure by some miracle or change in the established order. . . . Israel among the nations is as the heart among the members of the body—it is more sensitive to sickness than all of them and is healthier than all of them. (*Kuzari* 34–36)

Though Levinas invokes the "Passion" of the Jewish Holocaust many times in his essays, he nevertheless resists the sort of analogical aura such metaphors from biology can bestow, and it is useful to recall his words quoted at the beginning of this chapter about Judaism as a kind of disenchantment, dispelling the sorcery of nature and expropriative man alike. How often Levinas will cite Pascal, "'That is my place in the sun.' That is how the usurpation of the whole world began," as opposed to Halevi's naturalism.

Likewise, Levinasian being-for-others is also not quite what Maimonides meant by a "nation of proselytes" by giving such careful attention in his Code to the role of the convert ("righteous stranger"). As the medieval historian H. H. Ben Sasson has succinctly captured this attitude:

> Maimonides indicated two stages in the "conversion" of Israel, the first commencing when Abraham recognized the true God and taught the monotheistic concept to all who were prepared to accept it, without distinction to race, and the second occurring when Moses found the offspring of the patriarchs engaged in idolatry and brought them back to the true faith at Sinai. Those who have received the Torah by conscious choice are particularly honorable. (538)

Just as the Halakhah accords with the universal truths of philosophy— is logocentrist, in the argot of modern criticism—so Israel's particular-

ism is similarly normative for Maimonides: Jews model a life lived בצלם
אלה-ים, in God's image, which others can imitate and even adopt for
themselves.

The very structure of Maimonides's *Mishneh Torah* indexes how
fully the rationalist spirit presides over his concept of Judaism. Adjusted
to Levinas's inflection, a systematic presentation of the corpus of
halakhah, Maimonides's code is the Said of the Oral Law stripped of the
encumbrances of Saying. It codifies regulation without conversation, the
give-and-take of human speech that for Levinas is the essence of talmudic discourse. Thus, while Maimonides's thorough-going rationalism
cannot conceive of a relation to other humans unencompassed by reason, the core of Levinas's critique of such thinking revolves around an
ethical relation that precisely cannot be grasped by or expressed through
knowledge. The otherness of the other, the face of the other, the words
of the other, and our non-indifference to the other, our approach to its
otherness in the face of others: these are things, or rather events, that can
have only *moral* force; they are neither ontologically nor epistemologi-
cally derived but rather ethically produced.

Levinas insists on a Jewish peoplehood as a matter of "vocation,"
as I have quoted him in an earlier footnote, "not nationality." And yet
the political philosophy that led to the successful settlement and establishment in our century of the sovereign State of Israel, trumping
Halevi's and Maimonides's arguments alike, was political Zionism—the
argument from historical necessity and national right. Palestine was not
simply the regained birthright or household of every Jew in the world
should he or she wish it claim it. It was also a land where a new kind of
Jew was being made and born. The clearest sign that such was political
Zionism's animating impulse was the programmatic choice from its
inception of the adjective *ivri*, Hebrew, over *yehudi*, Jewish, in manifesto
after manifesto, essay after essay.

Levinas includes pieces on Zionism in all three of his books of
Judaic essays and readings. As far as movements and central personalities are concerned, in these too, he is . . . selective. One might expect, for
instance, a treatment of the famous skirmish between Levinas's philosophical predecessors, Martin Buber and Hermann Cohen, but such
names, like Gershom Scholem's, are mentioned in passing if at all.[120]
This is in part because Levinas's audience in his essays is restrictive: primarily, his nonreligious, non-Jewish colleagues at the annual Colloquium of French-Speaking Intellectuals. It is also because he does not
pretend here or elsewhere to a bonafide political philosophy, something
demonstrably clear in the attenuated political horizon sketched at the
end of *Totality and Infinity*; and thus I must acknowledge my own sporadic use of that term up until this point as something of a misnomer.

For in the final analysis, Levinas's Zionism is more ideological than philosophical, or, to use terms that have a greater poignancy here than perhaps anywhere else in this chapter, aggadic rather than halakhic. Levinas's Zionism is a distantly focused thing, the wide end of a sighting instrument placed closest to the eye, nowhere as sharp and crystalline as the "optic" he calls his ethical phenomenology. If I may, it is a Zionism conditioned by a diasporism, Levinas's diasporism, which is why, I think, he does not seem particularly interested in entertaining the political finer points of Jewish repatriation and reconceived nationhood as *philosophically* grounded.

By way of concluding this chapter, I will look at only two essays then (the latter only in passing), which seem to me particularly telling in their choice of source material: "The State of Caesar and the State of David" from *Beyond the Verse*, and "Moses Mendelssohn's Thought" from *In the Time of Nations*. The first essay treats the place of the political order in a truly humanist society and features one of only two explicit references to Maimonides in Levinas's work. Much like R. Soloveitchik's use of the *Nefesh haHayyim*, however, he includes a long excerpt from the chapter on kingship from the *Mishneh Torah* only to let it speak for itself in all its "rationalist sobriety." But before he arrives at Maimonides, he makes the sensible transit through the Bible (Deut. 17:14–20; I Samuel 8) and the Talmud's commentary on it (*Sanhedrin 99a–b*).

As always, his footing is solid, sure and expeditious, for he knows where he is going: a "Beyond" the State that Levinas describes in his lapidary way as an "anti-Machiavellianism anticipated in the refusal of anarchy" (*BV* 177). Would a decision for the State be equivalent to choosing life over the Law, while this Law aspires to be the Law of life? he asks. His answer—and it is Samuel's answer first (12:22)—is that religion grants a "concession" to political necessities, a "provisional abdication" precisely because "the Law entering the world requires an education, protection, and consequently a history and a State" (179) Jewish nationhood, guaranteed by a kingship before which God is always set, thus offers itself as exemplar to the seventy nations.[121]

Here, Levinas keeps pace exactly with the line of argument traced in the concluding pages of *Totality and Infinity* where the State as such, no longer biblical, approximates the values ascribed to it by talmudic culture—and this is the Rabbis' answer, in a world where their own state had been radically "suspended"—that is, fully answerable to ethical wisdom. Just as holiness comes to reside in the four cubits of *halakhah*, and rabbinic argument now legislates the social order, so "philosophy" in Levinas's sense of Saying and dialogical fervor "become[s] the rationale of the reduced responsibility of the state and of written laws" (Gibbs, 242).

In the Torah's terms, the political order is *invested* by religiosity in the form of the Davidic monarchy that, while now in interregnum, will be resuscitated and continually reinvested in the days of King Messiah, and beyond them as well.

> The Talmudic apologue [*Berakhot* 3b] becomes remarkably suggestive here: King David wages war and rules during the day; and at night, when men are resting, he devotes himself to the Law: double life in order to remake the unity of life. The political action of each passing day begins in an eternal midnight and derives from a nocturnal contact with the absolute. (*BV* 181)[122]

Since we have been introduced to such metaphysical wakefulness before, I would note here only its meaningful contrast with both the long night of antisemitism emblematized by the ever-Wandering Jew, and the wakening that for Herzl signified the advent of a Jewish state: "Now day is dawning. We need only rub the sleep out of our eyes, stretch our limbs, and convert the dream into a reality" (Mendes-Flor and Reinharz 533). As always for Levinas, Jews never sleep, paradigmatic of the ontological reform he wishes to introduce into general Western thought.

At this point, Levinas turns to Maimonides, recording in an endnote the Talmud's judgment that the messianic era will be of finite duration, and approvingly underscoring a vision of non-apocalyptic Messianism where "philosophical and rabbinical thought meet once more" (*BV* 181). Maimonides ends his great code with his vision of the messianic kingdom in which (as Leibowitz will not fail to remind us), "The one preoccupation of the whole world will be to know the Lord" (*Mishneh Torah, Hilkhot Melakhim*, 11:3–4). But after Levinas defers to Maimonides, he takes an additional step that Maimonides did not, signaled in the text by a section entitled "Beyond the State."

As in the *Mishneh Torah*, the political order ultimately serves the Divine Will, or in Levinas's words, "From behind the State of David, safeguarded from the corruption which already alienates the State of Caesar, the beyond of the State announces itself" (185). But taking his hint from the Talmud's suggestion that the messianic era will itself be surpassed, and specifically R. Hillel's "daring argument" that "There shall be no Messiah for Israel, because they have already enjoyed him in the days of Hezekiah," Levinas, Hillel-like, makes bold enough to claim that deliverance does not enter into the idea of kingship, and indeed surpasses it.

> We have here the highest hope, forever separated from political structures! Let the Messiah still be a King, and Messianism a political form of existence, and we have salvation through the Messiah as salvation through another—as if, having reached complete maturity, I could be

saved by another; or as if, on the other hand, the salvation of all others were not incumbent upon me, depending on the most precise significance of my personal existence! As if the ultimate end of a person were not the possibility of listening only to my own conscience and of rejecting reasons of State. A degree which modern man thinks he has reached and which is probably the best definition of modernity, but one which is perhaps more difficult than the "spontaneism" with which it is confused. A dangerous and tempting confusion which is undoubtedly the reason why the scholars condemned R. Hillel's daring argument. (186)[123]

The move is by now familiar, but I want to highlight how it takes place. For one of only two times in his work, Levinas defers to Judaism's supreme halakhist, only to spring back, not merely to the Talmud, but to a minority view within it that is rejected, and that is read as Levinasism. Need it be emphasized that the self described above is both the ethical self in Levinas's philosophy and the Jewish self in *Beyond the Verse, Difficult Freedom, In the Time of Nations,* and the *(New) Talmudic Readings*? And need it also be stressed that such a self, magnified to the dimensions of the State, but standing upright, and so projected vertically on the axis of religiosity, not horizontally on the axis of lowercase nationalisms, stands for the State of Israel?

Levinas makes much the same argument in his essay on Mendelssohn, whom he praises for a "lofty conception of human freedom" that devolves upon Judaism's "extraordinary history" that becomes, by implication, the entire world's. "In the desire for emancipation as expressed by Mendelssohn, the vocation of Israel is never forgotten. To be with the nations is to be for the nations" (*ITN* 144).[124] Mendelssohn's value for Levinas is, if I may, messianic, and thus, the nexus with Levinas's allusion to Maimonides. Like Franz Rosenzweig a century after him, Mendelssohn "heralds a new era in Jewish history" in which, paradoxically, assimilation (as with kingship in the previous example), enables its own overcoming while yet being "survived by its generous, innovative thought" (145).[125] To this degree, emancipation, like political messianism, is overseen by ethical destiny.

And yet, to return to the essay on the State, even here Levinas adds a coda, a concluding section entitled "Towards a Monotheistic Politics." And as it sufficiently compressed as to exemplify Levinas at his gnomic and aggadic, if one had to choose, one would say that here Levinas leaves Maimonides for Halevi (and Mendelssohn for Levinas). For he speaks of a formulation of political monotheism "that nobody would have formulated yet."

Not even the Talmudic scholars. Only the responsibility of a modern State, exercised on the land promised to Abraham's descendants, should allow his heirs to elaborate patiently, by comparing formula to facts, a political doctrine for monotheists. . . . Henceforth the commitment has been made. Since 1948. But all has just begun. Israel is no less isolated in its struggle to complete its extraordinary task than was Abraham, who began it four thousand years ago. But this return to the land of our ancestors—beyond solving any problem, whether national or domestic—would thus mark one of the greatest events of internal history, and, indeed, of all History. (*BV* 186–187)

From an argument over election that, reductively put, pits *zerah* (seed) against *mitzvah* (commandment), or *navuah* (prophecy) against *binah* (reason), the Halevian-Maimonidian polarity gets resolved by Levinas through a certain irrecusable awe before Israel's return to history, its *ontological* and *essential* singularity. Is this not Israel's and Jewish peoplehood's not–*Otherwise Than Being*, its not–*Beyond Essence*? And as such, is it not near to the "philosophical" sense of the blessing for ingathering in the Sages' fixed formula for daily prayer: "Blast on the great shofar for our freedom, and raise a mast for the ingathering of our exiles. . . . Blessed are You who gathers the dispersed of His people Israel," where a people's metaphysical unity—not its social or political constitutiveness—makes sense of and justifies attachment to a specific place?[126]

For even though "Israel" in Levinas's writing oscillates between referring to Jewish land or to Jewish peoplehood, its materiality—or "carnality" as he elsewhere terms it—remains a constant. Israel is the place where Jews and Judaism alike are perfected, a place, a people, a religion, a nation for all the others. Insisting on that linkage explains why Levinas justify both an Israel beyond politics and also an Israel singled out within history, the latter inspiring Levinas to the kind of rhetorical pitch that sounds, and I think is meant to sound, like prophecy.

> But perhaps the ultimate essence of Israel, its carnal essence prior to the freedom that will mark its history, this manifestly universal history, this history for all, visible to all, perhaps the ultimate essence of Israel, derives from its innate predisposition to involuntary sacrifice, its exposure to persecution. . . . It is an invisible universality! It is the reverse of a choosing that puts forward the *self* before it is even free to accept being chosen. It is *for the others* to see if they wish to take advantage of it. It is for the free *self* to fix the limits of this responsibility or to claim entire responsibility. But it can do so only in the name of that original responsibility, in the name of this Judaism. (*DF* 225)

This is the messianism that Levinas calls "ethical destiny" (*BV* 190).[127] And what I would emphasize one last time is that if it seems to speak outside the bounds of *halakhah*, that is because it expresses, rather, *aggadic faith*—the point at which Levinas seeks to outfit the Greek mouth with Hebrew vowels and consonants it cannot quite pronounce, and where, as it were, the commitment to providing for his own household appears to outpace his philosophy.

In an essay written in September 1979, shortly after the Camp David peace accord between Israel and Egypt, Levinas asks the question, "Has Sadat understood the human perfectly human which unfolds in historical events in the form of Judaism?" Although it is quite clear how he means its rhetorical force to be taken, the realistic answer to that question must be "very likely not." He continues:

> Did Sadat sense this all in Zionism, which is taken to be an imperialist endeavor, whereas it still carries pain and dereliction in its depths and, outside its truth, still has no reserved and inalienable patrimony which gives support to those who govern States elsewhere? (193–194)

Again, one must reply, "doubtfully." This, if I may, is a specimen of Levinas's own *difficult particularity*. And as he does so often through what I have have called his "Levinasism" (an infinition of his own ethical passion to voices and visions non his own), Levinas has lent Sadat his eyes and his mouth—in much the same way as he has, Moses Mendelssohn, Hayyim of Volozhin, and sundry Doctors of the Talmud.

Such extension of voice and the wisdom of love is the consistent feature of Levinas's thought that I have called *aggadic* in this chapter in order to stress both its affinity with and departure from a normative tradition of Jewish textuality. Whether Sadat sensed and understood in the way Levinas suggests he might have is, obviously, less important than the fact Levinas *wants* him to have. And the desire thus expressed, it seems to me, brings us to the limit-point of his discourse of "the neighbor" and its transcendence of the fences of *halakhah*, ideology, and political determinations. Indeed, whether R. Hillel and the other premodern Sages whose non in-difference to the non-Jewish other Levinas so approvingly cites, and whose "philosophy" so uncannily anticipates his own: whether this rabbinic culture sensed and understood in parallel ways Israel's "propensity for the outside" brings us to the exact same limit-point.

Such exorbitant Zionism, such generous Judaism, it seems to me, reflects Levinas's own modern intellectual itinerary from the Hebrew Bible to modern philosophy and back to classical Jewish sources, and thus bespeaks his own identity as much if not more than it does the tradition. His is a particularized Judaism because it is so obviously a personalized one—another way in which tradition can be said in Levinas's case to have been made *aggadic*.

The word for tradition in Hebrew, קבלה, also connotes "welcome" or "reception," as in the *mishna* from *Pirke Avot* that quotes R. Ishmael

בשמחה מקבל את כל האדם "Receive every person cheerfully" (3:16). Such welcoming and the other person who is its object are awarded their widest possible latitude by Levinas, signaling for him Judaism's absolute primacy as religion and philosophy. For us, it is also a boundary that signals a fence between religious thinkers. If we position ourselves now on the other side, the next setting and keeping, of wall, of boulders and gaps, of fences-and-neighbors, must belong to Yeshayahu Leibowitz.

CHAPTER 2

Mishurat HaDin:
Leibowitz, Nationhood,
and the Fence of Halakhah

*Two neighbors were blessed with daughters at the same time. One man
was a shoemaker by profession and extremely poor. The other was a thief,
and strange as it may seem, despite his profession he was equally poverty-
stricken. They would often lament their fate and discuss ways to help their
daughters when they were to reach marriageable age. A friend advised
them to save money, and the shoemaker took his advice. He bore a hole
in a crate, locked it up, and would daily place a penny inside this safe. In
those days, a long period of such savings would reap a goodly sum.*

*At the wedding of the shoemaker's daughter, the father of the bride
and his neighbor the thief again discussed money matters. "How did you
manage it?" inquired the thief. "I locked up a safe and placed pennies in
it day after day," responded the shoemaker. "And why did you not do
the same?" "I, who have no fear of other people's locks—why should I
fear a lock of my own?" replied the thief.*

—R. Yaakov Krantz, Maggid of Dubno

*One of the fundamental problems of language is that while it recognizes
the question mark and the exclamation point, it does not recognize other
necessary signs such as signs of amazement or irony.*

—Jorge Luis Borges[1]

ויעמד מלאך יי במשעול הכרמים גדר מזה גדר מזה:
... כי-מראש צרים אראנו ומגבעות אשורנו הן-עם לבדד ישכן ובגוים לא יתחשב:

*The angel of the Lord stood in the path of the vineyards, a fence on this
side and a fence on that side. . . . For from its origins, I see it rock-like
and from hills I see it. Behold! It is a nation that will dwell in solitude
and not be reckoned among the nations.*

—Numbers 22:24

עשו משמרת למשמרתי.
מועד קטן ה

Set a fence (guard) about my Fence (Guard).

—Tractate *Moed Katan* 5a

1. JUDAISMS

Altered slightly, the parable by the Dubner Maggid's in the first epigraph to this chapter suggests that thief and shoemaker are in identical positions when considered humanly, the latter's stroke of good luck notwithstanding. One man breaks into other people's safes; the other man breaks into his own safe: in both cases, the safes always hold out the possibility of their being cracked, the locks invite being broken into in the first place. That is because safes and locks, like shoes and promises made to oneself, are the stuff of human fabrication, and the human hand that grasps and aggrandizes is also the human hand that loses or finds itself emptied. The Halakhah, by contrast, is a set of safes and locks—or fences—instituted by Divine command, that entirely transcend a self-interested human calculus of gain and loss. It is minimally an anthropology because it concerns man. But it has no truck with *characterology*: as men, thief and shoemaker are equal before God.

I chose the Maggid's parable as an epigraph to this chapter not only because of the way it subtly implies an axial tenet of Leibowitz's philosophy—man's *standing* before God—but also because of implications in it that can be heard to speak over Leibowitz's head. That is, although the parable points in the same direction as Leibowitz's contumacious theocentrism, it is not the sort of discourse he would very likely use himself, for it is the stuff of storytelling—aggadic or biblical humanism—and thus ill-suits the lapidary formulations of his philosophizing. On Leibowitz's understanding of the Halakhah, a distinction between חפצא or חפץ (object) and גברא (person), is merely, or entirely, halakhic. So dogged is his antihumanism where ethics is concerned that from within its ambit and metaphysically considered, safes and shoemakers, locks and thieves, objects and persons, sometimes seem members of the same class of entity. It is only the fact that humans are made in the image of God that they have an opportunity thus to turn to God in worship and serve Him through the Torah and the *mitzvot*. But this, as one of the Sages says, is merely "because you were created for this purpose" (*Pirke Avot* 2:9). Or in the words of another: "Be like servants who serve the master without expectation of receiving a reward, and let the fear of Heaven be upon you" (*Pirke Avot* 1:3).

Thus for me, also, the relevance of Borges's aperçu: persons in Leibowitz's schema possess nothing approaching the creative *elan* of Soloveitchik's halakhic man or the existentialist immediacy of his lonely man of faith, or, finally, the awe before an Other expressed by Levinas's aggadic counterpart. God's imperatives are sealed by His exclamation points just as the question marks identifying His Halakhah promise certain and true answers. Amazement or irony are the very sort of modernist or existentialist virtues that in Leibowitz's strenuous monotheism trend away from God and toward something quasi-idolatrous, something truant, in His stead.

To parallel my initial phenomenological foothold in the previous chapter for halakhic man traversing the world, when the religious Jew arises in the morning the first thing uttered is a small prayer that reads, מודה אני לפניך מלך חי וקים שהחזרת בי נשמתי בחמלה; רבה אמונתך ראשית הכמה יראת יי שכל טוב לכל עשיהם תהלתו עומדת לעד: *I acknowledge You, living and everlasting King, for you have mercifully restored my soul within me; Your faithfulness is great. The beginning of wisdom is the fear of the Lord, Good understanding to all who perform [His commandments], His praise endures forever* (R. Moses ibn Makhir, *Seder Hayom*). Thanks are given for an indwelling spirit, and in doing so, an explicit connection is made between that soul, God's faith, and human discernment.

Leibowitz, by pointed contrast, emphasizes two other incipient moments in Jewish worship:

1. The morning prayer *Ribon haOlamim* which was originally part of the Yom Kippur service (*Yoma* 87b), and in which human intellect pales beside the givenness of God's grandeur:

> Master of all worlds! It is not on account of our own righteousness that we offer our supplications before You, but on account of Your great compassion. What are we? What is our life? What is our goodness? What our righteousness? What our helpfulness? What our strength? What our might? What can we say in Your presence, Lord our God and God of our fathers? Indeed, all the heroes are as nothing before You, the men of renown as though they never existed, the wise as if they were without knowledge, the intelligent as though they lacked understanding; for most of their doings are worthless, and the days of their life are vain in Your sight; man is not far above the beast, for all is vanity. (135–136)

2. The first sentence from the *Shulkhan Arukh*, Yosef Caro's authoritative sixteenth-century codification of Jewish law, which reads "Let him gird up strength like a lion to rise in the morning for the service to his creator" and which becomes a *leitmotiv* in essay after essay for Leibowitz because of its unvarnished depiction of prayer as worship, as service, as fixed and obligatory mandate. Since עבדה, *ministration*, defines religion for Leibowitz, so man is construed, fundamentally, as עבד, its *servant*.

Neither amazement nor irony. Instead, simply, duty and execution. Torah, *halakhah*, *avodah* (service) all for their own sake and thus all for God's. Is this, then, not also what Levinas means when he says that knowledge of God is not a dogma for Jews but a mode of action—knowing what to do? But Levinas also just as quickly asserts that a Jew can communicate just as intimately with a non-Jew (the Noachide) as with another Jew. Leibowitz, however, will sharply remind us of duty's full extent, as he anecdotally observes in a critique of David Hartman's *Joy and Responsibility*:

> During the intermediate days of Passover, I was summoned to a conference for the senior officers in the Israeli Defense Forces. . . . When one of the officers noted that we must not forget that we are in the midst of Passover, which is "a national spiritual treasure that all of us have in common, a symbol of our spiritual legacy, and the beginning of our people's history," I reminded him that if I visited his home on that same day, I could not even drink a glass of water with him. Thus Passover actually divides rather than unifies us. Even with regard to the normative content of Passover we have nothing in common, because for the officer and his friends its significance is sentimental, while for me and my family it is existential: this is a week during which we live differently than all the other weeks of the year. (qtd. in CV 81–82)[2]

It is thus not at all clear that Leibowitz and Levinas could have dined easily together themselves, for the hypothetical case described by Leibowitz here gestures *lifnim meshurat ha-din*, beyond the letter of law, as Hartman clarifies in his response:

> As a competent halakhist, Leibowitz surely knows that he could find ways of drinking water in the home of a sympathetic nonobservant listener. Were the secular Jew to provide paper plates, fruits, and other delicacies, Leibowitz could spend many pleasant hours eating and discussing the significance of Passover for both halakhic and nonhalakhic Jews. (CV 97–98)

This second chapter of *The Fence and the Neighbor* is therefore designed with two interdependent goals in mind: an explicit juxtaposition with Levinasian philosophy and a refinement of some of the previous chapter's central concepts (halakhism and ethicism, religion and the state, the content of peoplehood). I thought it helpful therefore to highlight at the very outset certain tangents with Levinas in order to show how the two religious thinkers align but also significantly differ. In his essay, "A Religion for Adults," for instance, Levinas seems to have made Leibowitz's second point above (R. Yosef Caro's paraphrase of the prophet Balaam in Numbers 23:24), in almost exactly the same terms:

> The law is effort. The daily fidelity to the ritual gesture demands a courage that is calmer, nobler, and greater than that of the warrior. We know the prophecy of Israel made by Balaam: "See! This people rises up like a leopard, it stands like a lion!" The talmudist does not hesitate

to link this royal awakening to the sovereign power of a people capable of the daily ritual. The shudder of the leopard rising, but not rising under the yoke. The law for the Jew is never a yoke. It carries its own joy, which nourishes a religious life and the whole of Jewish mysticism. (*DF* 9)

And yet, not only does Leibowitz ignore the metaphorics of regality completely. The very phrase, "Yoke of the Commandments," or "Yoke of the Kingdom of Heaven" becomes a constant refrain for him as the *essential* meaning of religiosity, as can be gleaned from the following restrictive definition of prayer from the same essay as the reference above to the *Shulkhan Arukh*: "The sole meaning of prayer as a religious institution is the service of God by the man who accepts the yoke of the Kingdom of Heaven" (31).

Moreover, in accentuating the primacy of the Halakhah next to which "all creativity within Judaism is fleeting and episodic," Leibowitz specifically singles out Jewish mysticism, as reclaimed for modern Jewish thought by Gershom Scholem, for its *subsidiary* contribution, and thus paradigmatic of all developments in Judaism that do not derive from or return to the Halakhah.

> Scholem believed he had proved that Judaism had a fundamental aspect in addition to the halakhic one. It would appear, however, that he inadvertently proved the opposite. The grand structure of the Kabbalah was created and developed after Judaism had already been delimited as a historic entity characterized by features which determined its continuous identity. Judaism existed long before the Kabbalah commenced and was not impaired after the wilting of the magnificent flowering of the Kabbalah and its almost total disappearance as a living pursuit. Moreover, even in its heyday, the Kabbalah was never identical with the whole of Judaism. Alongside it, and in opposition to it, grew various schools which rejected this mystical tradition. Thus the Kabbalah, probably the greatest, extra-halakhic growth within the framework of Judaism, was only an episode and not a constitutive element in its identity. (8)

Absent the fact that one of the driving forces within the contemporary *ba'al t'shuvah* (religious returnee) movement has been the mass-marketing of an esoteric, spiritual, "joyful" Judaism, or the fact the Chabad Lubavitch (whose founder R. Schneur Zalman of Lyady, fused Lurianic *kabbalah* and eighteenth-century *hasidut*) has engineered the most successful outreach in Jewish history and qualifies thus as a true phenomenon,[3] or, finally the always live wire of messianism in Israel and the Diaspora alike: absent all of that, and halakhic Judaism, normatively understood, is still Judaism, root and branch for Leibowitz; all else is efflorescence and epiphenomenality.

Of course, Levinas, a quasi-*mitnagid*, remains suspicious of religious joy before responsibility too: "Enthusiasm is, after all, possession by a god. Jews wish not to be possessed, but to be responsible" (*DF* 54).[4] But as we have seen, responsibility in Levinas's philosophy takes place in the light of day within the interhuman (the only legitimate "place" where one can even speak of God);[5] for Leibowitz, man stands simply *before God*.[6] Thus, Levinas will ask Cain's question, "Am I my brother's keeper," which he tells us rabbinical commentary does not regard "as a case of simple insolence." Rather, in Cain's response to God's sentence of judgment,

> [t]he rabbis pretend to hear a new question: "Is my punishment too great to be bear? Is it too heavy for the Creator who supports the heavens and the earth?" Jewish wisdom teaches that He Who has created and Who supports the whole universe cannot support or pardon the crime that man commits against man. (*DF* 20)

Leibowitz will, by contrast, repeatedly return to the figure of Abraham as called by God to bind Isaac for a sacrifice (the *akedah*), a summons pre-anchored, he says, in the verse, *And he had faith in God* (Gen. 15:6).[7] Or else he will turn to the Book of Job as, after Abraham, the Bible's preeminent expression of *yirat haShem*, fear of God, as echoed by Maimonides at the very beginning of the *Mishneh Torah*.[8]

Or, to take another instance in the same essay as the reference to Cain, Levinas makes one of his rare references to the Jewish calendar: the Festival of *Sukkot*, or "the cabins," as symbolizing Judaism's "freedom with regard to the sedentary forms of existence" (*DF* 23). The parallel move in Leibowitz involves, again, the reiteration of certain paradigmatic moments in which duty comes before joy or any other self-interested human motive: either the *Musaf* (additional) or the *Ne'ilah* (final) services of Yom Kippur, the first containing the prayer, "It is incumbent upon us to praise," which Leibowitz calls "the praise of thanks for Israel's privilege of worshipping God" (35) and the second, during which one *stands* for the duration, and which marks the end of the Holy Day and the recommencement of weekday worship. Leibowitz notes the transition this way:

> At the close of the Ne'ilah service with the public utterance of the verse of the Shema and the blowing of the Shofar—the first words of the evening prayer are uttered: "And he is merciful and forgiving of sin." Thus the basic situation of repentant man at the close of the Day of Atonement is exactly what it was the evening before. His sole achievement consists of the great religious effort invested in the day. Immediately after he must begin his preparations toward the next Yom Kippur. The cycle continues until the end of one's life. In like manner one's labor in study of Torah is not a means for the attainment of any other goal. (15)[9]

The analogy to Torah study, of course, is characteristic and deliberate, for at the core of Leibowitz's understanding of Judaism as
halakhic praxis lies an uncompromising criterion of *Torah lishmah* and
avodah lishmah. In the essay, "The Reading of the Shema," he says

> Care must be taken in how one follows the ways of God [for] we find
> in the Sephardic prayer book for the Days of Awe: "We performed
> Mitzvoth not for the sake of Heaven." The performance of Mitzvoth
> not for the sake of heaven is performed as a transgression in need of
> atonement. (43)

But when Levinas speaks of *mitzvah*, as we have seen, the imperative
aspect of God is linked directly to the commanding alterity of the other
person: "everything I can hear of His word and reasonably say to Him
must find an ethical expression. . . . The Justice rendered to the Other,
my neighbor, gives me an unsurpassable proximity to God" (17–18).[10]

Even at this preliminary point of the chapter, then, it should be clear
that the vanishing point of responsibility "opening up the beyond" for
Levinas also opens up the fissure between a philosophy of *lishmah* and
a philosophy of Torah-for-the-sake-of-the-Other, between Leibowitzian
halakhic man and Levinasian aggadic man. When the latter writes for
instance, "The harmony achieved between so much goodness and so
much legalism constitutes the original note of Judaism" (19),[11] it is not
at all clear that Leibowitz would assent, since goodness, as he explains
more than once, is not the exclusive religious or affective property of
Judaism.

As I intimated earlier, Levinas actually refers to Leibowitz in passing in an early essay entitled "The State of Israel and the Religion of
Israel," published in 1951. Citing a volume of essays in Hebrew, all
"eye-witness accounts . . . of the move from religion to ethics[, j]ustice
as the *raison d'être* of the State," Levinas singles out one piece in particular, by Leibowitz, entitled "Religion and the State," because of the
pivotal question it puts regarding the role of Jewish Law in a modern,
democratically instituted polity.

"But why, after all, should we get lumbered with Torah?" he asks
rhetorically. "And how can we apply it to a contemporary situation that
is so different politically, socially, economically from the order envisaged
by the Law" (219)?[12] Although the essay does not detail Leibowitz's
answer to his own question, Levinas evidently finds it satisfactorily
answered: "The social and political situation described by the Bible and
the Talmud is the example of a given situation that is rendered human by
the Law. From it we can deduce the justice required for any and every situation" (219). Whether Leibowitz in fact concurs is one of the questions
we shall pursue in the following pages as we try to satisfy our own curios-

ity about the alignment and incongruencies of both Levinas's and Leibowitz's Zionism and their halakhic/aggadic anthropologies.

For as I suggest in the introduction, what makes a juxtaposition of these philosophers intrinsically fascinating is that the two neither neatly converge nor diverge. "Doing philosophy Jewishly" in each case means something slightly oblique to the level plane of philosophical values— the meaning of "ethics"—and Jewish practices, specifically Torah for Torah's sake. Leibowitz, for example, will say of the creation of the State of Israel, "Privileged is the generation that has been summoned to this, the greatest of responsibilities," except that, to articulate the divide with Levinas once again, he is not speaking of Judaism's "universalist particularism" for which the State now exists to model justice and morality to other nations, but rather much more restrictively, of the need for newly legislated Halakhah equal to the unprecedented sociopolitical demands of a modern Jewish state (172–173).

And thus perhaps Leibowitz and Levinas's most dramatic difference: their viewpoints on Christianity or a common Judeo-Christian heritage—a concept Leibowitz wholly repudiates and Levinas endeavors, minimally, to retain. For nowhere more obviously than here, I think, can the impingement of place upon ideology be discerned, in the gap between Levinas's diasporist ecumenicism and Leibowitz's nationalized and self-sufficient Judaism. As anchored in reasoned judgment as these positions may be, as philosophically legitimate, I would point as well to a certain ideological tariff or tax imposed respectively by the State of Israel and the Republic of France on Leibowitz's and Levinas's intellectual autonomy.

Judaism is a religion of *demands*, says Leibowitz, Christianity, one of *endowments* (not surprisingly perhaps, Leibowitz makes no attempt to represent Christian faith, theology, or practice from within its own self-understanding—much in fact like Sartre's famously reductive analysis of Jewish identity in *Anti-Semite and Jew*). As Abraham personifies the former, the service of God through the Law, so Jesus embodies the latter, a free gift through the Incarnation and a price purchased subsequently through Crucifixion. The material transformation thus accomplished and the "economic" conversion thus wrought describe an alteration at the baseline level of human nature that halakhic Judaism cannot endorse. Rather, it imagines a mastery over nature, not its transfiguration, an adjudication not a redemption, and through the daily performance of the *mitzvot*, a recapitulation of the motivating spirit of the *akedah* in everyday life.

A restrictive link between Leibowitz and R. Soloveitchik becomes evident here, as the two Orthodox thinkers are similarly skeptical of Christianity's theological challenge to normative, halakhically circumscribed Judaism. Like Soloveitchik, Leibowitz construes the yoke of Torah and *mitzvot* as a permanent and endless task, "oriented as it is to the realities of human existence." For both of them an ideal world would be that in which the Halakhah matches empirical reality point by point, and fulfills it. But short of such eschatological perfection, "no religious achievement can change the human condition or the task" 15). (Bracketing Soloveitchik's existentialist dramatism, one discerns an additional connection to Leibowitz around the nodal point of Kant, who for both offers a philosophically far more respectable and defensible axiology than what each would see as Christianity's reversal of polarities between man's service and Divine transcendence.[13])

As the yoke of Torah and *mitzvot* defines Judaism and Jewish identity for Leibowitz and Soloveitchik alike, it follows that the programmatic revisionism of Christian Scripture must fundamentally and inarguably *mis-recognize* them, and "blasphemously, from the point of view of Judaism" (262). "[T]hat the Torah has a Christian meaning and that He who once gave the Torah then abrogated the Mitzvot" ensures Christianity's permanent strangeness to, and irrecuperable estrangement from, Judaism in Leibowitz's estimation, making any Judeo-Christian alliance chimerical. "Repugnance" is the word he uses to describe a justifiable Jewish attitude with regard to Christianity, something Soloveitchik deftly avoids by being so scrupulously particularist as to forego mentioning Christianity altogether (and through the construct of *homo religiosus* alluding to it only by implication).[14]

But as Eliezer Goldman rightly notes, Leibowitz adds an emotional, personalized component here that is absent in R. Soloveitchik if only because the latter's Orthodoxy flourishes contentedly in the *Bet Midrash* (albeit in Exile), as opposed to a halakhic contumacy lived from *within* a recrudescent *Eretz Yisrael*. Bluntly responding to a question about the meaning of Zionism, Leibowitz offers the following admission:

> My own answer [is] that Zionism is the expression of our being fed up with being ruled by *Goyim*. I am aware that this "we" does not extend to all Jews. Still, it is a motive shared by Zionist Jews who differ widely in their human values and in their conceptions of Judaism. Zionism is best defined as the program for the attainment of political and national independence. Now that this has been attained in the form of a sovereign state, Zionism consists in the effort to maintain this independence. This is the function the state of Israel performs for the Jewish people, in addition to inspiring "the fear of authority" as does every system of government to maintain peace and tranquillity. More than that should not be expected from any state. (116–117)

If one compares such clear-eyed vision of political allegiance to a state minimally defined, with the full import of Levinas's assertion that while

Judaism may be a particularism with regard to doctrines, anthropologies, axiologies, and theologies, it is not a limitation or other brought to bear on national allegiances, civic duty, and fraternity; or if one contrasts Leibowitz's declaration of independence with Levinas's arresting counterclaim that the entire non-Jewish world is in a very real way *dependent* on Jews and Israel, that at the very least it and Israel are co-implicated; if one pivots between them thus, the ideological abyss between Levinas and Leibowitz gapes wide.

The Jewish faith involves tolerance because, from the beginning, it bears the entire weight of other men (DF 173). Levinas italicizes that assertion, but it is not one likely to persuade Leibowitz, for whom the Halakhah that would sanction it does not appear at all self-evident. In "Antihumanism and Education," Levinas affirms, "ecumenicism seems to us a key idea not because it allows us to be recognized at our level by the Christian but because, when we have been brought back to the Law, we work for our Christian brothers" (286).[15] Such sentiments evince a practiced Levinasism that is consistent not only with the philosopher's discourse but with his biography as well—the lived realities that gave William Richardson such pause in our introduction, which, when Levinas introduces as "signature," are very far removed from apologetics.[16]

> The respect that we have for the Christian faith, the admiration provoked by the virtues of its saints and the righteousness of its many men of goodwill and courage who, notably, revealed themselves to us during the terrible years, invites an encourages us to reach this synthesis which must first of all be practiced like a friendship. Judaeo-Christian friendship: there is a phrase that embodies an absolutely proper use of this synthetic adjective. (279)

But such harmonization or kinship as Levinas endorses, especially under the umbrella of liberal humanism where "the Jew . . . feels he is the equal and the brother of the Christian" (279)[17] on both its cultural and liberal humanist merits remains alien to Leibowitz. This, despite the fact that Leibowitz becomes as much the heir of enlightenment liberalism as Levinas when defending against idolatries and inequities of the State. To that degree at least Leibowitz is also a "Westerner."[18] And yet, any supranational sense of fraternity, like any and all political and ethical considerations, must yield to the *differentia specifica* of the Halakhah, which remains always the final arbiter for Leibowitz. (I return to this point later in the chapter in respect to Levinas's short essay, "Exclusive Rights.")

Finally, to make the contrast with Levinas discursive as well as formal or substantive, only Levinas will scale such rhapsodic heights as these, where, in a short piece about the holiday of Hanukkah, he leaves Mitnagdism behind, as he does in his idiosyncratic reading of R. Hayyim of Volozhin, for something altogether more ecstatic:

> O! nocturnal existence turned in on itself within the narrow confines of a forgotten phial. Oh! Existence sheltered from all uncertain contact with the outside, a lethargic existence traversing duration, a liquid lying dormant on the edge of life like a doctrine preserved in some lost yeshiva, a clandestine existence, isolated, in its subterranean refuge, from time and events, an eternal existence, a coded message addressed by one scholar to another, a derisory word in a world given over to mixing! Oh! Miracle of tradition, conditions and promise of a thought without restraint that does not want to remain an echo, or brief stir of the day. Oh! Generous light flooding the universe, you drink our subterranean life, our life that is eternal and equal to itself. You celebrate those admirable hours, which are dark and secret. (*DF* 230)

Compare Leibowitz at his most astringent:

> Resting religion on Halakhah assigns it to the prosaic aspects of life, and therein lies its great strength. Only a religion addressed to life's prose, a religion of the dull routine of daily activity, is worth of the name. This is not to demean the poetic moments, the rare occasions when man breaks away from the routine, the experience of rising above the self spiritually and emotionally, the deeds performed fervently. It is quite possible that such moments mark the zenith of a human life. Nevertheless, the fundamental and enduring elements of human existence are in life's prose, not its poetry. (13)

No doubt Levinas would agree, as we have seen in both his scrupled regard for "the daily fidelity to the ritual gesture" and his interpretive commitment to the prosaic genius of Hebrew's "square letters," but here again, I think, cultural and intellectual temperament—the phenomenologist's and the biological scientist's, a certain *espirit intellectuel français* and the recalcitrantly mitnagdic—articulates a palpable divide. I will return to it (and what may bridge it) several times during the course of this chapter, but before shuttling back and forth any more between the two figures, I need to anchor Leibowitz firmly in the context of his own work for a moment.

Leibowitz's essays were published in Hebrew in two volumes, *Yahadut*, *"Am Yehudi, u-Medinat Yisra'el*, "Judaism, Jewish People, and the State of Israel" (Schocken, 1975) and *Emunah, Historyah, va-'Arakhim*, "Faith, History, and Values" (Academon, 1982). Collected into a one-volume translation into English by Eliezer Goldman, they are distributed under four headings: (1) Faith, (2) Religion, People, State, (3) The Political Scene, (4) Judaism and Christianity. "Religious Praxis: The Meaning of Halakhah" and "The Religious and Moral Significance of the Redemption of Israel" in the first section, and "Right, Law, and Reality" in the third are the most important in my view, and I will principally draw from those three, though all of the essays tend to echo each other in tracing out variations on a stable set of reiterated themes.

The decision to conflate the two Hebrew collections under the English title, *Judaism, Human Values, and the Jewish State*, is a sensible one on Goldman's part, for each domain thus bounded exercises its own territorial claims and can indeed be usefully construed, I think, *territorially*. Were I to schematize them reductively for argument's sake (like Leibowitz's dichotomy between Christian and Jew), hegemony belongs unquestionably to "Judaism." For "the Jewish State" is merely one of many places in which Judaism can be practiced and should not moreover be confused with an *Eretz Yisrael* halakhically understood. "Judaism" is contiguous with *halakhah*, and consequently any set of Jewish beliefs or practices not so encompassed cannot qualify as Judaism. Conversely, "Judaism" cannot be made isomorphic with social justice, national identity, ethics, or morality in a Socratic or Kantian sense, or any similar expression of "human values."

Of the three *terrae*, then, it is the middle one that remains most *incognita* for Leibowitz precisely because it can be made to signify almost anything. And in that very semiotic excess lies its idolatrous potential. "Judaism," by contrast, is a cartographer's paradise, mapped and charted down to the last ell and cubit. ("Dr. Leibowitz, I presume" one can almost hear R. Soloveitchik saying once again as the two meta-halakhists continue to cross paths that Levinas seldom traverses.) I begin my own progress through Leibowitz, then, with "Human Values," moving thence to a consideration of "the Jewish State" as Leibowitz defines it. The trajectory of this chapter's argument more or less approximates the previous chapter's in moving from the general as regards the conceptual boundaries of ethics to the particular in respect to nationhood. "Judaism," however, remains the mobile surveyor's level throughout.

2. THE PATHOS OF ETHICS

"Ethics, when regarded as unconditionally asserting its own validity, is an atheistic category *par excellence*" (13). The *par excellence* may sound Levinasian but the asseveration is pure Leibowitz. In Leibowitz's thought, ethics has not yet passed through the prism of postmodern critique let alone what Habermas called the philosophical discourse of modernity.[19] Indeed, it is pre-Hegelian, coming to rest ultimately in the moral philosophy expressed by Kant's second critique as bolstered by certain epistemological principles from the first. As a nonreligious modality, whether as praxis or meta-ethical argument, ethics can have only one of two meanings for Leibowitz: 1) the will as knowledge—"the ethics of Socrates, Plato, Aristotle, the Epicureans and especially the Stoics, and among the later philosophers Spinoza"; or the will as rational agency—"the ethics of Kant and the German idealists." Leibowitz summarily dispatches both by reference to the Shema:

> Among the passages of the Shema we find the words: *that you seek not after your own hearts and your own eyes: after your own hearts* is the negation of Kantian ethics; *after your own eyes* is the negation of Socrates'. The admonition: *I am the Lord your God* follows shortly thereafter. The Torah does not recognize moral imperatives stemming from knowledge of natural reality or from awareness of man's duty to his fellow man. All it recognizes are *Mitzvot*, divine imperatives. (13)

Should one think of appealing to Isaiah, Micah, or any other of Israel's prophetic voices, Leibowitz quickly reminds that the Torah and the prophets never appeal to the human conscience, "which harbors idolatrous tendencies." עקב הלב אכל ואנש הוא מי ידענו, *Weak is the heart above all, and deceitful; who can know it* (Jer. 18), is the sort of scriptural proof text he might adduce, for as he tells us, "The 'God in one's heart' which humanist moralists invoke is a 'strange god.'" (So much for Levinas's Pascal.) When Leibowitz does select *psukim* from the Torah he is careful to quote them in their entirety:

> *You shall love your neighbor as yourself* does not, as such, occur in the Torah. The reading is: *You shall love your neighbor as yourself, I am God.* . . . As misleading as the truncated quotation regarding love of neighbor is the distorted injunction, *And you shall do the good and the right.* The verse reads: *And you shall do the good and the right in the eyes of God!* (18)

Leibowitz's critique of ethics is not, however, predicated on a traditional Judaic dubiety about the efficacy of Western philosophical systems of thought, the devaluation manifested so clearly in a work like Halevi's *Kuzari* but held at some distance by contemporaries like Ibn

Ezra or Maimonides, Leibowitz's own paragon of Jewish rationalism. Indeed, while Immanuel Kant remains Leibowitz's counter-philosopher of choice whenever he propounds his antihumanist line of reasoning, he does not explicitly take up Kant's own critique of Jewish morality, which directly invokes the figure of Abraham, and the *akedah*, a point I take up myself below.

The Leibowitzian argument against ethics—interestingly enough, considering Levinas's stance here—is ontic: humanity is no less answerable to inviolable constitutive and regulatory laws of nature than any other instance or feature of physical reality. Leibowitz, like Soloveitchik, imagines a monistic world that is plural in its phenomena but unified in its raw, empirical givenness. Unlike Soloveitchik, however, the dydadic relationship of more philosophical import is not the dialectical movement between an *a posteriori* world and an *a priori* set of concepts—halakhic man in creative exercise of the Halakhah—but rather the all-defining antinomy between nature (which includes the human spirit), and God.

> Among the many definitions of human freedom, Spinoza's was the most profound: freedom is activity arising from the necessity of one's own nature. But does man have a nature of his own? As a natural being he is part of nature as a whole. His own nature is only the last link in a causal chain of the forces of inorganic and organic nature which act upon him and within him. Where then is man's autonomy? Man activated by his "own" nature is, in effect, nothing but a robot activated by the forces of nature, just like cattle grazing in the pasture, which are also "free from the Torah and the Mitzvot"; that is, from any law externally imposed. The Amoraite Rava tells us; "All bodies are sheaths; happy is he who has won the privilege of being a sheath for the Torah." (21)

Where Levinas will speak, counterintuitively, of being-in-one's-own-skin as already cramped or ill at ease and thus already for-the-other at the level of the corporeal, the epidermal, Leibowitz will defer to Rava's much simpler distinction between body-sheath and Torah-core.[20] Where Levinas will challenge both Heideggerian ontology (which for him takes the form of an anonymous, mere existing, a neutral and impersonal "there is") and philosophy's free-standing, autonomous Self by beginning with a more primordial *relationship*—the heteronomy of persons, "the relation of a being to a being, which is [not a rapport between subject and object but rather . . . a proximity, a relation with the Other" (*DF* 293)—Leibowitz imagines only material reality and its antithesis, God as mediated by Torah and the mitzvot.

The interhuman is merely the individually human multiplied many times. Indeed, every modality of the human—except that which actively chooses to cleave to God—is part and parcel of nature in its totality. And thus, "infinity," is Levinas's sense of a "metaphysical desire" for the Other, "the very opening to exteriority which is also an opening to Highness" (294) signifies an irrelevancy for Leibowitz. Infinity can only describe the Absolute: God purified of attribute or resemblance, God as not arithmetical but essential oneness:[21] אחד יי—*The Lord is One.*

So thoroughgoing is Leibowitz's monism and realism that a Levinasian distinction between Self and Other, from a religious standpoint, can only make *halakhic* sense, but otherwise sustains trivial significance. Ontically and phenomenally, selves do not *essentially* differ from one another. Matching textual meticulousness to philosophical consistency, Leibowitz writes,

> The well-known verse, which is nowadays usually quoted in a truncated form that perverts its meaning, does not confront matter with spirit but with the spirit of God: *not by might, nor by power, but by My spirit.* The human spirit is part of the "might" and "power." (22)

Superficially, this would seem to echo Levinas's definition of the Self (or the "Same," as he expresses the concept in Platonic terms) that we saw identified as the spirit of usurpation in the previous chapter, but that we also find characterized in terms of "imperialism," "*libido dominandi*" and "*pouvoir de pouvoir*," "primitive egoism," "sovereignty" and "homeland," a "wild and naïve liberty," "the itinerary of Ulysses" or "hegemony of Crusoe" (a complacency in and return to the Same) rather than Abraham (the archetypal going-toward, whether *a-Dieu* or *envers autrui*)—a first-person posited in the first place, self-conscious, self-interested, self-satisfied, self-possessed.[22]

But when Leibowitz speaks of "human spirit," he means it *comprehensively*. Neither a dualism between responsible self and approaching other nor a "We" whereby two-becomes-three, has any space allotted to it in the uniform asperity with which Leibowitz portrays the human condition. As for R. Soloveitchik, for Leibowitz there is only "man." By contrast, Levinas's entire philosophical edifice rests upon the deceptively simplest of armatures and foundations: grammatical number. Whether he is mounting a critique of ontology or of epistemology, whether he speaks in a flagrantly religious vocabulary or a resolutely academic one, whether he addresses Truth, Action, Testimony, Law, the State or any other sphere or relationality: whatever his theme or discourse, Levinas depends on an invariable triad of first, second, and third persons.

In *Totality and Infinity*, when Levinas introduces the notion of the "third party," who replots the coordinates of the face-to-face onto a third axis or dimension by which an original asymmetry now answers to multiple, competing symmetries, he says that the other "joins me" through a concatenating linkage of commandments, a "chain of command" if you will. The poor one, the stranger "commands me to command" by referring me to the public order where others are served; I am thus invested with the power to command for the sake of the third (*TI* 312). This is how a pluralism takes shape behind a two-person ethics, or as Levinas explains it in an early essay, "This reference from a command to a command is the fact of saying We, of forming a party."[23]

But to speak of commandments this way as human mutuality, as the investment of one person by another *ad infinitum*, as *metzavim* (commanders), is already to speak a language that has outstripped the plain sense—and purpose—of *mitzvah* as Leibowitz defines it (or understands it defined by both Torah and Maimonides). The imperative force of צו, *command*, has to be restricted to Divine insistence else its very exceptionality and exorbitance becomes meaningless. "No man would commit himself to such a way of life," Leibowitz writes, "if he did not regard the service of God as an end in itself serving no extrinsic purpose" (16). (The Sages, in *Sifra* and *Kiddushin* 29a, explain of the appearance of the word צו, in Lev. 6:1—when heretofore אמר, say, or דבר, speak, had been used for commandments involving the priestly offerings—that it connotes extra zealousness, and the warrant to be repeated constantly to ensuing generations.)

Levinas locates both the *power* of commandment and the very *event* (let alone meaning) of ethics as the property of the second person through whom the third—be it God or the another person—is revealed, for it is only in the interhuman that *mitzvah* assumes its signification as standard-bearer of a justice rendered to alterity. "To know God is to know what must be done."

> There is a Jewish proverb which says that "the other's material needs are my spiritual needs"; it is this disproportion, asymmetry, that characterizes the ethical refusal of the first truth of ontology—the struggle *to be*. Ethics is, therefore, *against nature* because it forbids the murderousness of my natural will to put my existence first. (*FTF* 24)

In other words, ethics *happens to me*; I *undergo* it; it comes from the outside, but in its very exteriority it derives the power to unseat me in my selfhood and compel my responsibility. And it is *this* wholly human moral force that is counternatural. Leibowitz, however, will quote the Tannaitic adage that "None but he who busies himself with the Torah is free" as signifying where the divide lies for him: "he is free from the bondage of nature because he lives a life which is contrary to nature, both nature in general and human nature in particular" (22).

The difference between Levinas and Leibowitz here is not simply a matter of nomenclature, as if *ethics* in its Levinasian sense were synonymous with *religion* or *Torah and mitzvot* in Leibowitz's. That is the case, of course, for Levinas, but the consequent correlation, between human and divine, represents a category mistake of the first order, in Leibowitz's view. Levinas writes,

> I do not want to define anything through God because it is the human that I know. It is God that I can define through human relations and not the inverse. The notion of God—God knows, I'm not opposed to it! But when I have to say something about God, it is always beginning from human relations. The inadmissable abstraction is God; it is in terms of the relation with the Other that I speak of God. . . . I do not start from the existence of a very great and all-powerful being. Everything I wish to say comes from the situation of responsibility which is religious insofar as I cannot elude it. If you like, it is like a Jonah who cannot escape. (*BPW* 29)

Leibowitz's starting point is completely different. *That God exists* is the first commandment of the Decalogue, and nothing outside of the knowledge of God can therefore lead man to the knowledge of God. "Why do I believe in God?" writes Leibowitz of Maimonidean first principles. "Because it is a *mitzvah*, a commandment, to believe in God" (*The Faith of Maimonides* 49).

Insisting thus on *commanded faith* is entirely consistent with Leibowitz's positivistic and normative account of revelation as the source of genuine value and choice (values and choices which therefore become *religious* values and choices) as opposed to an indifferent natural reality where even consensus and rational agency are conditioned and to that extent arbitrary.[24] For Leibowitz, too, *everything I wish to say comes from a situation that is religious insofar as I cannot elude it,* but that is because of God's Torah and mitzvot, which make sense of human relations, not human relations, which, in the opposite direction, make sense of religious duty.

It is significant also, I think, that Levinas should chose Jonah as an example of being unable to resist the force of command as opposed to, say, Abraham the Patriarch poised to slay his own son—Leibowitz's paradigm of self-nullification before the commanding Presence of God—and that when Levinas does make reference to Abraham, it is to the archetype of hospitality (Gen. 18) or leave-taking (Gen. 12). "The Akedah," writes Leibowitz on the other hand, "is man's absolute mastery over his own human nature."

> *Abraham rose early in the morning and saddled his ass . . . and set out* for the Akedah. Don Isaac Abravanel, commenting upon Gen. 22:3, explains *saddled his ass* means that he overcame his materiality, that is, his physical nature—a pun on the phonetically similar *hamor*, ass, and *homer*, matter. (14)

To articulate one last crucial bar rather than bridge between Levinas and Leibowitz, as we read in the essay, "In the Name of God according to a Few Talmudic Texts," the Oral Tradition's scrupulosity about effacing or pronouncing the name of God signifies for Levinas a "withdrawal" that points indexically to another sort of revelation. "According to the words of the prophet, to judge the cause of the poor and the needy, *Is this not to know me?* (Jer. 22:16). Knowledge of the unknowable: transcendence becomes ethics" (*BV* 123). Ethics can never be a category of transcendence for Leibowitz since by his definition it serves human ends; no matter how lofty the moral agency, "human values" will always act like a compass in search of a terrestrial magnetic North, an unguided and thus perplexed "seeking after one's own heart."

Both philosophers equate Judaism with transcendence and with infinite responsibility. Both insist on the authority of revelation through Torah and *mitzvot*. Both understand action in the world as religious praxis. Both, it could be said, strike a fourth blow to the modern subject, dethroned from its formerly sovereign, high Renaissance perch by successive Copernican, Darwinian, and Freudian usurpations. In both their *hashkafot* or outlooks, the self becomes *metaphysically unseated*, unable fully to justify itself in the sheath of its own skin. Levinas will invoke the Doctors of the Talmud as paragons of an authority reconceived not as force but rather self-restraint, having to accommodate themselves to a world where God seemed no longer to impose his will on history; Leibowitz will have habitual recourse to Maimonides who, in his observations on the Abraham of the *akedah* and Job, discloses a God wholly other, transcending both history and human need.

But a continental divide separates not only the way each philosopher will ascribe transcendence within Judaism and the illimitable obligation it therefore solicits or demands from the observant Jew ("solicits" being the operative Levinasian term, I think, and "demands" the more Leibowitzian). It also cleaves between the mandate for religious praxis each philosopher will defend, and the concomitant textual superstructure each will erect, whether philosophical or Judaic. On the latter score alone, perhaps even more than their conceptual differences, nothing more decisively differentiates the two as intellectual architects than the labyrinthine majesty of Levinas's phenomenological sublime, a many-roomed mansion of allusion, reference, and argument, and the monolithic spareness of Leibowitz's tent of meeting, where we encounter always and almost singly the voice of another Moses: Maimonides. Indeed how Levinas and Leibowitz each construes the *meaning* of philosophy for Judaism is a theme to which I am always returning, and take up in the concluding chapter to this book.

To recall the outlines of "holiness" traced by the previous chapter in my comparison of Levinas and Soloveitchik, the logic of Leibowitz's antihumanism but also the purity of his religious commitment, the need to define ethics as atheistic but at the same time a vigilance to all things potentially idolatrous, the fencing off of Torah and *mitzvot* but also the fencing out of other grounds for Jewish identity: such consistent dualism is predicated on that same differentiating impulse I have identified as normatively halakhic.

> Life molded on the halakhic model demarcates a domain of things and deeds that pertain to holiness. Holiness, in the religious sense of this word as against its figurative secular meanings, is nothing but halakhic observance; the specific intentional acts dedicated to the service of God. Any other deed-whether regarded as good or bad, material or spiritual—that a man may perform in his own interest or for the satisfaction of a human need is profane. Sacred and profane are fundamental religious categories. Within institutional religion, the religion of Halakhah, the distinction between them is an essential aspect of religious perception. Conversely, the idea of holiness as an immanent property of certain things—persons, locations, institutions, objects, or events—is a magical-mystical concept which smacks of idolatry. . . . Nothing is holy in itself. There is only that which is "holy to God"; that which is sanctified by the distinct purpose of serving God. Only this meaning of "holiness" can be accommodated by halakhic Judaism. "You shall be holy" is demanded at the beginning of a portion of the Torah concerned mainly with *Mitzvoth*. "For you are a holy people" occurs in a context devoted in its entirety to halakhic practices. (24)

That same discriminating machinery—what R. Soloveitchik calls the halakhic "*a priori*" and Levinas conjures in more abstract terms as "austere discipline" (*DF* 18)—is expressed in the benediction that marks the end of the Sabbath, when God is blessed for making a *distinction between the sacred and the profane, between light and darkness, between Israel and the other nations, between the seventh day and the six working days*. The *havdalah* (separation) is self-evident because the choices here are always only two—Judaism and idolatry.

And yet, this unswerving commitment to the Holy should give us pause before we contrast Leibowitz and Levinas too acutely. For is this not what Levinas means when he calls Judaism an irreducible modality of being present in the world, "a hope of holiness in the face of a scared that cannot be purified," where "sacred" signifies the world's propensity for appearance that falsifies what appears (*l'apparence altère l'apparaître*), for self-allegorization, mystification and enchantment?[25] He writes, "I have always asked myself whether holiness—that is separation or purity—can dwell in a world that has not been desacralized" (*NTR*

141) and his answer would seem to point precisely to the Halakhah: "the *separation* of the Pharisees . . . by means of prohibitions and rules" that promises an exit from—or at least a fence against—a world bewitched (153).

The conclusion of the Talmudic reading that discusses "the sacred" in relation to "the holy" suggests that all that Judaism will grant to the profane world perforce is the knowledge of its features, in order to mark the distinction, to erect the fence. Is this not then merely the corollary to what Leibowitz stipulates as the *ne plus ultra* of religious praxis and deliberation: the "understanding [that] requires the Halakhah to determine what is holy, from which we may infer what is not holy" (26)?

The difference, ultimately, and why ethics can seem pathetic, "an atheistic category *par excellence*" for Leibowitz, but signify a passion beyond pathos, "experience *par excellence*" (*DF* 293) for Levinas, I believe, lies with the notion of *lishmah*—in excess of which Levinas redefines the sacred as referring to "the Other's hunger" (xiv) but within which (*bifnim mishurat haDin*) Leibowitz squarely locates himself and the fence of meta-halakhah. To put this in theocentric terms, monotheism signifies God in his unity, oneness, and absolute transcendence for Leibowitz, the *bifnim mishurat* of Divinity; for Levinas, the fact that God is so often described anthropomorphically by the Torah and Talmud teaches another kind of monotheism: a finger pointing to human proximity, the *lifnim mishurat* (the *beyond*) of ethical good.

The next section explores the meaning of *lishmah* and *mishurat* for Leibowitz, and is followed by two separate treatments of the place accorded Maimonides and Kant in his thought, retrieving certain threads from my introduction. Rather than being limited exclusively to a face-to-face between Leibowitz and Levinas, the question of ethics will be opened up again to include "third parties" such as Rabbis Soloveitchik and Lichtenstein, David Hartman, and Emil Fackenheim.

3. LISHMAH

Leibowitz's analysis of Torah-for-its-own sake is distributed between two late essays, "The Reading of the Shema" and "*Lishmah* and Not-*Lishmah*." The former, the shorter of two, begins, in echo of Maimonides, with a definition of faith as its own legitimation: not a form of cognition, but rather a decision, a commitment, "a conative element of consciousness." As the *mitzvot* direct Jews to and educate them in religious faith, the purpose for which they have been designed becomes an end in itself, for faith has no other expression except the worship of God as realized through His commandments.[26] The service itself, as Leibowitz says, becomes the very purpose.

The distinction between means and end-in-itself is the distinction between לשמה and שלא לשמה (for-its-own-sake and not-for-its-own-sake), a dualism Leibowitz finds elaborated in the first two paragraphs of the *Shema*, where the first, *And you shall love the Lord your God with all your heart* . . . (Deut. 6:4–9) describes a self-validating categorical imperative (the love of God),[27] and the second, *If you will diligently hearken* . . . (Deut. 11:13–21), predicts a conditional set of rewards and corresponding punishments (God as the minister of health and security). The one delineates Judaism, the Halakhah, and the Torah as difficult freedom; the other as the wisdom of the feasible, the two being synthesized in the *Shema*'s third paragraph, the portion describing *tzitzit*, which commands remembering and doing as the baseline level of *mitzvot*, irrespective of whether one performs them *lishmah* or *she'lo-lishmah*.[28]

The essay "*Lishmah* and Not-*Lishmah*" is a polemical response to a review of Leibowitz's book *Judaism, the Jewish People, the State of Israel* and pointedly summarizes all his characteristic themes. After another explanation of the structure of the *Shema* and some obligatory references to Maimonides, Leibowitz quotes R. Hayyim of Volozhin— in Soloveitchikan rather than Levinasian mode—who, for him, expresses "the 'idea of Judaism' in its original sense, the spirit animating the world of Halakhah":

> For the reward of the *Mitzvah* is the *Mitzvah* itself given to one as a reward, and that is the light enveloping him, and he truly sits in Paradise . . . for he is *now in the world to come as he performs the Mitzvah*, and this is achieved by man himself, *for the Mitzvah is the very reward*, and the light is Paradise in the lifetime of man, and that is his reward. (67)

Again, the difference is sharp: Judaism as the service to human individuals and collectives, or Judaism as the service to God. "[T]he welfare of the body (ethics and politics!) which is only of functional and instrumental importance, and the welfare of the mind (the recognition of truth for its own sake!)" (68).

I suggest a contiguity with R. Soloveitchik rather than Levinas, and yet the purgative and nondialectical ethos Leibowitz demonstrates here is uniquely his own. For although Soloveitchik also defers to Hayyim Volozhiner, *sans commentaire*, in the concluding pages of his book's first part, part two begins an entirely new existential drama with a new, though necessarily related, role for the religious Jew: "Halakhic man is a man who longs to create, to bring into being something new, something original" (99). It is in this section that R. Soloveitchik alludes to *kabbalah*, and the concept that the world's given imperfection requires humanity's "fashioning, engraving, attaching, and creating" impulse and skill. And thus R. Soloveitchik will cast halakhic man against a second horizon, within a second landscape, superimposed upon those we saw at the beginning of the last chapter:

> When man, the crowning glory of the cosmos, approaches the world, he finds his task at hand—the task of creation. He must stand on guard over the pure, clear existence, repair the defects in the cosmos, and replenish the "privation" in being. Man, the creature, is commanded to become a partner with the Creator in the renewal of the cosmos; complete and ultimate creation—this is the deepest desire of the Jewish people. (105)

This partnership in creation—the command to create—is not unlike the partnership in revelation—the command to command—that for Levinas opens the ethical relation to a more encompassing world of justice and plurality—the *mitzavim* of "We" as more than the plurality of "I" (*CPP* 43). Indeed, Soloveitchik's closer alignment with Levinas rather than Leibowitz in this regard becomes all the clearer in light of the extended discussion that follows the passage above, which contains the talmudic *aggadah* about God's diminution of the moon that, as we saw, Levinas also glosses in his essay on the *Nefesh haHayyim*.

Soloveitchik understands this drive toward perfection as the actualization of the ideal Halakhah, filling the abscess that is the material world by contracting transcendence within it (108). The model here (though Soloveitchik uses the kabbalistic and exilic trope of *tzimtzum*) is ultimately scriptural—the *Bet ha-Mikdash* itself, the Temple Israel is commanded to build for God's *shekhinah*, His presence, to dwell on earth, in the holy city known as *sha'ar hashamayim*, or "gate of heaven." And however Levinas and Soloveitchik may differ in interpreting the meaning of such contraction—Levinas, as the overflow of Infinity that draws the self toward the other, Soloveitchik, as the realization

of קדשה (holiness) through halakhic creativity—each is equally far
removed from Leibowitz's manichean divide between Transcendent Will
and human action. For religious praxis in Leibowitz's understanding of
the halakhic life is first and foremost *obedience and submission*, if
Torah and *mitzvot* are to be understood normatively (as Divine pre-
scription) not factually (as adjusted to a natural world that is, religiously, speaking, indifferent).

But Leibowitz will clear a place for halakhic creativity, indeed, innovation, too. And it is exactly in the *political* sphere—where the establishment of a new Jewish state requires new halakhic strategies for regulating a new kind of Jewish polity—that, paradoxically, his asperity
bears fruit, as I emphasize in the final section of this chapter. But before
I address that dimension of his thought, where religious scruple—his
fierce anti-idolatry—and metahalakhic fidelity—his political pragmatism—become truly masterly in my view, Leibowitz's philosophical
prejudices warrant a closer reckoning. For what I have imprecisely
called manichean in Leibowitz's thought is properly *Kantian*: a rigid
dichotomizing between divine and human, religion and morality, norm
and fact, which he consistently deploys and assumes from the outset,
and which allow no room for mediation or dialectic.

At the same time Leibowitz's halakhic man begins where Maimonides does—with faith in an absolute and transcendent God—Leibowitz the philosopher retraces dividing lines in Kantian ethics and
epistemology that limn the interface between metaphysical and empirical (or practical) realms. And it is that same philosopher, as David
Hartman has persuasively argued, who mis-steps by failing to appreciate the value invested in philosophy by Maimonides himself, and who
is equally ill-served by a penchant for radical Kantian antinomies—
however he may repudiate Kant's moral philosophy—he is loathe to
part with. Ironically, such philosophical rigidity—philosophy in an
undercritical sense—prevents Leibowitz from imagining a more fluid
relationship between philosophy and the Halakhah, one that Hartman
finds most expansively and creatively theorized in Jewish tradition by
Moses Maimonides.

I turn to Maimonides first, and pivot thence to a Kantianism that
seems to me equal parts blindness and insight. I hope thus to underscore
the ontotheological bind in which Leibowitz traps himself which, as the
very sort of epistemic legacy from which Heidegger and Levinas in his
wake sought to free twentieth-century philosophy, is, finally, more Kantian than Jewish. It is *Jewish* philosophy, as metaphilosophically configured by figures like Maimonides in the twelfth century and Levinas in
the twentieth—or rather, it is doing philosophy *Jewishly* by rethinking
philosophical means and ends—that Leibowitz has failed to catch sight

of.[29] The very philosophizing that serves him in pitting Abraham against the Kantians leaves him as close in the final analysis to the Kantians as to Abraham. And even with Maimonides on his side, he has yet to find the *philosophical* third term bridging the distance between God and Man.

4. MOSES AND THE POST-KANTIANS[30]

One reason that Leibowitz's Maimonides and Hartman's Maimonides do not seem to coincide—indeed they are radically disjunct—is, very simply, that Maimonides's presence in Jewish philosophy looms both large and polyhedral.[31] Abraham Joseph Heschel tells an anecdote about the eighth hundred anniversary of Maimonides's birth in 1935 (*not* an innocent year), as celebrated interdenominatially by the Jewish community of Berlin.[32] The Reform rabbi referred to Maimonides as *Maimuni*, the Arabic name by which he was known to his contemporaries; the Conservative rabbi called him *Maimonides*, as he is known in the West; and the Orthodox rabbi called him the *Rambam*, the acronym for him in traditional Jewish literature.

To these three Maimonides(s) two more always need to be added as well: the author of the *Mishneh Torah*—Maimonides the halakhist—and the author of the *Moreh Nevukhim* (Guide for the Perplexed)—Maimonides the philosopher.[33] From Nachmanides to Leo Strauss, Maimonides has been read in a remarkably disparate number of ways by many different kinds of Jewish thinkers (and at least one Jewish philosopher has argued for a moratorium on just such exclusivist and conflicted focus).[34] Hartman has his own selective ambit for situating Maimonides, of course, and while personally I believe *The Living Covenant* accomplishes by far the most penetrating *symbiosis* between halakhic Judaism and the modern world, that ambit is wider than my immediate concerns here.

But Hartman is certainly correct to underscore the way in which Leibowitz habitually ascribes to Maimonides his own reified concept of halakhic observance—performance of *mitzvot*—as both the means and the end of divine worship. As he does capture the problem here both cogently and elegantly, I cite his extended conclusion:

> Leibowitz fails to give sufficient weight to the role of philosophy in Maimonides' conception of worship. He is mistaken in his claim that philosophy for Maimonides has only the function of helping one to overcome the dangers of idolatry. Love of God in Maimonides is related not to the will to worship, as Leibowitz would have it, but is a natural unfolding of the passion of the mind in its quest to understand God. For Maimonides, knowledge and performance of the *mitzvot* based on traditional authority lead one around, but not into, "the place of the king," as he puts it in *Guide* 3:51. You are still outside if the mitzvot are your only framework. It is philosophy that leads to Maimonidean intimacy with God. The end of the Guide does not offer a new understanding of how *mitzvot* lead from an anthropocentric to a theocentric focus. It shows, rather, how the philosopher can utilize the structure of halakhah to prepare for what is a meta-halakhic expe-

rience. . . . One cannot translate Maimonides' intellectualism into a
heroic existential attempt to free oneself from all that is natural within
the human world. . . . Leibowitz compresses the Maimonidean passion
into the will to worship, but in so doing he cuts off that passion from
the intellectual roots that nourish it. (*LC* 120–121)[35]

Indeed, even though Leibowitz transposes his consistent polarization of
opposites to an ideological plane by pitting Maimonides against Judah
Halevi[36]—the transcendentalist versus the historicist—it is actually the
latter whose totalized view of Jewish singularity envisions a reified
Halakhah—at the constitutive level—not unlike Leibowitz's.[37] Nevertheless, Leibowitz imputes to Maimonides a halakhic framework that
subsumes philosophy, or in which philosophical reflection merely serves
the Halakhah: faith is the rarefied, "philosophical" knowledge of God,
and thus faith and philosophy circularly, and conveniently, repeat each
other.

Any difference to be discerned lies thus not between *halakhah* and
philosophy (Maimonides of the *Guide* and Maimonides of the *Mishneh
Torah*), but within the Halakhah itself between two options for worship,
avodah lishmah and *avodah she'lo lishmah*, both mediated by the
mitzvot and thus, again, synthetically reconciled. In his book on Maimonides, Leibowitz even borrows from cybernetics the concept of a
feedback loop to describe this reciprocal relation between the practical
commandments and religious faith, or philosophy and *halakhah*. "The
halakhah, which is an instrument for educating man towards faith, is
then reconceived—by means of this faith—not as a means, but as the
purpose itself" (*Maimonides*, 24).

Not only is the hermeneutic circle here thus elegantly closed; the
mitzvot become the only conduit through which humanity makes contact with true Being, all other values being therefore neutral and religiously indifferent. Human freedom, paradoxically, takes the shape of
choosing the only available religious option over against human nature
and the material world in which it participates.

This is a Maimonides that bears only slight resemblance to the Jewish thinker, as interpreted by David Hartman, who praises philosophy
as the vehicle for extrahalakhic worship and who leaves room for "the
full presence of the human being in religious life" (130). Hartman's
Maimonides (after the fashion of "alignment" I suggest above) more
closely approximates the covenantal character of Judaism and the duple
structure of human striving articulated by Soloveitchik in *The Lonely
Man of Faith*. Instead of two Adams, figures of conquest and redemption, Hartman sees Maimonides as constructing two religious frame-
works, each mediating divinity and humankind, and so echoing an
Aristotelian distinction between moral and intellectual virtue.[38] The

first of these, *tikkun ha-guf*, is the body of *mitzvot*, oriented to the individual Jew and the covenantal community in history and the material world; the second, *tikkun ha-nefesh*, is contemplative, disinterested, a metahalakhic mode of rational excellence that Hartman rightly calls "philosophic eros."

Consider the following passage from Maimonides's letter to Rabbi Jonathan ha-Kohen of Lunel, which Leibowitz quotes as an index of how even philosophy must be subjected to a kind of בטל, or nullification (or at least subsumption) within a higher, all-encompassing devotion to Torah:

> *before I was formed of the womb* [Jer. 1:5] the Torah knew me, and before I came out of the womb she dedicated me to the study of the Torah and to spreading her thoughts abroad, and she is *the gazelle of my love and the betrothed of my youth* [Prov. 5:19]. Nevertheless, *many strange women have become her adversaries, women of the Moabites, Ammonites, Zidionites and Hittites* [1 Kings 11:1]. Yet God is my witness that I have not taken them from the beginning except *to be confectioners, and to be cooks, and to be bakers* [Talmudic expression for periods of sexual intercourse] since my heart has been divided into numerous portions by all kinds of wisdom. . . . [F]or I have put together things which have been scattered and strewn among the mountains and hills, and I have called them forth one of a city and two of a family.

Despite Leibowitz's uses for this passage, I do not think the metaphors of erotic love and consanguinity have been idly chosen.[39] Philosophy (like the phenomenology of eros in Levinas's schema in *Totality and Infinity*) exerts is own claims, and has its place outside the fence of halakhah. And thus I am further reminded of Levinas's reading of Gen. 30:30, *Now when shall I provide for my own household also?* Even in the framework of Jewish faith, those things that are *she'lo lishmah* assert themselves if only in being fenced off, for they can nourish the body and the heart. One declares one's fealty and devotion but always by means of the good fences that make good neighbors, that articulate intellectual or metahalakhic dividing lines in the first place. The world, in short, is not as religiously indifferent a place for Maimonides as it is for Leibowitz.

This is also Levinas's point in "Models of the West," in commenting on the *Tosefta* on *Avodah Zarah* (1:1) that says, "Go then and find a time that is neither day nor night and learn then Greek wisdom."[40]

> Does this mean that such an hour does not exist, and that Greek wisdom is being excluded from the Jewish universe? . . . Is it, on the contrary, an allusion to the hours of dusk, neither day nor night, hours of uncertainties where recourse to Greek wisdom would be possible, per-

haps even necessary? . . . This latter is excluded only from the hours where Israel is neither master of its difficult wisdom, or blindly subjected to its tradition. (*BV* 26)[41]

For Leibowitz, we could day, the Halakhah is entirely fenced off, or constitutively speaking, *is* a fence. Meta-halakhah would then be merely a descriptive and polemical enterprise, a fence around a fence. For Maimonides, by contrast, it signifies other possibilities for communion, the pleasures of intellection "in the dusk" and also a different way of being with God.

Where Leibowitz's Maimonides insists on Jews' transcendental homelessness in the world because of a prior metaphysical indemnity before the sheer fact of God, Hartman's Maimonides (and as I have implied a linkage with Levinas as well in terms of philosophy's intrinsic value) is a dialectician who moves deliberatively between theocentric and anthropocentric options, accommodating both "the betrothed [Torah] of my youth" and the "strange women" of Greek wisdom. Philosophical knowledge is eros in the sense that learning who God is outside of egocentric or anthropocentric needs reveals the Lord of the created world who therefore also transcends human history and even Jewish history; such knowledge, in Hartman's words, "provides the intellectual basis for self-transcending, relational love" (*CV* 124).

Leibowitz accords only the Halakhah such a means and end. As he configures Maimonides, so philosophy serves him as well as shunt or scaffold, leading to or merely supporting Torah and *mitzvot*. To frame the problem here genealogically, as a function of intellectual inheritance, Leibowitz's Maimonides looks at the world through a Kantian screen that has been back-projected by Leibowitz himself. But Maimonides was an Aristotelian, for whom the world was neither cloven into noumenal and phenomenal realms (with a consequent crisis for metaphysical knowledge) nor religiously indifferent. As Hartman writes,

> Maimonides' religious anthropology rather builds upon the ability of an individual to alternate between theocentricity and anthropocentricity, between solitude and social commitment, between silent reflection and social activism. Thus the appreciation of human self-realization within the life of *mitzvah* is not a *she-lo li'shmah* perception of worship. Man is not chosen *above* God. What the framework of the covenant mediates is man and woman *in the presence* of God. (*LC* 123)

Such synthetic thought, though premodern, picks up certain strains in talmudic culture, and is more plastic and faithful to the covenantal ethos of Jewish religiosity, Hartman argues, than even as dialectical a thinker as R. Soloveitchik will sometimes allow;[42] it is interdicted entirely in Leibowitz's case by the force of sheer incommensurablity. Maimonides's intellectual rapprochement between philosophy and Judaism is more seamless. In suggesting resemblances between the God of Halakhah and the God of Aristotle, it permits the sort of religious praxis that, in Hartman's words, "can withstand the critical passion of the philosopher," at the same time envisioning a model of worship that "captur[es] the relational intimacy of the covenant" (*LC* 179; *CV* 138).

For the latter, Hartman charts his reading of Maimonides's approach to prayer by showing how in both the *Mishneh Torah* and the *Guide*, the covenantal community is viewed as passing through a series of stages that sustain such intimacy—from the biblical institution of animal sacrifice as both bulwark against idolatry and vehicle for proximity (קרבן, offering, connotes closeness, a rapprochement of a different sort), through a second stage of petitional prayer as instituted by the Rabbis, to a yet higher level of worship, the contemplative and devotional communion with God that is *philosophical* perfection.

The second level corresponds to an anthropocentric dimension of religious experience that Maimonides accepts, even dignifies, and that Leibowitz will classify under the category of worship-not-for-its-own-sake but still allowable if mediated by *shmirat ha-mitzvot* (observance of the commandments). The third level designates not only the requisite reflective sophistication but also the best defense against idolatry since correct belief (philosophy) is crucial in order to identify God correctly, and thus to worship Him alone" (*CV* 129). The first level, finally, forever preserves the limit point reached in the *akedah*, where Abraham's hand is stayed by divine will and a ram is provided in place of Isaac. It also marks the limit point defining Jewish obedience for Leibowitz and, if I may, where Kantian philosophy takes the place of Maimonides and modern epistemology substitutes for medieval metaphysics.

With fascinating consistency, Leibowitz so radicalizes the fact of God's transcendence that is able to draw a continuous line between Maimonidean negative theology and an idealist epistemology that begins with a critique of synthetic knowledge, and leaves the world available to it only in a neutral, instrumentalizable sense. To know the world is to grasp it. To know God, as Levinas puts it, is to know what to do. Leibowitz takes such a model for knowledge as granted, and as it were overleaps entirely Kant's critique of practical reason (whose moral theory of human freedom as a causality undetermined by antecedent causal conditions draws on the epistemology of the first critique), and elects theological morality over moral theology, the reverse of Kant's conclusions at the end of the second critique. In doing so, he also excludes the very reopening and "saving" of metaphysics that Kant accomplishes in his moral theory through respect for the human autonomy revealed by my own existence as well as through the existence of others.[43]

Leibowitz cannot imagine an ethical discourse that does not in some part reflect the influence of Kant, because the "Kingdom of ends"—in whatever shape—defines ethical philosophy for him, intrinsically at odds with the Kingdom of Heaven. And yet his Kant, like his Maimonides, is selective, reified, idiosyncratically Leibowitzian. That is, in Leibowitz's thinking, Kantianism becomes as postivistic as *halakhah*. Consider for a moment certain points of tangency between Kantian and Levinasian ethics in order to appreciate the ideological distance separating Leibowitz from them both (see section 7 of this chapter, however, for the corollary to these speculations). While Levinas begins with the impeachablility of the rational subject, autonomy in Kant is nevertheless not as ironclad as may at first seem. As Adriaan Peperzak suggests, it signifies metaphorically: I am not able to establish the law by which I discover myself to be ruled; I can only appropriate it as if I had created it but the force and fact of its absolute claim precedes me.[44]

Kant, to this degree like Levinas, provides a way by which the other person escapes thematization; the other who inspires my respect and thus catches me, as it were, by surprise, produces an exceptional kind of awareness in me unlike any object-cognition.[45] The moral law transforms the cognizing self into an obliged self; Levinasian ethics puts that self into the accusative case. Being human means being answerable to moral necessitation that, for each philosopher (though obviously in different senses), suggests a law of holiness analogized to an unconditioned law of duty: self-willing in the face of a categorical imperative; the human face itself as *sollicitation* and command. (Levinas, of course, will make any universalist discourse about the rights of man, what he will call "an abstract peace," always answerable to, and derivative from, the rights of the other—"the dignity of goodness itself."[46])

By contrast, moral and religious realms do not form the parallax for Leibowitz that they do in Levinas's and Kant's philosophies. It would not be overtensing the strictures of Leibowitz's epistemology to imagine the face of the other, being part and parcel of the world, as possessing no intrinsic value except insofar as it is seen in the image of God (6).[47] But one never gains the vantage point of a face-to-face in Leibowitz; the phrase properly describes only Moses's converse with God (left unmentioned by Leibowitz and since vouchsafed to no one), not an encounter between persons.

The *rupture* the face signals, the *event* of ethics, the primordial claim of otherness, as all betokening a transvaluation of values in Levinas's schema, and the respect whose tribute we cannot refuse to pay, as Kant calls our practical mandate within the sphere of other persons: these alike for Leibowitz have everything to do with moral and legislative values that are as religiously indifferent as any other feature of nature, and nothing to do with religion. The holy and the sacred come from otherwise than and beyond *the human*, where God's remoteness and transcendence do not, *pace* Levinas, "turn into" anything—even *my responsibility*—but remain, simply, otherwise and beyond.

Is not the binding of Isaac Judaism's primordial object lesson in the antinomy of ethics and religion, the cleft that sunders human nature from worship of God? Leibowitz, as we have seen, answers with a resounding yes, with Maimonides's religious transcendentalism as axiom, and Kantian humanism as negative proof. But as we have also seen, Leibowitz is idiosyncratic in drawing upon Kant; his hostility to Kantian morality, and his categorical distinction between religious action and moral action, is counterweighted by a natural scientist's approbation of the philosophical critique of theoretical reason. It is time, then to turn to Kant not as epistemologist or ethical theorist but as moral theologian, and, realigning yet again, to investigate the divide that positions Kant on one side now, and *Avraham Avinu*, our father Abraham—with Leibowitz—on the other.

5. KANT AND THE SONS OF ABRAHAM

In a section of his book that precedes the footnote quoted in my intro-duction, Fackenheim treats at length Kant's rejection of Judaism as the equipoise between autonomy and heteronomy, a face-to-face between God and the Jewish people mediated by Torah and the *mitzvot*. In *Der Streit der Fakultäten* Kant appends a small footnote of his own to a dis-cussion of God's statutory and revealed will as intrinsically difficult to validate, and in some cases indubitably *not* the voice of God. "For if the voice commands man to do something contrary to the moral law," Kant writes, "no matter how majestic the apparition may be, no matter how it may seem to surpass the whole of nature, he must consider it an illu-sion." And then, the footnote:

> We can use, as an example, the myth of the sacrifice that Abraham was going to make by butchering and burning his only son at God's com-mand (the poor child, without knowing it, even brought wood for the fire). Abraham should have replied to this putative divine voice: "That I may not kill my good son is absolutely certain. But that you who appear to me are God, of that I am not certain and never can be, not even if this voice were to sound from visible heaven." (115)

The radical choice postulated by Kant pits theological morality—revealed, external, heteronomous law—against moral theology—law autonomously imposed and appropriated as though man were its cre-ator. Such are the precincts of practical reason, on the one hand, and the merely postulated, subjective condition of that reason, on the other. Representing God as moral author may satisfy a spiritual or psychic need, but it cannot substantively affect the moral law for a plurality of free wills united by reason.[48] In contradistinction to its exemplary pur-pose for Leibowitz, the *akedah* serves Kant as a proof text whereby every divine-human relation becomes, necessarily, interhuman, a matter for moral agents, equally answerable to the imperative force of the law because they have each been compelled to choose it for themselves.

Fackenheim distinguishes between two moments of morality in Judaism that therefore have no counterpart in Kant's moral philosophy: the "pristine" experience of revelation as vouchsafed to the Patriarchs and the Prophets (all of whom choose out of an unmediated encounter with God's Presence, but for the sake of that Presence alone and for no other reason) and the developed life of that morality through com-mandment and performance. It is in the latter that Fackenheim (and Lev-inas) locate a three-term relationship between a person, his human neighbor, and God Himself that Kant collapses into a two-term human interface alone, for which the moral law acts as bar not bridge between humanity and Divine source. If the latter were the case, says Facken-heim, it would be correct to say with Kierkegaard that for biblical faith and Kantian morality alike, one comes not "into relation with God but with the neighbor whom I love" (*Fear and Trembling* 78).

> The startling claim of the revealed morality of Judaism is that God Himself enters the relationship. He confronts man with the demand to turn to his human neighbor, and in so doing, turn back to God him-self. Michah's celebrated summary of the commandments does more than list three commandments side by side. For there is no humble walking before God unless it manifests itself in justice and mercy to the human neighbor. And there can be only fragmentary justice and mercy unless they culminate in humility before God. Here lies the heart and core of Jewish morality. (Fackenheim, 49)

It should be clear that another and quite simple way to restate the Levinas/Leibowitz cleavage is precisely in these terms of a religiosity predicated on three terms versus one predicated on only two: a worship of God that is also a human intersubjectivity versus either the interhu-man or man in service of God. As Fackenheim schematizes it, Divine commanding presence and appropriating human freedom still point dialectically to each other, and they do so through medial nodes—the leaven, if you will—of the commandments that disclose the neighbor and the neighbor who discloses the occasion for the commandments.

Appropriately enough, Fackenheim cites the midrashic *Pesikhta Kahana*—"Would that they had deserted Me and kept My Torah; for if they had occupied themselves with the Torah, the leaven which is in it would have brought them back to Me"—a midrash that Levinas quotes as well. Leibowitz, on the other hand will say, "the duty of love toward one's neighbor is not a corollary of man's position as such [the great rule of the atheist Kant] but of his position before God" (19).[49] And yet, it often seems, from Leibowitz's theocentric perspective, that the leaven of *ahavat re'ah* (love for one's neighbor) adulterates, so to speak, the purer *matzah* of divine service, such that others seem always to be configured as means and never ends-in-themselves. (I emphasize again that this is owing to the severity of Leibowitz's *religious* position, as his political writings reveal a different sensibility at work.)

To return to Fackenheim: Kant's moral philosophy presupposes its own wisdom of the feasible (as I characterized the Halakhah in the pre-vious chapter): humankind can do only what it is able to do, a matter of both ethical autonomy (what is virtuous or moral, the exercise of *free-dom*) and juridical legislation (what is right, from *necessity*). The force of divine commandment cannot therefore outstrip human agency, and "divine will becomes a moral redundancy" (52). Judaism, by contrast, and as Fackenheim argues, requires the intrinsic moral value of the commandments no less than it requires the absolute otherness of God; in order for neither to be redundant and for both to be reciprocally necessary, a mediation between them is crucial in order to counterbalance religion and morality, transcendence and the interhuman.

But as Kant makes divinity more or less an adjunct (he calls speculations about the existence of God or the immortality of the soul "practical postulates") to a transcendental human freedom legislated by the sovereignty of reason, the *akedah* represents for him something analogous to "the antinomy of practical reason," where "the highest good is impossible in accordance with practical laws . . . and the moral law, which commands us to promote it, must [therefore] be fantastic and directed to imaginary ends" (95). Fackenheim offers two examples that effectively localize the grounds on which Kant's objection to the *akedah* must be met by Jewish response. He notes that certain *midrashim* concur with what Kierkegaard called Abraham's pure subjective faith in what is objectively dubious (though with certain exceptions they do not support the notion of a teleological suspension of the ethical),[50] thus effectively removing Kant's concern with the indubitability of the voice or its source.[51] And he also cites Maimonides's ruling in the *Guide* (3:24) that the sort of extreme circumstance related in the Genesis story may justify child-murder in the name of religious sacrifice rather than self-evidently falling under the category of murder, thus qualifying Kant's assertion that Abraham's slaying of his son is normatively ruled out in any and every case.[52]

The Jewish response to Kant in regard to the *akedah* thus must be made on the grounds of a priori structures or conditions—a metaphysics of morals—and in Kant, the rectitude and authority of the Categorical Imperative as established by practical reason provides the basis for any moral theology. Revelation answers to the touchstone of that concept— *Act in such a way that you always treat humanity, whether in your own person or the person of others, never simply as a means, but always at the same time as an end*—whose original purity, as Kant says in *Religion within the Limits of Reason Alone*, must also be our source for the contempt of idolatry (95). By means of Kant's example of suicide (in *The Groundwork of the Metaphysic of Morals*) as illustrating the inviolability of the moral maxim, Fackenheim suggests that sacrifice in a religious sense becomes a logical contradiction for Kantian moral theory, and thus its possibility "as a direct gift to God motivated by the pure love of God remains totally unexamined" (62). The same incoherence attaching to sacrifice would apply to martyrdom as well for Kant (though not for Kierkegaard),[53] who can find no moral justification for it.

It is precisely such a link from *akedah* to *kiddush haShem* (sanctification of God's name through martyrdom) that Fackenheim considers, in the course of contrasting Kantian two-term morality and the three-term religiosity of Judaism, and that Leibowitz explicitly rejects. Here is Leibowitz:

> Emancipation from the bondage of nature can only be brought about by the religion of Mitzvoth. It cannot be accomplished by overcoming one's inclinations by rational or secular ethical considerations. True, the tendency to secularize all the traditional value-concepts has affected even the Aqedah. The term is prevalently used to designate heroic acts of self-sacrifice lacking any religious import, such as those of parents who sacrificed their children, or at least consented to their death, in the 1948 war of liberation. This is a misleading usage. The parents who overcame their pity and love suspended a human value out of deference to another human value which they themselves considered superior and justifying any sacrifice—the nation and the fatherland. This is entirely different from the Aqeda, in which all human values capable of being subsumed under the categories of human understanding and feeling were set aside before the "glory of the majesty" of God. (22)

And the Fackenheim "rejoinder":

> What [is] there to explain? That, given a choice between apostasy and death, a Jew must choose death? Jews in Nazi Europe were not given this choice. . . . That God does not break His covenant with Israel? This was the lament of the angels when Abraham raised his knife, but God stayed Abraham's hand and stilled their lament. What did the angles do when they saw Auschwitz, Bergen-Belsen, Maidenek, Buchenwald? And where was God? A Jew after Auschwitz cannot and dare not give answers. He may and must give a response. The core of every possible response is that just as Abraham . . . and countless and nameless others who refused to abandon their Jewish past, so must he—but that after the martyrdom of Auschwitz, forever unfathomable and without equal anywhere, Jewish life is more sacred than Jewish death, even if it is for the sanctification of the divine name. (77)

It should not be surprising that the impasse here is identical to the one I record in my introduction, when Fackenheim rises in the name of martyred European Jewry—and what he elsewhere calls the 614th commandment: *the authentic Jew of today is forbidden to hand Hitler yet another, posthumous victory*[54]—to answer Leibowitz and "give a response." It should not be surprising that Leibowitz would exemplify quasi-*akedot* by reference to the Israeli war of Independence as opposed to the medieval martyrologies of Mayence or Worms or those of the Holocaust itself. And it should not be surprising that Leibowitz construes the *akedah* as a present demand in terms of submission to the Yoke of Heaven embodied by the Torah and the 613 *mitzvot*—that is, as *mimesis*, a model of religious duty—and that Fackenheim, conversely, should entertain "the staggering leap from intention to execution" (73)[55] whereby the *akedah* ends in a human sacrifice that no substitution can mitigate nor any religious covenant reasonably inculcate.

And yet Fackenheim's answer to Kant, if not to the choice between apostasy or death, is that Abraham's behavior during the *akedah* continues to possess moral force for Jewish believers precisely because of its *mimetic* function: what it teaches is not indeterminacy or counterethical murderousness but rather perpetually reenacted radical surprise, in terms not merely of the event itself but also of the perpetuity it institutes through the Torah as the inheritance of Israel and the instrument reflecting God's choice.

> To receive the Torah on account of Abraham's merit is, first, to have called all things into question in light of the Divinity, the intrinsic value of humanity included; second, it is to accept that some things are in question no longer; and third, it is to receive, in surprise as well as gratitude, the value of humanity as a gift that Divinity might have withheld and that is given forever. (70)[56]

Does Leibowitz have as forceful an answer? He might defer to Maimonides who, in the same section of the *Guide* devoted to Job that I cited earlier, suggests that the command to sacrifice Isaac is God's announcement of Himself as transcending even the specificities of Jewish history, of his promise to Abraham's seed "throughout their generations." As Hartman expresses it, "The experience of the *akedah* symbolically demonstrated that the ultimate goal of Torah lay outside history. The archetypal act of love of God consists in the ability to abandon history" (CV 33).

Is this what Leibowitz has in mind when, in "*Lishmah* and Not-*Lishmah*," he clearly distinguishes between Jewish religiosity as "perfection [that] consists in the very effort to serve God by observance of the Torah and its Mitzvoth," and "the contention of the greatest of all ethical theorists (Kant) that a 'morality' based on religious faith is no morality at all" (63)? Leibowitz is not unaware of debt to Kant. Indeed, he repays it over and over again. In "The Religious and Moral Significance of the Redemption of Israel," he acknowledges that in the treatment of philosophical questions, despite being a believing Jew "whose intention is to assume the yoke of the Kingdom of Heaven and the yoke of Torah and Mitzvoth," he does not draw upon Jewish sources but rather "the atheistic antisemite Kant" (106).

The break that Fackenheim is able to make with Kantianism and also the *akedah* in staging an encounter between Judaism and modern philosophy never becomes a possibility for Leibowitz. For Fackenheim follows his chapter on Abraham (and Kant) with a chapter on Moses (and Hegel). The previous section to this one in my own book, "Moses and the Post-Kantians," refers of course to Maimonides not the Moses of the Pentateuch. Crucially, I think, the figure of Moses also occupies the most minimal of presences in Leibowitz's essays. Three times in three different places his name is invoked but only in order to make a pointed contrast with the faith and Judaism of Korach ("all the congregation are holy"); twice he is mentioned with regard to his or Israel's failure.[57] The three other instances where Leibowitz names him are all in passing.

In contradistinction to R. Soloveitchik who mentions Moses often in *Halakhic Man* and *the Lonely Man of Faith* and several of the essays collected in *Reflections of the Rav*, and Levinas, for whom the Exodus narrative occupies his attention in more than one Talmudic reading, Leibowitz has almost nothing to say about the figure through whom and facing whom Israel became a nation and accepted the Torah. Nor, for that matter, does Kant. More than six hundred of the six-hundred and thirteen commandments—the yoke of Torah and Mitzvot, in Leibowitz's parlance—are mediated by Moses as the vehicle through which the Jewish people merits the *zerah v'aretz*, the seed and land vouchsafed to Abraham, Isaac, and Jacob.

To be sure, as Fackenheim asserts so powerfully, it is on account of Abraham's merit that the Torah is received. But the covenantal intimacy and its futurity of which Fackenheim speaks in his resounding Judaic response to Kant's dismissal of Judaism, that three-term religiosity that Levinas configures in terms of persons, and Soloveitchik in terms of two Adams and Divinity (a Divinity whom the Torah, after Genesis, calls the God of Abraham, Isaac, and Jacob, the God who elevates Israel from the land of Egypt to be holy): this communal, multifaced, Mosaic and Siniatic Judaism is flattened and collapsed by Leibowitz into the stark two-dimensionality of the *akedah*. (As if in compensation for the silence that the Torah assigns Isaac during most of the *akedah*, *midrashim* and talmudic *aggadot* dilate and amplify his role; Leibowitz, significantly, mentions only Abraham.)

There is a certain irony here, considering the singular and sometimes singularized role that the Torah, both Written and Oral, typically assigns to Moses. In the episode regarding the status of Moses's wife (or wives) that I allude to in the last chapter, the Rabbis read God's rebuke to Moses's brother and sister, Aharon and Miriam, as signifying the special and exclusive relationship between Himself and Moses which even marital cohabitation might compromise.[58] But it is Abraham, the procreative *pater gentis* at the moment when he is being asked to sacrifice his "only son," that Leibowitz selects out, not Moses.

Something analogous to this aporia is what explains Hartman's frustration with Leibowitz's treatment of the other Moses, which he regards as cramped, reductive, anti-anthropological, and, self-admittedly on Leibowitz's part, inhuman. This becomes starkest in Leibowitz's normative, prescriptive account of prayer: "The same set of eighteen benedictions is required of the bridegroom as of the widower returning from his wife's funeral. The same series of psalms is recited by one enjoying the world and one whose world has collapsed" (32). Indeed, Leibowitz invokes by analogy Maimonides's explanation of the exact details of the Temple sacrifices as normatively not factually based to justify the rabbinically instituted form and content of Jewish prayer as "ritualistically determined."

In effect, prayer answers to God's commands, not human needs. Again, however, one comes away from Leibowitz's observations on prayer with the distinct sense that he is referring to prayer in the third-person singular. "One prays," "he who prays," "Prayer not imitated by him, but one imposed upon him." The dialogism (if I may borrow a literary term from Mikhail Bakhtin) of *tefilah b'tzibur*, or congregational prayer—the very reason that the wording of the eighteen benedictions has been *ritualistically determined* in the first-person plural—much like a larger religious congregation of Israel mediated before the face of God and his Torah by Moses, makes but little sound in Leibowitz's writing.

The loneliness and sheer impersonality of halakhic man standing before God, which R. Soloveitchik soothes and softens by emphasizing the covenantal, the communal, the dialogic between persons as well as between Adam and God, is what one chiefly takes away from an encounter with Leibowitz. And it is a loneliness rigorously halakhic but also philosophic, in the Kantian rather than full Maimonidean sense. This is how Kant ends his second great critique, with the Kantian counterpart to a "mitnagdic phenomenology" we have seen several times thus far:

> Two things fill the mind with ever new and increasing admiration and reverence, the more often and more steadily one reflects on them: the starry heavens above me and the moral law within me. . . . The first begins from the place I occupy in the external world of sense and extends the connection in which I stand into an unbounded magnitude with worlds upon worlds and systems upon systems. . . . The second begins from my invisible self, my personality, and presents me in a world which has true infinity but which can be discovered only by my understanding, and I cognize that my connection with that world (and thereby with all those visible worlds as well) is not merely contingent, as in the first case, but universal and necessary. (133)[59]

In place of Kant's self-delighted moral agent, Leibowitz places not himself, a first-person singular, but Abraham standing in the presence of

God, a third-person plural that is, as it were, composite and *a fortiori*. Only the Torah and the *mitzvot* can be said to populate this spare landscape, and even in their case, the personificatory, corporeal, and even libidinal meanings that Levinas's Doctors of the Talmud attached to the pneuma and lifeblood of Scriptural Text are scrupulously purged by Leibowitz.[60] What Torah, Talmud, and Prayerbook call חיים עץ, a tree of life, or what R Hayyim of Volozhin called חיים נפש, the soul of life, is, with drumbeat insistence, a Yoke. And in such insistence, if one is forced to personify against the Leibowitzian grain and speak in terms of *dramatis personae*, one discerns (behind or alongside the figures of Abraham and Maimonides), the looming shadow of the Sage of Königsberg.

The reckoning with that shadow, in my view, is less an encounter between Judaism and modern philosophy, to use Fackenheim's construct, than a struggle with the angel, in Levinas's sense. And as Levinas says of Jacob, it is Leibowitz's religion that remains a little lame when the Angel's grip is released. One will remember that Levinas speaks, in that context, of even the most generous thought as threatened by its own totalitarianism, praising the casuistry of the Talmud as watching over the general in light of the particular, and thus a fence against ideology.

In its rigidity, Leibowitz's Kantianism, like his Maimonideanism, sometimes risks such danger: like the Herodian walls built around an already fortified Temple in Jerusalem, the fence of *halakhah* in his hands often seems a kind of battlement. And yet to belabor the metaphor just a little, his moral courage in the political sphere can appear at the same time Maccabean, making the kind of stand in public space that Kant might well have too, had he been born at a different time in a different place and against the horizons of a different culture.

Having reached a limit point ourselves as well, the next two sections take up two final legacies of Kantian philosophy as they bear on Leibowitz's intellectual allegiances. The first returns to the essay from my introduction, "Does Jewish Tradition Recognize an Ethic Independent of Halakhah?" to ask a related question about halakhic Judaism's architectural impregnability to structural vicissitudes of the modern world. Can the Halakhah boast its own *point d'appui* within a public discourse riven into the seemingly disjunct realms of private morality and state-derived rights and powers, a cleft formalized by Kant? The second section takes the opposite tack: might the Halakhah, in its best sense, act as a buttress: a fence against all unreason, which in the modern world takes ideological and idolatrous form as the *Shwärmerei* of nationalism and state-sectarianism? Might Leibowitz thus model a severer Kantianism, in the sense of a public morality accountable both to itself and to transcendent command?

6. LEZAD HA-HALAKHAH; OR, META-HALAKHIC MAN

Toward the beginning of his essay on ethics and *halakhah*, R. Lichten-stein quotes the Talmud: "Rabbi Yochanan stated: if the Torah had not been given, we would have learned modesty from the cat, [aversion to] robbery from the ant, chastity from the dove, and [conjugal] manners from the dove" (62).[61] *Pace* Leibowitz, nature does appear to possess certain of its own brakes on Hobbesian inclinations—what *Pirke Avot* (cited more than once by Levinas), calls the tendency of men to "swallow each other alive" [3:2]).[62] Like Maimonides after them, the Rabbis recognized both natural religion, which presupposes idolatry, and the possibility of natural morality, which need not.

R. Lichstenstein's essay assumes a minimal definition of *mos naturalis* at the outset. Leibowitz, as we have seen, restricts axiological values to the yoke of Torah and *mitzvot* alone.[63] When the Oral Tradition speaks of peace or *derekh eretz* (rectitude) or any other "moral virtue" in reciprocal relation to itself, it seems at least to allow for a dialogue with the Halakhah, a "feedback loop" more broadly defined. R. Lichtenstein calls this a contextual, rather than formal, morality. The question of whether the case can be argued for such an ethic as *independent* of the Halakhah ultimately matters less to Lichstenstein than its practicable utility for Jews bound by the *mitzvot*: whether, in other words, the Halakhah should be seen as self-sufficient, containing within itself the very impetus for *lifnim meshurat hadin*.[64] Phrased simply: do "ethics" and "religion" describe the same territory, differently policed, or different but perhaps adjoining territories. What are the boundaries of *halakhah*? How comprehensive is its fence?

In addition to specific Torah precepts and implicit principles (*kevod habriot*, respect for human dignity, for example, as following from *briah betzelem Elo-him*, the creation of man in God's image), the Talmud provides a critical vocabulary: *din* (law, judgment) and *lifnim meshurat hadin* (the line of the law and its "beyond") R. Lichstenstein distinguishes between the two this way:

> *Din* consists of a body of statutes, ultimately rooted in fundamental values but which at the moment of decision confront the individual as a set of rules. . . . [T]he basic mode is that of formulating and defining directives to be followed in a class of cases—it is precisely the quality of generality that constitutes a rule—and applying them to situations marked by the proper cluster of features. . . . The contextualist, by contrast, will have noting to do with middle-distance guidelines. He is directed, in theory, at least, only by the most universal and most local of factors. . . . Only direct ad hoc judgment . . . can serve as an operative basis for decision. (78–79)[65]

While noting a terminological distinction to be kept in mind—that "*halakhah*" (lowercase and without the definite article) in the Talmud typically denotes rules, laws, and the process of deducing specific instances from a general class, as in the first case above, and "Halakhah" will often connote something more axiological and inductive, as in the second—he concludes with a concise answer to his own titular question, "You define your terms and take your choice" (83).[66] As a way of life committed to holiness, halakhic Judaism means the dialectical complement to the procedural directives of *halakhah*; the fence of Law, *strictu sensu*, articulates its own "beyond."[67]

We seem to have found our niche once again in the comforts of the dialectic, comparable perhaps to the interplay R. Soloveitchik locates between the participial *merachem*, one who performs charitable acts, and the adjectival *rachaman*, one whose attribute is to act compassionately, who, in other words, cannot act otherwise (Besdin, 192). Yet I have not turned again to R. Lichstenstein's essay because I think he offers the necessary sublation for a Levinas/Leibowitz polarity (let alone an aggadic/halakhic one in the loose sense that I have deployed those terms). *Din* and *lifnim meshurat hadin* do not so efficaciously take the place of the terms "religion" and "ethics," if indeed we should wish to style Leibowitz the more "religious" philosopher and Levinas the more "ethical" (a simplistic and misleading contrapositioning anyway).[68]

Moreover, R. Lichstenstein's aims are methodological, not meta-halakhic. But by framing his inquiry in terms of legality and some supralegal ethic, and prompting in turn a rejoinder from Reform Judaism by Eugene Borowitz entitled "The Authority of the Ethical Impulse in Halacha" he has opened it to a larger (or different) question about philosophy's investment in the spheres of politics and the law.

That is the case put by Gillian Rose in her short but extremely suggestive essay, "Jewish Ethics and the Crisis of Philosophy." Rose's interests are, frankly, meta-halakhic. The utility she identifies in two very different formulations of ethics for Jewish religious life (R. Lichtenstein's and Eugene Borowitz's) has less to do with the relative merits of each (she does not pretend to resolve the debate) than with the mirror thus held up to a parallel split between moral philosophy and social theory, outside the boundaries of Judaism entirely.[69] As Emil Fackenheim might put it, one of modernity's most characteristic ellisions becomes thereby self-exposed to Judaism: Shem, the religious spirit of Judaic thought, is accorded a place of honor in Japheth's tent (5).[70] Or, to expand on an image from Levinas, the human sciences are invited to walk Judaism's tightrope (*DF* 50).

The rise of the modern nation-state and its institutional potencies, Rose argues, can be seen as a kind of discursive separation of powers:

ethics and moral philosophy go one way, law and social theory go another. (*In Sources of the Self*, Charles Taylor makes an analogous point about the shift in the concept of freedom from substantive justifications to those that are procedural [86].) Genealogically speaking, the source for such a split can be traced to the influential distinction introduced by Kant between heteronomous legality and autonomous morality, a counterpoint, as it were, between two different models or realms of freedom. As a result, public and private spheres grow increasingly disjunct, as the enrichment and maintenance of individual rights is fostered at the price of ever more massive edifices of state authority and domination. Filling a vacuum opened up by Kant's moral agent who polices only himself, the State effectively "separates instrumental means from the evaluation of substantive goals, and increasingly inhibits the reformulation of ethical and political ends."[71] Not only do moral philosophers and social theorists accede thus to a kind of intellectual partition; even within sociology, Rose points out, a split can be noted in the different approaches to law as "normative sanction," and as "meaningful orientation" (169).[72]

It is at this point in her argument that Rose turns to the Halakhah, for in her view the dynamic of freedom and necessity and the division into separate legal and ethical spheres become as problematical for modern Jewish thought as for secular modernity, generally. She leaves unstated, however, an important premise that Soloveitchik, Leibowitz, Levinas take for granted. The Halakhah is a comprehensive human framework. At its best it *unifies* social and individual practices, legitimating them both morally and legally. As a "wisdom of the feasible," it also demonstrates how the Rabbis sought to accommodate the historical revelation of Torah and *mitzvot* to a political and social order very different from that envisioned by Moses and the Prophets.[73]

Rose, however, speaks of "a *halakhah* beyond *halakhah*, and only then an ethics" (167), a phrase left tantalizing undelineated, but that (and this is my own extension) we might correlate with both Levinas's refusal to let go of messianism, and Leibowitz's pragmatic call to innovate halakhically in the wake of Israeli statehood. The former I have already discussed; the latter limns this chapter's final horizon.

Rose has something at once more restrictive and less particularist (not specifically Judaic) in mind, however, which follows her fair and lucid presentation of the two polarities:

Prima facie, Lichstenstein asks whether halakhah is *equitable* by inquiring into the *status* of equity within halakhah, whereas Borowitz asks whether halakhah is *egalitarian* by inquiring into the *flexibility* of halakhah. Lichstenstein focuses on the ethical potential *within* halakhah, whereas Borowitz focuses on the ethical potential *of* halakhah. Yet, paradoxically . . . its is Lichstenstein who demonstrates the flexibility of halakhah, while it is Borowitz who demands that ethics be as "categorical" (unconditioned) as halakhah, and not a secondary kind of imperative. (170)

In other words and to bring Leibowitz back into the picture, in allowing for a productive interplay between *din* and *meshurat hadin*, it is the Orthodox thinker Lichstenstein who resists the Kantian bifurcations, and Borowitz (the exponent of Reform Judaism) who imports the Kantian categorical ethic back into Judaism—"the same ethic that has itself been fundamentally questioned by modernity, and displays the qualities of absoluteness, unconditionality, formality, and imperativeness that [Borowitz] otherwise deplores in the idea of law" (170).

I draw two conclusions from this:

1. Modern Jewish thought has tended to hold itself hostage to a philosophical legacy that rabbinic culture obviously—and thus the Halakhah—safely avoids. (I say as much in my introduction when I single out Levinas from among the more familiar twentieth-century Jewish philosophers because of the role the Talmud plays in his thought). This is not to say that Halakhah does not know or recognize its *own* binds. But they take an entirely different *philosophic* shape.

2. Paradoxically enough, it is the epistemological underpinnings of that same ethic (as well as a certain Kantian sensibility or affinity, as I suggest in the next section) that consistently haunt Leibowitz's philosophical method and hold him something of a hostage as well. As a comparison with other Orthodox figures like R. Lichstenstein and Hartman clarifies, Leibowitz, for all his caviling with the "atheistic, antisemite Kant," permits a Kantian string the proprietary claim on a halakhic kite.[74]

While R. Lichstenstein's essay thus holds its own instructive mirror up to Leibowitz, Eugene Borowitz's counter-thesis raises the issue of gender, which for Rose's purposes, discloses the blind spot in both halakhists' analyses. However women's changing status might be addressed by Reform and Orthodox Judaisms, each must still reckon, outside the Halakhah, with the "modern problematic of freedom together with its conceptual and political antinomies," one that the structured differential in power between men and women makes self-evident.

For what determines the meaning of law and ethics is not what is posited, or even how it is posited, by its jurisconsults, rabbinic or other, but how it is configured within the modern separation of state and civil society, which reappears in the separation of philosophy and social theory with which Judaic and non-Judaic ethics are infected. (172)[75]

One direction in which such a critique points, obviously, is contemporary feminist theory, an exemplary instance of which can be found in Seyla Benhabib's *Situating the Self: Gender, Community, and Postmodernism in Contemporary Ethics*.[76] For Benhabib, the exclusion of the female other stands as the most compelling index of liberal universalism's "epistemic failure." To base communal interaction on restrictive or biased definitions of public and private space (the sort demonstrated, say, by Charles Taylor's otherwise expansive study, *Sources of the Self*) promises a universalism in name only. Although such a topic takes my own inquiry too far afield, I will say something briefly about its relevance for the present discussion.

None other than Leibowitz himself calls the question of women's role in religious Judaism "more crucial today than all the political problems of the people and its state" (129–131). Unfortunately for religious feminists who seek to redress structural inequities in the Halakhah by challenging duties assigned by law or custom to men, Leibowitz's reasoning is entirely consistent on this point: such actions (the public reading of Torah, all *mitzvot* limited by time restrictions such as morning or afternoon prayer, for example), possess no value in themselves, and as "[t]heir entire significance derives solely from the fact that the Torah prescribed them," they cannot be called discriminatory (129). He draws the analogy of duties or proscriptions specific to priests as opposed to they laity in order to emphasize that his interests here are, as always, formalist and positivistic, and not sexist or patriarchal.

Indeed, he is just as quick to open the world of *talmud Torah* as widely as possible in order to make it available to women—and they to it. And in this regard—what he will call a *mitzvah*, too, "of utmost importance"—he demonstrates the kind of political pragmatism about which he is as consistent as his halakhic formalism. In "The Status of Women: Halakhah and Meta-Halakhah" (significantly enough, the only one of essays to feature that term or concept), Leibowitz writes,

> Jewish religious society will not be able to survive if, for pseudo-religious reasons, we continue to deprive Jewish women of their due rights. This is the point at which we—those of us resolved to practice Torah—cannot perpetuate the halakhic decisions of our fathers dating from a social reality which differed radically from our own. (131)

One of the things that makes Leibowitz endlessly fascinating to me is how he counterbalances his realism and his formalism, his answerability to the claims of both *halakhah* and modernity. For as the contemporary world discloses a Western culture and Jewish existence that not only interpenetrate but also each lie open to men and women alike, to bar women halakhically from Torah study and participation in the public-political sphere is to confuse stiffneckedness with "the yoke of the kingdom of heaven," and obstinacy with the wisdom of the feasible. "Keeping women away from Talmud Torah," he insists, "is not to exempt them from a duty but is rather to deprive them of a basic right" (129).

But to speak thus is already to gesture in a second direction as regards the critique that Rose initiates above, and it is the one I shall pursue at greater length here: politics and political philosophy in its plain sense. Rose makes the point, inarguable as it is halakhically vexed, that as fully one-sixth of the Talmud is given over to the "status" of women, "Judaism . . . cannot dissemble its assumptions and impositions." Whether a structural problem for halakhah or more broadly a matter for modernity, "[t]he status (sic) 'woman' will continue to explode any surety it is made to stand for on the way" (172).

Amplifying Rose's purview here from the systemic actualities of civic society—the fence (among others) of gender—to geopolitical destinies and decisions—the fence of nationhood—we arrive at that peculiar entanglement of patriotic feeling and libidinal cathexis so neatly captured by the phrase, "foreign affairs." In the unfortunate but by no means unique case of the Jewish State, that means domestic reality as well: the competing or irredentist claims of rival nations and peoples.

It is here, within a political horizon, that I believe Leibowitz finally and fully comes into his own, as strict a Westerner as an halakhist. If "we are equally steeped in Western culture," and if "modern humanist man is man in a State," who must therefore concern himself with other men's discourses before he lets himself be moved by the men themselves (*DF* 217, 239),[77] then the encounter between Judaism and modern philosophy, in the person of Leibowitz, needs to justify itself as a politics, not just as a halakhics. In order to explain why I believe it does, the next section complicates Gillian Rose's thesis by identifying another crisis for liberal society that may also be said to trace its roots to Kant's moral philosophy: nationalism. My discursive *vade mecum* this time will be an essay by Isaiah Berlin entitled "Kant as an Unfamiliar Source for Nationalism."

7. THE IDOLATRY OF IDEALISM

Nationalism is, it seems to me, the sense—the consciousness of nationhood in a pathological state of inflammation: the result of wounds inflicted by someone or something on the natural feelings of a society, or of artificial barriers to its normal development. . . . This leads to the transformation of the notion of the individual's moral autonomy into the notion of the moral autonomy of the nation. . . . The doctrine of the free self with which Kant attempted to overcome what seemed to him the danger to moral freedom from acceptance of a mechanical, impersonal, determined universe, in which choice was illusory, became magnified, and indeed perverted, into the doctrine of quasi-personalised history as the carrier of the collective will, the will to growth, to power, to splendour, a vision half-biological, half-aesthetic, at the centre of which is the notion of the interest and the purpose of the nation State as a kind of creative, self-developing work of art. (247)

Isaiah Berlin captures with forensic precision here what Levinas might call the *conatus essendi* of the body politic.[78] I note the correspondence if only to realign philosophical allegiances once again by angling Levinas away from rather than parallel to Kant.[79] For, like Levinas, Isaiah Berlin suspects another root-system for the doctrine of autonomy besides a politics of liberal universalism and a metaphysic of moral reason, and at cross purposes with the kind of cosmopolitanism, the spirit of *Foedus Amphictyonum*, that Kant advocates elsewhere.[80]

And perhaps not so coincidentally, the sources Berlin traces are biographical and sociocultural: Kant's religious upbringing and a divided Prussian empire at the end of the eighteenth century. Kant was brought up in a Lutheran and Pietist household at a moment in European history Berlin calls "a time of humiliation and political impotence for the Germans in their divided land" (241), a country veined by several hundred fractious suzerainties, few distinguished for their enlightened rule.

For Kant and those like him for whom Pietism offered both a stronghold and a retreat, political impotence, says Berlin, meant spiritual freedom; material defeat earned moral victory. Unlike the vulnerable self in Levinas whose very skin expresses the exposure to alterity, or the free-ranging, impervious subject of Kant's moral philosophy, this self, rooted in history and culture, announces rather, "By contracting the vulnerable area, I can make myself free of nature and of man, as the early Christians did who escaped to the Theban desert."

This note of austere self-insulation is very deep in Kant. In him it takes quietist forms. But in his successors it becomes defiance, resistance against anyone and anything that seeks to diminish or degrade my inner kingdom, the sacred values by which I live, and for which I am prepared to suffer and die. (242)

Berlin is careful to distinguish the direction of Kant's own thought from that of contemporaries like Herder or epigones like Fichte. But the seeds for what takes root afterwards are sown by Kantian predilection, nevertheless, even if inadvertently. Call this the genealogy, if not of morals, then of autonomy. And as I stated a similar case for Levinas and Leibowitz at the beginning of this book, place impinges upon the philosopher, and exacts its own tolls and tariffs. Geography more often exerts a gravity than allows a buoyancy. Leibowitz illustrates such a principle with respect to Maimonides, and Berlin applies it to the case of Kant here as well.

In section 4 of this chapter, I suggested that Leibowitz's Kant, like his Maimonides, will often betray the hand, the voice of his ventriloquist. And yet a certain affinity in their philosophical sensibilities can be detected as well. Perhaps nowhere is that more apparent than in their similar perspectives on nature, which are a world away from Aristotle's, and thus disclose again the debt Leibowitz continues to pay to modern philosophy over against his arrears to rabbinic and medieval Judaism. Berlin explains the Kantian attitude as follows:

> if Kant is right, and the forces of nature, if we surrender to them, reduce us to mere turnspits (as for him, things and animals are), then the very notion of nature is revolutionised. Nature is no longer what it was for the French Enlightenment—the beautiful model which, with the help of science, we shall understand and accept, and ourselves fit into frictionlessly. For Kant, nature is either neutral stuff that we must mould to our own purposes as free, choosing creatures; or something more sinister and ambivalent: a power which . . . threatens our freedom, and is therefore to be kept at bay, to be resisted, if we are to rise to our full human nature as free, self-determined moral beings. (240)[81]

If, as Berlin goes on to say, it takes but two steps from here to reach the ideology and idolatry of nationalism—one that at first glance seems so very far removed—it also takes but two in another direction to reach Leibowitz's Abraham—no less far removed, it would appear at first. Hostility to the phenomenal world runs comparably deeply in both philosophers. Leibowitz, of course, takes a third and momentous step that for Kant, as we have seen, represents a philosophical betrayal. Abraham saddles his ass and thus subdues his nature, in heed to divine commandment. Human "freedom" in Leibowitz's philosophy belongs to nature, too: religiously indifferent, instrinsically neutral, or even "something more sinister and ambivalent." At any rate, it represents part and parcel of the "materiality" Abraham overcomes by binding Isaac.

And it is at this same limit point where Leibowitz becomes the severer Kantian, and where I believe his political philosophy does him greater justice than his theology or his halakhic formalism. Leibowitz absolutely interdicts the two-step process that Berlin tracks as following directly from the doctrine of autonomy to its "inflammation" at the level of nation and state—an inflammation all the more dangerous because of the unconditioned, categorical split between morality (the autonomous self) and legality (the body politic), having its roots in Kant. Such moral self-inoculation, moreover, ensures a kind of complacency with regard to the pathologies of nationalism, for to recall Gillian Rose's argument, in the modern nation-state, greater moral or subjective freedom continues to be purchased at the price of less objective or ethical freedom (168).

How does moral autonomy lead, however improbably, to ideologies, even pathologies, of nationalism? The first step is taken when I prize the values I hold not because they are universalizable (whereby my autonomy mirrors that of every responsible moral agent), "but because they are my own, express my particular inner nature. . . . In short, there is now some sense in which I can be said to create my own values" (243). In other words, the "metaphor" of autonomy is abandoned for an ideological and rationally precarious literalism.

The second step requires a new conception of the chooser: distended, projected, autonomy now becomes imperialistic—*L'État, c'est moi*, the correlation Levinas draws numerous times. Idealism surrenders to ideology,[82] and in a debased form of spiritual election thereby risks idolatry. "It is this collective self," writes Berlin—whether expressive of nation, land, people, history, or destiny—"that generates the form of life lived by individuals . . . an authority from which there can be no appeal" (244).

However much such idolatry may represent a perverted form of autonomy, its genealogy in Kant—from its roots in his Pietism and anti-naturalism—points unerringly to the inflamed need "to be and do something, to win a place a sun"[83] as the raison d'être of the state. A coda at the end of Berlin's essay offers a minor qualification—"ideas are not born of ideas only; there is no parthenogenesis in the history of thought" (247). We can, however, reasonably sustain a different etiological analysis (Levinas's): that "the consciousness of nationhood in a pathological state of inflammation" has merely magnified "a pathology and sensibility and ill will" already residing in a margin of "incoercible spontaneity" within the private, autonomous self (*Outside the Subject*, 122).

Cultural-studies critic Homi Bhabha has written of the ambivalent nature of the Nation, revealed when its "people" address or narrate it, when they articulate a gap between their *a priori* historical presence and something more performative, more enunciatory—the difference between people-as-object and people-as-subject, between nation and *dis-*

semi-nation (299). The danger of the Nation, in this view, is its *metaphoricity*, as Derrida himself suggests in *L'Autre Cap*, where he finds Europe tellingly *envisaged* by Valéry: as a face [*visage*], a leader [*chef*], a head [*cap*] (20), Europe—not *L'Europe*—like a person with a proper name (113). Both theorists want to pluralize, de-monumentalize the Nation, exchange its metaphors for metonyms, supplements, *dis-semi*-nation. "Can the incommensurable act of living," Bhabha asks, "change the way we identify the symbolic structure of the western nation" (303)? Isaiah Berlin's nonpostmodern answer (and in parallel ways, Levinas's and Leibowitz's alike), is: only if that "act of living" begins by immunizing itself against inflammation of any kind, by resisting the blandishments of the imperial self and sustaining the metaphor of autonomy as *metaphor*—not idolatry in the guise of ideology.

8. HALAKHIC MAN REVISITED: "HIS POLITICAL ACUMEN"

Perhaps it goes without saying that in tracking a schism between ethics and law or a bridge between autonomy and the state, neither Berlin nor Rose assumes a transcendent reality beyond the sum total of multiple freedoms, rights, and enfranchisements. Even when Levinas addresses the rights of man (though invested by the more primordial rights of the other), he anchors it not on Divine Revelation, as though it proceeded from the sternness or the grace of God, but rather the reverse: "the coming of the idea of God on the basis of the patency of the rights of man" (118).[84] To that extent at least (paraphrasing Leibowitz again), Levinas, along with Gillian Rose, Isaiah Berlin, and all morally responsible subjects of the Kingdom of Ends, is a Kantian.

But it is Leibowitz, the paradoxically Kantian antihumanist, who, as a Zionist and citizen of an embattled but also militarized Israel, more than any of these thinkers, wrestled with the *political* consequences of the Kantian legacy in the double sense I have outlined here. And it is Leibowitz, too, who asks whether society is validly a religious concern and whether the social order possesses aspects that elevate it to the level of a religious task.

Such questions galvanize him beyond the contours of mitnagdic phenomenology, as embodied by R. Soloveitchik's halakhic man, because Leibowitz confronts a very different demand on his analytic powers: bridging a gap not between the a priori of *halakhah* and material reality, but rather between a sociopolitical system minutely described by the Torah, and one that has been configured in the same space but at a radically different moment in history.

In light of such concerns, an early essay written a year before statehood, "The Social Order as a Religious Problem," poses perhaps a more foundational question: does the sociopolitical legislation in the Torah describe society and the state as they ought to be or as they are (148)? As the question aims at answers that are pragmatic not academic, it differs profoundly from the rhetorical structure of R. Soloveitchik's panegyric to Maimonides in *Halakhic Man*:

> When Maimonides describes the order of events on the fifteenth night of Nisan, he "forgets" temporarily that he is living approximately one thousand years after the destruction of the Temple and paints the image of the service of this holy festival night in a wealth of colors that dazzle the eye, that reflect the Passover service as it was celebrated thousands of years ago in ancient Jerusalem and as it once again will be celebrated in the era of the Messiah. . . . The *seder* with which Maimonides is dealing is an ideal conception of Passover night. Our great master pays no attention to the cruel and bitter present. (26–28)

R. Soloveitchik does not ask Leibowitz's question because he inhabits the halakhic version of non-Euclidean space, an idealized real. Leibowitz, on the other hand actively presses for answers because he stands in the midst of a soon-to-be created Jewish sovereignty.

Is there, perhaps, some merit in wondering whether R. Soloveitchik dwells at length on the kabbalistic trope of *tzimtzum* (divine self-contraction) toward the end of *Halakhic Man* in part because, as Leibowitz puts it, "[t]he separation of the circumscribed world of the individual, which can be regulated by Halakhah, and his political and social ambitions, which cannot, was first imposed on the Jew from without and gradually internalized" (151)?[85] To contract the ambit of the world thus and project an idealized real bounded by the individual will and faculties of reason recapitulates, quite uncannily, the quietistic Kantian self Berlin describes, for whom political impotence means spiritual freedom and material defeat means moral victory. Here, however, there is no inflammation, and if pathology, it is the sort of ingrained proclivity that Leibowitz wants to challenge by calling for halakhic horizons corresponding to the dimensions of a new sociopolitical reality.

One Kantian attribute that cannot be charged to Leibowitz, obviously, is quietism. While he states the maximalist case in this essay for a Torah and *mitzvot* geared to specific social, politic and economic conditions that no longer obtain, he does not defend it. Consistent with such a fundamentalism is the view that "positions taken in the present on social and political issues have no religious implications and cannot be determined by halakhic decision" (152). Hence, Maimonides's purposefully anachronistic *seder*, and its mimetic value for Soloveitchik.

An alternative, a hybrid (or bastardization), which allows for religious legislation on religious matters, but leaves the ideological apparatuses of the state to administer themselves, forfeits a religious task for a clerical politics (Leibowitz's phrase). The dependent relationship of the Rabbinate, Rabbinic Court, and Ministry of Religious Affairs upon a government apparatus for economic subsidization—an innovation of the newly established State—and the progressive intertwining of the fates of religious and political parties, fulfilled some of Leibowitz's deepest dread and misgiving. In his words, that a "sector of the religious public organized as a political movement lacks a religious program for the conduct of the state deprives its religious struggle of all value and significance" (154).[86]

Leibowitz's position is clear enough, and it forms the essay's concluding paragraph:

> Whoever acquiesces in the restatement of Halakhah for application to the problems of contemporary society and state in the spirit of the written Torah and the tradition, and in the light of the halakhic paradigm

which was formulated in circumstances other than our own, has no
alternative to being guided by his understanding of the spirit of the
Torah and the intentions and purpose of its Mitzvoth. (157)[87]

As he goes on to note, such understanding is neither uniform nor perhaps easily consolidated, for even within the fence of the Halakhah, different theological, moral, sociopolitical, and functionalist conceptual-
izations of the Torah's "spirit" have always existed side by side.

How, then, can such implicit trust in a halakhic wisdom of the feasible, and the evident elasticity it sanctions for precedents in the social
order be reconciled with what up until this point I have referred to as
Leibowitz's halakhic positivism—a seeming incongruence that I confess
myself at first to have been puzzled by? How can one sort of halakhic
mandate transcend history, and another discover its warrant there? The
answer does not lie with an inconsistency in Leibowitz's understanding
of individual as opposed to collecting *standing before God*, but rather
with the advent of a new nationalized entity *within* the bounded framework of Jewish religion and Jewish religiosity (on principle, Leibowitz
will speak of "the place of the state in religious life," and not "Jewish
religion in the state of Israel").

Political autonomy and nationhood represent twentieth-century
phenomena for religious Jews who have resided within the four cubits of
halakhah ever since the destruction of the *Bet ha-Mikdash*. It is this historical eventuality that explains the palpable difference in the alternately
retrospective and messianic horizons surveyed by R. Soloveitchik[88] (no
less a diasporic or postexilic Jew therefore than R. Hayyim of Volozhin
or Maimonides or Emmanuel Levinas for that matter), and the fence of
halakhah that ideally should surround and inform the perimeter of the
Israeli state for Leibowitz, its citizen. The former are either prehistoric
or poshistoric, a semimythical past, as Leibowitz puts it, or a vision of
the end of days (164). Leibowitz's horizon, by contrast, spatializes the
present.

A citizen of the "West" as well of Jerusalem, Leibowitz is, in Anto-
nio Gramsci's useful phrase, a genuinely organic intellectual woven into
the tissues of the polity and its conscience. There is, thus, no "normative" or halakhically mandated religious response to the creation of a
new Jewish state (which is exactly Leibowitz's point of departure: "The
whole magnificent structure of sovereignty, the judiciary, and procedural law laid down in the talmudic tractate *Sanhedrin* was never intended
to function under historical traditions"[89]). Halakhic Judaism *accommodates* a new Jewish state; it does not and cannot *predict* it.

"In fact," writes Aviezer Ravitzky, "contemporary Orthodoxy
offers a wide range of attitudes toward the State of Israel, from radical
delegitimation to virtual beatification."

It is said to be a "Satanic act," an "anti-Jewish state," a "regime which calls itself Israel," a "state ruled by Jews," "the state of the Jews," "the state of the Jewish people," "the state of the Congregation of Israel," "the pedestal of God's throne in this world," and finally, "a divine state!" . . . Indeed, the question of the State of Israel has proved even more divisive than the issue of modernity.[90]

Raison d'état, as Leibowitz understands its post-Enlightenment motivations, is neither an expression of the Halakhah nor a guarantor of essential, absolute, intrinsic values. Function—the diversity of individual and national needs fulfilled by a state—steps into the vacancy left by essence. Here, then, halakhic procedures become paradigm rather than blueprint, the Torah is actualized as an all-encompassing way of life rather than preserved as if in amber, hidden or distant, in heaven or across the sea (Deut. 30). Indeed, the concept of *et la'asot*, or "time to do"—modifying *halakhah* toward a more perfect inculcation of Torah—is an already imagined possibility within the Oral Law itself.

And thus Leibowitz can, with perfect consistency, advocate a Judaism that manifests itself in "a *particular way of serving God, and not in any particular conception of man, of the world, or of history*" (96), and simultaneously defend a Zionism that "is not an ideology but a complex of activities undertaken to restore independence to the Jewish nation in its own land" (191)[91] and therefore a "legitimate Jewish aspiration" (118). To appreciate the philosophical and halakhic heroism of such equipoise—and why Levinas singled it and Leibowitz out for especial mention (*DF* 220)—one must, however, turn finally to that land, that nation, and that aspiration.

9. TOWARD A POLITICAL RELIGIOSITY

A "nation" is not a natural entity amenable to objective definition. A "nation" is a being of the mind, which exists insofar as there is mental awareness of its existence. It has no being apart from this awareness. Is there a British nation, or perhaps only an English nation, a Scottish nation, and a Welsh nation? Is there an objective answer to this question? . . . The answer is determined by the *consciousness* of those who feel that they constitute a national entity. A mental entity has no rights in the legal sense. Its rights exist only in the minds of those involved. The link between a "nation" and a particular country is not a nexus created by law, and thus is differs fundamentally from the bond between a legal "person" and his property. Likewise, a connection between a nation and a particular country is not a natural datum. A particular country is the country of a particular people insofar as it is such in the collective consciousness of that people, not because of any objective facts. Fortunate is the people whose conception of its tie to its country is recognized by others, for should this connection be contested, no legal argument could establish it. Even the fact that at a particular historical moment a particular territory is populated by members of a certain nation does not constitute a valid legal claim. In Talmudic law there is a sound maxim pertaining to the law of presumptive title: "Without a claim, possession cannot confer presumptive life." And there is almost no nation in history or in the present, whose claim to a right to a certain territory by virtue of its inhabiting that country could not be contested: "Is it yours only by dint of robbery" (in the midrashic formulation). The attempt to justify such a right on historic grounds has neither legal nor moral validity. The historic past does not live in the present except as an act of consciousness. (230–231)

Thus Leibowitz the philosopher. And thus, also, the halakhist. I have begun this last section with an extended quotation because, to repeat myself from the introduction, Jewish history, Jewish experience, and Judaism *in its metaphysical integrity* need to be given voice and be heard speaking in that voice. The voice that expresses all these things most probitively for me when speaking about the State of Israel belongs to Yeshayahu Leibowitz. In the previous section I wondered aloud how Leibowitz can reconcile the Yoke of Torah and *mitzvot* with such a ductile and disinterested analysis of the relationship between nations and the lands they occupy, and how such pragmatism can be made to appeal to the same Halakhah Leibowitz disassociates from human values, interests, and needs. Since he emphasizes the evidentiary and empirical over the abstract or ideological, I will follow suit, beginning with one of two additional and pointed contrasts with Levinas in this section, followed by some concrete particulars.

Readers will recall that an analogue to Leibowitz's point above is ventured by Levinas in "A Religion for Adults," alluding to Rashi's commentary on the fifth verse of Genesis:

> [T]he ancient response that Rashi proposes consists in maintaining that, in order to possess the Promised Land, man must know that God created the earth. For without this knowledge, he will possess it only by usurpation. No rights can therefore ensue from the simple fact that a person needs *espace vital*. (*DF* 17)[92]

The exegesis is, plainly, aggadic; more importantly, it also entirely omits the end of the *midrash* that says, "It was God's desire to give it to [the Cananites] and then it was His desire to take it from them and give it to us." Leibowitz's example, on the other hand, is halakhic in the strictest sense. "Nationhood" and "peoplehood" designate features or facts of consciousness, not empirical realities. They cannot, therefore, be expressed according to the same pragmatic concepts employed by the Halakhah to mark the fence between one person's property and another, or around *property*, and thus substantiatable *right*, in the first place. The immediate talmudic context for Leibowitz's point of law about presumptive title is worth citing in full:

> R. 'Anan's field was flooded through the bursting of a dam. He afterwards went and restored the fence, on land belonging to his neighbor. The latter sued him before R. Nakhman. He said to [R. 'Anan]: "You must restore the land." "But," [R. 'Anan] rejoined, "I have become the owner of it by occupation?" Said R. Nahman to him: "On whose authority [do you rely]? On that of R. Ishmael and R. Judah, who both lay down that [if the occupation takes place] in presence of the owner, it constitutes a title at once. The law, however, is not in accordance with their ruling." R. 'Anan thereupon said: "But this man has tacitly waived his right because he came and helped me to build the fence?" R. Nahman replied: "This was a waiver given in error. You yourself, had you known that the land was his, would not have built the fence on it. Just as you did not know, so he also did not know." (*Bava Batra* 41a)

Not only do fences sometimes *not* make good neighbors, one could say, but the Halakhah here seems to go so far as to protect unwitting neighbors from even their own mistakes. In other words, possession that is חזקה שאין עמה טענה (unaccompanied by a claim), may constitute *espace vital*, but it does not confer ownership. Or, to recall the verses that stand at the head of this book, *setting and keeping the wall between neighbors, to each the boulders that have fallen to each, apple trees that will never get across and eat the cones under their neighbor's pines*: while such contingencies may describe Frostean pastoral, they do not necessarily correspond to halakhic realism, let alone brute geopolitical fact.

When, therefore, Leibowitz extends the reach of the talmudic principle to the country of Israel as constitutionally established, the severity of his logic dictates that not even the three legal purchases recorded by Scripture—the Cave of Machpelah, the Tomb of Joseph, and the Temple in Jerusalem—demonstrate a *necessary and sufficient* claim to override completely "the perverse course of history, which is incorrigible," by which "an analogous bond was created between the same country and *another* nation" (231).

Eretz Yisrael/Falastin. Yerushalayim/Al Quds. The same place, or two different countries, cities, in palimpsest? What happens when a people loses its country, but retains its national consciousness? Whose "right" to the land takes precedence? Since, according to the logic again, neither legal nor moral categories of justice can adjudicate a solution based on the relative rights of the claimants—for no law or categorical imperative grounds a nation's *rights* to its geography—surely, we wonder, that same perverse but incorrigible history that Leibowitz invokes can be invoked as the final court of appeal. For how exactly can one *history* replace another? Indeed, how can one speak of multiple or conflicting histor*ies*, of 1400 years of Arabic history superimposed onto 2000 years of Jewish history? Is there not just History, perverse, incorrigible, but also disinterested, neutral, and therefore *just*? "In a world that has become historical," writes Levinas, "shouldn't a person be as old as the world?" which represents for him the eternity of Israel, an eternal youth "attentive to reality and impatient to change it, and an old age that has seen it all and is returning to the origin of things" (*DF* 212).

And yet history, as a modern relation to the past, is no less a construct, in Leibowitz's sense, no less an institutional mentality, as Levinas might put it, than law, politics, or ethical philosophy, for that matter; it does not confer identity, but rather practices a "means of identification," a conventionalized and at some level arbitrary system of differences, comparisons, approximations. In his book on collective remembering, *Zakhor: Jewish History and Jewish Memory*, Yosef Hayim Yerushalmi observes that in the case of Jewish history especially, the modern impulse to historicize and the appeal to History in an absolute sense signify radical departures. They replace, or intervene in, a completely different relationship to the past, that of memory. From being the physician of memory, as Eugene Rosenstock-Huessy movingly called him, the Jewish historian (or historicist Jew), becomes the clinician of history. The discourse of history occupies the space vacated by faith for myriad sons of Abraham and Moses who identify just as strongly as sons of Hegel and Kant. "For the first time," writes Yerushalmi, "history, not a sacred text becomes the arbiter of Judaism[, now] inseparable from its evolution through time, from its concrete manifestations in history" (90, 92). Signaling philosophical and Judaic losses to Leibowitz and Levinas alike, *Wissenschaft* assumes the mantle of *talmud torah*.

It is precisely such scientific *appeal* to history that Leibowitz rejects out of hand as having no more clarifying ultimacy than legality or ethical humanism. For it represents yet one more element in a scale of values having man at its pith and height. The God of Judaism is the God of Torah and mitzvot, not of history; where the former effectively ground Jewish identity, the latter necessarily shifts according to perspective.

> Are we dealing with the people of Israel as an a priori idea, or with the Jewish people as a historical entity? . . . If the subject is the historical people of Israel, are we concerned with the continuum of its history, or with the present generation, whose problems do not necessarily coincide with those of the preceding ones? In other words, is the "uniqueness of the people of Israel" conceived as initially determined or as a contingent factuality? Is it an entelechy predetermining Israel's vocation or a product of its history? Which came first, the uniqueness that produced a people or a people that shaped its own uniqueness? (80)

Like Levinas (though with different justifications, obviously), Leibowitz cannot accept a universal, inexorable History as telos or totality, any more than he can countenance any other improperly venerated idol of world, mind, or spirit.[93] העולם מנהגו נוהג, *The world pursues its natural course*, says the Talmud; בדרך שאדם רוצה לילך מוליכין אותו, *Man is led by the path he wishes to pursue*. Within such course and on such path—which may well manifest their own perversity—nothing, not even historical progression, can confer absolute value in the sense exercised by the Commandments (217).

If legal title, morality, and historical precedence all fail to establish a necessary and sufficient link between a people or nation, and its land, certainly the Halakhah must, finally, confer and justify such a right. For not only does the Torah records God's promise of land and seed to the Patriarchs, tying a people's continuity to the land in which it will in perpetuity. It also contains specific *mitzvot* that direct the Israelites to *conquer* and *inherit* the land (Num. 33:52ff., Deut. 12ff.).[94] Even if history in a modern sense is not constitutive of the Halakhah, the Torah clearly mandates a Jewish presence in Israel: an obligation to possess, settle, inherit, and thus serve God in it.

The midrashic *Yalkut Shimoni* on the Book of Jonah, for example, says that only in Israel does God's presence dwell and prophecy flourish. Is this not how Levinas understands the return to Zion in our century, a picking up *exactly* where Holy History left off—the resumption of an original right that is also an infinite responsibility? Jonah repre-

sents Levinas's prophet of choice for the subject who cannot escape ethical address; so he likewise turns to the prophecy and revelation made
possible by a modern Jewish state, going so far as to suggest (in the same
essay that mentions Leibowitz) that "an Israeli experiences the famous
touch of God in his social dealings" (*DF* 218). In "Promised Land or
Permitted Land" (a selective reading of *Sotah* 34a–35b), he writes,

> You see, this country is extraordinary. It is like heaven. It is a country
> which vomits up its inhabitants when they are not just. There is no
> other country like it; the resolution to accept a country under such con-
> ditions confers a right to that country. (*NTR* 69)

Jewish assumption of national rights does not correspond to possession
or ownership in the ordinary sense. It sacralizes instead. For there is an
elevation of the land in the name of justice, but also, conversely, "a worship of the earth and a shame attached to this worship," whereby even
biblical Zionists can be rebuked in the name of truth (56). The "nation"
of Israel can mean only a state ever-anxious about its origins, an
"extreme consciousness" over coveting the land in which it dwells or
collapsing permission into unconditional promise.[95]

Leibowitz shares Levinas's anti-idolatrous sentiments unequivo-
cally, but I think it should be obvious by this point that he would balk
at the particularism Levinas seems to smuggle in, as well as the correspondence he draws between the *Eretz Yisrael* of Scripture and the *Medinat Israel* of human will and invention. Nor would he tolerate the blurring of a distinction so essential for him, both philosophically and
halakhically: the Jewish people as the bearer of Judaism on the one
hand, and the sovereign state instituted by this people as its instrument
of self-government on the other. Here, conversely (and counterintuitively), is Levinas again, from the same essay:

> One can also suppose . . . that the explorers [Num. 13–14], confronted
> by the inhabitants of Palestine, had misgivings—about what Vigée said
> yesterday and what many others have said when they speak of Israeli
> children. Perhaps the explorers caught a glimpse of *sabras*. Fear seized
> the; they said to themselves: this is what awaits us there; these are the
> future children of Israel, those people who make holes wherever they
> set foot, who dig furrows, build cities, and wear the sun around their
> necks. But that is the end of the Jewish people! (61)

(An irony worth noting here: *sabra* is the term for Israeli-born Jew,
named after the fruit of the prickly pear cactus. But the plant itself is not
native to Israel; it was imported from Mexico by Spaniards. Moreover,
the rows of such cacti one sees while driving throughout Israel are the
traces left by pre-1948 Palestinian peasants that fenced off fields belonging to neighboring clans.) I can think of few other instances which so

solidly, unmistakable, uncannily position Levinas—like the *meraglim* (explorers) themselves—*outside* Israel while fondly gazing *in*, peering at his Beloved through the lattice (Song of Songs 2:9), the most romantic of romantic Zionists.

Necessarily, Leibowitz stops short of such quasi-inflamed passion because inflammation, at least of the nationalist kind, is always moving away from sacralization and toward enchantment—something, as we know, Levinas believes just as strongly (136–160), but for whom the pragmatic, the normative, and the halakhic still defer to the more pressing claims of metaphysics and meta-*aggadah*. Leibowitz believes rather that any argument about the state *as it has taken shape in our century* appealing for sanction to Torah and *halakhah* uses religion as a camouflage for nationalism. Writing in an essay published after the annexation of the territories in 1967 he says, "Counterfeit religion imputes to the state—which is only an instrument serving human needs—supreme value from a religious standpoint" (226). Since the state *from its inception* has favored the interests of a clerical politics instead of striving for a political religiosity, it cannot at the same time appeal to the imperative demands of *mitzvot* that understand a relationship of a wholly different order to the land. Either a modern Jewish state conforms to dimensions specified by the Halakhah—the idealized template rhapsodized by R. Soloveitchik—or it locates its bearings according to other systems of reckoning. It cannot, however, do both.

Twin rationales support Leibowitz's position here, one having to do with the holiness of the land, the other with its sovereignty. The argument for the former is again halakhic and is based on the discussion of the sacrality of the Temple precincts and its ritual objects in *Kelim* 1:6:

> The land of Israel is the Holy Land and the Temple Mount is a holy place only by virtue of the Mitzvoth linked to these locations. These Mitzvoth were not associated with the land and the mountain because these are "holy." On the contrary, their "holiness" derives from the Mitzvoth associated with them. The idea that a specific country or location have an intrinsic "holiness" is an indubitably idolatrous idea. . . . Nationalism and patriotism as such are not religious values. (227)

The second thesis follows from the first: a return to Zion by world Jewry in the twentieth century can only possess *potential* religious significance. To the extent that the land is fenced at the whim of government policy, patriotic fervor, and *raison d'etat*, rather than the norms of Halakhah, the state forfeits that much of its claim to being a nation founded upon קדשה, holiness. A Holy land reclaimed in Holy History (Levinas's terms), must regulate itself, indeed must express itself, accordingly, through service to God.

Levinasian Zionism and Leibowitzian Zionism thus only partially coincide. To recall my introduction, it is Leibowitz's *Judaism*—bent through both Kantian and Maimonidean optics—that prevents him from following Levinas into the metaphysical beyond of *human values* and *the Jewish state*. What for Levinas is visionary far-sightedness is an oddly clarifying, saving astigmatism in Leibowitz's case instead. In his essay, "The Uniqueness of the Jewish People," Leibowitz runs through all the possibilities that confer unity and self-identity upon a people: biological, linguistic, territorial, temporal. Unsurprisingly, he concludes, "Unlike the identities of the peoples that are characterized by race, language, territory, or state, the national identity of the historic Jewish people is Judaism, the actuality of which is life according to the Torah" (83).

Consider on the other hand the way Levinas defines the same terms in the essay from which I have already quoted. "What we call the Torah provides norms for human justice. And it is in the name of this universal justice and not in the name of some national justice or other that the Israelites lay claim to the land of Israel" (*NTR* 66). In the course of this essay, Levinas suggests an explicit correspondence between an Israel espied and an Israel recognized, a biblical "promised land" and a modern "permitted land." Such a link is one already sanctioned by iconography, which has transformed the image of grape clusters borne on a double pole from the episode Levinas discusses (Num. 13:23) into a familiar national symbol of fecundity and national regeneration. Now, although Levinas will say that his reading "does not describe a problem of history," he will find a place in the Bible for a very modern metaphysic of Zionism, folding one into the other nevertheless. The ill-fated touring of the land described by the Torah results ironically, in an exile from it, a sinfulness the entire congregation once again is made to bear on their vexed passage from bondage to difficult freedom. Because of the explorers' faintheartedness, the generation of the Exodus is punished with forty years' wandering; only Caleb and Phineas survive to enter the Promised Land under the leadership of Joshua.

Moreover, as the explorers' "evil report "elicits widespread lamentation in the camp on the ninth of Av, so God is said to decree in the talmudic extract Levinas selects, "[because the assembled congregation] cried without cause, I will make this a permanent day of lamentation."[96] And indeed, the ninth of Av marks the date of not only the destruction of the First and Second Temples and the sack of Jerusalem, but uncannily, the expulsions from England in 1290 and from Spain in 1492, and the start of the first World War, the first act in an extended tragedy for twentieth-century European Jewry. From this *midrash* Levinas draws the meaning for modernity, which he expresses in a contemporary vocabulary of national loss and entitlement: "Only those who are always ready to accept the consequences of their actions and to accept exile when they are no longer worthy of a homeland have a right to enter this homeland" (69). Diaspora, an original deprivation or bar, signifies an indemnity that must precede the restored claims of occupation and ownership.

Fore-echoing, in a way, Moses's own admission at the end of Deuteronomy, "I can no longer go out and come in" just before his death (31:2), but anticipating more closely and by counterexample the word for the modern return to Zion, *aliyah*, or ascent, the explorers conclude their report on a cowardly note: לא נוכל לעלות, *we cannot go up*; ארץ אכלת יושיבה הוא, *It is a land that devours its inhabitants* (Num. 13:31–32). Their hearts fall within him as they compare their dwarfed stature to the Canaanites, whom they magnify accordingly: ונהי בעינינו כחגבים היינו וכן היינו בעיניהם, *we were like grasshoppers in our eyes, and so we were in their eyes* (Num. 13:3).[97]

Levinas's reading of the Talmud's gloss on these verses characteristically indulges certain "anachronisms," as he candidly calls them (just as, again, he disembeds a single story from its larger aggadic context within the tractate). Besides references to biblical "Zionists," he will speak of discovering in the explorers' great fear "anxieties more familiar to us." As the Israelites are made vermiform through the Canaanite gaze, so contemporary Israel is miniaturized perceptually, ontologically, by its modern enemies:

> It is a remarkably contemporary passage. That way of taking human faces for grasshoppers! Or that way of taking the historical act of Return for a movement of grasshoppers. Oh, the forewarned intelligence of realists! Always, at the beginning, there is a dance of grasshoppers. On this point, the explorers tell the truth. They knew the inhabitants took them for grasshoppers. (68)

At the risk of duplicating Levinas's own move in relation to the talmudic text by recontextualizing his (it dates from 1965),[98] I find myself tempted nevertheless to update "being taken for grasshoppers" by recalling the phrase used by former Israeli Defense Minister Ariel Sharon to describe the Palestinian insurgents during the Intifada: *cockroaches*. Not for every Israeli then will Jewish thought, like Jewish conscience, know "every scruple, every remorse, even [regarding] the most sacred rights of the people troubled by this thought" (54). The inflammations of nationalism produce a "dance of grasshoppers" no matter who draws the boundaries or how.

But as I have myself destabilized the grounds for a corrective appeal to history, I will make a stronger case for qualifying Levinas here by turning back to Leibowitz, following his lead as he frames a critique of nationalist rights in terms of the halakhic restrictions cordoning off holiness—the fence of *kedushah*. The specific sin committed by the spies (*chet hameraglim*, as it is traditionally known) is seen by certain commentators as deriving from the internally faulty nature of the mission itself. The men are sent, (1) to gather information about the nature of the land and, (2) to assess the feasibility of military conquest, making theirs a twofold purpose that translates easily, however, into an evident contradiction. This is borne out by the Talmud's comparison of the two versions of the episode related in Num. 13 and Deut. 1:22ff., something Levinas notes as opening a window onto the human crisis of the story, and which we can interpret—following the commentary of Isaac Abravanel, Leibowitz's frequent model of halakhic probity—as at least partly a result of Moses's own conflicting intentions. (Rashi proffers the related argument, generally accepted by other commentators, that the Israelites should have relied completely on Divine Providence—thus no reason for a "scouting party" in the first place.)[99]

The Talmud already implies something like that: "R. Yohanan said in the name of R. Shimon bar Yochai: the going is compared to the return. The return happened with 'bad intentions'; the going was already with these 'bad intentions.'" On the one hand, the reconnaissance was divinely ordained (Num. 13:1–3), a mission to survey the land for prospective division among the princes of the twelve tribes. On the other hand, it was *reformulated* by the explorers themselves in purely *utilitarian* terms as a military operation (Deut. 1:31), for which an entirely successful (and contrastive parallel) is narrated in Josh. 14, and as a result of which, prospective advance turns into retreat, the unwarranted fear of an outsize enemy.

As R. Yaakov Medan interprets the sense of the verse about the explorers' admitted distortion in perception, "it testifies to our lack of understanding of an exchange of glances with military significance."[100] Or, anchoring glances in faces as Zornberg does in *The Beginning of Desire*, "one who is too much affected by other's faces finds his own face turning all colors, blushing and paling in response to their changing expressions" (206). Levinas is thus *partially* right in his reading: the explorers' fear betokens a justified fear, but not because the inhabitants *disparage* them but rather because they *suspect* them, having inferred their ulterior motives that they meet with soldierly wariness and hostility. The more important point, however, and its relevance for a Leibowitzian critique, is that an act commanded by God—*avodah lishmah*—has been compromised in the direction of human values and interests; as the Rabbis say elsewhere (in line with Deut. 4:2), כל המוסיף גורע, "Whoever adds thereby diminishes." On the model of the halakhic recourse Leibowitz finds by adducing prohibitions against mistaking the mundane for the holy in tractate *Kelim* (Vessels), the explorers' mission can be said to have committed a kind of *me'ila* (trespass, as in Deut. 32:51), *the unlawful use of consecrated property*—in this instance, the vessel of divine commandment adulterated by mere expediency and weakness of spirit.

I am not sure that this is what Gillian Rose has in mind when she speaks of a *halakhah* beyond *halakhah*. But the close-grained apperception of things and place that constitutes "the fence around the law" taps roots in Jewish thought and conscience surely as deep as those mined by Levinas, and maybe deeper. For though Levinas's reading is gorgeous, nuanced, exquisitely attuned to the harmonics of the text, it brings its own agenda *al peshuto shel mikra* (not in the plain sense)—an ethics *before the halakhah*. Quasi-hasidically, he reads the redundancy of "bad intentions" as actually signifying good intentions, the "extreme consciousness" of an overly pure conscience. This is the sort of moral sensibility he calls the possibility of atheism in this essay as well as elsewhere in his philosophical writings because it demonstrates an ethics concerned first and foremost with "the other man," the worry over the exigencies of conquest by an absolutely moral people bound to the word of God. "It begins to doubt God because God's command asks us either what is above our strength or beneath our conscience. The Promised Land is not permitted land" (64).[101]

A Leibowitzian reading (one conducted in the *spirit* of Leibowitz's habitual concerns), would regard the note of ambiguity on which Levinas concludes—either the explorers were too pure in their belief that rights to the land were not theirs to claim, or else their right lacked might (the conquest seemed too utopian to them)—as itself symptomatic (or mimetic) of the halakhic flaw embodied by the explorers' very mission, *independent of the philosophical scruples Levinas wishes to impute to the explorers themselves*. God proposed, and man disposed, or more Jewish-accented, *a mensch trakht un Got lakht*. Unless the *mitzvah* is its own reward (R. Hayyim of Volozhin), Judaism, as *avodah lishmah*, becomes the ancilla of human autonomy, whether individual or collective, impelled by bravado or cowardice. In her commentary on this Torah portion, Leibowitz's sister, Nehama, writes,

> In other words, their sin lay in making their own selfish calculation of the material prospects ahead of them. They were afraid of the responsibilities of freedom, the dangers involved in securing it. Far better it was to wander the wilderness and even return to Egyptian bondage. The slave has no responsibility and his fate is decided by others. (*Studies in Bamidbar*, 146)[102]

Not only does the error here point, by counterexample, to the absolute necessity of political maturity and sophistication. The conflation of purposes in the *chet hameraglim* also teaches a larger lesson about the gulf dividing transcendent imperative from the already admixed mundane. And thus, as if in rejoinder to Levinas's ingenious *philosophical* reconciliation between bad intentions and good, Leibowitz will turn to the fence of later rabbinic wisdom:

> Don Isaac Abravanel, commenting upon Gen. 22:3, explains: "saddled his ass" means that he overcame his materiality, that is, his physical nature—a pun on the phonetically similar "hamor" (ass) and "homer" (matter). This "matter" or nature includes all the benevolent sentiments as well as man's conscience; all the factors in man's makeup which an atheistic humanism regards as "good." In the morning benedictions, recited prior to reading the narrative of the Aqueda, we find the request; "Compel our *Yetzer* [inclination] to subject itself to you"—a request meant to apply to our benevolent as to our evil inclinations. This would be a banal supplication were it concerned with only the evil inclinations. (14)

"Oh beautiful incorruptible consciences," Levinas chants. "What, then, does the Talmud want?" The Leibowitzian answer (if I may): an *aggadah* within the *halakhah*, and only then an ethics.

As we saw in the last chapter, halakhic man's "heroism" proves its mettle, for R. Soloveitchik at least, in the most private of spheres: the couple that must postpone conjugality on their wedding night because of the laws of *niddah*. Yet projected and magnified according to the dimensions of public space, that courage assumes a grandeur for me here, in Leibowitz's scrupulosity, exactly proportionate to the stakes vested in the gross identities of lands and peoples for which good and bad intentions alike bow to the Yoke of the Kingdom of Heaven. If Leibowitz "girds up strength like a lion" to hold forth against the irreligiosities of nationalism, he does so certainly in large part because they can have no place for him in the service of his Creator. Levinas is absolutely right when he says "The daily fidelity to the ritual gesture demands a courage that is calmer, noble, and greater than that of the warrior" (*DF* 19), and yet I would apply these words to Leibowitz here. Thus, at the same time, Leibowitz's sense of what the Halahkah can and cannot do, and his commitment to civic and political morality, evince something on the order of philosophical majesty, comparably leonine.

Above, I speak of Leibowitz as the stricter Kantian. To invoke that curiously uncanny ante-type one last time, I mean that Leibowitz takes the dauntless aspect described at the end of the *Critique of Practical Reason*—the heroic moral agent—and retools it to the lineaments of halakhic man. On the political plane, he echoes the answer Kant supplied to his own question in the essay, "What is Enlightenment?": "to be grown-up," but resists all blandishments that might seduce him into a complacent interiority. In this way does Leibowitz, too, insist upon a *difficult freedom* that earns for Judaism its worth as a religion *for adults* (*DF* 16; *NTR* 15).

Leibowitz's Zionism is hard-won, a mix of migrancy and civic icon-oclasm, perhaps not so very far, in the final analysis, from the meta-physics of exile Levinas posits in "Promised Land" or "Permitted Land." It is his Judaism, however (all its formalist excess notwithstand-ing), that acts as his Zionism's safeguard and custodian—ever-wakeful, insomniac, a religious praxis perhaps best rendered by the compound sense of the Hebrew verb שמר: *to watch, to observe, to keep, to wait, to be vigilant*. Leibowitz understands that while to be authentically Jewish may mean apportioning fences and neighbors according to religiously framed statute and limitation, Jews must not only still reckon with an already lived-in world—a world of fences and neighbors defined other-wise. They must also resist the pull of modern ideologies that twist Judaism from a task and vocation into a fictitious objectivity. "Values are not rooted in reality," he writes. "They are objects of aspiration beyond reality toward which one must strive from within reality" (80). Few dec-larations speak more pointedly (and multiply) to current socio-political conditions *within* Israel—possibly more factionalized than ever before in its fifty-year history as it begins to negotiate peace with its neighbors.

In his review of Leibowitz's book, Moshe Halbertal explains such a refusal to ground religious belief in propositions, intriguingly enough, by analogy to a famous text of modern philosophy, the *Tractatus Logico-Philosophicus*:

> Wittgenstein, another believer, ended his reflections on the limits of metaphysical knowledge with the famous statement that "whereof one cannot speak thereof one must be silent." Leibowitz's view might be said to be, "whereof one cannot speak, thereof one must act." (37)

I agree with Halbertal's intertextual instincts here, and yet, remaining now within the ambit of modern philosophy—the topic of my epi-logue—perhaps the case of Leibowitz more closely approximates the later Wittgenstein, of whom Stanley Cavell observes in *The Claim of Reason*, "It can seem sometimes that Wittgenstein has undertaken to voice our secrets, secrets we did not know were known, or did not know we shared" (20). In Cavell's interpretation, the "pitch" of philosophy's own voice in the work of Wittgenstein shows how the case of philoso-phizing itself can be out of tune with the words of ordinary human beings; and yet in being so, it poses the very problem or challenge of attunement in the first place (34).[103]

However we want to identify the pitch at which Leibowitz philosophizes, he lays claim to a Judaism that, similarly, becomes all the more
compelling for the way he brings its foundation stones—like the contempt for idolatry—newly to light: a secret, let us say, that we did not
know we knew or shared with such rectitude and courage. The analogy
to Wittgenstein, of course, ceases to be instructive as soon as we remember that morality, or attunement, for this school of philosophy assumes
the form of a wholly human problem: what is in doubt or jeopardy is
not God (a matter, as in Kant, for the theologians) but rather the link
between selves and human others. And yet, here too, I think a connection with Leibowitz does suggest itself. "Healthy radical monotheism"
of Leibowitz's kind presupposes a necessary, given, even if only initial,
lack of attunement between divine commandments and human wishes
or inclinations. It is only thus that idolatry in all its possible shapes can
be made suspect from the start.

> Had the rationale of the Mitzvoth been national welfare, fulfilling them
> would express love of Israel. Had it been social, observing them would
> indicate the love of mankind. Had it been social, observing them would
> serve important human needs. . . . Their justification is *not* "national"
> and *not* "moral" and *not* "social." Their sole point is the service of
> God. (73)

Ideally, one moves ever-toward some ultimate rapprochement. But to
begin with disjunction and asymmetry—Levinas's prerequisites for the
drama of ethics and religion as well—means, while anchored on one side
of fence, to be always already haunted by what lies beyond it, wary, vigilant, observant, peering through the lattice.

Clearly, as Jews and as distinct practitioners of the same vocation,
Leibowitz and Levinas peer from dissimilar positions, through dissimilar fences, and at dissimilar objects. The Torah verse that may best
express such nonattuned "peering" is probably Deut. 1:17, in which
Moses repeats his instruction to judges, לא תכירו פנים, *not to show
favoritism in judgment*, an admonition more literally translated, *You
shall not recognize a face*. The (Levinasian) seat of human majesty and
destitution merely obscures the (Leibowitzian) rectitude of litigation at
hand. For both philosophers, however, the seriousness with which such
scrutiny is engaged suggests one way that Judaism attunes itself, as an
extreme consciousness, to the provocation of human values and the
uncompleted vocation of a Jewish state. The concluding chapter specu-
lates on how the virtues of religious fidelity may permit Judaism's values to speak to philosophy's, leaving them at the very least audible to
one another, and perhaps at the most, neighbors who set the wall
between them and keep it as they go.

Thus, in one last and perhaps freest application of Robert Frost's poem, let us imagine the stones of such a wall as limestone-faced and golden in the sun: like those in the midst of Jerusalem marking the site of former glories and tragic ruinations, the twinning of Judaism's home and its estrangement into foreign places—making the appellative "Western Wall," in this context, especially apt. But let us also hold out the possibility that Judaism and philosophy, in the persons of Levinas and Leibowitz, can engage each other apart from such enrootedness, too. That relationship would be something like the metamorphosis traced in a midrash about Serah, daughter of Asher (mentioned in Gen. 46:17 and said to have survived through Moses's lifetime in *Sota* 13b), a figure that symbolizes for R. Soloveitchik a living link between generations. "Our eyes," he remarks, "seeing our teachers, so to speak" (*Shiurei HaRav,* 52). And so, appropriately enough in the *midrash,* walls become filters and finally windows:

> R. Yohanan explained that the waters [at the splitting of the Red Sea were [opaque] like a wall. R. Yohanan explained that they were like a net. Serah bat Asher looked down from heaven and said, "I was there and they were like clear windows" (Pesikhta d'Rav Kahana).

EPILOGUE

The Present of
"Future Jewish Thought"

Let me object, at the outset, to any attempt to explain anyone's views by where he comes from or who he is. I object as well to any attempt to distinguish between those who come from a milieu shaped by Western culture and others whose cultural and spiritual origins lie in Eastern Europe. I, too, belong to the Western world, although, geographically speaking, I come from the East.

Maimonidean anthropology, with its emphasis upon man's individuality, is at least partially a product of the historic situation of Jewry in exile, a community divested of independent social functions and deprived of civic roles and obligations.

—Yeshayahu Leibowitz

Perhaps I am not Jew enough and too much of a Germanic intellectual, full of reverence for the heroes of late Greece and their modern heirs. Perhaps the love for a motherly tradition in which one can feel at home prevents me from a more courageous exodus. It seems, however, worthwhile to meditate on what unites us with the heritage of our Greece-inspired modernity and to plunder it as much as we can before we leave it behind—before we are renewed by the arid sufferings of a desert.

—Adriaan Peperzak

The problem of Judaism is the problem of opening a way to Judaism that will show it to those who being blinded are now outside. I speak of those who, unlike the wicked men of Sodom, are knocking at the gate and seeking to enter; and even those who are not yet seeking entrance.

An Aggadah promises the reconstruction of a Jerusalem in its glory, a reconstruction by the very means which were used to destroy it, precisely through fire, become protector. But where is the glory of His presence among us, if not in the transfiguration of consuming and avenging fire into a protective wall, into a defensive barrier.

—Emmanuel Levinas

Rabbi Yochanan said, A man's feet are responsible for him; they take him to the place where he is wanted.

—Tractate *Sukkah* 53a

עמר רב חסדה למדנו מקום ממקום ומקום מניסה וניסה
מניסה וניסה מגבול וגבול מגבול וגבול מחוץ וחוץ מחוץ

עירובין נא,א

Rav Hisda said, we learn place from place, and place from flight; flight from flight, and flight from border; border from border, and border from beyond; and beyond from beyond.

Eruvin 51a, [elucidating Ex. 16:29 (Shabbat boundaries)
with reference to Ex. 21:13 and Num. 35:26
(cities of refuge) and Num. 35:5 (Levite cities)]

My heart is the East though I am in the uttermost West.

—Yehudah Halevi

אמר רבי יוחנן רגלווהי דבר איניש ערבין ביה לאתר דמיתבעי תמן מובילין יתיה.

סוכה נג,א

Yehudah Halevi wrote, "In the East is my heart, and I dwell
 at the end of the West."
That's Jewish travel, that's the Jewish game of hearts between
 east and west,
between self and heart, to and fro, to without fro, fro without to,
 Fugitive and vagabond without sin.

—Yehudah Amichai

FROM PROPER NAME TO PLACE NAME

Since in one respect this has been a study in proper names (some more familiar than others), a conclusion seems an appropriate place to recall the *dramatis personae* that have figured prominently in the foregoing pages. Emil Fackenheim, Emmanuel Levinas, Yeshayahu Leibowitz, R. Joseph Soloveitchik, R. Aharon Lichstenstein, Halevi, Hayyim Volozhiner Maimonides, David Hartman, Stanley Cavell, Ludwig Wittgenstein, Immanuel Kant. To all except the last (recalling that Wittgenstein converted) can one apply the sobriquet, "Jewish philosopher"; if we are to follow Levinas's lead, the Sages of the Oral Law, or Doctors of the Talmud as he typically calls them, deserve the appellation as well.[1]

In *Noms propres*, Levinas asks, "The proper names in the middle of all those common names and common-places—do they not help us speak" (4)?[2] Inasmuch as my stated task in this book has been to provide a voice for two Jewish philosophers for whom Judaism and philosophy do not neatly coincide, the answer is, yes. But maybe the names have merely eased the problem of the role in each case, as though the proper name validates, fills in, bears out, the title. Does a more insistent problem inhere in the relationship between Judaism and philosophy, or within modern Judaism and modern philosophy themselves?[3] I cannot lay claim to the kind of thoroughgoing answer such a question really demands, and can only proffer the preceding pages of inquiry and speculation in lieu of something more categorical and conclusive. It may be more faithful to the spirit of such inquiry, therefore, to conclude with some summary thoughts about how the question can be framed, indeed asked in the first place. So properly speaking, this epilogue is really propaedeutic or heuristic—a final meditation on the reach of place and the migrancy of words.

Levinas confesses in several places that although the classical topics for modern continental philosophy may have been exhausted under pressure from successive Nietzschean, Heideggerean, and Derridean critiques, philosophy in its other sense of critical speculation and interrogation, continues; and in the very putting of itself into question that characterizes its contemporary situation, "it has found a new lease on life" (*FTF* 33). Defined thus, philosophy finds an analogue in rabbinic Judaism, with its distinctive methods of critical speculation and interrogation.

Certainly, the parallel explains the peculiar mutuality of Levinas's twin vocational imperatives: for a place in the Bible and for "the face" in philosophy.[4] The comparison, of course, has not gone unobserved, least of all by Levinas himself, who speaks to it directly in several essays.[5] And if, with one of Levinas's interviewers, we were to entertain a rapprochement between Western and rabbinic modes of philosophizing as a contrast of languages,[6] we would merely have inverted the argument built on comparison. As for Judaism in the sense of halakhic praxis, which at bottom means not just observance but continued study, it has not needed a new lease on life for it has yet to exhaust its old one. It remains unclear, however, whether the bridging of philosophy in its rabbinic or talmudic sense and philosophy in its modern or postmodern sense can assume a form independent of the unique syncresis Levinas was able to accomplish in his own person and vocation.

Even his readers who share Levinas's dual identity of Jew and academic philosopher have addressed that singularity mostly in terms of the sobriquet "modern Jewish philosopher," which, while it may have the advantage of cueing a set of related proper names—Rosenzweig, Buber, Cohen—still does not fully take on the challenge posed by Fackenheim in the subtitle to his book paraphrased here for my epilogue. That challenge, it seems to me, is perhaps best captured by Levinas himself when he speaks of Judaism as *anachronistic*—as both youth and old age, impatient to change reality but also indefatigably cognizant of origins. The future of Jewish thought is also its past, just as Moses's ostensibly repetition in Deuteronomy of events already narrated in the three Pentateuchal books preceding it, is a formula for future action.[7]

I have tried to capture such anachronism myself in this book by linking Levinas and Leibowitz in the present, linking each of them to a common halakhic/aggadic past that remains a living tradition, and linking each of them again to the projective sociopolitical aspirations of a modern Jewish state. Taking up the gauntlet at the end of my preface, and preferring to be Zusya rather than a Moses who repeats, and rather than using proper names to solve the problem of proper titles, I will follow my own rhetorical and Frostean instincts and go behind or even ahead of my father's saying. And although this last chapter does indeed return to the work of Stanley Cavell, it is not the logic of returning full circle that prompts me to invoke him once again here.

Speaking of the philosophic vocation generally, Cavell distinguishes several times in his books between philosophy as a set of problems and philosophy as a set of texts. He also calls philosophy's investment in ordinary life, as embodied by the everyday words we use (and the agreements derived from or situated beneath them), a search for *community*, an exploration of how we can be party to the establishing of criteria unrecognized by us beforehand.[8]

What if we indulge the thought experiment of a *tertium quid* on this model and think of philosophy neither as a set of problems nor as a set of texts, but rather (in a restrictive postliberal context) *as a certain set of Jews*—as such, making an attendant appeal to community, albeit differently conceived? A bold-faced proposal, no doubt, and one I do not at all intend glibly. Let me elaborate what I have in mind here by returning to Fackenheim. Fackenheim's inquiry, readers will recall, is motivated by redress. Modern philosophy in the West, he argues, is flawed by a parochialism it demonstrates with regard to a Judaism it continues to know in flattened or distorted form. More than just a flaw in the architecture of its rationalism, such insensitivity signifies a loss for civilization as a whole inasmuch as philosophy claims Athens and Jerusalem alike to be its twin cities, the latter, of course, according to its Judeo-Christian pedigree (a fusion which Leibowitz, as we saw, explicitly rejects).

At least since Epicurus, whenever Western philosophy has said the word "God" or contemplated religion, it has had Christianity at least subliminally in mind; whenever it has quoted Scripture (Pascal, Kant, Hegel, Kierkegaard), it does so by means of a translated and recomposed Bible. In our own century, while Heidegger, after Nietzsche, may have pointed the way back to a pre-Judeo-Christian paganism, he just as surely assumes a foothold in a non- or anti-Hebraic Christianity.

Self-evidently in this ideological age, however, Fackenheim's charge can be leveled from quarters having nothing to do with Judaism. On the plane of race and culture, I think of a book like Anthony Appiah's *In My Father's House: Africa in the Philosophy of Culture*, which studies the consequences of an entire continent left out of the Athens/Jerusalem equation. Or through the optic of feminism, Seyla Benhabib's *Situating the Self* and Andrea Nye's *Philosophy & Feminism: At the Border*, and Martha Nussbaum's *Sex and Social Justice* all come to mind. Western civilization is "Western" by exclusion and "civilized" according to a socially constructed, restrictive inheritance of fathers and sons—the law of patrimony.[9]

Fackenheim, however, appeals to the same history Walter Benjamin famously linked to barbarism and catastrophic wreckage—"Ever since the Nazi holocaust it is Western civilization that is on trial" (5)—a history in which Levinas implicates modern philosophy also—"None of the generosity which the German term '*es gibt*' is said to contain revealed itself between 1933 and 1945" (*DF* 292). (This, of course, ventures the standing rebuke to Richardson and Scott in my introduction, unanswerable on its face, I think.) Though certainly the West can be held to account for unconscious parochialisms of other sorts that have sanctioned different historical calamities, there has been only one *Führer* in this century, says Fackenheim, and in his wake modernity can no longer afford to keep itself "unexposed" to Judaism. That encounter, conducted on behalf of Western philosophy, would therefore describe one possible path for "future Jewish thought" (223–229). This epilogue paraphrases Fackenheim because my express purpose in the preceding chapters has been to voice the encounter he advocates, but at the particular philosophical pitch vocalized by Levinas and Leibowitz. Fackenheim's own epilogue is existentialist; the encounter between Judaism and modern philosophy concludes more or less with the year 1945—a very prolific year for civilization's dark side. The book's final words, however, gesture to a proximate but different temporal arc (or segment of the same arc) that was signaled by the inaugural year of 1948. The "bearing witness unto the nations" Fackenheim ascribes to a contemporary Jewry that has survived the Holocaust Kingdom, Levinas and Leibowitz both ascribe, with equal fervor, to the establishment of a modern Jewish state, and the place it consequently assumes again among the nations.

By asking us to think of philosophy *as a set of Jews that appeals to a particular image of community* (a claim still in need of warrant), no doubt I have seemingly parochialized it all over again from just another standpoint. Admittedly, I have not sought in this pages to extend the range of Judaism itself very far, leaving questions like pluralism and denominational or ethnocultural conflict among Jews themselves unasked let alone unanswered. Demographically speaking, I have concentrated on a small sliver of Jewish phenomenal life loosely configured by me as *halakhic and aggadic*—that is, rooted in classical Jewish texts and the practical implications for lived Jewish experience they contain. The community thus described, however—observant Jews and scholars—is tiny.

But I have also assumed a concomitant population maybe even more miniscule in endeavoring "to extract the secret scent" from the work of two contemporary thinkers who were religious Jews as well as classically trained philosophers. I have done so for all the reasons I candidly voice in my introduction. The middle epigraph to this chapter offers at least a self-conscious explanation of the closure from philosophy's side. But on the Judaic side, too, the languages of choice have tended primarily to be German or French rather than Hebrew and Aramaic. In neither case, have halakhic praxis or aggadic commentary played an informing or central role. Few writers have actually *followed* Levinas's lead; even fewer *know of* Leibowitz. And thus by default but also providing me with an opening, the appeal I have made in this book to Jewishness and community has been restrictive.

It is telling, too, if we recall Cavell, that he also confines his dialogue with continental philosophy to Heidegger alone, mentioning Levinas only once in passing, and having little to say, beyond the anecdotal and cultural, about Judaism. In his books, Cavell speaks in the most general sense about humanity's universality, its "commonness," as he calls it, and like Gillian Rose and Isaiah Berlin in the last sections of my chapter on Leibowitz, seems to bracket or suspend religious experience entirely. (He does say suggestively, however, that atheism, like ahistoricalness, portends a desire for awakening, which calls to mind Levinas's definition of atheism as a break with participation in Being—as though "the separated being maintains itself in existence all by itself"—and also the converse midrashic idea that God is to be defined by insomnia, "[a]s if, in the impossibility of sleeping, the ontological rest of being were to be torn and entirely sobered up" [*TI* 58; *BV* 112, 210–211].[10])

To state the task I have proposed once again as Cavell might himself put it: say that philosophy is a set of Jews; and call their predilections an appeal to community. Community in Cavell specifies an edging of private and public realms: the finding of one's own voice, and, in turn, its attunement to others', an act visibly—and audibly—at risk, he says, in philosophy, in politics, and in autobiography. For in each case, one invokes either communal consent or representative speech, a speaking with, or for, others.

The possibility that such consent can fail Cavell calls *skepticism*, or alternately, *tragedy*, for it manifests a natural possibility that takes shape within the ties binding person to person.[11] Freeing such a notion from its home-context (and at the risk of simplifying Cavell's purposes), such a fantasy of inexpressiveness—dramatized by literature, studied by philosophy—cannot assume realistic shape within the boundaries of religious Judaism because an arrogation of voice (Cavell's figure for philosophers or tragedians who force the familiar into strangeness) is demanded by the tradition itself as halakhic duty.[12] The Talmud explicitly rebukes those who are too shy to ask questions. What I mean is that Jews are religiously bound to become *mefarshim* (expounders), and thus in Levinas's sense, also *metzavim* (commanders)—that is, to personalize, and thus give verbal consent to, criteria never placed in jeopardy. Cavell might call this Jewish Emersonianism, where one writes not "Whim" on the lintels of one's doorpost, but perhaps one's own *mezuzah*.[13]

"In every generation a person should look upon himself as if he personally had come out of Egypt," says the Passover *Haggadah*—a word, as we have seen, that means to tell or relate, and in context, to renarrate.

> Even if we were all wise, all understanding, all experienced, and all verse in Torah, we would nevertheless be obligated to recount (*l'saper*) the story of the departure from Egypt; and who greatly recounts it (*hamarbeh l'saper*) it is worth of praise.[14]

Even if one were mired in religious doubt of the most fundamental kind, that is, does God really exist? was Moses a prophet?, the Halakhah presupposes a fundamental *entanglement* of voices over and above an attunement, a self that remains present and accounted for in its performance of *mitzvot* and the obligations of *talmud torah*. A perfect expression of such commingled voice and deed is the *mitzvah* above to retell the story of Exodus annually on Passover, which not only re-enacts an event, but also implicitly re-echoes the declaration of agreement and communal consent that followed it at the foot of Mount Sinai: *na'aseh v'nishmah*, we will do and we will hear. And that one-time acceptance or *kabbalat Torah*, undertaken by each generation in turn (as Levinas suggests in "Means of Identification" and Leibowitz throughout his essays), means both compulsion and choice, natural instinct and the willed labor of cognition.[15]

Halakhic study of the text—an almost infinite regress of commentaries—and the translation of it into praxis begins with the assumption that there is nothing that cannot *not* be expressed within a community defined by a pre-agreement to converse, to demur, to expound, except perhaps the sacred name of God. And as Levinas says of the latter,

> But writing and reading, tracing and uttering, protecting and studying, are observances. They come and take their place among all those other observances—ritual, ethical, and liturgical—that Scripture commands in the Name of this very God that it reveals. (*BV* 117–118)

As if in rejoinder to the loss signaled in the modern world by skepticism, Levinas says that names, terms, and words *express* relations.

Being Jewish in this sense means to occupy one's place in a community of Jews diachronically (across generations) and synchronically (through the Halakhah). It means to philosophize accordingly (Levinas) because the shared framework of religious praxis—even up to and including disputation—ascribes to each person the validity of a voice and the obligation to lend it. But it also means that all such acts, including disputation, are performed for the sake of Heaven, *avodah lishmah* (Leibowiz), defining the parameters of agreement, attunement, and acknowledgment at the outset. It means, finally, that one's utterances successfully sign the world and their utterer in it. Cavell will say that acknowledgment or attunement permits the belief that in addition to meaning what we say, we are *in* what we say, expressed by it, and in an uncanny formulation, he notes that ignorance of self has to be worked at and studied, in Levinas's words, "like a dead language." In other words, one is fated, metaphysically, to take a stand in relation to oneself and risk becoming strange in order to become attuned; but I ask greater losses as well, for to the same degree that I cannot "just" know myself, I open up possibilities through which others can become lost to me, "a cascade of catastrophes or diversions of catastrophe" (389).[16]

If the preceding two chapters have done their work, clearly, something very like the opposite prevails for halakhic man and aggadic
man. To take Cavell's suggestive metaphor first, it is the *living* quality
of biblical Hebrew, talmudic Hebrew, and Aramaic, of course, that
Levinas, because of his audience, takes such pains to stress and Leibowitz assumes as a given, the sine qua non of religious praxis. Second, attunement at the base level of shared language realized through
the Halakhah ensures that individual and community practicably
align, and that selfhood or otherness signify ethical demands (Levinas)
or religious duties (Leibowitz) before metaphysical crises; as Levinas
puts it, "one just is a Jew," an adherence that pre-exists allegiance (*DF*
50).[17] Third and perhaps most important, the Torah itself underlies
and inhabits any expression, both founding and grounding it. The
Mishnaic tractate *Pirke Avot* says that not only for ten persons or for
two who interchange words of Torah but even for one, the Divine
Presence indwells.[18]

"Words come to us from a distance," Cavell writes in *The Senses of
Walden*. "Meaning them is accepting the fact of their condition" (64).
In this way, but Jewishly, a community is both claimed and owned. The
Yoke of the Kingdom of Heaven and the Yoke of Torah and *mitzvot* can
be a yoke, in the sense of linkage (Leibowitz) that is also not a yoke, in
the sense of burden (Levinas). Even in the mismatch between halakhic
ideal and material real that R. Soloveitchik describes in *Halakhic Man*
(though he places a misrepresentative pressure on the solitary observer)
the *trompe l'oreille* effect Cavell punningly ascribes to a world fraught
with misattunement cannot have descriptive force (*The Claim of Reason*, 424–425). Within its fences, the Halakhah unites *talmidim* (students) and *hakhamim* or *poskim* (authorities and adjudgers) alike in a
discursive world of projective seamlessness and sonority. In short, and
to recall my own governing metaphor once again, while concentric or
expanding boundaries around the Torah may signify a converse reality
of "not-Torah," the fence still marks a limit beyond which the religious
Jew does not step.

I have yet to explain, however, what *philosophy as a set of Jews*
might mean; a disclaimer is probably in order since I have in mind neither number nor type, as if I had said something on the order of "the
American entertainment industry as a set of Jews" or New York "psy-
chiatrists as a set of Jews," or "diamond merchants as a set of Jews" or
the like).[19] Let me clarify then by turning to the philosopher-Jews whose
voices I have used all along, Yeshayau Leibowitz and Emmanuel Levinas. Leibowitz, so far as I am aware, makes a passing connection
between "Jew" and "philosophy" only once, in an anecdotal preface I
have quoted before, the full text for which reads as follows:

> I spent my childhood in Russia, but am familiar with Western science, philosophy, literature, and society no less than are the "Westerners." I recall a public debate more than thirty years ago between myself and the late Dr. Isaac Breuer, one of the most interesting thinkers among religious Jews in the generation preceding ours, for whom I had great respect despite the considerable differences between our respective views. In that debate we drifted off to general philosophical problems, and although they were relevant to the issues that were close to our hearts, Judaism, Torah, and faith, they were fundamentally ontological and epistemological problems. Since Breuer argued persistently from the Jewish viewpoint, I said to him, "Dr. Breuer, why should we deceive ourselves? You know as well as I that in our treatment of philosophical questions both of us—who consider ourselves believing Jews, whose intention is to assume the yoke of the Kingdom of Heaven and the yoke of Torah and Mitzvoth—do not draw upon Jewish sources but upon the atheistic antisemite Kant. We cannot do otherwise!" Breuer conceded at once that it would be impossible—even he could not do it—to discuss philosophical problems without recourse to Kant. (106)

Whether the final claim is disputable (clearly, Levinas presumes so), Leibowitz acknowledges both the irony and necessity of a dual loyalty to different intellectual masters. (It is from the same essay, also, that the first epigraph to this chapter is taken, directly preceding the passage above.) And thus the two issues of intellectual and geographical itineraries are connected self-evidently for Leibowitz, but also toward a particular end for me.

But the passage above is somewhat misleading. Unlike R. Soloveitchik or Levinas, Yeshayahu Leibowitz never addressed "philosophical questions" as such. Compressed arguments about epistemology and ontology, short syllogisms (and sometimes enthymemes) about intentionality and agency are pressed into service in essays whose primary focus is variously, the nature and function of *halakhah*, biblical text, Jewish identity, Zionism, political morality. As the previous chapter was meant to show, Leibowitz's claim above for the centrality of Kant is borne out—with a paradoxical vengeance—in the philosophical premises he takes for granted.

It is almost as though Leibowitz moves from Kantian idealism to an analytical positivism while skipping all the intervening steps in the history of philosophy on either side of the Atlantic or the British Channel. Hegel's historicist critique of Kant, Marx's concepts of ideology and dialectical materialism, Nietzsche's antifoundationalism, its extension by poststructuralists, modern philosophies of action, language, and religion, humanism both at the point that Fackenheim leaves off in his book and subsequent to Sartre: in other words, almost the entire philosophical discourse of modernity seems to pass Leibowitz by, or he it.

Leibowitz's philosophy, pietistic in its fervor, is obtusely self-unaware. It staunchly refuses reflexivity. And so I am not sure how ultimately persuasive is his admission that "we are all equally steeped in Western culture," since at least within the context of his essays, any immersion more often seems like a quick cold shower. As discourse, philosophy for Leibowitz never reaches the point of *Kritik*. It does not suspect itself sufficiently, does not perform its own archaeology, which is why I have risked borrowed from Levinas in describing it as threatened from within by its own "Stalinism," a drive toward reification that overtenses both Kantian and Maimonidean dimensions of his thought. In short, for all its subordinate or merely instrumental worth in relation to the Torah, philosophy carries a peculiarly *authoritative* weight for Leibowitz, in the sense of an ideological *assimilation* of other(s') words.[20] Leibowitz's Judaism is anything but Emersonian.

One might at first think of the Hebrew Bible and the Oral Law as quintessential examples of such discourse. And yet, quite aside from the Sages' famous statement, "Torah has been given and Halakhah innovated" (*Shabbat* 135b), I think my characterization of Leibowitz not unfairly accounts for his *ideological* commitment to a certain way of philosophizing and a certain rhetorical sensibility. Despite his own protestations—or rather, preferring to follow the implications of the second epigraph to this chapter rather than the first—I am thus venturing a tie between Leibowitz's worldview and the places where, as Cavell might say, he came into possession of a world viewed.

It is not finally a distinction between Eastern and Western Europe that matters here and that Leibowitz is entirely correct in gainsaying. Rather, it is Leibowitz's own provenance *as a Westerner*, Germanically influenced, that affixes itself to his Judaism, laming it a little, yet again, as the Angel does Jacob. My question would be: is such laming the mark of philosophy?[21] In Leibowitz's case especially, because he identifies himself so vehemently as discursively halakhic rather than aggadic (I mean this in the same plastic sense I have applied throughout), "belonging to the Western world" signifies a voice that speaks through a prior discourse, authoritative, distanced.

Partly, of course, this is a matter of the specific community in and to which Leibowitz (and more so, even Levinas) speak, thickening the notion of community I have sketched so far. I am not sure that Leibowitz ever saw himself as a "Jewish philosopher" in the sense associated with Rosenzweig or Levinas. Rather, he directly addressed contemporary cultural and politic contexts within Israeli society, and as such spoke to the citizenry of Jews in *Eretz Yisrael*. Levinas, too, as I have intimated for the writings discussed here, addressed an ambient community of French intellectuals (other examples of French-Jewish voices within that same community would be Albert Memmi, Alain Finkielkraut, Benny Lévy, Shmuel Trigano).

It is in this sense that place could be said perhaps most concretely to impinge upon the philosopher as he hears himself addressing someone specific, some specific community—vividly captured in the anecdote from Emil Fackenheim quoted in my introduction. Neither thinker, that is, philosophizes (in un-Jewish fashion) to the cosmos. But then both belong to an ancient Jewish genealogy in which a pietist-speaker speaks to and from within a locally constituted community standing for something grander and more capacious.

There is no question that Leibowitz felt the deep truth of Moses's words at his journey's end on the plains of Moav, כי קרוב אליך הדבר מאד בפיך ובלבבך לעשותו, For the matter is very near you, in your mouth and your heart, to perform it (Deut. 30:14).[22] And similarly, there is no question that he felt as well the proximity of the Sages as mediated by the figure of Maimonides, in both the realization of the Halakhah through mitzvot, and his meta-halakhic justification for it. And yet, to refer to Moses again before the assembled congregation of Israel, if indeed this commandment that I command you today is not hidden from you and it is not distant (Deut. 30:11), then perhaps it is not wholly inaccurate to situate the distant and the hidden (in the sense of subliminal) in the context of rhetorical claims on Leibowitz's allegiance imposed upon him by philosophy. Writes Cavell in the same passage quoted above, "To discover what is being said to us, as to discover what we are saying, is to discover the precise location from which it is said; to understand why it is said from just there, and at that time" (64).

And from this, I believe, we learn a modern lesson about genealogy in its non-ancient sense. In Levinas's case, of course, discursive provenance, the filiality of intellectual traditions, is not only enacted but referenced, and thus reflexive in the best sense. As I have suggested, while Levinas's philosophically trained readers tend for obvious reasons to defend his own distinction between the two dimensions of his work as offered in an interview from 1984, the cleavage is bridged by him too often elsewhere for us to fall complacently into the breach. In the passage that follows, for instance, he proposes the resemblance between midrash and philosophical inquiry that I mention above, each style of thought alternately self-evident and dependent on exegesis:

A way of speaking that incorporates, and enlivens, that more confidential, closed and firm manner more closely linked to the bearers of meaning—bearers who will never be released from the duties of the signified. . . . Such are the biblical verses, and even the terms used in their first, ancient deciphering by the sages of the Talmud. Tireless signifiers! But one day it is discovered that philosophy is also multiple, and that its truth is hidden, has levels and goes progressively deeper, that its texts contradict one another and that the systems are fraught with internal contradictions. Thus, it seems to me essential to consider the fact that the Jewish reading of the Scriptures is carried out in the anxiety, but also the hopeful expectation of *midrash*. (*ITN* 169)

An *anxiety* of method: the phrase does perfect justice to what I earlier called the twofold vocational imperative that Levinas consistently measured himself against.

As we know, philosophy and Judaism are always linguistically differentiated for Levinas, one speaking in Greek, the other in Hebrew. And yet "Greek" philosophy is pre-Christian philosophy, just as "Hebrew" Judaism is, as it were, prediasporic, before the saturation into other geographies and the languages of those geographies. *Philosophy as a set of Jews* by no means need connote Jews whose linguistic loyalties are identical to those narrated by the Bible. To clarify: by restricting themselves to the Levinasian (or Arnoldian) terms of opposition, what "Greek" readers of Levinas fail to mark, however, is the very arc of modern history that underpins philosophy's closure, in its blind/deafness, to Judaism. If we think of Judaism as not just a biblical or even talmudic discourse, but say, a modern-exilic discourse that therefore speaks Yiddish, Ladino, and even Judeo-Arabic in addition to Hebrew, its very plenitude of language and dialect *opens beyond what modern French, German, and English philosophy can see and perhaps beyond what they are willing to know.*

Levinas, like Leibowitz, was born into a Jewish Eastern European family where Yiddish shadowed Hebrew as Judaism's other tongue, the language of exile spoken in living room, in study hall, in the street. And although Levinas's writings do not speak in that tongue—nor do Leibowitz's—it would nevertheless do both of them an injustice to forget the whole world of language Yiddish opened up for them and gave them access to, a *tertium quid* that unsettles the neat, binary simplicity of Greek/Hebrew, Athens/Jerusalem, or Shem/Japheth.

In language, one is always on surer ground speaking of dialect rather than dialectical synthesis, or antonyms (and thus also homonyms and synonyms), rather than antinomy. That is to say, there are linguistic truths and there are philosophical truths, and sometimes the truths demonstrated by linguistic evolution and fecundity *just are* their philosophical truth. To propose that philosophy is a set of Jews is also to propose that in this instance the Jews who became philosophers *spoke Yiddish*, in addition to reading biblical Hebrew or speaking its modern counterpart. And it is to propose implicitly that the advent of something like Yiddish in Jewish history demonstrates the most powerful evidence for place, for geography, for diaspora, on and within consciousness. It is in Yiddish that we come upon lexical and semantic differences pointing out a world in which Jews have been dispersed—in, but not necessarily of, any number of adopted homes.

Take, for instance, the difference between the separate words in Yiddish for book—בוך, *bukh*—and holy book—ספֿר, *seyfer*, where Hebrew, both rabbinic and modern, would know only the single word ספר, *sefer* (which aptly enough connotes "boundary mark" in addition to "writing" and "telling"). Or, conversely, the non-synonymous relation between Yiddish חגא—*khoge* (non-Jewish holiday)—and יום-טוב—*yom-tov* (Jewish holiday)—whereas the two words possess an identical meaning in Hebrew. Or the difference, in Yiddish, between חכמה—*khokhme* (wisdom)—and װיסן—*vissn* (knowledge)—the latter of which, in its European provenance, possesses no real analogue in Hebrew. Or finally, the Yiddish שטאָט—*shtot* (city)—which discloses a world unimaginable from within the ancient confines of the Hebrew עיר, its ostensible synonym. For the Hebrew word denotes Enoch (the city built by Cain, son of Adam, and the first biblical city mentioned as such), Jerusalem in the time of the Prophets, and twentieth-century Tel Aviv alike.

My point of course, is that the Greek/Hebrew or Athens/Jerusalem polarity, useful perhaps for schematic purposes, offers no way of voicing the very sort of intellectual, geographic, and lingual itineraries Emmanuel Levinas and Yeshayahu Leibowitz can claim for themselves as traditionally educated Jews who practice philosophy. In Levinas's case, that means: from Yiddish, Hebrew, and Russian, to German and French; or concomitantly, from Kovno to Freiburg to Paris, In Leibowitz's case, that means: from Yiddish, Hebrew, and Russian to German and French; or concomitantly, from Riga to Basel to Jerusalem. And even if the Jewish demotic of Yiddish never becomes an explicit focal point for either thinker, like Aramaic, and indeed modern Hebrew, it inflects, if only subliminally, the way each *speaks* to philosophy in a Jewish voice. For it is, after all, how each first spoke in a Jewish voice.

Thus, while Levinas's essay on S. Y. Agnon explicitly reserves for Hebrew the status of a "living, resuscitated language, whose birth was a resurrection" (*PN* 8), through whose "sonority" a bygone Jewish way of life is voiced and heard—to sharp ears, the expressive *beyond* of which this essay speaks invokes a *mameloshen* alongside the *fotershprakh*, shadowing and haunting it. Levinas begins the essay by saying that poetry's essence is to signify "only between the lines—between times—like . . . an echo preceding the sound of a voice" (7). Such is also Yiddish, Hebrew's echo in a certain sense, but also assuredly the most tragically sonorous echo of the bygone life mourned by Agnon's stories. In those stories "what is at stake is resurrection. Closer to us than any present, the Unrepresentable will not be represented in the poem" (12). Likewise, but conjured between the line's of Agnon's fiction and Levinas's essay alike, the unvoiced, the unheard, the *beyond*, the trace, also leads us inevitably to the common tongue in which Agnon and Levinas (had they met), would have no doubt conversed.[23] One of its proper names, designating the language otherwise known as Yiddish, is "Jewish."[24]

TOWARD JERUSALEM . . . AND "MYSELF"

I expected to be questioned, and was attentive and curious in advance. Your first words appear to direct the conversation more particularly toward myself. Judaism and philosophy: I was thinking of their manifestation in history. But you seem to want to lead me to speak of myself. (*ITN* 167)[25]

This is Levinas in an interview that makes up the essay "On Jewish Philosophy" from *In the Time of Nations*. To be sure, what I have called the reach and portage of place for the philosopher throughout this book is not what Levinas means when he says in *Beyond the Verse* that all philosophical thought rests upon prephilosophical experience. He would probably be no less vigorous than Leibowitz in rejecting any attempt to explain someone's views by where he comes from or who he is. But then, I have been interested not so much in "explaining" Levinas or Leibowitz in this inquiry as in *projecting, filling out their voice*, and breaking it down into its several planes or idiolects.

"The proper names in the middle of all those common names and common-places—do they not help us speak?" Such has been the implicit interrogative burden every time I have written the name "Levinas" or "Leibowitz," "Emmanuel" or "Yeshayahu," Jewish vocables, all—though in the case of "Levinas" (like "Kaunas" or "Vilnius"), remapped by means of a Lithuanian suffix. With Levinas at least, I discover a minor affinity, as I come full circle finally to the end of this inquiry. West rather than East to Palestine and much further West than France, emigrating to America entails a particular struggle with the angel modernity whereby my own family name, *Novogrodsky*, becomes lamed by its metamorphosis into the anglicized *Newton*.

Such change of name is perhaps what the character David Levinsky has in mind in Abraham Cahan's novel when he speaks of the marvelous transformations possible in the New World—the place that Jews with deeper roots to Eastern Europe and further East to Jerusalem called *a treifene medine*, a profane land. It certainly discloses a Jewishness that walks a tightrope: between an immemorial past and an historical present, between home and an estrangement into foreign places. In my own family's case, it marks the difference between a Novogrodsky whose patrimony lay in the small town of Strezgowo in southern Poland but was transplanted to New York City, and the Novogrodskys who remained in the country of their birth, to perish there when the Jewish community of Strzegowo was annihilated except for fifteen souls in the final years of the Second World War.[26]

Beneath that same tightrope are spanned not just the signs, attributes, contents, qualities, and values of a comparatavist mentality

Levinas assigns to the University—a means of identification "defined by its refusal to adhere to anything until it performs an act of adhesion." Traversed as well are family histories and places—a means of identification "which is founded on an adherence that pre-exists any form of allegiance": *Levinas, Leibowitz, Latvia, Lithuania, Eretz Yisrael*—proper names and also inescapable and utterly specific syllables.

This is the tightrope maneuvered by the philosophers to whom I have endeavored to give voice here, however they themselves made sense of their national or geographic allegiances. It is, less loftily but still a matter of record, the tightrope walked by my own reterritorialized family as well. Through an awareness of how Jewish identities can thus be forged midst striated Jewish and non-Jewish realities—the fences and neighbors of idiom and culture—rather than by means of a facile dividing line between (Hebrew) Judaism and (Greek) philosophy, we better appreciate Levinas's and Leibowitz's standing—their place—as Jewish philosophers, philosopher-Jews, or simply vocational exemplars of "doing philosophy Jewishly." It is in this way, I would suggest, that we reach the outermost boundaries, mother-lingual and natal, of "The Fence and the Neighbor: Israel among the Nations." For Kovno, Riga, and even Strezgowo: these are proper names, inescapable and utterly specific syllables, too.

NOTES

PREFACE: FENCES AND NEIGHBORS

1. I follow the spirit of Richard Poirier's expert reading of the poem in *Robert Frost: The Work of Knowing* (New York: Oxford University Press, 1977), 104–106.

2. See the essay, "On Extravagance" in Robert Frost, *Collected Poems, Prose, and Plays* (New York: Library of America, 1995).

3. The word, שכן, is also used in the Oral Torah to signify neighbor, in the sense of settler, as in *Shabbat* 39b and *Avot* 1:7; relevantly enough, this term for neighbor derives from the same root as *Shekhinah*, the rabbinic term for Divine Presence (see, for instance, Num. 35:34). Ernst Simon's essay, "The Neighbor (*Re'a*) Whom We Shall Love," in *Modern Jewish Ethics: Theory and Practice*, ed. Marvin Fox (Columbus: Ohio State University Press, 1975), 29–57, teases out many of the ambiguities here, as does Harold Frisch's response, 57–61; see also Jacob Katz, *Exclusiveness and Tolerance: Studies in Jewish Gentile-Relations in Medieval & Modern Times* (New York: Oxford University Press: 1961).

4. Walter Benjamin says something very similar in his essay "Unpacking my Library": "For such a man [the book-collector] is speaking to you and on closer scrutiny he proves to be speaking only about himself." *Illuminations*, trans. Harry Zohn (New York: Schocken Books, 1969), 59.

5 Levinas's oblique autobiographical coda to *Difficult Freedom: Essays on Judaism*, trans. Seán Hand (Baltimore: The Johns Hopkins University Press, 1990) is entitled "Signature."

6. Cavell's phrase for philosophy's arrogation of the right to speak for us, the demand placed on the philosopher to "autobiographize or sign the world" (*Pitch*, 35). While distinct from "pitch" in this sense, compare Peter Fenves's excursus on "tone" in *Raising the Tone of Philosophy* (Baltimore: Johns Hopkins University Press, 1993).

INTRODUCTION: SIGNING THE WORLD

1. Richardson adds the following: "On another more formal occasion, someone with the same experience asked: 'What do you see in Heidegger? What can you hope for as a Christian from the thought of that God-less man?' In effect, the same question lies behind Dr. Jonas's reproach to the theologians at Drew: 'My theological friends, my Christian friends—don't you see what you are dealing with? Don't you sense if not see the profoundly pagan character of

Heidegger's thought?'" "Heidegger and God—and Professor Jonas," *Thought* 40 (Spring 1965): 13–40. Richard Cohen discusses Jonas's critique of Heidegger's paganism in *Elevations: The Height of the Good in Rosenzweig and Levinas* (Chicago: University of Chicago Press, 1984), 300–304.

2. "The defense of [Richardson's] book's theses has passed into legend (or apocrypha): almost every important anyone in what is now known as "continental" philosophy was there (Ricoueur, Levinas, etc., as well as several contributors to the present collection) and its author delivered himself of the same *tour de force* that continues to characterize his every public presentation" (Babette E. Babich, *From Phenomenology to Thought, Errancy, and Desire: Essays in the Honor of William S. Richardson, S.J.* [Dordrecht: Kluwer Academic Publishers, 1995], xi). This particular public presentation was published in *Ethics as First Philosophy: The Significance of Emmanuel Levinas for Philosophy, Literature, and Religion*, ed. Aadrian Peperzak (New York: Routledge, 1995), without reference to the earlier article from *Thought*.

3. John Murray Cuddihy's concept of Jewish authenticity in its encounter with a "Protestant esthetic and Protestant etiquette" as shaping forces in modern culture, from *The Ordeal of Civility: Freud, Marx, Lévi-Strauss, and the Jewish Struggle with Modernity* (Boston: Beacon Press, 1987). In the *Mishneh Torah* (*Hilkhot De'ot* 6:6–9), discussing the Levitical commandment (19:17) to rebuke one's fellow Jew in his errancy, Maimonides distinguishes between warranted censure and public shaming. He quotes '*Arakhin* 16b: rebuke should stop short of causing a person's "face to change," a Levinasian *regard de l'regard* of basic importance in the Oral Law (see also Mishna *Avot* 3:14, *Bava Metzia* 58b and the Rashba (R. Solomon ibn Adret): "Be aware that a soft spoken word shatters bones, and different ways will clear a path before the people to remove obstacles from them."

4. In *Otherwise Than Being; Or, Beyond Essence* (The Hague: Martinus Nijhoff, 1987), Levinas says of the self's ab-original position vis-à-vis others, "One must not think of it as the state of original sin; it is, on the contrary, the original goodness of creation" (155) the classical stance in Judaism. Compare "From the Rise of Nihilism to the Carnal Jew," in *Difficult Freedom*: "To be persecuted, to be guilty without having committed any crime, is not an original sin, but the obverse of a universal responsibility—a responsibility for the other that is more ancient than any sin. It is an invisible universality! It is the reverse of a choosing that puts forward the self before it is even free to accept being chosen. It is for the others to see if they wish to take advantage of it. It is for the free self to fix the limits of this responsibility or to claim entire responsibility. But it can do so only in the name of that original responsibility, in the name of this Judaism" (225). The Talmudic reading in the same volume, one of Levinas's most exquisite and complex, "Messianic Texts," contains its own luminous disquisition on the meaning of "fallenness," 75–76. In a parallel historicist vein (in the light of Toynbee, say), it is equally disconcerting to run across such obtuseness about Jewish self-understanding in a work like Marcel Gauchet's *The Disenchantment of the World: A Political History of Religion*, trans. Oscar Burge (Princeton: Princeton University Press, 1997). In this otherwise powerful critique, Judaism is seen as either "Mosaic" or "Prophetic" (i.e., biblical), but in

any event superseded by the advent of Christianity; the whole of the Oral Tradition remains unacknowledged; see by contrast, "The Ark and the Mummy" (*DF* 54–55). To be sure, post-Biblical Judaism (like Koranic Islam), acknowledges an existential "fall," from the Garden into the quotidian and from human immortality into the capacity for death (as for example, in the midrashic *Seder Eliyahu Rabbah 5* and *Deut. Rabba 9.8*). But this is still distinct, both discursively and theologically, from the programmatic Christian concept of inherent and disseminated sinfulness.

5. "Thus it is that the voice of Israel is at best heard in the world only as the voice of a precursor, as the voice of the Old Testament that—to use a phrase from Buber—the rest of us who are Jews have no reason to consider either a testament or old, or something to be situated in the perspective of the new" (*DF* 13). "The Old Testament does not prefigure the New: it receives its interpretation from the Talmud . . . which is no longer treated archaeologically or historically but as a form of teaching" (161). Also, "For a Jewish Humanism," 273–276, and "Judaeo-Christian Friendship," 202.

6. *Openings* includes the essays, "Judaeo-Christian Friendship," "Israel and Universalism," and "Religion and Tolerance." Also, the essays "A Voice on Israel" and "Poetry and the Impossible," a critique of Paul Claudel, in the same volume.

7. In his letter, Richardson's interlocutor writes, "when we philosophers do our job . . . we see the hopelessness of life-on-its-own (if there is such a thing) and its requirement that we forgive each other (including Heidegger and Levinas) as we all participate in disasters and in other events of lesser injury and wrong that arise out of our fallenness and separation from God, i.e., out of a loss of God that is originary in our actions" (230). But the simple, morally peremptory thrust of Levinas's rebuke was that in 1943, he, a Jew, was in peril of his life, while Heidegger, a German Christian and member of the Nazi party, enjoyed the benefits of the Third Reich. The two cannot possibly be symmetrical partners in a retroactive act of forgiveness that even others stage for them, nor can the particularity of Levinas's disaster be commensurated with "other disasters and events of lesser injury and wrong." Interestingly enough, Robert Eaglestone, in his book *Ethical Criticism: Reading After Levinas* (Edinburg: Edinburgh University Press, 1998), quotes this same passage by Fackenheim, only to reach the opposite conclusion: Levinas's particularity ultimately "stands for" the universal. In the same way as he implicitly elides the particularity of rabbinic Judaism for Levinas by speaking rather of a common Western heritage embodied by "the Bible," so he writes in the context of twentieth-century history of "a Judaism at the heart of Levinas's thought . . . a 'Judaism' which is not limited to the Jewish people, but to all peoples" (6). That the Holocaust was an event not confined to Jews does not, however, make Judaism common metaphorical property. Indeed, though Levinas does speak from time to time of "the Jew in every man" as analogous to "the proletarian, the stranger, the persecuted," he makes his own ambivalence on this score eloquently clear on the dedicatory page to *Otherwise Than Being; Or, Beyond Essence*—one epitaph, in French, dedicated to "victims of the same hatred of the other man, the same anti-semitism" (which Eaglestone quotes) the other, a *Yizkor* prayer in Hebrew, ded-

icated to the memory of relatives who perished in the Nazi occupation (which Eaglestone does not). The Hebrew, in other words, does not translate the French. It should be remembered that Levinas's Lithuania saw the destruction of 94 percent of its 240,000 Jews, the highest percentage of any European during the war. See the preface and "Demanding Judaism" in *Beyond the Verse: Talmudic Readings and Lectures*, trans. Gary D. Mole (Bloomington: Indiana University Press, 1994), 3–10; and also *She'elot U'Teshuvot Me'Ma'amakim (Responsa Out of the Depths)* by R. Efraim Oshry of Kovno (Levinas's birthplace).

8. Even the title of Rüdiger Safranski's *Martin Heidegger: Between Good and Evil* (Cambridge: Harvard University Press, 1997), seems to answer Richardson's own, *Heidegger: Through Phenomenology to Thought* (The Hague: Nijhoff, 1974), but on its own merits it makes a valuable companion-piece in interrogating just how "prolific" Heidegger's years were during the Nazi ascendancy and afterwards.

9. *Testimony: Crises of Witnessing in Literature, Psychoanalysis, and History* by Shoshana Felman and Dori Laub (New York: Routledge, 1992), is an immediately relevant companion text here.

10. The papers have been collected in *Ethics as First Philosophy: The Significance of Emmanuel Levinas for Philosophy, Literature, and Religion*, the first two of which situate Levinas within Jewish contexts. Yet the book is arranged in such a way that none of the essays under the heading "Religion" discusses Judaism. Richardson's contribution is perhaps best answered with reference to Levinas's own elegy, "Nameless," from *Proper Names*, trans. Michael B. Smith (Stanford: Stanford University Press, 1996), 119–123. The following excerpt from Charles Scott's paper, "A People's Witness Beyond Politics," 25–35, sad to say, speaks for itself: "Although I believe that Levinas's work is moved by the persona of the rabbi who is also a philosopher, the neighbor is not dependent on the rabbi. The rabbi is dependent on the neighbor. More than dependent, the rabbi stands in unnecessary indebtedness before the other, and, as rabbi, kills what is to be killed as surely as the nonrabbi kills. And kills in his or her effort to free the other as other" (32). Perhaps even sadder to say, six years later at the 1999 conference at Emory University, "Addressing Levinas: Ethics, Phenomenology, and the Judaic Tradition," the situation had changed little if at all. If we take the conference title to signify place or location, a Jewishly specific *address* for Levinas was distressingly absent, "the Judaic Tradition" having been shunted into a single, sparsely attended panel.

11. Solecisms in the translations of Levinas's essay are only the most obvious instance of such disregard. Similarly, much of the premier scholarship by philosophers and postmodernists this late in Levinas's reception indicates little or no attempt to consult classical rabbinic sources even in translation. Recent examples in English are: Adriaan Peperzak, *Beyond: The Philosophy of Emmanuel Levinas* (Evanston: Northwestern University Press, 1997), Simon Critchley, *Ethics, Politics Subjectivity: Essays on Levinas, Derrida, and Contemporary French Thought* (New York: Verso, 1999), Dennis Keenan, *Death and Responsibility: The "Work" of Levinas* (Albany: State University of New York Press, 1999), and Jill Robbins, *Altered Readings: Levinas and Literature*

(Chicago: The University of Chicago Press, 1999); in French and German: Fabio Ciamerelli, *Transcendence et éthique: Essai sur Lévinas* (Brussels: Ousia, 1989, Thomas Freyer, ed., *Emmanuel Levinas: Fragen an die Moderne* (Vienna: Passagen-Verlag, 1996). An exception is Tamra Wright's conspectus (briefly adducing Leibowitz, R. Lichtenstein and Fackenheim), *The Twilight of Jewish Philosophy: Emmanuel Levinas' Ethical Hermeneutics* (Singapore: Harwood Publishers, 1999).

12. Levinas pointedly preferred to be identified himself not as a Jewish thinker but as "a Jew who thinks, and also thinks Judaism," as can be gleaned from his conversations with Richard Kearney in *Face to Face with Levinas* , ed. Richard Cohen (Albany: State University of New York Press, 1986), and with François Poirié in *Emanuel Lévinas—Qui êtes vous?* (Lyon: La Manufacture, 1987). Significantly, the philosophical writings and the Jewish essays are brought out by different publishers. But even if we honor Levinas's allegiance to giving "Greek" form to "Hebrew" wisdom while preserving the distinction between the two, the interpenetration of discourses is unmistakable. See the essays by Richard Cohen, Jonathan E. Bauer, and Ephraim Meir on Levinas's place in the academy in *Jewish Philosophy and the Academy*, ed. Emil Fackenheim and Raphael Jospe (London: Associated University Presses, 1996), and by Robert Gibbs, Ze-ev Levy, Ephraim Meir, and Annette Aronowicz on Levinas's position in modern philosophy in *Paradigms in Jewish Philosophy*, ed. Raphael Jospe (London: Associated University Presses, 1997).

13. "On Jewish Philosophy" in *In The Time of Nations*, trans. Michael B. Smith, (Bloomington: Indiana University Press, 1995), 167–183, is insistent, however, about *"making the implicit philosophy of rabbinic study explicit."* In "Messianic Texts" from *Difficult Freedom*, he writes, "But we none the less begin with the idea that this [religious] meaning is not only transposable into a philosophical language, but refers to philosophical problems. The thought of the Doctors of the Talmud proceeds from a meditation that is radical enough also to satisfy the demands of philosophy" (68). Marc-Alain Ouaknin's *The Burnt Book: Reading the Talmud*, trans. Llewellyn Brown (Princeton: Princeton University Press, 1995) is a marvelous companion book to Levinas here (it quotes him often) since it actively merges traditional rabbinic self-understanding with postmodern criteria.

14. See the essays by Menachem Kellner, Barry Kogan, Norbert Samuelson, and Steven Schwartzschild in *Studies in Jewish Philosophy: Collected Essays of the Academy for Jewish Philosophy, 1980–1985*, ed. Norbert M. Samuelson (Lanham, Md.: University Press of America, 1987). Kellner makes a useful distinction (though not hard or fast) between medieval Jewish "philosophy" seen as *product* and modern Jewish "thought" understood as *process*. "To think politically about Judaism and to think Jewishly about politics" (David Novak, in a review), is the thrust of an extraordinary volume published as this book was going to press—*The Jewish Political Tradition: Vol. 1: Authority*, ed. Walzer, Lorberbaum, and Zohar (New Haven: Yale University Press, 2000.

15. Compare also by Schwartzschild, the essay "The Lure of Immanence—The Crisis in Contemporary Religious Thought," in *Tradition* (Spring 1997): 70–99. As an obvious example, Levinas's ethic of being responsible for the

other's responsibility fairly parallels the basic halakhic concept of *arvut* (guar-anty)—that Jews are obligated in and for the religious obligations of others: unless every person's obligations have been fulfilled, none has.

16. See Richard's Cohen's introduction to *New Talmudic Readings* (Pitts-burgh: Duquesne University Press), 25. A classic instance is the case of the idol-atrous city in Deut. 13:15: *you shall smite the inhabitants of that city . . . lay it waste.* Maimonides, following the Talmud, rules that after two Torah scholars are sent to the city, if its people repent, it is no longer the same city—i.e, "*that city*"—and must not be destroyed (*Hilkhot Avodah Zara* 4:5).

17. Compare Schwartzschild: "I have no doubt in my mind that the most important living Jewish philosopher today is Emmanuel Levinas. . . . Now, Lev-inas is, of course, a very self-conscious and knowledgeable Jew, and he writes a good deal about matters specifically Jewish. But there is a peculiar twist to this: Levinas often and rather vehemently asserts that what he does philosophically is not specifically Jewish, and vice-versa. Just about all his philosophical explica-tors take their cue from him about this. But this is demonstrable rubbish" (104).

18. Fackenheim's essay is included in the volume *Jewish Philosophy and the Academy*. Despite my qualification above, Robert Gibbs's *Correlations in Rosenweig and Levinas* (Princeton: Princeton University Press, 1992) and Richard Cohen's *Elevations: the Height of the Good in Rosenzweig and Levinas* are exemplary treatments of Levinas's place in modern Jewish philosophy; Cohen is especially good on a Judeo-Christian bias that Levinas and Rozenzweig share. See also Michael Oppenheim, *Speaking/Writing of God: Jewish Philo-sophical Reflections on the Life with Others* (Albany: State University of New York Press, 1997); Susan Handleman, *fragments of Redemption: Jewish Thought and Literary Theory in Benjamin, Scholem, and Levinas* (Bloomington: Indiana University Press, 1991); and the web journal *Textual Reasoning* spon-sored by the Postmodern Jewish Philosophy Network.

19. Even in his more recent books, Fackenheim has yet to devote an extended treatment to Levinas, who, when mentioned, is coupled with Leo Strauss as an example of post-Holocaust Jewish philosophy. In addition to *Jew-ish Philosophy and the Academy*, see the chapter, "What Is Jewish Philosophy?" in *Jewish Philosophers and Jewish Philosophy* (Bloomington: Indiana University Press, 1996); and also *Dark Riddle: Hegel, Nietzsche, and the Jews* (University Park: Penn State University Press, 1998) by Yirmiyahu Yovel and *Altared Ground: Levinas, History, and Violence* (New York: Routledge, 1996) by Brian Schroeder for more recent encounters between Judaism and modern philosophy (specifically, Hegel, Nietzsche, and Heidegger).

20. Levinas, I think, clarifies the terms in dispute here, a first glimpse of the distance separating himself and Leibowitz (or in this instance, his closeness to Fackenheim): "But this is why we must follow with more confidence everything that in our young generation is attracted to generous actions, even when this young generation no longer bears the label of Judaism or expressly rejects it. There are abnegations that atone for denial. By closing ourselves to the Jews who are without Judaism but who, without Judaism, act as Jews, we risk end-ing up with a Judaism without Jews" (271).

21. A certain clandestinity does as well (though I do not imply an analogy),

when the Lubavitcher Rebbe writes in his 1974 book on faith and secular knowledge, "It is very dangerous and harmful to see the Torah—as is done by a certain professor in Jerusalem—as something separate from the world and distinct from everyday life." Aviezer Ravitsky's surmise in *Messianism, Zionism, and Jewish Religious Radicalism*, trans. Michael Swirsky and Jonathan Chipman (Chicago: The University of Chicago Press, 1996), coincides with my own that the "certain professor" here is almost definitely Leibowitz himself (189). R. Schneerson's remarks can be found in *Emunah u–Mada: Iggerot Kodesh* (Kfar Chabad, 1974), 51, 146.

22. Fackenheim offers his own anecdotal explanation for his umbrage at Leibowitz: "Some lessons of the three months in Sachsenhausen were to become part and parcel of my thought. The concentration camp first taught me to dislike theologies (Christian as well as Jewish) that are concerned with the fate of Judaism but are indifferent—or so high-minded as to be above concern with—that of Jews" (243).

23. The cities are less than a hundred miles apart. The first (Kaunas, its Lithuanian name) is located in south–central Lithuania, the second, a seaport, is the capital of Latvia. From the perspective of Jewish Eastern Europe, of course, the two cities are more or less neighbors. Both were German-influenced on account of the Prussian Empire's reach, though because of its location within the Pale of Settlement, Kovno was arguably the more Slavic of the two. It is a difference borne out, I think, in Levinas's and Leibowitz's respective intellectual loyalties. Where the former considered himself the cultural legatee of Russian literary tradition (Levinas often alludes to Tolstoy, Dostoevsky, Gogol, and Vassily Grossman), the latter demonstrated a wholly Germanic pertinacity, having been educated, moreover, in Germany and Switzerland before making *aliyah* in 1934. On the roots of their shared cultural background—*litvisch* (Lithuanian) sensibilities, maskilic leanings (more so for Levinas than Leibowitz), and mitnagdic austerity—see Allan Nadler, *The Faith of the Mithnagdim: Rabbinic Responses to Hasidic Rapture* (Baltimore: The Johns Hopkins University Press, 1997), together with the same author's disparaging critique of Leibowitz's "legal positivism" in *Commentary* 95.5 (November 1992): 57–59.

24. Both use the figure of Abraham contrastively. Levinas, in his philosophical writings (*Totality and Infinity*, for example) and his essays on Judaism, measures Abraham against Odysseus (the type who comes full circle as opposed to moving ever outward from the self and toward the Other). Leibowitz, rather, pits the binding of Isaac against the Crucifixion as antithetical models of human submission: Abraham is the fullest expression of man's absolute mastery over his own nature (Leibowitz cites Abravanel: "He overcame his materiality"), in contradistinction to Jesus-as-medium through which God fulfills man's need for salvation. Leibowitz's use of the *akedah* is habitual, almost compulsive, and always serves the one-dimensional thrust of his argument. Jerome Gellman's *The Fear, The Trembling, and the Fire: Kierkegaard and Hasidic Masters on the Binding of Isaac* (Lanham, Md.: University Press of America, 1994) offers a much less monothematic approach, by contrast.

25. Alain Finkielkraut's *The Wisdom of Love*, trans. Kevin O'Neill and David Suchoff (Lincoln: University of Nebraska Press, 1996), is one of the few

attempts to situate Levinas thus, but even Finkielkraut confines his presentation of Levinas's thought to the strictly philosophical writings, and for the most part eschews the Talmudic readings and essays on Judaism. For discussions of Levinas's place against a background of more classical Jewish texts, see Jacob Meskin, "Critique, Tradition, and the Religious Imagination: An Essay on Levinas' Talmudic Readings," in *Judaism* (Winter 1998): 91–106, and responses to it in the web journal *Textual Reasoning* 5.3 (1996); the introductions by Annette Aronowicz to *Nine Talmudic Readings by Emmanuel Levinas* (Bloomington: Indiana University Press), 1990 and Richard Cohen to *New Talmudic Readings*; and Ira Stone's looser treatment, *Reading Levinas/Reading Talmud* (Philadelphia: Jewish Publication Society, 1998).

26. See Hartman, *A Living Covenant: The Innovative Spirit in Traditional Judaism* (New York: The Free Press, 1985), and *Conflicting Visions: Spiritual Possibilities of Modern Israel* (New York: Schocken Books, 1990); Avi Sagi, "Contending with Modernity: Scripture in the Thought of Yeshayahu Leibowitz and Joseph Soloveitchik," *Journal of Religion* 77.3 (July 1997): 421–441, and also the related studies by Eliezer Berkovits, *Crisis and Faith* (New York: Sanhedrin Press, 1976), and *Major Themes in Modern Philosophies of Judaism: A Critical Evaluation* (New York: Ktav, 1974). The estimations, upon his death in 1994, of Leibowitz's place in Jewish thought vary considerably. Haim Marantz's eulogy, in "Bearing Witness: Morality and Religion in the Thought of Yeshayahu Leibowitz," *Judaism: A Quarterly Journal of Jewish Life and Thought* 46.1 (Winter 1997): 35–45, lauds him both as committed intellectual and Zionist. Avishai Margalit's "Prophets with Honor: Israelis Martin Buber and Yeshayahu Leibowitz," in *The New York Review of Books* 4.18 (November 4, 1993): 66–71, positions him in the company of a counterfigure of similar though very different stature; and Moshe Halbertal's review of Leibowitz's collected essays in *The New Republic* 208.11 (March 15, 1993): 35–38, offers, in my view, the most perspicuous judgment of that stature, generally. Yehudah Mirsky's review of the same book in *The New Leader* 75.11 (September 7, 1992): 18–20, on the other hand, is censorious and unimpressed. For surpassing contempt, probably nothing approaches Hillel Halkin's "Israel against Itself: Yeshayahu Leibowitz and Israel's Trading of Land for Peace," *Commentary* 98.5 (November 1994): 33–39, which reckons Leibowitz a mediocre thinker and a misguided polemicist who defaults into the hands of the dovish Israeli Left while lending it the mantle of undeserved religiosity.

27. Isaiah Berlin himself, in his important essay I treat in chapter 2, "Kant as an Unfamiliar Source of Nationalism," enjoys an instructive proximity to the austere antisubjectivism of both Leibowitz and Levinas. It is precisely in his ethical humanist-anthropology, Berlin argues, that Kant lays an ideological foundation for state idolatry through magnified or perverted versions of (1) the doctrine of autonomous will, and (2) a surrogate absolutism that modulates from an axiological duty to universal reason to self-legitimating notions of national will. The rational, and therefore moral subjective agent, by analogy, presents a model for quasipersonalized, *volkish* concepts of history and the State. See *The Senses of Reality: Studies in Ideas and Their History* (London: Chatto and Windis, 1996), 32–248. David Hartman's *A Living Covenant* gives an explicit

and critical reading of Leibowitz's radicality in relation to Maimonides on one side and Rav Soloveitchik on the other. Jonathan Sacks's *Crisis and Covenant: Jewish Thought after the Holocaust* (Manchester: Manchester University Press 1992) assigns Leibowitz a place in contemporary Jewish thought he calls "radical orthodoxy." Finally, Aviezer Ravitsky's *Messianism, Zionism, and Jewish Religious Radicalism* clarifies the ambient Orthodox climate in Israel from within which Leibowitz's iconoclasm so singularly stands out.

28. Leibowitz's "halakhic man" and R. Soloveitchik's (discussed in the next chapter) articulated famously in his *Halakhic Man*, trans. Lawrence Kaplan (Philadelphia: Jewish Publication Society, 1983), are not identical, nor is their purchase on the centrality of Maimonides in Jewish thought. Compare Allan Nadler, "Soloveitchik's Halakhic Man: Not a Mithnagged," in *Modern Judaism* 13 (1993): 119–147; Aharon Lichtenstein, "R. Joseph Soloveitchik," in *Great Jewish Thinkers of the Twentieth Century*, ed. S. Noveck (Philadelphia: Jewish Publication Society, 1963); Moshe Koppel, *Meta-Halakhah: Logic, Intuition and the Unfolding of Jewish Law* (Northvale, N.J.: Jason Aronson, 1996); Eliezer Berkovits, *Not in Heaven: The Nature and Function of Halakha* (New York: Ktav, 1983); Joel Roth, *The Halakhic Process: A Systemic Analysis* (New York: Jewish Theological Seminary of America, 1986); and Avi Sagi, "Contending with Modernity," and *Yeshayhu Leibowitz: Ha Ish, Olamo, VaHaguto* (Jerusalem: Keter, 1995).

29. Yeshayahu Leibowitz, *The Faith of Maimonides*, trans. John Glucker (New York: Adam Books, 1987). See also David Hartman's *Maimonides: Torah and Philosophic Quest* (Philadelphia: Jewish Publication Society, 1976), and Norman Lamm's *Torah Lishmah: Torah for Its Own Sake in the Work of Rabbi Hayyim of Volozhin and his Contemporaries* (Hoboken, N.J.: Ktav, 1989). Not coincidentally in this regard, the only post-talmudic Jewish text to which Levinas makes constant recourse is the *Nefesh ha-Hayyim* by Hayyim of Volozhin, published in Vilna and Grodno in 1824.

30. "One cannot, in fact, be a Jew instinctively; one cannot be a Jew without knowing it. One must desire good with all one's heart and, at the same time, not simply desire it on the basis of a naive impulse of the heart. Both to maintain and to break this impulse is perhaps what constitutes the Jewish ritual. Passion mistrusts pathos, and becomes a *consciousness*! Belonging to Judaism presupposes a ritual and a science. Justice is impossible to the ignorant man. Judaism is an extreme consciousness" (*DF* 6).

31. "The other" is Levinas's term of choice (with the common orthographic distinction between human or divine other, *autrui*, and "other" as distinct from "the same," *autre*). But *neighbor* (*prochain* in French and closer to *k'rov* than *re'ah* in Hebrew in the multiple sense of "drawn near, attracted, offered"), more exactly captures the determinate sense of alterity as a constant approaching. The neighbor is a provocation—always "on the way toward" the self, but never commensurate with it.

32. Compare A. J. Heschel's paean to Jewish temporality, *The Sabbath* (New York: The Noonday Press, 1951).

33. Significantly, when captured by the Nazis in 1940 Levinas wore the uniform of a French soldier, which thus saved his life. At the end of his essay,

"Space Is Not One-Dimensional," a response to French charges of double loyalty after Israel's victory in 1967, he writes, "To 'go up' [the translation of Heb. *aliyah*] into Israel for a French Jew is certainly not to change nationality, it is to respond to a vocation" (*DF* 264). In this connection, the following recent studies of French Jewry are immensely helpful: Pierre Birnbaum, *Jewish Destinies: Citizenship, State and Community in Modern France*, trans. Arthur Goldhammer (New York: Hill and Wang, 2000); Vicki Caron, *Uneasy Asylum: France and the Jewish Refugee Crisis, 1933–1942* (Standford: Stanford University Press, 1999), and Paula E. Hyman, *The Jews of Modern France* (Berkeley: University of California Press, 1998).

34. See also "Education and Prayer," "For a Jewish Humanism," and "Anti-humanism and Education" in the same volume. I do not address Buber or Heschel in this book, although they are clearly towering figures in modern Jewish thought. Heschel, for instance, like R Soloveitchik (and the Lubavitcher Rebbe Menachem M. Schneerson, for that matter) made the formative intellectual trek from *ostjudische* beginnings to a more "Westernized" cultural consciousness in Berlin. Such westward migration of traditionally educated *talmidei hochamim* coincided with a more or less inverse phenomenon—the first intellectual encounter in the West with Eastern European Judaism. Unlike R. Soloveitchik and R. Schneerson, however Heschel veered markedly away from his roots to a more individualized and syncretic rapprochement between Orthodoxy and modernity. In addition to his many books and essays in theology, his biblical study of the Prophets, and a biography of the great Hasidic rabbi, Menachem Mendel of Kotsk, Heschel penned a monumental work on revelation in rabbinic texts, *Torah Min Ha'shamayim B'aspakalariyya Shel Ha'dorot (Torah from Heaven in the Mirror of the Generations)*, which eschews *halakhah* for more visionary and "poetic" midrashic literature (Heschel also wrote poetry in both Hebrew and Yiddish). See Yehudah Mirsky's helpful analysis of Heschel's place as philosopher-Jew in his article "The Rhapsodist," *The New Republic* (April 19, 1999): 36–42.

35. An abbreviated version of this *aggadah* is recounted by Alain Finkielkraut in his superb book on Levinas and cultural alterity, *The Wisdom of Love*. As Finkielkraut elegantly puts it, "Whether we bow before his craft or ridicule his clumsiness, Judah the tailor always reassumes his status as descriptively *qualified*. That is the fundamental violence of the scene . . . : to speak of a being is to inflict upon him the treatment as a third person singular. . . . We categorize him rather than respond to his summons: such is the essence of calumny, and lies are nothing but an intensified version of this fundamental evasion" (18–19).

36. The name given to this prohibition in the Oral Torah is שפיכות דמים, the spilling of blood. Maimonides says in *Rotze'ach* 1:4, "There is nothing about which the Torah is so insistent as *shfichut damim*." In legislating that it is preferable to give up one's own life than do murder, the Talmud (*Sanhedrin* 74a, *Pesachim* 25b, et al.) makes one of its most eloquent statements about human equality that Levinas surely sees inscribed in the injunction against murder: "What evidence do you have that your blood is redder—it may be that the other man's blood is redder?" Not unrelatedly, the talmudic term for the violence done to another through slander is מלבין פנים, "to whiten the face," that is, as if

one had drawn blood (*Bava Metzia* 58b) a connection drawn, for instance, by the eleventh-century commentator Abraham Ibn Ezra in explaining Ex. 20:13 as signifying murder by either hand or tongue. A later *perush* foucuses on the alternate vocalization of the word for murder—with a *patach* or open vowel in private recitation and *kamatz* or closed, for public reading—as intimating that where bodily (open) harm is forbidden even in private, so shaming someone, closing them up in the company of others, transgresses no less.

37. Intriguingly enough, this is the same kind of heavenly voice that the famous *aggadah* in *Bava Metzia* 59b declares as having ceded authority over Torah to human commonsense understanding.

38. "[When Rav Shimon died], all that day, the fire did not desist from the house, and no one approached it, since they could not as the fire was all around" (*Zohar Ha'azinu, Idra Zuta* III:296b). The fire serves as the basis for the custom of lighting bonfires on *Lag Ba-omer*, the traditional anniversary of Shimon bar Yochai's passing. But the implication here is similar to that of the Talmud's story: fire threatens to consume anyone not totally devoted, "like Rav Shimon and his colleagues," to תורה לשמה, Torah for its own sake (*Shabbat* 11a). Compare *Berakhot* 35b, in which the meaning of the verse in the *Shema*, "and you will gather your grain and grapes and oil," R. Ishmael interprets as a blessing and Bar Yochai regards only as a mixed one at best (Torah study precludes even the gathering and enjoying of God's bounty)—a view the *gemara* rejects as too stringent; also *Yevamot* 63b, in which Ben Azzai, upon being questioned about his apparent disregard of the *mitzvah* enjoining procreation, replies "What can I do? My soul cleaves to Torah, and the world can be sustained through others." On bar Yochai, see Rav Asher Meir, "Lag Ba-Omer and the 'Sefrirat ha'Omer Jew," *Yeshivat Har Etzion Virtual Beit Midrash*, Alon Shevut, Gush Etzion, Israel, May 13, 1998 http://www.vbm-torah.org/. For a helpful introduction to the genre of *aggadah* (which cites Bialik as well), see Joseph Heinemann, "The Nature of the Aggadah," in *Midrash and Literature*, ed. Geoffrey Hartman and Sanford Budick (New Haven: Yale University Press, 1986), 41–55. Finally, to buttress my own approach to aggadic narrative here and in the next chapter, I would cite David Stern's essay, "Midrash and the Language of Exegesis" in Hartman and Budick (105–124), adapting his remarks on *chavivut* (intimacy between exegete and God's word or voice) to an ethic about religious text as situated among persons; and also, the exquisite essay by Gerald Bruns, "The Hermeneutics of Midrash," in Regina Schwartz, *The Book and the Text: The Bible and Literary Theory* (Cambridge: Basil Blackwell, 1990), which locates midrashic practice as a search for criteria (in Stanley Cavell's terms) that ends up as a search for society: "What midrash finally concerns itself with is the question of what it is to be a Jew. In the political and cultural turmoil of the Diaspora, to say that understanding is a mode of being is no longer an abstract principle. Call it the criterion of a form of life" (204). Levinas's aggadic ethicism and Leibowitz's halakhism converge at exactly this point.

39. Steven S. Schwartzschild (*Studies in Jewish Philosophy*, 105). But see Jill Robbins's counter-statement, "Alterity and the Judaic" in *Prodigal Son/Elder Brother* (Chicago: The University of Chicago Press, 1991), on the reinscription of tradition—a Talmudic *rereading* and thus, "mediated" Judaism—in Levinas.

CHAPTER 1. *AGGADIC MAN*

1. A verse from Song of Songs (2:9) Levinas quotes often. See note 10.

2. Distinguishing halakhic man as *reader of text*, enactor of *mitzvah*, from *posek*, who issues legal decisions, R. Soloveitchik writes: "The foundation of foundations and the pillar of halakhic thought is not the practical ruling but the determination of the theoretical Halakha. Therefore, many of the greatest halakhic men avoided and still avoid to serve in rabbincal posts. They rather join themselves to a group of those who are reluctant to render practical decisions. And if necessity—which is not to be decried—compels them to render practical decisions, this is only a small, insignificant responsibility which does not stand at the center of their concerns" (24).

3. In *Kaddish* (New York: Alfred A. Knopf, 1998), 26–27. Leon Wieseltier criticizes this precedence of commandments over sense-experience. But for Levinas also, what must precede the purely sensate and subjective, mediating the physical and metaphysical, is precisely *obligation*—to the Halakhah directly or to its raison d'être, human Others. (Of Levinas too, Wieseltier is likewise, and characteristically, censorious, in his afterword to Zvi Kolitz, *Yosl Rakover Talks to God*, trans. Carol Brown Janeway [New York: Pantheon Books, 1999].)

4. Levinas's essay, "Contempt for the Torah as Idolatry," in *In the Time of Nations*, discusses this concept at length, "the toil of the mouth, the toil of the word," 67–71. On the phrasing of the daily *birkat hatorah*, "who commanded us to be *engaged* in the study of Torah," R. Soloveitchik remarked that it connotes a constant, latent immersion and attachment—an extreme consciousness as Levinas might say.

5. In that essay, heroism takes the form of marital abstinence when the newly married bride discovers she is menstruating: "The heroic act did not take place in the presence of jubilating crowds; no bards will sing of these two modest, humble young people. It happened in the sheltered privacy of their home, in the stillness of the night. The young man, like Jacob of old, makes an aboutface: he retreats at the moment when fulfillment seems assured" (*Tradition* 17.2 [Spring 1978]: 46).

6. As if to embolden Emil Fackenheim's critique by reversing its polarity, the final endnote to *Halakhic Man* reads as follows: "An echo of the longing for creativity, the ultimate desire of Judaism, which makes itself heard in the philosophy of Kant . . . and in the neoKantian school of Hermann Cohen. . . . This concept of the obligatory nature of the creative gesture, of self-creation as an ethical norm, and exalted value, which Judaism introduced into the world, reverberates with particular strength in the world views of Kierkegaard, Ibsen, Scheler, and Heidegger. In particular, the latter two set the idea of creation at the very center of their philosophies" (164).

7. Eliezer Berkovits's *Not in Heaven: The Nature and Function of Halakhah*, Moshe Koppel's *Meta-Halakhah*, and David Harman's masterly, Maimonidean dialectical synthesis of Soloveitchik and Leibowitz in *A Living Covenant* all offer meta-halakhic models of halakhic systematicity that differ strategically, and more important, ideologically from Soloveitchik's *frum* (religious) existentialism. To take an example I have reserved until this point, Jacob

Neusner's *Judaism as Philosophy: The Method and Message of the Mishna* (Columbia: University of South Carolina Press, 1991), would seem at least superficially congruent with Soloveitchik's model of Halakhah as *a apriori*, and his hermeneutic drive to pure theory. But Soloveitchik's prose speaks in an entirely unique register: sometimes deliberately continuous with certain recognizable stylistic and rhetorical traits of mishnaic Hebrew, it speaks through, rather than about, Mishna and Talmud; moreover, it *personifies* its inquiry and imbues it with pathos in a way that Neusner's entirely more academic project completely eschews. The following offer helpful treatments of R. Soloveitchik's thought: Eugene Borowitz, "The Typological Theology of Rabbi J. B. Soloveitchik," *Judaism* 15 (1966); Marvin Fox, "The Unity and Structure of Rabbi Joseph B. Soloveitchik's Thought," *Tradition* 24.2 (Winter 1989): 44–65; Hillel Goldberg, *Between Berlin and Slobodka: Jewish Transition Figures from Eastern Europe* (Hoboken, N.J.: Ktav, 1989); Lawrence Kaplan, "The Religious Philosophy of Rabbi Joseph Soloveitchik," *Tradition* 14.2 (1973): 43–64; Zvi Kolitz, *Confrontation: The Existential Thought of Rabbi J.B. Soloveitchik* (Hoboken, N.J.: Ktav, 1992); Emmanuel Rackman, "Clarifying Soloveitchik's Halakhic Ideal," *Sh'ma* 16 (1985): 2–13, 16; Morris Sosevsky, "The Lonely Man of Faith confronts the *Ish haHalakhah*," *Tradition* 16.2 (1976); Shubert Spero, "Rabbi Joseph Dov Soloveitchik and the Philosophy of Halakha," *Tradition* 30.2 (Winter 1996): 41–64; and the essays by Moshe Sokol and Walter S. Wurzburger in Sokol, ed., *Engaging Modernity: Rabbinic Leaders and the Challenge of the Twentieth Century* (New York: Jason Aronson, 1997).

8. In *The Lonely Man of Faith*, Soloveitchik contrasts the two Adams as differentially related to God and to human partners as allegorized by Eve. The cognitive, aesthetic, and legislative dramas of Adam the first differ from the roles specific to the man of faith—"Adam in his dual role as a lonely individual and as one committed to a peculiar community idea" (34) who prefigures the faith community of Israel "which reached full fruition in the covenant between Abraham and God" (37). *Loneliness* remains a necessary coefficient of that covenant, and for Soloveitchik never entirely disappears even in the amplitude of love and community.

9. And thus Hartman asks the following pointed questions: "What happens to the emotional life of a person who, like Aaron, is commanded to extinguish all natural sentiments of love for his or her children? . . . Can Abraham allow himself freely to love his son, knowing that the command of God can at any time again instruct him to kill him? Can there be natural joy and spontaneous love in the relationship of husband and wife if in the moment of deepest passion they must deny their natural instincts? Can the intellect be encouraged to feel its own strength, but also to deny its own ability to create a moral a conception of life" (87–88)?

10. Coincidentally enough, Levinas will revert again and again to the verse from Song of Songs that makes a felicitous counterpoint to the R. Soloveitchik's epigraph: *Here he stands, behind our wall, gazing through the windows, peering through the lattice (2:9).*

11. Compare the discussion of the *'ir hanidakhat* in R. Menachem M. Schneerson, *Torah Studies* (New York: Kehot, 1996), *Parashat Re'eh*, 305–310.

12. *Totality and Infinity: An Essay on Exteriority*, trans. Alphonso Lingis (Pittsburgh: Duquesne University Press, 1969).

13. It also mediates divine transcendence through the ethics of the interhuman. In "A Religion for Adults," Levinas quotes a *gemara*: "'God never came down upon Sinai, Moses never ascended to Heaven. But God folded back the heavens like a cover, covered Sinai with it, and so found Himself on earth without ever having left heaven.' There is here a desacralization of the sacred. The Justice rendered to the Other, my neighbor, gives me an unsurpassable proximity to God" (18). R. Soloveitchik quotes the identical *midrash* (*Mekhilta, parshah* 9 on Ex. 20:19), in order to emphasize the fundamental antitranscendentalism of the Halakhah and its preoccupation with the lower, not supernal regions. "Homo religiosus ascends to God: God, however, descends to halakhic man. The latter desires not to transform finitude into infinity but rather infinity into finitude. He brings down the divine presence into a sanctuary bounded by twenty boards, holiness into a world situated within the realms of concrete reality. . . . Transcendence becomes embodied in man's deeds, deeds that are shaped by the lawful physical order of which man is a part" (45).

14. Ibid., "Israel and Universalism," 176–177. Compare the sense of place in *Totality and Infinity*: "To posit oneself corporeally is to touch an earth, but to do so in such a way that the touching finds itself already conditioned by the position, the foot settles into a real which this very action outlines or constitutes—as though a painter would notice that he is descending from the picture he is painting" (128). In an ethical sense, this kind of footing would always be temporary, and necessarily "unsure."

15. In "A Religion for Adults," Levinas writes, "The beginning of Genesis is, for a second-century commentator, less interested in what a man may expect than in what he must do. It is an object of astonishment: why does the Revelation begin with the account of Creation when God's commandments apply only to man? This astonishment is still to be found in the eleventh-century commentator Rashi, who for a thousand years now has been the way into the Bible for Jews throughout the world. And the ancient response that Rashi proposes consists in maintaining that, in order to possess the Promised Land, man must know that God created the earth. For without this knowledge, he will possess it only by usurpation. No rights can therefore ensue from the simple fact that a person needs *espace vital*" (17). In his "Levinas's Thinking on Religion as Beyond the Pathetic," in Fackenheim and Jospe, eds., *Jewish Philosophy and the Academy*, Ephraim Meir notes that the Jewish festival of *Sukkot* (Tabernacles), prophesied by Zachariah as a holiday for all the nations in the Messianic era, annually recapitulates this displacement from home (149).

16. In the forward he writes, "'Of great importance is the mouthful of food,' says Rabbi Johanan in the name of Rabbi Jose b. Kisma [*Sanhedrin* 103b]. The Other's hunger—bit of the flesh, or of bread—is sacred; only the hunger of the third party limits its rights; there is no bad materialism other than our own!" (xiv).

17. R. Aharon Lichstenstein elegantly sums up the multifaceted role of *talmud Torah* in Jewish tradition. At one level, "it is an halakhic act, entailing the realization of a divine commandment," both "positing specific goals . . . and

prescribing clearly defined conduct" and also serving as an end in itself, or rather a service to God apart from ritual and prayer. At another level, it is viewed "axiologically," the intrinsic value of "contact with the revealed and expounded divine Word." This is also a covenantal value, in Soloveitchik's sense, of binding together a community before God. Finally, it is understood cosmologically and mystically, "as a metaphysical factor affecting the fabric of reality, as that which supports and sustains the very existence of the universe." See "Study," in Arthur Cohen and Paul Mendes-Flohr, eds., *Contemporary Jewish Religious Thought: Original Essays on Critical Concepts, Movements, and Beliefs* (New York: Charles Scribner's Sons, 1987), 931–938, as well as the essay "Prayer in the Teachings of Rav Soloveitchik" (*Yeshivat Har Etzion Virtual Beit Midrash*, Alon Shveut, Gush Israel, 1997, http://www.vbm-torah.org.). William Kolbrener discusses this and other dimensions of Soloveitchik's hermeneutic—as well as drawing a link to Levinas—in his very valuable essay, "No 'Elsewhere': Fish, Soloveitchik, and the Unavoidability of Interpretation," *Literature and Theology* 10.2 (June 1996): 170–190.

18. The word for "heritage" is ירושה or מרשה, the former betokening "conquest," and the latter read by the Sages in *Pesachim* 49b homiletically (in different vocalization) as מורשה ("married") to suggest espousal between the Jewish people and the Torah.

19. *Peshat* (plain sense), *remez* (allusive), *derash* (allegorical), *sod*, the acronym for which, *PaRDeS*, spells the word for orchard and signifies Paradise in the Oral Tradition.

20. Ephraim Meir pertinently glosses this as the "fatigue of responsibility, a stiff neck—like Atlas—that supports the universe" (*Jewish Philosophy in the Academy*, 150).

21. *Halakhic Man*, 158–159. Levinas devotes an entire Talmudic reading, "And God Created Woman" to the Sages' explanation of the anomalous spelling, and the ensuing discussion about the creation of Eve in *Berakhot* 61a (*NTR* 161–177).

22. "The interhuman relationship emerges with our history, with our being-in-the-world, as intelligibility and presence. The interhuman realm can thus be construed as part of the disclosure of the world as presence. But it can also be considered from another perspective—the ethical or biblical perspective that transcends the Greek language of intelligibility—as a theme of justice and concern for the other, as a theme of love and desire, which carries us beyond the infinite being of the world as presence. The interhuman is thus an interface: a double axis where what is "other world" qua *phenomenological intelligibility* is juxtaposed with what is "not of the world" qua *ethical responsibility*" (*NTR* 20).

23. In "The Temptation of Temptation," Levinas comments on an *aggadah* about assiduousness in study, "As if by chance, to rub in such a way that blood spurts out is perhaps the way one must 'rub' the text to arrive at the life it conceals" (*Nine Talmudic Readings*, 46). Aronowicz's introduction brilliantly explains the secularizing ethos here; see also Ouaknin's discussion of *makhloket* (translated as "open dialectic") in *The Burnt Book*, 82–99, 155–185.

24. In "Damages Due to Fire," a reading of *Bava Kamma* 60a–b, Levinas

writes, "But in the text itself, the Halakah, without calling into play the inter-pretation of the reader, is transfigured into an Aggadah, into a homiletic text, which, as you know, is the way philosophical views, that is to say, the properly religious thought of Israel, appear in Talmudic thought. . . . And this aggadic interpretation of a Halakha concerning fire will end with a new Halakhic teach-ing: the text thus goes from Halakha to Aggadah, and from Aggadah to Halakha" (*NTR* 182). Within the tradition, a precedent for Levinas's concen-tration on *aggadot* over *halakhot* can be found in the *Ein Ya'akov*, a medieval compilation by R. Jacob Ibn Khabib of all the rabbinic legends, parables, and homiletic lessons in the Talmud, following the order of certain major tractates. Commentary for some can be found in two volumes by Dovid Landesman, *As the Rabbis Taught: Studies in the Aggados of the Talmud* (Northvale, N.J.: Jason Aronson, 1996). But see also Judah Goldin, "The Freedom and Restraint of Haggadah," in *Studies in Midrash and Related Literature* (Philadelphia: Jew-ish Publication Society, 1988), 253–270.

25. But as the redactor of some of R. Soloveitchik's lecture-*shiurim* observes, he was "also a brilliant expositor of Aggadah," a latter-day counter-part to those Torah sages "who were accomplished in both fields" of legal anal-ysis and nonlegal wisdom (Abraham Besdin, *Reflections of the Rav: Lessons in Jewish Thought*, adapted from Lectures of Rabbi Joseph B. Soloveitchik [Jerusalem, Dept. for Torah Education and Culture in the Diaspora of the World Zionist Organization, 1981], 9). I imply as much, of course, in my presentation of *Halakhic Man* and *The Lonely Man of Faith*. To quote finally from Eliezer Berkovits's plain-sense guide to halakhic meaning, "The term 'Halakhic Judaism' . . . is not to be understood as a form of Judaism that is opposed to Aggadic Judaism, a distinction which has been propagated by some authors. There is no such thing as Aggadic Judaism. Halakha and Aggadah are intrinsi-cally interrelated. The great Halakhists of the Talmud are also the great Aggadists" (*Not in Heaven: The Nature and Function of Halakhah*), 1.

26. Not only does the Hebrew differ slightly (mishnaic versus biblical), but the rhetoric of *Mishna* and Talmud is famously lapidary and elliptical, the liv-ing hermeneutics of speech as opposed to the engraved majesty of Holy Writ. The Oral Torah "transforms" textual monuments into living reality by adding to the written voice inside the Torah the voices of its Doctors and practitioners from without. Or as Levinas defines "the essence of Judaism": "something that is laid down in square letters and something that illuminates living faces" (*DF* 25; and also tractate *Pirke Avot* 6:2 and *Eliahu Zuta* 4). Compare the chapter "Halakhah and the Autonomy of Man" in Moshe Koppel's *Meta Halakhah* (which discusses the identical passages from *Hagigah* 3b and *Pesikta Rabbati* 21:21 that Levinas comments on in "Demanding Judaism"), and also my "At Play in the *Piels* (and *Hiphils*) of the Lord; Or, the Home of the Free and the Graven(n): A Passover Story of Freedom and Command," in *Narrative* 4.3 (October 1996): 265–277.

27. R Soloveitchik's untranslated essay is *Shiurim le-Zecher Abba Mari*.

28. "Revelation in the Jewish Tradition" is the essential text to consult here. In his essay that builds on it, "Teaching Rosenzweig as a Philosopher and Levinas as a Jewish Thinker," Robert Gibbs describes the revelatory dimension

in ethics and Torah study this way: "Levinas interprets Jewish textual, commandment, commandment focused, intellectual tradition as an expression of the basic ethical perspective. The polysemia of the texts, the intellectualism of *pilpul* [argumentation], the focus on halakhic questions that do not admit of any practice in our world—these are the traits of revelation that display the social ethics of his philosophy. He gives us access to the Talmud as the adjudication of infinite responsibilities, while he makes rabbinic thought the norm for social reflection. The talmudic text serves revelation because over it two people, myself and an other, Levinas and his Talmudic master, R. Shushani, meet to explore the difficulty of fixing what is due to whom" (*Paradigms in Jewish Philosophy*, 241). The *chavruta* relationship Gibbs describes—the classical Jewish texts are always studied by two readers facing each other with the text in between—models the face-to-face relation, which, as inflected by the trace of "the third party" who thereby introduces justice into the world, exactly parallels the mediation of Scripture—the sign of *illeity*, the trace of the unseen God. In Ze'ev Levy's article in the same volume, "How to Teach Emmanuel Levinas," a somewhat similar point about philosophy and the Jewish tradition is made; Ouaknin's description of the "bidimensionality" of both the talmudic text and *yeshivah* learning in *The Burnt Book*, 83ff., is also pertinent here.

29. See also "Judaism and the Present" (*DF* 213).

30. Norman Lamm, *Torah Lishmah: Torah for Torah's Sake*, 29. See also Nadler, *The Faith of the Mitnagdim*, chap. 7, "The Centrality of Torah Study in Mithnagdism." The other works on the *Nefesh HaHayyim* are all in Hebrew: Immanuel Etkes, "*Shitato U-faalo She Rabi Hayyim mi-Mi-Volozhin ki-Teguvat ha-Hevrah ha-Mitnagdit la-Hasidut*," *Proceedings of the American Academy for Jewish Religion* 38 (1972): 1–45; and Jonah ben Sasson, "*Olamam ha-Ruhani u-Mishnatam ha-Hinukit Shel Meyasdei ha-Yeshiva ha-Litait*," in *Hinukh ha-Adam ve-Yiudo* (Jerusalem, 1967): 155–167.

31. As Lamm explains, R. Hayyim takes the Zohar's bifurcation of God's relation to the worlds as *memale* (immanence, or God's point of view) and *sovev* (transcendence, or humanity's perspective), an opposition whose valences R. Scheur Zalman of Lyady, the founder of Habad Hasidism and the opponent of the Vilna Gaon, completely reverses. "More than semantics is involved here. Whereas for the Hasidim the 'real' world, where Halakhah applies, is the one in which God is immanent, for R. Hayyim, the immanence of God results in the ontological annihilation of these worlds and removes them from consideration altogether; man's thinking and acting, and consequently the Halakhah, are concerned with and become meaningful only in relation to God as He is beyond the world" (82–83).

32. *L'Ame de la vie*, trans. Benjamin Gross (Paris: Éditions Verdier, 1989), vii–x. See also the brief mention in "Means of Identification" (*DF* 51) and *New Talmudic Readings*, 49.

33. Most modern *yeshivot* follow the Volozhin model. Moreover, as Alan Nadler notes of R. Hayyim's book, "although he stated the case for Talmud Torah in unusually bold and creative terms, R. Hayyim of Volozhin in fact innovated very little. . . . There is no question that the fourth section of *Nefesh ha-Hayyim* is a most remarkable panagyric to the supreme religious value of Torah

study, Nevertheless, it was not the first such work published by the rabbinic opponents of Hasidism. Moreover, while it introduced some novel kabbalistic delineations of the cosmic status of Torah and the powers of study, as a rejoinder to the Hasidic demotion of intellectual study it advanced virtually nothing that was entirely original in the practical rabbinic championship of the supremacy of *Talmud Torah* over other religious acts. In fact, every one of R. Hayyim's claims . . . can be found in a work published thirty-six years earlier, R. Phineas of Polotsk's *Kether Torah*" (153).

34. Only a partial English translation of the entire work can be found, in *An Anthology of Jewish Mysticism*, ed. R. Ben-Zion (New York: Yessod Publishers). The only secondary source that comments on Levinas's use of the *Nefesh haHayyim*, Stone's *Reading Levinas/Reading Talmud*, merely rehearses Levinas's own argument, and does not seem to have consulted the work in the original. (Kolbrener briefly mentions R. Hayyim in connection with R. Soloveitchik in "No 'Elsewhere,'" 182–183.)

35. Compare *Zohar* I:243b, which distinguishes among three kinds of articulation: *dibbur*, "verbal speech"; *amirah*, "saying," which comes from the heart; and *aggadah*, "relating," the voice of the soul.

36. These bear comparison on their own account, with some truly fascinating affinities. "On the Name of God in a Few Talmudic Texts" (*BV* 116–128) and "The Three Biblical names of God" (*Reflections*, 13–22); "Promised Land or Permitted Land," (*NTR* 51–69) and "The Singularity of the Land of Israel" (117–126); "The Temptation of Temptation" (*NTR* 30–51) and "Mt. Sinai—Their Finest Hour" (89–116); "The Youth of Israel" (*NTR* 120–135) and "Who Is Fit to Lead the Jewish People?" (127–138); "The Nations and the Presence of Israel" (*ITN* 93–107) and "A Stranger and a Resident" (169–177); "Beyond Memory" (*ITN* 77–91) and " The *Mitzvah* of *Sippur Yetzi'at Mitrayim*" (207–218). The Rav's essay on *hister panim*, God's hiding of his face, "The World is not Forsaken" (31–39) elegantly counterpoints Levinas's constant theme of the human face as the site of ethical responsibility, and thus speaks to the important essay, "Revelation in the Jewish Tradition" (especially 144–145). Still, essays like Soloveitchik's "Imitating God," "Man is Vulnerable," and "The Torah Way of Justice" show Soloveitchik at his most aggadically normative. And it is there, I think, that we find the most conspicuous difference with Levinas's brand of *aggadah*, especially when the sequence of subject headings in Levinas's books with those in R. Soloveitchik's essays in *Reflections of the Rav* is compared. Levinas offers phenomenological categories that are complexly pluralized, with rabbinic text, significantly enough in the case of each book, bracketed in the middle; R. Soloveitchik speaks in singularities: God, Man, Creation, Justice, Wisdom, Prayer.

37. See Hartman, *LC* (chap. 4) and *Conflicting Visions* (part 3).

38. In *Sanhedrin* 21b, R. Isaac says, "Why were the reasons of the commandments not revealed? Because the reasons of two commandments were revealed to the greatest man in the world [Solomon] and he stumbled on account of them." The construct known as *taamei ha-Mitzvot*, the reasons for the commandments, though contemporary with rabbinic Judaism, is most commonly associated with Maimonides in his *Commentary on the Mishnah* and *Hilkhot*

Mamrim. He distinguished between five classes of laws aside from those in the Pentateuch: פירושים מקובלים, hermeneutic principles, הלכה למשה מסיני, *halakhah* also received at Sinai, היקש, rabbinic deductions, גזרות, safeguards for the Halakhah, and תקנות, societal ordinances, the last three being collectively known as דברי סופרים or *divrei soferim* (synonymous with *derabbanan*, rabbinic in a categorical sense, as opposed to *divrei kabbalah*, or *de'oraita*. See Koppel's *Meta-Halakhah* on this point together with the related discussion in Roth's *The Halakhic Process*, and also Avi Sagi, "Halakhic Praxis and the Word of God," *Journal of Jewish Thought and Philosophy* 1 (1992): 305–324.

39. David Stern "Aggadah," in Cohen and Mendes-Flohr, 7–12. See also Stern's *Parables in Midrash: Narrative and Exegesis in Rabbinic Literature* (Cambridge: Harvard University Press, 1991); "Midrash and the Language of Exegesis," in Hartman and Budick (1986), and the excellent introduction to Chaim Nahman Bialik's *"Sefer Ha-Aggadah": Legends From the Talmud and Midrash* (New York: Schocken Books, 1992); also, Daniel Boyarin, *Intertextuality and the Reading of Midrash* (Bloomington: Indiana University Press, 1990); Gerald Bruns, "The Hermeneutics of Midrash," in Schwartz (1990); Judah Goldin, "The Freedom and Restraint of Haggadah"; and Jacob Neusner, *Invitation to Midrash: The Workings of Rabbinic Bible Interpretation* (San Francisco: Harper & Row, 1989). As Stern points out, the heterogeneous material of rabbinic *aggadah*—narrative, allegory, proverbs, poetry—bespeaks the sort of formal traits associated with traditional oral literature. The same *aggadot* may in fact appear in multiple contexts, such as the *targumim* (Aramaic translations of the Pentateuch), *midrashim*, postmedieval rabbinic homilies, and so on, where the meaning changes according to the context—a Judaized version of folk-myth, an apologetic proof-text, a homiletic "fence" around the Halakhah. But for the Rabbis as well as for contemporary readers, the Aggadah remains complexly unsystematic, unlike its older, stricter sibling, the Halakhah, but for that very reason, to recall Bialik's distinction from my introduction, it remains in dialectical tension with the Law and normative theology. Stern writes, "[t]he present-day theological significance of *aggadah* lies in the way its chaotic richness resists being organized into orderly discourse—in its open preference for homily over theology, for impassioned assertion over reasoned argument. Most playful and novel in form precisely when it is most commonplace in content, *aggadah* represents all that is quintessentially untheological about Judaism. As such it is the point of discontinuity against which the theology of Judaism must take a stand in order to make its own beginning" (12). Contrariwise, Marvin Fox points to passages in the Palestinian Talmud (*Ma'asrot* III:10, 51a and *Shabbat* XVI:1, 15c) that evince a deep distrust of aggadic exegesis that has the capacity "to interpret a single Biblical verse in contradictory ways" and "that turns true teaching upside down" (*Modern Jewish Ethics*, 17). Finally, in *Carnal Israel: Reading Sex in Talmudic Culture* (Berkeley: University of California Press, 1993), Daniel Boyarin argues for a confluence of aggadic and halakhic eddies through the method he calls cultural poetics. "We cannot read the aggada as background for the halakha, but if anything, the opposite: the halakha can be read as background and explanation for the way that the rabbinic biographies are constructed—not, I hasten to add, because the halakha represents 'reality'

which the aggada 'reflects,' but only because the halakha as a stipulated nor-mative practice is, almost by definition, ideologically more explicit" (16).

40. A famous passage from *Eruvin* 13b is also included in *Pirke Avot*: "Any controversy which is in the name of Hevaen is destined to result in something permanent; any controversy which is not in the name of Heaven will never result in anything permanent. Which controversy was in the name of Heaven? The controversy between Hillel and Shammai." Of that controversy Levinas writes, "The great disagreement between the school of Hillel and the School of Sham-mai (in the first century before Christ) is called the discussion or disagreement 'for the glory of Heaven'. Despite all the care it takes to reach an agreement, the Talmud never ceases to apply to the differences of opinion between Hillel and Shammai—and to the flow of divergent ideas which proceed from them through the successive generations of scholars—the well known phrase: 'These and those alike, are the words of the living God'" (*BV* 37). And thus a related passage in *Yevamot* 14b: "The School of Shammai did not refrain from marrying women of the families of the School of Hillel. Nor did the School of Hillel refrain from marrying those of the School of Shammai. This is to teach you that they showed love and friendship towards one another, thus putting into practice the Biblical text 'Love truth and peace' (*Zech* 8:19)." See also *Tosefta* on *Sotah* 7:14, which concludes, quite beautifully, "So make yourself a heart of many rooms and bring into it the words of *Bet Shammai* and the words of *Bet Hillel*, the words of those who declare unclean and the words of those who declare clean"; and M. Fish-bane's "Reading Rabbinic Texts," *The Jewish Political Tradition*, xxxix–lv.

41. The meaning of this phrase underwent a change from its use by the Sages to the sense in which Maimonides deploys it. In the former, it refers to the Torah's seeming linguistic redundancy, the prevalence of doubled or amplifica-tory expressions. And best to interpret it: as conveying additional meaning with halakhic consequences (R. Akiva's view), or merely rhetorical emphasis, as in ordinary speech (R. Ishmael's view). Although the occasion for the dispute revolves around the correct use of formalized rules of interpretation, the import here is whether a sacred text has its own language, and thus distinct from "the language of men." In Maimonides's hands, the phrase refers not to stylistic peculiarities of the Torah's language, but rather to the way in which the Torah speaks about God—that is, in a language comprehensible to people despite the metaphysical looseness thereby incurred. Thus, the "language of men" is anthropomorphic because of the need for ordinary language to use material terms even when referring to the transcendent and ineffable. See *The Guide for the Perplexed* 1:1.

42. See *Sifre* on Deut. 82, *Berakhot* 19b, *Shabbat* 23a, and Maimonides's *Mishneh Torah*, *Mamrim*, 1:1–2.

43. *Freedom on tablets of stone* is the epigraph to *Difficult Freedom*. In "On the Jewish Reading of Scriptures," Levinas quotes tractate *Makkot*: "Three things were enacted by the Tribunal below, and the Celestial Tribunal on high have given their assent to their action; who has gone [to Heaven] and come [back with this information]? Only, we [by] interpreting these texts; and in this instance, too, we so interpret the texts" (*BV* 108).

44. Levinas's interpretation here of the Talmud's intertexual references to

the Scrolls of Esther and Ruth and Nehemiah 10:39 is paradigmatic: each
instance becomes an illustration of his own philosophical tropes, the forcing
upon, through interpretation, of the secret of transcendence, the face of the
Other, and giving as anonymous goodness and justice.

45. He continues, "A personal and unique God is not something revealed
like an image in a dark room! [Rather,] ethics and principles install a personal
relationship worthy of the name. Loving the Torah even more than God means
precisely having access to a personal God against Whom one may rebel—that is
to say, for Whom one may die."

46. As David Hartman puts the problem this raises: "How the person of
learning becomes a person of action is a serious question. He rejects the notion
that *talmud torah* in effect substitutes for *mitzvot* that take place outside the
study hall. The world of thought can be an island to which one escapes from the
often tragic failures that may result from attempts to do something in the world.
Thought always confers a feeling of completeness and purity that material
involvement in the social and economic evils of the world might promise. That
intellectual involvement in Torah study might be a source of alienation from the
real world is not given serious consideration in Soloveitchik's essay" (74).

47. A similar theme is drawn out by Levinas in his reading of *Shabbat* 88a
in "The Temptation of Temptation" (*NTR* 30–50). In "Israel under the Mountain: Emmanuel Levinas on Freedom and Constraint in the Revelation of the
Torah," *Modern Judaism* 18.1 (February 1998): 35–47, Lawrence Kaplan
points out Levinas's heterodox approach to this *sugya* when comparing it with
the interpretations given by the Tosafists and Nachmanides, but also its affinities with a *perush* like that of the Maharal of Prague. Kaplan notes, "The Ram-
ban's explanation reflects his well known emphasis on the central theological
and metaphysical significance of the land of Israel. . . . Levinas's explanation
reflects his fundamental perception of the Torah as the 'no' to violence, and his
deep awareness of the inevitable price paid by those who, upholding the Torah,
say that 'no'" (45). The two opinions, however, converge around the idea of
exile: where Nachmanides understands exile geographically and modern Orthodoxy understands it theologically, Levinas sees it in political terms. "To be in
exile," Kaplan says, "is to be exposed to the threat of genocide." (Interestingly,
Kaplan's paper ends with a reference to John Llewelyn's book *Emmanuel Levinas: The Genealogy of Ethics* [New York: Routledge, 1995], mentioned in my
introduction as correlating Levinas with Fackenheim.)

48. See the essays collected in *Tradition* 17.2 (Spring 1978), "Majesty and
Humility," 23–37; "Catharsis," 38–54, and "Redemption, Prayer, Talmud
Torah," 55–72, and also R. Lichtenstein's "Prayer in the Teachings of Rav
Soloveitchik."

49. Levinas makes only one extended reference to Maimonides in "The
State of Caesar and the State of David" from *Beyond the Verse*, an essay on
Zionism. Other allusions to Jewish philosophers like Spinoza, Moses Mendelsohn, or Rosenzweig are similarly confined to essay-polemics rather than *expli-
cations du texte*.

50. Abraham R. Besdin, *Reflections of the Rav: Lessons in Jewish Thought*;
Nehama Leibowitz, *Studies in Genesis, Exodus, Leviticus, Numbers, Deuteron-*

omy, trans. Aryeh Newman (Jerusalem: Dept. for Torah Education and Culture in the Diaspora of the World Zionist Organization, 1982). Avivah Gottleib Zornberg's more recent *The Beginning of Desire: Reflections on Genesis* (New York: Doubleday, 1995) brilliantly and elegantly weaves the classic Jewish commentaries together with modern philosophy and poetry.

51. *Ha'amek Davar*, commentary on the Pentateuch, but also noted by Zornberg in The *Beginning of Desire*, xvi.

52. Compare the far more traditional approach to text modeled by Nachman Cohen's *Master a Mesikhta Series* from the Torah Lishmah Institute (distributed by Feldheim)—commentary-and-study guides keyed to *yeshivah*-style learning, or Dovid Landesman's *A Practical Guide to Torah Study* and *As the Rabbis Taught: Studies in The Aggados of the Talmud* (distributed by Jason Aronson); and also Richard Cohen's introduction to *New Talmudic Readings*, which beautifully extrapolates the duties incumbent upon the student of Jewish texts through a just engagement with Levinas's writings. Contrariwise, I would note Llewelyn's *Emmanuel Levinas: The Genealogy of Ethics*, more or less paradigmatic of its kind in its complacence about Judaic particulars. The hermeneutic scheme of *PaRDeS*, for example, is not "cabbalistic" (221) but rabbinic. Calling R. Hayyim of Volozhin by the nickname "Volozhyn" makes as much sense as calling Levinas "Kaunas" or "Paris"; in any event, the sobriquet is entirely of Llewelyn's invention. The Vilna Gaon is the Gaon of Vilna, not "Vilnyus" (29), the Lithuanian, that is, *non-Jewish* name for the city.

53. Levinas studied the traditional rabbinic sources later in his life, in 1947–1951 (see Cohen's *Elevations*, 115).

54. "Face" is one of the Torah's premier examples of what Max Kadushin in *The Rabbinic Mind* (New York: Bloch & Co., 1972) calls a " value concept," or what Buber and Franz Rosenzweig in their essays on biblical translation call the *Leitwort* or "leading word" principle, also known in Hebrew as *mila maancha*. Fortuitously enough, in the introduction to his translation of the *Five Books of Moses* (New York: Schocken Publisher, 1995) based on the Buber-Rosenzweig approach, Everett Fox selects the following verses from Gen. 32:21 to illustrate the leading-word principle as a whole: "For he said to himself: I will wipe [the anger from] his face with the gift that goes ahead of my face; afterward when I see his face, perhaps he will lift up his face! The gift crossed over ahead of his face." In Hebrew, the word for face also means presence or selfhood, and as such appears in numerous scenes of encounter in the throughout the Hebrew Bible, but it takes other forms as well, from Gen. 6:13, *for the earth is filled with robbery through them*, which means literally, robbery "from their faces," to Psalm 34:6, *They looked at him and were radiant; and they* [their faces] *shall never be ashamed.* As Moses "hides his face" from God on Sinai, so God's answering threat of absence from the plane of human events is called *hister panim*—the hiding of face—in Deuteronomy. (Indeed, the many instances of "falling on one's face" in the Pentateuch and Prophets, and "shame-facedness," as in Daniel 9:17, are the human expression of such self-veiling.) Perhaps the most stunning negative proof of Levinasian physiognomic ethics can be discerned in the verses from Genesis, *And Jacob saw that Laban's face was not with him, as it had been in the best* (31:2) and *Laban's face is not to me as it*

was previously (31:5), brilliantly glossed by Zornberg in *The Beginning of Desire*: "Laban's face is part of Jacob's world; he carries its impress, its changing looks around with him." Zornberg adduces R. Nachman of Bratslav on a related talmudic passage (*Berakhot* 6b) that metaphorically represents the self-consciousness induced by the gaze of others in terms of the "*kroom* bird," who, when the sun rises, turns many colors: "one who is too much affected by other's faces finds his own face turning all colors, blushing and paling in response to their changing expressions. . . . At its truest, that is what the human face represents—a forceful integration of the authentic self that can confront other selves, other faces, without fear or favor" (206). Finally, a *midrash* from *Pesikta de Rav Kahana* (12:25) translates such self-presence into property of the Divine: "R. Levi said: The Holy One appeared to them as though he were a statue with faces on every side. A thousand people might be looking at the statue, but it would appear to be looking at each one of them. So too, when the Holy One spoke, each and every person in Israel could say, The Divine word is addressing me. Note that Scripture does not say (Ex. 20:2) *I am the Lord your God* [plural] but *I am the Lord thy God* [singular]."

55. The approach here echoes my method of ethical poetics in *Narrative Ethics*. See, however, Jeffrey L. Rubenstein's superb *Talmudic Stories: Narrative Art, Composition, and Culture* (Baltimore: Johns Hopkins University Press, 1999), the richest and most informed study of aggadic narrative to date.

56. Compare Isaiah 3:5–6. Ironically enough, sententia of R. Yohanan are themselves cited in *Berakhot* 17a as his world-weary pronouncement after finishing the Book of Job.

57. See also the essays in Judah Goldin, *Studies in Midrash and Related Literature*.

58. See *Yoreh De'ah* (section of *'Arba'ah Turim* and *Shulkhan 'Arukh*, 385). A companion parable (about R. Eliezer's illness) is related in *Sanhedrin* 101a; of four elders here, it is R. Akiva who succeeds in citational sense and sensibility.

59. See also "The Temptation of Temptation," 46–47 and Robert Eaglestone's critique of Martha Nussbaum in chapter 3 of *Ethical Criticism: After Levinas*.

60. David Hartman's *A Living Covenant* and *Conflicting Visions*.

61. For the purposes of argument, I am consciously skewing the more dialectical picture Soloveitchik refines in *The Lonely Man of Faith*, at the end of which, he writes, "If one would inquire of me about the teleology of the Halakha, I would tell him that it manifests itself exactly in the paradoxical yet magnificent dialectic which underlies the Halakhic gesture. When man gives himself to the covenantal community, the Halakha reminds him that he is also wanted in another community, the cosmic-majestic, and when it comes across man while he is involved in the creative enterprise of the majestic community, it does not let him forget that he is a covenantal being who will never find self-fulfillment outside of the covenant and that God awaits his return to the covenantal community. I would also add, in reply to such a question, that many a time I have the distinct impression that the Halakha is considered the steady oscillating of the man of faith between majesty and covenant not as a dialectical but as

a complementary movement. . . . I am prompted to draw this remarkable inference from the Halakha has a monistic approach to reality and has unreservedly rejected any kind of dualism" (83–84).

62. The Torah's uncanny way of attuning concepts to one another can be glimpsed in the repeated verses that combine the ideas of ללכת בדרכיו, to *walk* in his ways, and לשמר מצוותיו, to *observe* (or *guard*) *his commandments* (and those, likewise, the verses that link this same concept of *shmirat mitzvot* with God's own desire that he should התהלך בתוככם, *walk among you*.) In his *Sefer ha-Mitzvot* (Book of Commandments], Maimonides writes of the commandment to love one's fellow in Lev. 19:18 "that God commanded us to resemble Him as much as possible and that is the meaning of *and you shall walk in his ways* (Deut. 28:9). This commandment was repeated [in the verse] . . . *to walk in all His ways*, and the explanation was given that just as God is called compassionate so you should be compassionate; just as God is called merciful so you should be merciful; just as God is called kind, so you should be kind."

63. The original promise to Abraham in the Covenant between the Parts (Gen. 15:17) correlates the land (*ha'aretz*) with conquest (*yerushah*), reflecting a historical and national mission to establish sovereignty. In the Covenant of Circumcision (Gen. 17:3–8), the Promised Land (*eretz Canaan*) is specified as an inheritance (*achuzah*) between intimates and God's special Providence. Nachmanides concludes that possession is a separate *mitzvah* in its own right, a normative obligation (see also Lev. 18, Num. 33:53, and *Ketubot* 110b). As Nehama Leibowitz puts it, "the Torah cannot be observed in its entirety except in a society wholly governed by its precepts and not in an alien framework ruled by other ideals. Admittedly there are personal and religious obligations that can be observed anywhere, even by a Jewish Robinson Crusoe on his desert isle, but the Torah, as a whole, implies a complete social order, a judiciary, national, economic, and political life. That can only be achieved in the Holy Land and not outside it" (*Studies in Bamidbar*, 399–400). Leibowitz cites the *midrash* in *Bereshit Rabbah*, "*Return unto the land of the fathers, and to thy kindred; and I will be with thee* (Gen. 31:3)—your father is waiting for you, your mother is waiting for you—I myself am waiting for you" (77) as another example of the Torah's sense of possession as double edged: one takes control of the Land only because God has taken control of him. Finally, Rashi will interpret Gen. 28:21, *and the Lord shall be a God unto me*, as signifying Jacob's desire for God's name to rest upon him eternally—that God become a *possession* "to me." (Three related terms in Torah describe this relationship: מורשה, heritage—mentioned above in relation to Deut. 33:4—נחלה, inheritance, and אחזה, holding, whose etymology emphasizes a sense of grasping, seizing, taking hold, as in Lev. 25.)

64. The Talmud consists of the *Gemara*, or "completion" together with the Mishna (Oral Law) whose sequence in the six orders it follows, as redacted by R. Judah HaNasi in at the beginning of the third century C.E. The Sages known as *Tana'im*, whose conversations are in mishnaic Hebrew, presided from roughly the third century B.C.E. through this redaction. The *Amora'im* were a later generation of Rabbis from 220 C.E. to the end of the fourth century who conducted their discussions in Hebrew and Aramaic (often around sayings

called *baraitot* omitted from the *Mishna*), which were finally written down c. 500 C.E. The *Tosefta* is the earliest commentary on the Mishna. *Midrashim* are both halakhic (*Mekhilta* on Exodus, *Sifre* on Deuteronomy, *Sifra* on Numbers) from the third and fourth centuries, or aggadic, redacted for the most part in the fifth and sixth centuries. The Talmud as it has been known since Maimonides consists of both the Tannaitic and Amoraic tiers together with the eleventh century commentary by Rashi, and that of his students, the Tosafists. See Maimonides's *Hakdamah l'Perush haMishnayot*, trans. Zvi Lampel (New York: Judaica Press, 1975) and *Mebo haTalmud* by Zvi Hirsch Chajes, trans. Jacob Shacter (New York: Feldheim, 1962). Adin Steinsalz's *Reference Guide to the Talmud* (New York: Random House, 1989); David Kraemer's *The Mind of the Talmud: An Intellectual History of the Bavli* (New York: Oxford University Press, 1990); and E. Urbach's *The Halakhah* (Israel, 1986) are all helpful.

65. The same verse explains why days in the Hebrew calendar are calculated from the night preceding.

66. This is, technically speaking, the terminal *sugya* (line of argumentation, from the same root, *sug*, denoting "fence"). The very last paragraph of the Talmud, which directly follows it, is simply the very last mishna in *Taharot* (the last of the six orders in the Mishna), a general blessing for peace that ends, "R. Shimon ben Chalfta said: the Holy One, blessed be He, found no vessel that could contain blessing for Israel save that of peace. As it is written (Ps. 29:11) *The Lord will give strength unto his people; The Lord will bless his people with peace.*"

67. "The great demand, to worship God and not to worship anything other than God, requires of man that he not refer to his sense perception or to his imagination, but that he *know*. The first phrase of the first *halakha* of *Yesodei ha-Torah* after the introductory words, 'The fundament of fundaments and the pillar of wisdom,' is 'to know.' It is the duty of man to know that there is none beside him" (*The Faith of Maimonides*, 41). See also the chapter, "Knowledge of God as Commandment," 45–52. It has been observed that Maimonides's wording for this essential principle differs between the *Mishneh Torah* and the *Sefer ha-Mitzvot*. The former enjoins belief, while the latter stresses the intellectual basis of this precept. In the words of the nineteenth-century commentator Malbim, "They are innate Ideas. A man has only to look into his own soul to discover them just as he develops all the rest of his faculties. There was no need to receive them from Moses as an act of faith. They were therefore imparted directly by God who fashioned man's soul." As such, they can be seen in spirit with Levinas's reading of the passage in Descartes's *Third Meditation* as the idea of the Infinite placed within thought but overflowing it, and thus a type for the Metaphysical Desire for the Other; see *Totality and Infinity*, 25–30 and "Signature" (*DF* 294).

68. This is as far from a purely philosophical assessment of Judaism's "truth" according to independent veridical criteria, of course, as can be imagined. See, for example, Hermann Cohen's *Religion of Reason Out of the Sources of Judaism*, trans. Simon Kaplan (New York: Ungar, 1972), as well as the chapters on Cohen in Eliezer Berkovits, *Major Themes in Modern Philosophies of Judaism* and Novak, *The Election of Israel: The Idea of the Chosen People* (Cambridge: Cambridge University Press, 1995).

69. The *taryag mitzvot* consist of 248 positive and 365 negative command-ments, and an additional 7 fixed by rabbinic decree. Other such medieval com-pilations besides Nachmanides's *HaSegot HaRambam* and the *Sefer haHinuch* are the *SeMaG* (large book of *Mitzvot*) by R. Moses of Coucy, and the *SeMaK* (Small Book of *Mitzvot*) by R. Issac b. Joseph of Corveil (thirteenth cent.)

70. Also, the verse ends like many other verses in Leviticus with the refrain "I am the Lord," His name, the *shem Hayava* or Tetragrammaton (*hameforash*), identifying His importance as covenant-partner over and above Creator-God (*shem eloh-im*).

71. *Sifre* on *Re'eh* 112:2, where "neighbor" excludes non-Jews and "kins-man" excludes resident aliens (*gerim toshavim*).

72. *Mishneh Torah*, *Nizke Mamon* 8:5. See the superb general introduction to Maimonides by Marvin Fox, *Interpreting Maimonides: Studies in Methodol-ogy, metaphysics and Moral Philosophy* (Chicago: The University of Chicago Press, 1990).

73. Simon points finally to the case of the *Shulkhan Arukh* of R. Scheneur Zalman, the founder of Habad Lubavitch which states that "the dwelling of a non-Jew has the legal status of the dwelling of an animal"; similarly in his *Likkutei Amarim*, the Rebbe quotes Malachi 2:10, *Have we not all one father?* as applying to all *"Israelites as real brothers."* On the other side of the balance sheet, Simon lists the thirteenth-century legal theorist, R. Menachem ha-Meiri who advocates abolishing all forms of legal discrimination against non-Jews on the basis of the obsolescence of certain talmudic rulings (though he yet agrees with *Bava Kama* 113b that Jews are under no obligation to return the lost prop-erty of non-Jews); the Malbim, who interprets Lev. 19:18 in the light of Kant's categorical imperative; and R. Jacob Zvi Mecklenberg, another nineteenth-cen-tury commentator, who says forthrightly that *re'ah* signifies "every human being." All these progressively more liberal interpretations exemplify the kind of halakhic plasticity that Eliezer Berkovits sees as a defining feature of the Jewish legislative and juridical framework. The *prosbul* (innovated by Hillel to circum-vent the cancellation of debts in *shmittah*, the sabbatical year); the *heter iska* (circumventing the biblical prohibition against loan-interest); and the modern debates over *agunot* (abandoned wives deprived of a legal divorce) and *mamz-erim* (illegitimate issue from an incestuous or adulterous union), are pragmatic instances of the same recursive spirit. In his reply to Simon's essay, however, Harold Frisch offers the valid counterclaim that the command to love, תואהבה, "is a category that surely belongs to the particularistic dimension of Judaism," the only other commandment incorporating it being that which specifies love of God (Deut 6:5); in both cases, specific reference is made to the Jewish people as objects or subjects of such love. Frisch prefers the concept of *hesed*, goodwill, as the sort of universalist ethical standard Simon wishes to apply here, which, how-ever, cannot then be made to bear on Lev. 19:18, and how the Rabbis have tra-ditionally interpreted the meaning and status of "neighbor." The problem with this view, however, is that *hesed* is treated by the Sages as a specific command-ment that is part of the Law, there being universal agreement among the Rab-binic authorities that it is mandated within the community of Israel, and not simply voluntaristic outside of it. See "A Response to Ernst Simon," in Fox,

57–61, and also R. Lichstenstein's essay, where he cites *Hullin* 33b, "Is there anything which is permitted to the Jew but prohibited to the Gentile?" (a minimum, universal moral standard) as one pole of a dialectic, and Maimonides's statement in *Commentary on the Mishna* that halakhah incorporates natural morality (superseding it) as the other.

74. Comparable speculations underpin the essay "The Will of God and the Power of Humanity" (*NTR* 47–77), which also selects its talmudic text from tractate *Makkot*.

75. למקל, on the lenient side, and לחמרה, on the stricter, represent two poles of Talmudic adjudication. The Rabbis by no means always opt for leniency. Two related principles here affect halakhic decision-making: (1) when a doubt exists regarding the application of a Torah law, one makes a restrictive, stringent decision; and (2) when a doubt exists regarding the application of a *rabbinic* law, one makes a lenient, less stringent decision.

76. *Pace* Levinas, the immediate reference in the preceding *mishna* in *Makkot* is the Nazirate, and even allowing for the categories of resident alien, Canaanite slave, and Samaritan who can also be banished (v. *Makkot* 8b–9a), the talmudic text does *not* generalize in terms of "neighbors."

77. During this time Israel fell under two distinct periods of Roman supremacy, and the diasporic community of Babylonian Jewry flourished, authors of what came to be the authoritative Talmud. What is called the Palestinian Talmud (the shorter of the two) was composed when Imperial power had weakened greatly, and increased state taxation and increasing pressure from an expanding Christianity severely depleted Jewish resources in *Eretz Yisrael*. Emigration and a general decline in Torah study were some of the more dire consequences, resulting in an incompletely edited Talmud (and thus the lesser of the two bodies of Amoraic commentary and exegesis in Palestine and Persia).

78. However, in the ninth-century *Seder Eliahu Rabba* we read, "I call heaven and earth to witness whether one be gentile or Jew, man or woman, male slave or female slave, in accordance with the merit of his deeds does the Holy Spirit rest upon him" (10:48).

79. See Gordon Lafer, "Universalism and Particularism in Jewish Law: Making Sense of Political Loyalties," in *Jewish Identity*, ed. David Theo Greenberg and Michael Krausz (Philadelphia: Temple University Press, 1993), 177–211; also Silberstein and Cohn, *The Other in Jewish Thought and History*.

80. The Talmud uses the acronym, נשג"ז (menstruant, slave, non-Jewess, and prostitute) to refer to a set of severely prohibited sexual relations, second only to the *arayot*, incestuous and adulterous unions as specified in Lev. 18 and 20, and punishable by excision (cf. the hierarchized list of persons in *Horiot* 13b).

81. Two dietary examples, סתם יינם (wine touched or even looked at, by a non-Jew) and בשול נכים (food cooked by non-Jews even when the *kashrut* is indubitable), demonstrate the operative power of fences in halakhic Judaism. Tractate *Avodah Zarah* lists a whole series of laws designed by the Rabbis to limit social intercourse between Jews and Gentiles.

82. Boyarin discusses how women are figured and represented in Mishna and Talmud (in particular, *aggadot* in the Palestinian Talmud about women who aspire to study Torah), and how in the homosocial world of rabbinic learn-

ing and argument, the Torah itself was itself the object of libidinal energy.

83. See "And God Created Woman" (NTR 161–177), and "Judaism and the Feminine" (DF 30–37). On the other side of the ledger, see the essays by Tina Chanter, Catherine Chalier, and Luce Irigaray in Re-Reading Levinas, ed. Robert Bernasconi and Simon Critchley (Bloomington: Indiana University Press, 1991); and by Chanter and Alison Ainley in The Provocation of Levinas: Rethinking the Other, ed. Bernasconi and Wood (London: Routledge, 1988). Also: Judith Z. Abrams, The Women of the Talmud (Northvale, N.J.: Jason Aronson, 1995); Mieke Bal, Lethal Love (Bloomington: Indiana University Press, 1987) and Murder and Difference: Gender, Genre, and Scholarship on Sisera's Death (Bloomington: Indiana University Press, 1988); Rachel Biale, Women and Jewish Law: An Exploration of Women's Issues in Halakhic Sources (New York: Schocken Books, 1984); Leila Leah Bronner, From Eve to Esther: Rabbinic Reconstructions of Biblical Women (Louisville: Westminster John Knox Press, 1994); Blu Greenberg, On Women & Judaism: A View from Tradition (Philadelphia: Jewish Publication Society of America, 1981); Judith Hauptman, Rereading the Rabbis: A Woman's Voice (Boulder, Colo.: Westview Press, 1998); Judith Wegner, Chattel or Person? The Status of Women in the Mishnah (New York: Oxford University Press, 1988).

84. Note how Levinas interprets this term (which denotes "unbeliever" or "disdainer," that is, a follower of the School of Epicurus): "Nothing could be more natural than the refusal of an Epicurean to recognize the giving of the Torah by God. But the Gemara that prolongs the text translated for the present lesson identifies the apikoros, disdainful of the Torah, with one who offends his fellow in the presence of a rabbinic doctor. Contempt that does not remain a theological attitude, but immediately becomes contempt for humanity and a defiant challenge to one's fellow" (ITN 62). One might also compare the corrolary account in Berakhot 28 of the added nineteenth blessing to the Daily Prayer which asks that "all heretics (minim) be eradicated immediately": "Rabban Gamliel said to the Sages: Is there no one who knows how to draft the birkat ha-minim? Shmuel HaKatan stood up and drafted it. The next year, he forgot it, and paused for two or three hours (trying to remember it), but they did not replace him." That is, while the imprecation against evildoers may be warranted, it should come not easily but with hesitation and ambivalence.

85. See Virginia Dominguez, People as Subject/People as Object: Selfhood and Peoplehood in Contemporary Israel (Madison: University of Wisconsin Press, 1986), and Alouph Hareven, Every Sixth Israeli: Relations between the Jewish Majority and the Arab Minority in Israel (Jerusalem: Van Leer, 1983).

86. It is in the episode of Korach (Numbers 16–17) that the word for "choose" (יבחר), otherwise appearing in the Pentateuch in connection with place God will choose to make His name great (Deut. 12) or the people He has taken to Himself (Deut. 7), describes Moses's response to Korach's declaration of Jewish egalitarianism, For the entire assembly—all of them—are holy and the Lord is among them (16:5): In the morning God will make known the one who is His own and the holy one, and He will draw close to Himself, and whomever He will choose, He will draw close to Himself (16:6). This episode, moreover, immediately follows the mitzvah of tzitzit that locates holiness in and through

the Halakhah alone—a religious task, not an ontological given.

87. On this point, Gordon Lafer remarks, "So too rabbinic law's just-price doctrine, and its restrictions on profiting from trade in subsistence goods, pertained only to trade within the Jewish community" (*Bava Batra* 90a); Maimonides, *Mishneh Torah, Hilchot Mechirah*, 14. Lafer quotes Moshe Greenberg: "'these aids to the poor were the expression of solidarity among Israelites; outsiders could neither be expected to share such obligations, nor expect to enjoy their benefits'" (192).

88. One of thirteen instituted by R. Ishmael in the introduction to the *Sifra* (midrashic commentary on Numbers) that the Rabbis chose to include in daily worship in order to satisfy the minimum requirement for Torah study.

89. The immediate background for this is a discussion in *Sanhedrin* 98b of Isaiah 60:2.

90. *Avodah Zarah* 2b. Compare *Sifre* on Deuteronomy 41: "If one learns an interpretation from the least learned of the Israelites (*katan*, lit. a small person), he should consider it as if he had learned it from a sage."

91. A good example is *Taanit* 7b: "Rav Sala said, Every arrogant person will eventually sin. . . . Rav Nachman said, It is evident that an arrogant person is one who has already sinned." Rav Sala states that arrogance causes wrongdoing, and Rav Nachman asserts that wrongdoing causes arrogance; psychological truth inheres in both observations. (See Ouaknin on *makhloket*, 83ff., 159ff.)

92. In the radio interview quoted above, Levinas says "Innocence is not the zero degree of conscience, but merely an exalted degree of responsibility, which is perhaps the final nodal point of the Jewish conscience among all those symbolized by the knots of our *tzitzit*: the more innocent we are, the more we are responsible" (*The Levinas Reader*, 291).

93. In 24:18–33, Eliezer is addressed as "master" and "the man," not "servant."

94. *Bava Metzia* 31a–33a, and Maimonides's *Mishneh Torah* (*Hilkhot Deot* 6).

95. "Today I will no longer say refugees, but Palestinains. Zionism is not at an end, for all that. It is not finished. If Jews and Israelis recognize that if the State of Israel is to exist it needs the recognition of the Arab world and, for Israel, an entrance into the intimacy of this world" (*BV* xvii).

96. Levinas discusses the Scroll of Esther and the talmudic concept of "making the hands impure" by touching the uncovered scroll of the Torah—a figure Levinas interprets as the text's own revenge on instrumentality, on the grasping, scientific, impatient hand.

97. It is in the book of Ruth that we see the practice known halakhically as *yibbum* (levirate marriage), explained in Deut. 25:5 and also instanced in the episodes of Judah and Tamar and the family of Lot. In each of these cases, however, the *yibbum* is nonstandard, for technically the process involves the brother of the deceased marrying his widow. Additionally, the perpetuation of family is linked to the purchase of the field: "When you acquire the property from Naomi and from the Moabite, you must also acquire the wife of the deceased so as to perpetuate the name of the deceased" (4:5). One of the themes of Ruth, then, is

that, is that inheritance depends on the passing down of property from generation to generation. There is a final thematic link to the verse about Jacob that
Levinas cites. In one of the Torah's great strokes of interconnection, the act of
"resurrecting the name of the dead on his property" links the story of Lot (the
genealogy of Moab), and of Judah to the narrative of Ruth the Moabite and
Boaz from the Hose of Judah; and because King David traces his lineage back
to Ruth, the land of Israel itself is also symbolically included in this same idea
of possession in perpetuity. See Rav Yaakov article's "Redemption in *Megillat
Ruth*," *Yeshivat Har Etzion Virtual Beit Midrash*, Alon Shevut, Gush Etzion,
Israel, May 29, 1998 <http://www.vbm-torah.org/>, and Julia Kristeva's discussion of Ruth in *Strangers to Ourselves*, trans. Leon S. Roudiez (New York;
Columbia University Press, 1991), 69–76.

98. In "Contempt for the Torah as Idolatry," Levinas comments on a
gemara in *Sanhedrin* 99b that expatiates on the seemingly superfluous figure of
Timna, sister of Lotan (Gen 36:22) and concubine of Eliphaz (Gen 36:12):
"Timna tried to convert. She went to Abraham, Isaac, and Jacob. They turned
her away. She became the concubine of Eliphaz, Essau's son. She must have said
to herself; 'It is better to be a servant in this nation than to have lordly rank in
another.' Amalek issued from the union—who cause Israel so much suffering.
For what reason? Answer: Timna should not have been turned away." Levinas
reads the Talmud's moral in terms of the "vocation of Israel" and a "superb
spirit, a movement of openness," and yet the text (following the discussion of
Timna with a reference to Reuven, Jacob's son) plainly extols the virtue of
assimilating into the network of family ties and bloodlines. From Ruth who con-
verts comes the House of David and the Messiah to follow; from Timna, who is
turned away comes Amalek, Israel's eternal enemy from within the Nations. The
former would be precisely Maimonides's model for how Jewish particularism
becomes universal: actually entering into Jewish peoplehood. The latter, for Levinas (if I read him correctly here), becomes an object lesson in remaining open
to the lesson taught by alterity.

99. Robert Bernasconi raises an important question in this essay about the
route to universalism from Levinas's Jewish particularism, for as he says, "This
is not to say that Levinas's attempt to negotiate between Jewish election and
Jewish universalism is clear." Bernasconi holds Levinas to the connection
between persecution and election (the former being more that just "a formal
structure or an elaborate metaphor" and "more even than an ontic fundament"), but rightly notes that this also prevents Levinas's notion of philosophy
from being genuinely pluralistic: "to my eyes quite scandalously, Levinas
excludes the possibilities of most cultures from contributing to philosophy. . . .
He does not acknowledge the existence of philosophies outside the Greek and
Hebraic traditions; still less does he admit the possibility that they might put
into question the dominant tradition, as a 'Levinasian' hermeneutics—were such
a thing admitted—would surely proclaim" (84–85).

100. See also in the same volume, "On Jewish Philosophy," 171. Levinas's
analysis of the instrumental relationship between hands and objects in the section entitled "Possession and Labor" is nicely anticipated by the coincidence of
words for "work" and "hand" in the very portion of the Torah portion describ-

ing Jacob's service for Laban that he cites. As Robert Gibbs puts it, "Working, as opposed to enjoying, is to risk alienating my self in the work produced. We consign the work to others and abandon our control over it" (236). And the entire ensuing analysis of "dwelling," "habitation," and "hospitality" in *Totality and Infinity* evokes those scenes in Genesis that detail the domestic exigencies of Abraham and Sarah, Isaac and Rebekah, Jacob and Rachel—events and decisions in the most private of spheres that found God's relationship with Israel. Finally, as Elaine Scarry perceptively notes in *The Body in Pain: The Making and Unmaking of the World* (Oxford: Oxford University Press, 1986)—a book unfortunately marred by its "Judeo-Christian" over more purely Judaic reading of Hebrew Scripture—the material (human) and disembodied (worlds) are manifestly intertwined at this point in the Genesis narrative, as "Jacob appropriates the gifts of both fathers, the flocks of Laban and (in his animal husbandry) the cultural authorship and authority of God" (196).

101. From the text of the Passover *Haggadah*. In my "At Play in the Piels (and Hiphils) of the Lord," I focus upon the *Haggadah* text and its rabbinic extension of biblical demands as a reconsecration through renarration. See also Menachem Kasher, *"Hagadah Sh'lemah": The Complete Passover Hagadah* (Jerusalem: Torah Shelema Institute, 1967).

102. In the *Politics*, Aristotle says of Plato's model of brotherhood, "it is better to have a cousin of one's own than a son in the sense indicated" (2.3).

103. Although commentators disagree on this point, I see Levinas's treatment of eros, and his specific vocabulary of espousal and consanguinity "father," "son," "feminine," "beloved," as expressing metaphysical rather than biological correlates, and proceeding in exactly the same spirit as the Sages' allegorical reading of Song of Songs. In *Totality and Infinity* he says, "If biology furnishes us with the prototypes of all these relations, this proves, to be sure, that biology does not represent a purely contingent order of being, unrelated to its essential production. But these relations free themselves from their biological limitations" (279).

104. See also Levinas's *Time and the Other*, trans. Richard Cohen (Duquesne: Pittsburgh University Press, 1987), 90–94.

105. R. Soloveitchik's essay, "Engaging the Heart and Teaching the Mind," from *Reflections of the Rav*, makes this very point in relation to this identical passage: "What is the difference between a teacher and a nursing-father (or mother)? A teacher instructs a child and a nursing mother also teaches a child. The latter, however, in addition to teaching, also carries the child in her bosom, *behekekha*; she submerges her identity in that of her child, making her ambitions secondary or nullifying them completely. . . . There is an emotional fusion of two identities. A teacher, however, retains his own identity and personality; his is an intellectual communication of specific knowledge" (157).

106. See also "The Nations and the Presence of Israel" (*ITN* 92–108).

107. See also (*NTR* 67–68).

108. See also "Ethics and Exegesis" (*BV* 109–113).

109. "Who Is One-Self" (*NTR* 109–115), Levinas's last, from 1989, explores this inveterate theme in light of Abraham's assertion, *I am ashes and dust* (Gen. 18:27).

110. When Levinas does imagine a spatial binomial, it is that of *height*—a vertical "elevation to the heavens" as opposed to a "Euclidian space . . . the forward of a horizontal march." See "Beyond the State in the State" (*NTR* 83–87 and 102).

111. He continues parenthetically, "When thinking of Judaism, one must always catch sight of humanity as a whole, just as it is appropriate to anticipate in Abram Abraham, the father of many nations."

112. Ouaknin makes a similar point about the meaning of *Ivri* ("Hebrew") in *The Burnt Book*: "*The Hebrew is not in time; he produces time*" (73–74).

113. See also the extended passage on "insomnia" and "awakening" in "God and Philosophy" (*BPW* 132–133).

114. See also "Beyond the State in the State" in *New Talmudic Readings*.

115. "The ethical call of conscience occurs, no doubt, in other religious systems besides the Judeo-Christian, but it remains an essentially religious vocation," Levinas says in his dialogue with Richard Kearney, but it is not entirely clear how any but a monotheistic faith can have the transcendent oneness to "turn human nature inside out" (25). See also "Monotheism and Language" (*DF* 178–180).

116. He mentions Maimonides indirectly in "A Figure and a Period," *ITN* 146–149).

117. In the Bible, בחירה—"*bechira*," chosenness or selection, as in כי עם קדוש אתה ליי אלהיך בך בחר יי אלהיך, *For you are a holy people to the Lord your God; the Lord your God has chosen you* (Deut. 7:6)—appears thematically in Genesis in the form of God's ברכה—"*berakha*," blessing of *zera v'aretz* (seed and land) to the Patriarchs—and in Deuteronomy in the repeated formulaic description of the Temple as *the place which the Lord will choose* [יבחר] to *proclaim his name there*. Steven Novak points out in *The Election of Israel* that, as with the neither autonomous nor fully heteronomous nature of the covenant between God and Israel, chosenness is not simply a one-way proposition. He cites the *midrash* on Ps. 135:4, *for the Lord has chosen Jacob for himself*, that states (because of a grammatical ambiguity): "the matter is still inconclusive, for we do not know whether it is God who has chosen Israel or it is Israel who has chosen God" (*Sifre*). Compare Deut. 26:16–19: "You have singled out the Eternal this day to be your God . . . and [He] has singled you as His treasured people to keep His commandments," along with its commentary by Rashi and the Rambam.

118. In *Reflections of the Rav*, R. Soloveitchik explains the meaning of *segula* as "an ontological merger," as instanced for the love of Jacob for Rachel over Leah or of Jacob for Joseph and Benjamin. *Idolatry* by Moshe Halbertal and Avishai Margolit (Cambridge: Harvard University Press, 1992) considers the issues of chosenness and specialness in the context of biblical interdicts against idolatry.

119. Strictly speaking, according to Halevi, "choice" is a human not divine category of action. It is more accurate to say that God willed Israel's election outside of history and not that he chose it within history; supernaturally speaking, the primacy of Israel is *inevitable*. As Novak formulates the distinction, Halevi's notion of "substantial distinctiveness" vies with the "authentic biblical-

rabbinic teaching" of "relational distinctiveness," which is Maimonides's position as well. The two positions are synthesized in modern times by R. Abraham Isaac Kook (whom Leibowitz explicitly classes with Halevi), but they are not exclusive to Maimonides and Halevi, and (loosely conceptualized), again provide an illustration of strictly halakhic judgments on one hand, and aggadic inclinations on the other. It is a principle upheld by the Sages that prophecy was and always will be exclusive to the Jewish people. And yet, a famous *midrash* in *Tanna Debei Eliyahu* claims that any person, Jew or Gentile, man or woman, slave or maidservant, may achieve prophecy. For R. Kook, the Pentateuch's terms of chosenness and *segula* are expressed in terms of a unifying and wholly singular "national spirit" that is the dialogic partner to God's *yichud* or oneness: "The congregation of Israel is the concentrated essence of all of existence, and in this world this essence is actually contained within the Jewish nation" (*Orot Yisrael* in *Orot* 138). In "Halakhic Praxis and the Word of God," 313–319, Avi Sagi contrasts Halevi and Maimonides in terms of their respective philosophies of *halakhah*: as disclosing or revealing the word of God versus a "creative" model of halakhic truth as human convention. See also Novak, *The Election of Israel*, 207–225; Menachaem Kellner, *Maimonides on Judaism and the Jewish People* (Albany: State University of New York Press, 1986).

120. "Politics After!" (*BV* 187–195), narrates a short history of Zionism pointedly ending with a reference to Scholem. See also the "Debate on Messianism and Zionism" between Cohen and Buber in Paul Mendes-Flohr and Yehuda Reinharz, *The Jew in the Modern World: A Documentary History* (Oxford: Oxford University Press, 1995), 571–577, in which Buber argues for a supranational destiny of "infinite striving" that can be concretized only in the land of Israel by Jews, and Cohen counters with a never-to-be exhausted "political religiosity" that can transpire only in the diaspora where Jews point the way to a "universal humanistic Jewish nationality that transcends the State." As Stephen Novak puts Cohen's position, "election is consistently subordinate to revelation"; in the messianic end of days, "the nations will for all intents and purposes become one with Israel in all her singularity. The content of their life will become Jewish" (77). By contrast, Buber believed that Exile forever postponed a realization of Judaism, which requires the "firm sod" of Palestine where nature becomes spirit.

121. In chapter four of *The Election of Israel*, Novak contrasts "extensive" Jewish eschatology (Maimonidean) with "apocalyptic."

122. I should emphasize here a point I have left to treatments of Levinas like Gibbs's and Cohen's: Levinas's talmudic selectivity derives in part from a purely philosophical desire to remotivate modern ontological and epistemological categories. Here he is perhaps most like Spinoza (despite his own declaration that his philosophy lies "at the antipodes of Spinozism"), in bringing to Jewish thought a reformist passion for philosophy itself. Cohen's introduction to *New Talmudic Readings* sheds light here.

123. See also the lengthy reading "Messianic Texts" (*DF* 59–96), which ends with the following important passage: "The messianic sensibility inseparable from the knowledge of being chosen (which is perhaps, ultimately, from the very subjectivity of the subject) would be irremediably lost—and this will be my

final remark—if the solution of the Stare of Israel did not represent an attempt to reunite the irreversible particularist acceptance of universal history with the necessarily particularist messianism. This universalist particularism (which is not Hegel's concrete universal) can be found in the aspirations of Zionism, and associated with a recognition of History and a collaboration with it. This collaboration begins with a withdrawal, a movement out of History in which we have located ourselves as assimilated Jews ever since the Emancipation." But it also involves (for "collaboration" cannot be an innocently chosen term for a French survivor of Hitler's Europe) a return to History in the form of Israeli Statehood. I return to this passage in the next chapter.

124. Refer to the helpful essay by Ephraim Meir, "Teaching Mendelssohn's Concept of Jewish Singularity," in Jospe, *Paradigms in Jewish Philosophy*, 147–165, and Raphael Jospe, "Jewish Particularity from Ha-Levi to Kaplan: Implications for Doing Jewish Philosophy," in Jospe and Fishman, eds., *Go and Study—Essays in Honor of Alfred Jospe* (Washington, D.C.: Ktav, 1980), 312–314. Levinas's view of Mendelsohn should be compared with that of the great, and underappreciated, exponent of Judaism's diacritical legacy, Hermann Levin Goldschmidt, who champions its fusion of decided particularity (belief-centeredness) and decisive universality (History as Messianism) in his *Das Vermächtis dutschen Judentums* (Vienna: Passagen Verlag, 1994). I thank David Suchoff for this reference.

125. See in the same volume "The Philosophy of Franz Rosenzweig," 150–160, "Between Two Worlds" in *Difficult Freedom*, 181–201, "Franz Rosenzweig: A Modern Jewish Thinker," in *Outside the Subject*, 49–66; and also Novak's discussion of both Rosenzweig and Cohen in *The Election of Israel*.

126. See the brilliant essay, "The Meaning of *Shemona Esrei* #15," by R. Ezra Bick, *Yeshivat Har Etzion Virtual Beit Midrash*, Alon Shevut, Gush Etzion, Israel, October 17, 1999, <http://www.vbm-torah.org/>.

127. Consult, however, Gillian Rose's trenchant critique of Levinas in *The Broken Middle: Out of Our Ancient Past* (Oxford: Blackwell Publishers, 1992).

CHAPTER 2. *MISHURAT HADIN*

1. I am indebted to Prof. Shalom Rosenberg of the Philosophy Department at Hebrew University for these references.

2. Also see the companion essay, "Yeshayahu Leibowitz's Vision of Israel, Zionism, and Judaism," in *A Heart of Many Rooms* (Woodstock, Vt.: Jewish Lights, 1999).

3. Aviezer Ravitsky provide a superb treatment of the Lubavitch movement and twentieth-century messianic religious Zionism in *Messianism, Zionism, and Jewish Religious Radicalism*.

4. Here, I allude to the title of David Hartman's *Joy and Responsibility*, quoted above. Of Jews, irrespective of nationality, Levinas writes, "Their moving fate, which is played out above history, is played out within history. Their participation in the terrestrial world is, believe me, the essential factor in this

supernatural history. I believe that their role, in this history, consisted above all in creating a society, a type of man who lives in a demystified, disenchanted world, a type of man to whom, as it is somewhat vulgarly put, *one has nothing more to say.*" See also Levinas's essay "Martin Buber's Thought and Contemporary Judaism" (*OS*, 4–19).

5. "Transcendence and Height," 11–31, and "God and Philosophy," 129–148, in *Basic Philosophical Writings.*

6. "Those who perceive themselves as 'standing before God,' in the sense of the prayer that concludes the Day of Atonement, interpret the meaning of this 'standing' in different ways. Some see it as a gift. Others regard it as a demand. Some people perceive their 'standing' as 'receiving,' whether in the sense of something given or in the sense of expecting, wishing, intending, or making an effort to be given something. In any case, this person's standing before God is for his own good. . . . Others, however, may regard themselves as being called upon to 'give,' because the 'standing' is itself the end, the service of God for the sake of which all man's resources, material and spiritual, are but means" (54–55).

7. The verse ends with the hemistich, *and He reckoned it to him as righteousness,* which Rashi interprets as God's judgment of Abraham, and Nachmanides reads in reverse: God's generational promise as a manifestation of His righteousness.

8. Leibowitz notes that the place name associated with Job, Uz, is only mentioned again in relation to Abraham in Gen. 22:20–21, and quotes *Midrash Tanchuma* to Gen. 18:23, "That which Abraham said is what Job said." Hartman acknowledges Leibowitz's probity on this score, citing Maimonides's discussion of Job; and yet even here, Hartman finds support in the *Guide* (3:22) for a framework of Jewish worship that accommodates extrahalakhic options, something Leibowitz explicitly rejects: "In the *Guide* [Maimonides] shows how scientific knowledge and metaphysics make possible the highest worship of God. Thus, when he says of Job that he possessed moral virtue but not knowledge, wisdom, and intelligence [as opposed to Abraham's powers of 'reasoning and speculation'], the implication is that Job's worship of God was characterized by practice rather than philosophical knowledge. This was why Job spent so much time bemoaning his incomprehension of why great suffering had befallen him" (127). Compare Avi Sagi's observations on R. Soloveitchik's treatment of the Book of Job in "Contending with Modernity," 428–436.

9. "Fear of God in the Book of Job," 48, "The Individual and Society," 91–92, "Religion and Science," 137–138, are also instructive here.

10. In "God and Philosophy," he writes, "Does God signify as the theme of the religious discourse which names God—or as the discourse which, at least to begin with, does not name him but says him with another form of address than denomination or evocation" (*Basic Philosophical Writings*, 135). See also "The Name of God According to a Few Talmudic Texts" (*BV* 116–128).

11. "The psalmist, in a striking way, associates the verse's profound human distress to a call made to the divine commandment, to the *Mitzvah*, to law: *I am a sojourner on earth; hide not thy commandments from me* (Ps. 119:19) as he unites the intimate elation of the soul that thirsts after God with the austere

vision of divine justice: *My soul is consumed with longing for thy ordinances at all times* (Ps. 119:20)."

12. The allusion is to Leibowitz's essay, "The Crisis of Religion in the State of Israel," originally published in *Beterem* in 1952 as "Religion in the State and the State in Religion."

13. Gillian Rose terms Soloveitchik's position "Cohenian Neo-Kantian," and Leibowitz makes Kant his principal partner in counterpointing Jewish religiosity and ethical humanism, an antithesis Emil Fackenheim captures as follows: "How can man appropriate a God-given law or commandment, accepting and performing it as though it were his own, while yet remaining, in the very act of appropriation, essentially and receptively related to its divine Giver? How can a man *morally* obey a law that is, and never ceased to be, *essentially* revealed? According to Kant, this is clearly impossible. Puzzlement and wonder arise for the Jewish philosopher because—if he is to believe the testimony of both Jewish life and thought—what Kant thought impossible is real" (44–45).

14. Leibowitz's view of Christian antisemitism follows from his theological and philosophical critique: "From the standpoint of Christianity, the existence of Judaism apart from Christianity has ceased to be legitimate. Its continued existence can only be interpreted as a deviation from the proper divine order of the world. The Church could be reconciled to the continued existence of the Jewish people only to the extent that this existence was severed from the proper existence of mankind, that of the Christian world, whose members are the 'true Jews.' The Jewish people could be permitted to exist only if their existence were disfigured, cursed, and degraded. The entry of Jews into the mainstream of the life of Christian society while still remaining Jewish, a process which began with the emancipation, must appear in the eyes of the Church as challenge to the very root of Christianity. Christianity regards itself as the legitimate heir of Judaism, and the heir cannot take possession of his inheritance while the testator is still alive. The Church did not desire the physical annihilation of the Jews. It was interested in the liquidation of Judaism, and every Jewish convert was precious as testimony to its truth" (253).

15. Even in his most polemical pieces that insist on the particularism of both Jewish suffering and Jewish religiosity, Levinas takes pains to emphasize a fraternity linking one monotheism to another. While it may derive in part from Rosenzweig's Judaeo-Christian philosophic fusion in *Star of Redemption*, Levinas's view also speaks to the cultural politics informing his identity as postwar French intellectual.

16. As for instance, the remembrance of a Catholic priest whose prayers over the Stalag-grave of a Jewish comrade "were in the absolute sense of the term, Semitic" (*DF* 12).

17. See also "Jewish Thought Today," 159–166.

18. An allegiance Levinas defines as "the expression of belonging to a high form of society that is more than a coalition of interests, a professional or confessional grouping, more than adherence to local customs, a philosophical or literary credo, or even a Review, a study circle, an 'original' doctrine all of which, furnished with a social reason, quoted according to the roles of the passionate game of letters in the neighboring Review or study circle, gave their adherents,

collaborators, and subscribers the illusion of entering history and renewing civilization." "Being a Westerner" (*DF* 47). In "Means of Identification," 50–53, Levinas will compare this secular, rationalist model of an "absolute society . . . of first-rate minds" with Judaism's adherence or adhesion that preexists any "allegiance" (the milieu and mentality of the university). Compare Leibowitz's observation that "we are all equally steeped in Western culture" (106–107).

19. Jürgen Habermas, *The Philosophical Discourse of Modernity: Twelve Lectures*, trans. Frederick Lawrence (Cambridge: The MIT Press, 1987).

20. *Otherwise Than Being*, 109ff., and also "Substitution" in *Basic Philosophical Writings*, 84–87.

21. Compare Leibowitz's analysis of Maimonidean knowledge of God as worship of God and God as necessary (nonconditioned) Being in *The Faith of Maimonides*, chapters 2 and 4.

22. See, for instance, *TI* 198, the excerpt from *Time and the Other* in *The Levinas Reader*, 46–48, "Dialogue with Richard Kearney" in *FTF* 24, "Transcendence and Height," "Meaning and Sense," "Substitution," in *BPW*.

23. The passage, from "The Ego and Totality" in *CPP*, reads in its entirety, "To respect is not to bow down before the law, but before a being who commands a work of me. But for this command not to allow any humiliation—which would take from me the very possibility of respecting—the command that I receive must also be a command to command him who commands me. It consists of commanding a being to command me. Because of the reference from a commandment to the other, We is not the plural of I" (48).

24. Eliezer Goldman provides a succinct explanation of what he calls "a curious dialectic of autonomy and heteronomy" at work in Leibowitz's thought (present also though refracted otherwise in Levinas): "The religious value of an act consists in its being performed because it is a divine command. Yet the very idea of a divine commandment and acceptance of any specific system of norms as a body of divine prescriptions can only follow from an autonomous decision. The very ascription of normative force to a divine command is a matter of decision. . . . Decision is not merely a condition for entertaining value; it is constitutive of value. Only what is freely chosen—a goal to which one aspires or a property one seeks to embody in reality—is, properly speaking, a value. In Leibowitz's opinion, a need cannot possibly be a value since it is given, not chosen. Freedom of choice is not a value in its own right, but a condition of all valuation. . . . The heteronomous force of the Torah and its Mitzvoth is dependent upon continued autonomous commitment (either explicit or tacit) on both communal and personal level" [xv].

25. See the very important lecture, "Desacralization and Disenchantment" in *NTR* 136–160, especially in concert with the diametrically opposed viewpoint in Marcel Gauchet's *The Disenchantment of the World*. "Ethics and Spirit" in *DF* 3–10 also discusses the sacred in terms of violence, the numinous, and the irrational, as does Leibowitz's short essay, "Idolatry," in Cohen and Mendes-Flor, 445–449.

26. See *The Faith of Maimonides*, 18–25, and "Religious Praxis," 27–28.

27. I link Leibowitz's analysis of love and fear of God to Levinas's in the section on Kant later in this chapter. In his essay, "On Religious Language and

the Fear of God," which discusses *Berakhot* 54a and 60b (relating to the first paragraph of the *Shema*), Levinas offers the following characteristic commentary: "[The love of God is a]n attachment which is also a sense of gratitude felt in the consciousness of a proximity at a level that is higher than the intimacy of satisfaction. A sense of gratitude for proximity-itself lived in gratitude, and as if the very meaning of the word God and the possibility of evoking and invoking it—the transcendent discourse—were to arise in this attachment. This proximity and this gratitude called love characterize monotheism, as if the possibility of the ethical good, above and beyond the difference between natural good and evil deeds, were the opening of transcendence and the source of all religious language" (*BV* 92). Clearly, this line of reasoning points in a direction both foreign and in a decisive way unthinkable for Leibowitz, and betrays a very different intellectual sensibility.

28. David Hartman objects strenuously to Leibowitz's formalized concept of worship, which collapses *kavanat ha-lev* (heartfelt devotion) into *kavanat latzet* (the intention of discharging one's duty to God). The overriding antinomy by which Leibowitz polarizes not only divine and human realms but also worship either for-its-own-sake or not-for-its-own-sake cannot accommodate the covenantal aspect which Hartman locates at the very pith of Jewish life and belief. For Hartman, reciting the *Shema* allows, indeed demands, more than simply the fulfillment of divine will; it reenacts communion at both personal and collective levels, historically but also for all time. "In reciting the Shema, we hear God addressing the community. . . . In the Shema and its benedictions, one captures the felt immediacy of the revelatory moment of Sinai. God invites the community to enter into the covenant. Th[is] does not create a sense of helplessness, but rather it is followed by the *Amidah* prayer with its many petitions, in which the community gives expression to its security and confidence in God's accepting love" (*LC* 165).

29. Linking Levinas and Maimonides in such a way finds a quiet legitimation in Hartman's discussion of Maimonides and Soloveitchik as Jewish thinkers with parallel commitments to *Torah u-madah*, Torah and secular knowledge, in "The Resurgence of Orthodoxy" (*CV* 117–120).

30. The heading refers to Maimonides in light of Leibowitz, Soloveitchik, and Levinas, but also tropes on the chapter heading "Moses and the Hegelians," 81–169, from Emil Fackenheim's *Encounters between Judaism and Modern Philosophy* ("Kant and the Sons of Abraham," which follows next in this chapter, takes its cue from Fackenheim's "Abraham and the Kantians," 33–77).

31. In a way, this is the pure power (or scandal) of mimesis, since as Leibowitz points out many times, Maimonides will often make of Abraham or Job "mouthpieces" for his own theological determinism that knowledge and love of God constitute faith itself.

32. Quoted in David Novak, "Maimonides on Judaism and Other Religions," the Samuel H. Goldenson Lecture at Hebrew Union College (Cinncinati, 1997), 1.

33. Besides the lecture on Maimonides, see Novak's *The Image of the Non-Jew in Judaism: An Historical and Constructive Study of the Noahide Laws* (Lewiston, N.Y.: Edwin Mellen Press, 1983) and *The Election of Israel*.

34. Collette Sirat, "Should We Stop Teaching Maimonides?" in Jospe, *Paradigms in Jewish Philosophy*, 138–144. Compare "How to Teach Judah Ha-Levi as a Jamesian, a Nietzschean, or a Rosenzweigian" by Warren Zev Harvey in the same volume, 129–135.

35. Although he does not pursue the issue at any length, Hartman also locates the blind spot in Leibowitz's epistemological premises. Because the natural world possesses a religious significance to premodern Maimonides that it cannot for post-Kantian Leibowitz, the latter is reduced to making *halakhah* both constitutive of, and absolutely necessary for, worship. In his review of Leibowitz's essays in *Commentary* (November 1992): 57–59, Alan Nadler is more pointed: "in no school of Judaism did the rule of law rule out the rest of life, or exclude entirely all other manifestations of spirituality. Indeed Leibowitz's strict legal positivism is without precedent in Jewish thought, and impossible to reconcile with almost an reasonable interpretation of the canonical sources of Judaism" (58). Moshe Halbertal voices a similar criticism: "An examination of the *halahkah* itself reveals an extensive interest in human needs and values. . . . Talmudic deliberation is hardly the inhuman ratiocination of its Christian and post-Christian caricatures; it is replete with references to real human values and weaknesses, which it incorporates into its legal reasonings. Leibowitz errs in the strictness of his insistence on the transcendence of the *halakhah* above human values and needs. He is too strict" (37).

36. "For Halevi, God is conceived through history: we believe in God who has revealed himself to us within the historical reality of our people. . . . But if God is to be conceived in terms of His relation to the people of Israel and to the history of the people of Israel, it follows that belief in God—for Maimonides—a belief not-for-its-own-sake [*lishmah*]. In the whole of the *Hilchot Yesodei ha-Torah* (Laws Concerning the Foundations of the Torah), the historical destiny of the people of Israel is never mentioned. Even the word 'Israel'—the fundamental principle in the world of the thought of Rabbi Judah Halevi—is never mentioned in the first four chapters of *Yesodei ha-Torah*. It appears suddenly in the first *halakhah* of chapter 5: 'The whole of the House of Israel is commanded to sanctify the great Name of God. . . .' Knowledge of God (like knowledge of the world and of man himself) is a task incumbent on man qua man: the unique religious position of *Jewish man* is *the commandments*" (124).

37. In "Ahistorical Thinkers in Judaism," one of several essays contrasting Maimonides and Halevi, Leibowitz includes history as another category of Jewish experience that, from a religious perspective, must be seen as *she'lo lishmah*. This explains the tremendously antiteleological—and antimessianic—thrust of his ideology, although significantly, he does not therefore insist on an inflexible framework of *halakhah* impervious to change. His argument, again, is predicated upon a *philosophic* distinction between necessary being and contingent reality. "Judaism in its actual embodiment as the service of God in the form of halakhic practice is ahistorical. This ahistoric character remains unaffected by the changes and transformations of the Halakhah corresponding to the historical changes and transformations in the course of time. If halakhic rules and regulations changed—or were even deliberately modified—in accordance with changes and innovations in historical conditions, that does not indicate that his-

tory is constitutive of Halakhah or a determining factor" (104–105). In a similar connection, Leibowitz highlights the different ways in which Halevi and Maimonides interpret *I am the Lord your God, who has brought you out of the land of Egypt*: "But whereas to Judah Halevi the *second* half of this verse, *who has brought you out of the land of Egypt, out of the house of bondage*, is the significant part of the verse, for Maimonides, the first few words, *I am the Lord your God*, are the key words, and it is quite intentionally that he does not refer in the context to the second half of the verse, "who has brought you out of Egypt, out of the house of bondage" (47). Compare Novak's helpful article, "Does Maimonides Have a Philosophy of History?" in Samuelson, *Studies in Jewish Philosophy*, 397–415, and Avi Sagi, "Halakhic Praxis and the Word of God: A Study of Two Models," 313–317.

38. In his essay "Soloveitchik's Response to Modernity," Hartman speaks about the interdependence of internal religious meaning and communal norm in terms of *aggadah* and *halakhah* (*CV* 153).

39. Or as R. Abraham Isaac Kook describes the matter kabbalistically, Maimonides's "strange women"—the Greek to his Hebrew—are so many *klippot* (husks) which, however, contain sparks of divinity. My argument here complements Boyarin's in *Carnal Israel*: "In order for there to be desire and thus sexuality at all, there must be the possibility of illicit desire. Desire is one, and killing off desire for illicit sex will also kill off the desire for licit sex, which is necessary for the continuation of life" (62). Boyarin's discussion treats the "dialectics of desire" as the interplay between *yetzer hara* and *yetzer hatov*—the inclinations toward evil and good in rabbinic anthropology.

40. Hartman discusses the same passage, along with the *gemara* about R. Shimon ben Yochai quoted in my introduction in "The Resurgence of Orthodoxy" (*CV* 113).

41. Following these speculations, Levinas reads the *gemara* (*Menachot* 99b–100a) as distinguishing between Greek wisdom and Greek language, the latter signifying rhetoric capable of dissimulation: "Greek wisdom, therefore, is an opening, but it is also the possibility of speaking through signs which are not universally understood and which, as signs of complicity, thus have the power to betray. . . . That is why, in the reply to Ben Damah ["Cursed be a man who rears pigs and cursed be a man who teaches his son Greek wisdom!"], the exclusion of Greek wisdom would be radical. Not because it would be knowledge, but because, in purely human knowledge without Torah, in pure humanism, this deviation already slips toward rhetoric and all the betrayals against which Plato himself struggled. Perhaps the Talmudic style whose interpretation is causing us so much difficulty is also precisely this struggle with rhetoric; [Jewish wisdom] is opposed above all to the sorcery of language" (28).

42. Hartman extends his critique of Soloveitchik's rarefied existentialism to what he regards as an unnecessarily constricted attitude toward prayer as *tefillat hovah*, the obligatory worship of God through self-sacrifice and surrender. See the discussion of both *The Lonely Man of Faith* and the latter essay *"Ra'ayonot al ha-tefillah"* in chapter 6 of *The Living Covenant*, "The Spirit of Judaic Prayer," 131–159. The classic *gemara* counterbalancing divine providence with a world free to develop on its own is found in *Avodah Zarah* 54b:

Our rabbis taught: Philosophers asked the elders in Rome, "If your God has no desire for idolatry, why does He not abolish it?" They replied, "If it was something of which the world has no need that was worshipped, He would abolish it; but people worship the sun, moon, stars, and planets; should He destroy the universe on account of fools? The world pursues its natural course [*Haolam ke-minhago noheg*], and as for fools who act wrongly, they will have to render an account. . . . Another illustration: suppose a man has intercourse with his neighbor's wife; it is right that she should not conceive, but the world pursues its natural course and as for the fools who act wrongly, they will have to render an account." This is similar to what R. Shimon b. Lakish said, "The Holy One, blessed be He, declared, 'Not enough that the wicked put My coinage to vulgar use, but they trouble Me and compel Me to put My seal thereon.'"

43. Adriaan Peperzak, "Some Remarks on Hegel, Kant, and Levinas" (*FTF* 205–217). In the *Groundwork*, Kant distinguishes between the *a priori* principles of pure ethics (the metaphysic of morals) and the subjective conditions of applied ethics (moral anthropology), a difference Levinas also recalls when he differentiates reason and ideology in "Ideology and Idealism," in Fox, *Modern Jewish Ethics*, 123.

44. Peperzak continues: "Once again the highest (the lawyer, the rule of human existence) and the lowest (the hostage, the slave) converge into something that cannot be circumscribed conceptually but that produces itself—albeit awkwardly—in the half-contradiction of opposite metaphors. The exaggeration of a transcendental self-determination together with the emphatic being-for-the-other that no longer belongs to itself seem to point to the same orientation: a 'being-for' that includes a nonphenomenal and unknowable, but practical, awareness of the absolute orienting the subject's life."

45. *Critique of Practical Reason*, trans. Mary Gregor (Cambridge: Cambridge University Press, 1997), book I, chap. 3, "On the Incentives of Pure Practical Reason," 62–75.

46. "The Moral law is, in other words, for the will of a perfect being a law of *holiness*, but for the will of every finite rational being a law of *duty*" (75). Obviously, a comparison between Kantian and Levinasian ethics proceeds only so far before breaking down. "The universality of the maxim of action according to which the will is assimilated to *practical reason* may not correspond to the totality of good will," writes Levinas in "The Rights of Man and the Rights of the Other." "Is it so certain that the entire will is practical reason in the Kantian sense? Does the will not contain an incoercible part that cannot be obligated by the formalism of universality? And we might even wonder whether, Kant notwithstanding, that incoercible spontaneity, which bears witness both to the multiplicity of humans and the uniqueness of persons, is already pathology and sensibility and 'ill will'" (*OS* 122).

47. "Those who would ground morality on the image of God in man may remember that Adolf Hitler and Adolf Eichmann were created in God's image like you and me, and also every rapist and murderer, as well as the most righteous of men" (107).

48. *Critique of Practical Reason*, book II, chap. 2, 92–135. Compare Maimonides:

It should not be thought that what . . . [prophets] hear or what appears to them in a parable is not certain . . . just because it comes about in a dream or vision. . . . A proof for this is the fact that [Abraham] hastened to the slaughter, as if he had been commanded, his son, his only son, whom he loved, even though this commandment came to him in a dream or in a vision. For if a dream of prophecy had been obscure for the prophets, or if they had doubts or incertitude concerning what they apprehended in a vision of prophecy, they would not have hastened to do that which is repugnant to nature, and [Abraham's] should would not have consented to accomplish an act of so great an importance if there had been doubt about it. (*Guide* 3:24)

49. "[There is no Hebrew word for "ethics" . . . Neither in Scripture nor in the language of the Sages is there a word for ethics, even as there is no biblical term for the concept 'conscience.' . . . Ethics is not a program of behavior. In itself an act is morally indifferent" (114).

50. In *The Fear, the Trembling, and the Fire: Kierkegaard and Hasidic Masters on the Binding of Isaac*, Jerome Gellman cites the cases of Mordechai Joseph of Izbica and Zadok Hacohen of Lublin who invoke the halakhic concept of *aveirah lishmah*, transgression committed for the sake of Heaven (*Nazir* 23b), in their readings of the *Akedah*. Where the Izbicer distinguishes between God's commandments and circumstances when the will of God seems to override them, R. Zadok contrasts those who repent out of love or out of fear in relation to sins that can be characterized as having been committed for the sake of God's will. Compare, however, R. Lichstenstein's demurral on the halakhic grounding for such a concept in Fox, *Modern Jewish Ethics*, 85.

51. Kierkegaard abstracts Abraham from not only the faith community he shares with Sarah, Isaac, and the kinship network of fellow believers, but also the perpetuity of Jewish peoplehood as instituted by *brit milah* (circumcision—Gen. 17:9) and *brit ben ha-betarim* (the covenant of the parts—Gen. 15:17), God's covenantal promises to the Nation of Israel. Gellman argues that the Kierkegaardian scenario of a clash between morality and religion is secondary to the act of self-definition before the face of God; see also Levinas's own essay "A Propos of 'Kierkegaard Vivant'" (*PN* 75–79), and Derrida's *The Gift of Death*, as well as *The Jewish Political Tradition*, texts and commentary, 3–107.

52. Gellman calls these the problems of hearing (raised by Martin Buber as well as Kant) and the problem of choice, respectively (2–21).

53. Fackenheim quotes the essay by Kierkegaard entitled "Does Man Have the Right to Let Himself be Killed for the Truth?" (73–74).

54. See *To Mend the World* and *The Jewish Return to History* (New York: Schocken Books, 1978), 19ff.

55. For an historical account of such tragic leaps in Jewish history, see Shalom Spiegel, *The Last Trial* (New York: Pantheon, 1967).

56. Fackenheim continues, "Kant's common reason and the Torah emerge thus as being in a significant contrast. Immune to surprise from any source,

Kant's common reason is *wholly* invulnerable so long as it is not questioned and *indiscriminately* vulnerable once it is questioned. Self-exposed to surprise, the Torah embodies for eternal reenactment the fear and trembling that once gripped Abraham. But precisely this self-exposure makes it *absolutely* immune to any child sacrifice, no matter what voice might demand it." Jacques Derrida's essay on Hermann Cohen, "Interpretations at War: Kant, the Jew, the German," *New Literary History* 22:1 (1991): 39–96, would also be relevant here.

57. "The law-giver of Israel said on the day of his death: behold while I am yet alive with you this day you have been rebellious against God and how much more after my death? . . . for I know that after my death you will surely be corrupted (Deut. 31:27–29). More than three thousand years have elapsed since then—and the words of Moses remain true" (108). "The redeemed people failed so completely that they caused their 'first redeemer,' Moses to fail along with them" (124).

58. Assembling several tannaitic *midrashim* and a parallel account in *Shabbat* 67a on the Pentateuchal story in Numbers 12 and *Sifre*, Daniel Boyarin writes, "Even the Patriarchs, Abraham, Isaac, and Jacob, were not expected or allowed to be celibate. Only Moses, with whom God spoke 'mouth to mouth'— in itself, a highly erotic attribute—only he was required to withdraw from marital life. He is either only slightly below the angels or even more spiritual than they, and no other human being was ever like him" (*Carnal Israel*, 164).

59. Charles Taylor discusses such Kantian moral heroism in *Sources of the Self: The Making of the Modern Identity* (Cambridge: Harvard University Press, 1989), 77–88.

60. See the chapter "Lusting after Learning" in *Carnal Israel*.

61. Discussing the same proof text from *Eruvin* 100b in his consideration of R. Lichstenstein's inquiry about an ethic idenependent of *halakhah*, J. David Bleich demurs from such a generalized assumption about natural morality: "Yet, the very formulation of the conditional phrase, 'if the Torah had not been given,' indicates that the content of these maxims of natural morality are identical with the moral precepts of revealed Sinaitic law" (*Studies in Jewish Philosophy*, 538). He refers us to Marvin Fox's corollary observation in *The Philosophical Foundation of Jewish Ethics: Some Initial Reflections* (Cincinnati, 1979), 14, and Richard Wollheim's article on "Natural Law," *The Encyclopedia of Philosophy* V (New York, 1967), 451. He also underscores the shortcut to Leibowitz from within the bounds of rabbinic theology: "Recognition of the inherent difficulties associated with a concept of natural morality leads to a position which can be best described as halakhic formalism or halakhic positivism. Such a position recognizes the norms of Halakhah as constituting the sole constraints upon human conduct" (539).

62. Compare also R. Soloveitchik's "A Stranger and a Resident," in Besdin, *Reflections of the Rav*, 170.

63. I am following R. Lichstenstein's lead by compressing a feature of his argument (the status of natural law in rabbinic theology), about which scholars do not have uniform opinions. Leo Strauss's *Natural Right and History* (Chicago: University of Chicago Press, 1953), for example, takes a Maimonidean perspective, while David Novak's *Law and Theology in Judaism*,

(New York, 1974), and Bleich's "Is There an Ethic beyond Halakhah?" both analyze the early rabbinic background.

64. Some sources for a supralegal ethic Lichstenstein cites are: Nachmanides on Lev. 19:2, Rashi on Deut 6:18, *Mekhilta Yitro, Masekhta d'Amalek* (the primary rabbinic source), Maimonides in *Mishneh Torah, Hilkhot De'ot* 1:5, 1:6, 1:7, and *Bava Metzia* 83a (which Levinas's adduces in "Judaism and Revolution" *NTR*, 94–119). In *Ketubot* 103a, the Sages speak of *midat S'dom*, denoting the sort of privatized and proprietary *amour propre* Levinas regards as counterethical in an ontologic sense—" What is mine is mine, and what is yours is yours . . . this is the trait of Sodom" (*Avot* 5:13). It is proscribed by the Sages under the general rubric of *lifnim meshurat ha-din* whose true scope R. Lichstenstein describes as comprehending both "rigorous obligation" and "supreme idealism" (75–76). Compare Jacob Petuchowski's defense of self-interest in the same volume, "The Limits of Self-Sacrifice," 103–118.

65. Lichstenstein notes the linguistic distinction articulated by the Rabbis in the *Mekhilta* source: "'*And the action*—this is the line of *din; that they shall take*—this is *lifnim meshurat ha-din*'—the reified static noun being used in relation to the one and the open-ended verb in relation to the other. In observing *din*, the Jew rivets his immediate attention upon the specific command addressed to him. His primary response is to the source of the prescribed act. With respect to *lifnim meshurat ha-din*, he is, 'looking before and after,' concerned with results as much as origins" (79).

66. He notes, however, that a distinction between *halakhah* and Halakhah or *din* and *lifnim meshurat hadin* should not make the mistake of identifying duty as merely or wholly legalistic, and a supererogatory ethic as consequently optional or pietistic, which does "a disservice to Halakhah and ethics alike."

67. In "Halakha and Other Systems of Ethics: Attitudes and Interactions" in *Modern Jewish Ethics*, 89–102, Nachum L. Rabinovitch suggests the following set of polarities: "moral code" (restrictive) as opposed to "ethical theory" (paradigmatic), individual halakhic decision-making versus standardized norms, God's attribute of mercy in relation to that of justice, and finally, a Halakhah truncated by sociopolitcal exigencies versus one that sanctions needed innovation.

68. See David Sidorsky's "The Autonomy of Moral Objectivity," in *Modern Jewish Ethics*, 153–173 and Steven S. Schwartzchild's "Authority and Reason Contra Gadamer" in Samuelson, *Studies in Jewish Philosophy*, 161–190.

69. She thus disputes Schwarzchild's claim that far from being "the tail to secular philosophy's kite," Jewish practical reason secures the string to lead it. While thus positioned perhaps to resolve the internal crisis of modern moral philosophy, this view still fails to account for the rift Rose locates between philosophy and social theory. See Schwartzchild, "Modern Jewish Philosophy," in Cohen and Mends-Flohr, 629–634, and "Authority and Reason contra Gadamer" in Samuelson, *Studies in Jewish Philosophy*, 161–190.

70. *Midrash Rabbah* on Genesis 9:27 explains that "many things Greek (deriving from Japheth) are welcome within Judaism (deriving from Shem)."

71. Lamenting the institutional divide between philosophy and social theory, Rose segues from Kant to Max Weber who analyzes how the modern appa-

ratuses of "legal-rational authority" leave human freedom fully or merely autonomous, and thus extraneous to the public discourses of administrated power (168). This link between Kant and Weber is neatly echoed by Eliezer Goldman in his introductory exposition of Leibowitz's intellectual history in *Judaism, Human Values, and the Jewish State*, where he suggests that Leibowitz's distinctively positivistic cleft between fact and norm resonates according to Weberian principles as much as Kantian (xiv).

72. "[I]t is Kant's emphasis on the priority of practical reason or subjective freedom that has itself undermined ethics. It is this disjunction between the moral discourse of rights and the systemic actualities of power in modern states and societies—that is, the disjunction between 'morality' and law—that has given rise to the separation of philosophy and social theory. . . . [T]he disjunction is perpetuated in the spectrum of competing approaches to conceiving of law and the reinsinuating of ethics into science: from law defined normatively as sanction, to law defined ideal-typically as meaningful orientation" (169).

73. Robert Gibbs argues for a philosophical exploration of *halakhah* as illuminating the task of social and political liberation in *Correlations in Rosenzweig and Levinas*, 251: "The development of institutions that would replace the sacral practices of the Temple in Jerusalem and priestly authority required a mode of reflection that holds particular interest for an attempt to develop social institutions that could replace the totalizing proclivities of modern states." Drawing from the traditions of rabbinic thought about such institutions, Gibbs suggests, might have thickened and complicated the drive to economic justice abstractly envisioned by Levinas and linked too dangerously by Marx to a totalized view of revolution. The question of Zionism, however, as Gibbs freely admits, is not his concern (243).

74. I paraphrase Schwartzchild's formulation from "Modern Jewish Philosophy" (Cohen and Mendes-Flohr 628).

75. Rose explicitly mentions Levinas and Rosenzweig as bearing much of the blame for failures to integrate for social and political history into their ethical philosophies (170). When, for instance, Levinas speaks of grounding "the rights of man" in something "more legitimate than any legislation, more just than any justification," that expresses personhood "suspended of all reference," he is positing, in Rose's terms, a law beyond the law, and only then an ethics. See "The Rights of Man and the Rights of the Other," *OS* 116–125.

76. Compare also Jean Bethke Elshtain, *Public Man, Private Woman* (Princeton: Princeton University Press, 1981) and Martha Nussbaum, *Sex and Social Justice* (New York: Oxford University Press, 1999).

77. "The State of Israel and the Religion of Israel" (*DF* 217), and "Exclusive Rights" (239). In "Transcendence and Height," apropos of a discussion about the State, Levinas remarks in passing, "There are, if you like, the tears that a civil servant cannot see: the tears of the Other" (*BPW* 23).

78. The organicist metaphors suggest a natural bridge to Levinas as well: art is known by its "bewitching rhythms" and its idolatrous ability to "lend face to things"; the self, in ethical experience, is revealed as "an irritability, a susceptibility, or an exposure to wounding and outage," "a particularism of the enrooted vegetable being," "a tree that grows without regard for everything it

suppresses and breaks, grabbing all the nourishment, air, and sun." See "Signature" (*DF* 93); "Is Ontology Fundamental?" and "Substitution" (*BPW* 10, 86); "Ethics and Exegesis" (*ITN* 110); "Place and Utopia" (*DF* 100).

79. Section 4 in this chapter.

80. "Idea for a Universal History from a Cosmopolitan Point of View," in *On History* (New York: Bobbs Merrill, 1963); see also Julia Kristeva's comments on Kant in *Strangers to Ourselves*, 170–172.

81. In *Sources of the Self*, Charles Taylor writes, "This is a root and branch rejection of all ancient moralities. We cannot accept that the cosmic order, or even the order of ends in human 'nature,' should determine our normative purposes. . . . In spite of some resemblances to ancient stoicism, Kant's theory is really one of the most direct and uncompromising formulations of a modern stance" (364). Compare Stanley Cavell's analysis of the Kantian divide in *In Quest of The Ordinary: Lines of Skepticism and Romanticism* (Chicago: University of Chicago Press, 1998), and J. B. Schneewind, *The Invention of Autonomy: A History of Modern Moral Philosophy* (Cambridge: Cambridge University Press, 1997).

82. "Idealism and Ideology," in Fox, *Modern Jewish Ethics*, 121–138. The former term, of course, represents the visible face of an ontologic interruption (ethical alterity), while the latter, Levinas suggests, can be complicit in the very discourses of Universal Reason—essence, totality, subjectivity—it ostensibly critiques. "The modern world is even more shaken by this [the other man]—shaken to the very depth of its religious sensibilities—than by the denunciation of ideologies, although this movement, like Harpagon crying, 'Stop, Thief!' is quick to suspect itself of ideology. To demand justice for the other man, is this not to return to morality" (130)? This is one of the few essays in which Levinas explicitly mentions Marx, though his description of the proletarian other, whose economic deprivation models the absolute stripping of the other *as other*, is a common theme

83. Berlin quotes Fichte here. This, of course, is the counterfable to Pascal's as chosen by Levinas for the epigraph to *Otherwise Than Being*: "'That is my place in the sun.' That is how the whole usurpation of the world began." The parallel maxim in Leibowitz is perhaps just as relevant: "Gird up strength like a lion to rise in the morning for the service of your Creator."

84. Levinas cites *Sanhedrin* 37a: "Grandeur of the Holy One Blessed be He: Behold! man, who strikes coins with the same die and gets coins all alike; but behold the King of kings, the Holy One Blessed be He, who strikes all men with the die of Adam and not one is the same as another. That is why each is obliged to say: The world was created for me!"

85. "The Social Order as a Religious Problem," 151. Hartman offers a parallel claim in his discussion of Soloveitchik's essays "Majesty and Humility" and "Catharsis," in which withdrawal, defeat, and recoil exemplify halakhic heroism (*LC* 81–88), and compare the critique of Soloveitchik's later observations on prayer, 141–159.

86. "Leibowitz offers a Jewish categorical imperative for the religious community: Act in such a way that you could wish all Jews to act in the same fashion. . . . Any Jewish perspective that does not imply the possibility of observance by the total community is a false application of the Judaic tradition. . . . There-

fore, religious Jews who embrace the State of Israel must build a Judaism that can govern the entire community" (*A Heart of Many Rooms*, 273–274). Compare the connection Levinas draws between community and consecrated individuals in "The Youth of Israel" (*NTR* 120–135).

87. Also, the essay cited by Levinas in *DF*, "The Crisis of Religion in the State of Israel," 159–173.

88. R. Soloveitchik's grandfather and father, whom he mentions with such reverence in *Halakhic Man*, are quoted by Aviezer Ravitsky as each decrying the advent of Zionist Jews: "They are a new sect like that of Shabbatai Zevi, may the names of evildoers rot" and "the people of Israel should take care not to join a venture that threatens their souls, to destroy religion, and is a stumbling block to the House of Israel" (13).

89. "What the Halakhah never envisaged was the emergence of the state of Israel in real history, in the year 1948, unaccompanied by any theophany (as pictured in popular tradition), or even by the emergence of the perfected human type (as depicted by Maimonides). The ineffectiveness of religious Jewry today in dealing with the real phenomenon of the state of Israel is rooted in an incoherent attempt to view it through the prism of a system which never reckoned with the possibility that such a phenomenon would exist" (164)! Compare also A. B. Yehoshua's essays on national identity in *Between Right and Right*.

90. Ravitsky's study of the historical background and the current radical religious climate in Israel is masterly, and should be consulted for placing Leibowitz in context. His conclusion merits quotation in that regard: "[N]one of the religious outlooks discussed in this book acknowledge an intermediate historical model—a concrete mode of Jewish being that is neither exile nor redemption. They all maintain a dichotomous approach (*galut* or redemption), thereby rejecting entirely the more complex option of a partial Jewish revival within history that continuously hovers between the two extremes. By contrast, the alternative, moderate approaches seek religious significance specifically within the realm of historical, premessianic realization, precisely because of what such a realization opens up and invites, demands and promises. The advocates of this viewpoint [Leibowitz being paradigmatic, of course] see the present return to Zion as taking place in an 'opportune moment,' as a halakhic challenge based precisely on this maverick condition—that is no longer 'exile' but not yet 'redemption'" (208). Compare also "The Celebration of Statehood," in Hartman's *Conflicting Visions* and *A Heart of Many Rooms*, 267–296.

91. He continues: "There are only anti-Zionist ideologies, for the purpose of denying that the Jewish nation is a nation."

92. The *midrash*, in the name of R. Yitzchak, asks, if the Torah is a book of Laws, why does it not begin with the commandment regarding the new moon. It establishes, rather, God's sovereignty as Creator. If the nations accuse Israel of banditry for seizing one of the seven nations of Canaan, Israel can respond, "The entire universe belongs to God. He created it and He granted it to whomsoever he deemed fit."

93. Levinas, (*TI* 244–247); "Demanding Judaism" and "Who Plays Last" (*BV* 4, 63); "Judaism and the Present" (*DF* 212–213); and Leibowitz, "Ahistorical Thinkers in Judaism," especially 96–98 and 102.

94. Nachmanides criticized Maimonides for not including the injunctions to conquer, possess, and settle the land in his *Book of Commandments*. *Mitzvot la'asot b'aretz* like the *Shmittah*—Sabbatical—year of fallowness or the *ma'aser sheni* tithe to be eaten in Jerusalem can be performed only in *Eretz Yisrael*, hence the force of statements like the following from *Ketubot* 110b: "Whoever dwells outside the Holy Land is regarded as if he worshipped idols" (see also *Avodah Zara* 8a, *Sota* 14a, *Bava Batra* 91a, and Maimonides's *Hilchot Melachim* 5:9–12 in the *Mishneh Torah*. For the halakhic background, see Hershel Shachter, "The *Mitzvah* of *Yishuv Eretz Yisrael*," in *Religious Zionism*, ed. Shubert Spero and Yitzchak Pessin (Jerusalem: World Zionist Organization, 1989), 190–212, and the essays collected in *Israel as a Religious Reality*, ed. Chaim Waxman (Northvale, N.J.: Jason Aronson, 1994).

95. "The inhabitants of Canaan—farmers as spontaneous as the forces of nature and yet capable of organization—are also builders of cities. To build, to dwell, to be—a Heideggerian order. This then was what awaited the children of Israel there" (60). Compare Heidegger's "Building, Dwelling, Thinking," in *Poetry, Language, and Thought*, trans. Albert Hofstadter (New York: Harper & Row, 1972).

96. Also *Ta'anit* 29a, and *Megillat Eichah* (Lamentations) 2:17.

97. They are called the *Nephilim*, deriving from the root נפל, to fall, and are also mentioned in Gen. 6:4, which the medieval commentator Abraham Ibn Ezra reads in the way I adduce here, but which Rashi interprets as "they fell [through sinfulness] and caused others to fall."

98. In his introduction to the *Quatre lectures talmudiques* (Paris: Les Éditions de Minuit, 1968) Levinas refers to the present reading: "The third lesson, about the birth of the State, precedes by two years the discussions generated everywhere by the Six-Day War, which the State of Israel was forced to win in 1967" (*NTR* 3). In her introduction, Aronowicz cites this essay as representative of Levinas's purposefully secularizing hermeneutic.

99. Rashi follows *Sota* 64:2, *Sifri*, and *Midrash Tanchuma* 5. In her *Studies in Bamidmar*, 135–155, Leibowitz's sister, Nehama, draws on several midrashic and later rabbinic sources to substantiate the majority view that either cowardice or outright rejection of the Promised Land motivates the action in this episode. In the same vein as the argument about *me'ila* below, the fifteenth-century Torah commentary *Akedat Yitzhak*, for example, blames the spies for mixing factual report with opinion. Levinas's reading interprets against the grain of this and other standard commentaries. Not unlike his un-mitnagdic use of the *Nefesh ha-Hayyim*, however, it does echo a Hasidic approach that sees the spies as loathe to leave the wilderness, the site of revelation, for the mundane plane of material responsibilities. See, for example, the *Likutei Torah* of R. Schneur Zalman of Lyady (New York: Kehot, 1987, 72, *Sefat Emet* (on *parashat Shelach*), and R. Menachem Schneerson, *Torah Studies* (New York: Kehot, 1996), 245–251.

100. R. Yaakov Medan, "The Mission of the Spies: On *Parashat Shelach*," *Yeshivat Har Etzion Virtual Beit Midrash*, Alon Shevut, Gush Etzion, Israel, June 18, 1998, <http://www.vbm-torah.org/>.

101. Consider in this light Deut. 26:1–11 (the first-fruits testimonial)

together with the *mitzvot ha-teluyot ba-aretz* like *terumot* and *ma'aserot* (dedicated portions of food and produce) keyed to inheritance of the Land: possession depends on a kind of dispossession, as the land, never owned, becomes *deserved* through a web of obligations. Increase ultimately belongs to the land, not its occupants. Compare R. Ezra Bick's "This Land Is My Land," *Yeshivat Har Etzion Virtual Beit Midrash*, Alon Shevut, Gush Etzion, Israel, February 9, 1999, <http://www.vbm-torah.org/>. (The Oral Law does not assign the same object status to land as to other propertied articles—certainly not to Israel as Divine inheritance, justified as such through the legatee's "oneness with its owner" [*Bava Batra* 65a, *Zevachim* 4b]. Still, the concept of *kinyan* (ownership and its transfer) as elaborated in tractate *Bava Metzia*, might also be considered here, especially in so far as such property rights are formalized *spatially* by the Rabbis in terms of the customary "four cubits." In the case of *kinyan*, the immediate area of which a person can legally dispose functions to extend the self into physical space as a mode of acquisition. See also Hillel Zeitlin, "The Concept of Property and Acquisition in the Holy Scriptures" in *Sifran Shel Tzadikkim* [Jerusalem: Mossad HaRav Kook, 1973].)

102. The final affirmation dovetails with Kant's declaration of political maturity, cited by Berlin: "The man who is dependent on another is no longer a man. He has lost his standing, he is nothing but the possession of another man" (237).

103. *The Pitch of Philosophy*, "Philosophy and the Arrogation of Voice" (111–113) and "Counter-Philosophy and the Lease of Voice" (125–126). Avi Sagi also remarks on a Wittgenstein-Leibowitz link in "Contending with Modernity," 433.

EPILOGUE

1. Cavell address his Jewish identity at some length in *A Pitch of Philosophy*, and it is taken up by Rael Meyerowitz in chapter 4 of *Transferring to America: Jewish Interpretations of American Dreams* (Albany: State University Press of New York, 1995). On Wittgenstein, see Brian McGuinness, *Wittgenstein, A Life: Young Ludwig, 1889–1921* (Berkeley: University of California Press, 1988).

2. Also cited by François Aremengaud in "On Jewish Philosophy" (*ITN* 170).

3. Besides the two volumes edited by Jospe, *Paradigms in Jewish Philosophy* and *Jewish Philosophy and the Academy*; Kellner, Samuelson, and Schwartzchild in *Studies in Jewish Philosophy*, see Kenneth Seeskin, *Jewish Philosophy in a Secular Age* (Albany: State University Press of New York, 1990), and the excellent *Reasoning after Revelation: Dialogues in Postmodern Jewish Philosophy*, ed. Steven Kepnes, Peter Ochs, and Robert Gibbs, and Yudit Greenberg (Boulder, Colo.: Westview Press, 1998). *The Society for Textual Reasoning* and its electronic journal, *Textual Reasoning* (*TR*, Postmodern Jewish Philosophy Bitnetwork), pick up substantively where my admittedly heuristic notion of community for the present of "future Jewish thought" leaves off. See especially

Aryeh Cohen, "Talmud and Postmodern Jewish Philosophy: Framing Women/Constructing Exile," in *TR* 3.1 (1994), together with responses to it in *TR* 3.2 and 3.3 (1994); Jacob Meskin, "Critique and the Search for Connection: On Levinas' Talmudic Readings," in *TR* 5.2 (1996), together with responses in *TR* 5.3 (1996); and the discussion of Ira Stone's *Reading Levinas/Reading Talmud* (Philadelphia: Jewish Publication Society, 1998), in *TR* 8 (1999).

4. In addition to the other references noted earlier, see Levinas's careful explanation of such duality in "On Jewish Philosophy" (*ITN* 167–183).

5. See also Susan Handelman, *The Slayers of Moses: The Emergence of Rabbinic Interpretation in Modern Literary Theory* (Albany: State University of New York Press, 1982); and Daniel Boyarin, *Intertextuality and the Reading of Midrash*.

6. Françoise Armengaud also asks Levinas about the Maimoinides/Halevi antinomy as offering perhaps another way to formulate the relationship between Scripture and critique; his response entails a by now familiar, characteristically Levinasian (and very non-Leibowitzian) equation of terms, "To me, religion means transcendence. . . . The relation to God is already ethics."

7. In the classical sources, the Book of Deuteronomy is known as *Mishneh Torah*, the root for which, שנ, means "to repeat." The nominative concept, however, *shinun*, does not necessarily describe a past action but rather an iterative future: the need to repeat *mitzvot l'dorot*, commandments throughout the generations, whether *chovat haguf* (personal) or *chovat karkah* (pertaining to the Land).

8. The distinction, like skepticism and the problem of acknowledgment, remain abiding concerns in Cavell's work, explored in a range of contexts and intellectual figures. See especially *In Quest of the Ordinary* and *This New Yet Unapproachable America: Lectures after Emerson after Wittgenstein* (Albuquerque: Living Batch Press, 1989).

9. Appiah, *In My Father's House: Africa in the Philosophy of Culture* (New York Oxford University Press, 1992); Nye, *Philosophy & Feminism: At the Border* (New York: Twayne Publishers, 1995).

10. See *The Claim of Reason*, 370, 372, 393–395. As I suggest in *Narrative Ethics*, Cavell and Levinas do uncannily overlap in the way each dignifies the move of skepticism. By means of a radical separation, one initiates the possibility of a greater communion or attunement: what Levinas calls "proximity" and Cavell, "acknowledgment." Failures, losses, and denials of attunement, however, bring out very these contours, and not unlike atheism in Levinas, attest to a representativeness that is at the same time a limitedness, in Cavell's words, conditions of impossibility (to block skepticism, to grant presence) that are simultaneously conditions of possibility (to recount a world, one shared) (*A Pitch of Philosophy*, 12, 119–120). For an intervention that builds on some of these tangencies between Cavell and Levinas, and traces a unique helix of avoidance-as-acknowledgment, see Doris Sommer, "About-Face: The Talker Turns," *boundary 2* 23.1 (1996): 91–134.

11. The power of skepticism for Cavell is the power of being odd and getting even, of existential or expressive aloneness. "The fantasy of a private language . . . can be understood as an attempt to account for, and protect, our sep-

arateness, our unknowingness, our unwillingness or incapacity to know or to be known. Accordingly, the failure of the fantasy signifies: that there is no assignable end to the depth of us to which language reaches; that nevertheless there is no end to our separateness. We are endlessly separate, for no reason. But then we are answerable for everything that comes between us; if not for causing it then for continuing it; if not for denying it then for affirming it; if not for it then to it" (*The Claim of Reason*, 369). See also *A Pitch of Philosophy*, 97ff., and the chapters on Kant, Coleridge, and Poe in *In Quest of the Ordinary*. The "claim of reason," as a search for origins, might also be compared to Levinas's definition of philosophical rationality as "archaeology." Like Cavell, too, Levinas enlists Shakespearean drama along with philosophy as addressing the same problems of "the human condition" albeit in different languages (*ITN* 168).

12. Cavell says that such a fantasy solves a simultaneous set of metaphysical problems: "it would relieve me of the responsibility for making myself known to others—as though if I were expressive that would mean continuously betraying my experiences, incessantly giving myself away; it would suggest that my responsibility for self-knowledge takes care of itself—as though the fact that others cannot know my (inner) life means that I cannot fail to. It would reassure my fears of being known, though it may not prevent my being under suspicion; it would reassure my fears of being known, though it may not prevent my being under indictment. The wish underlying this fantasy covers a wish that underlies skepticism, a wish for the connection between the claims of knowledge and the objects upon which the claims are to fall occur without my intervention, apart from my agreements. In the case of my knowing myself, such self-defeat would be doubly exquisite: I must disappear in order that the search for myself be successful" (351–352). Compare 380ff.

13. The last of the 613 *mitzvot* commands every Jew to write his own Torah scroll. For the Cavell, see *This New Yet Unapproachable America* and also *The Senses of Walden* (San Francisco: Northpoint Press, 1981), especially the appended essay "An Emerson Mood," 156.

14. See again my own "At Play in *Piels* of the Lord"; "The *Mitzvah* of *Sippur Yetiziat Mitzayim*," in Besdin, *Reflections of the Rav*; Menachem Kasher, *Haggadah Sh'lemah*; and Yosef Hayyim Yerusahlmi's *Zakhor*, chapter 1, and *Haggadah and History* (Philadelphia: Jewish Publication Society, 1976).

15. Commenting on the famous *aggadah* in *Shabbat* 88 in which God threatens the Israelites at the foot of Sinai with death if they do not accept the Torah—thus is "notice served notice on the Torah"—the Ketzot, following the Maharal, suggests that God compels devotion to the Torah in order exactly to provide an unshakeable basis for conscious understanding—identity and adherence as *guarantors* for subsequent "identification and adhesion." A beautiful explanation of the tension here can be found in a *shiur* on *Parashat Yitro* by R. Elyakim Krumbein, *Yeshivat Har Etzion Virtual Beit Midrash*, February 2, 1999, Alon Shevut, Gush Etzion, Israel, June 18, 1998, <http://www.torah-org./>.

16. Cavell draws an explicit tie between his Jewishness and his Americanness, the latter (through Emerson and Thoreau) illuminating his understanding of the former in terms of "a philosophy of immigrancy, of the human as stranger

[that takes] an interest in strangeness, beginning no doubt with the strangeness of oneself" (*A Pitch of Philosophy*, xv).

17. The Mishna in *Pirke Avot* says, אל תפרוש מן הצבור, *Do not keep apart from the community* (2:5), and also אל בינתך אל תשען, *do not rely on your own understanding* (4:14). That is, again, the fence gestures to an outside that nevertheless remains an unlikely possibility—further solidified textually, one could argue, in that each of the sixth chapters of the tractate returns to the same opening refrain, כל ישראל יש להם חלק לעולם הבא, *All Israel has a share in the world to come*, and the fact the entire tractate begins by outlining the *shalshelet kabbalah*, the chain of tradition, binding generation to generation, Jew to Jew.

18. *Pirke Avot* 3:3–4 and 7, 5:20, all of chapter 6. See also R. Soloveitchik's allusion to this *mishna* in "The *Mitzvah* of *Sippur Yetiziat Mitzayim*," *Reflections of the Rav*, 215. On the Torah as tradition not identity, ethical necessity before biological accident, assent over descent (the sense of this chapter's final epigraph also drawn from *Pirke Avot*) see Leon Wieseltier's *Kaddish*, 258–295.

19. Meyerowitz speaks to the last element of this series in *Transferring to America*, which treats the cases of Harold Bloom, Sacvan Bercovitch, and Stanley Cavell; the introductory and concluding chapters discuss a Jewish presence in the humanities generally.

20. In a very important essay for modern literary studies, the Russian critic and theorist Mikhail Bakhtin distinguishes between "authoritative" and "innerpersuasive" discourse. "The authoritative word demands that we acknowledge it, that we make it our own; it binds us, quite independently of any power it might have to persuade us internally; we encounter it with its authority already fused to it. The authoritative word is located in a distanced zone, organically connected with a past that is felt to be hierarchically higher. It is, so to speak, the word of the fathers. Its authority was already *acknowledged* in the past. It is a *prior* discourse" (*The Dialogic Imagination: Four Essays*, 342). Compare the texts from what is known as Bakhtin's Nevl'/Vitebsk period, *Art and Answerability: Early Philosophical Essays by M. M. Bakhtin*, trans. Vadim Liapunov (Austin: University of Texas Press, 1990), and *Toward a Philosophy of the Act*, trans. Vadim Liapunov (Austin: University of Texas Press, 1993). For relevant treatments of these issues, see Caryl Emerson, *The First Hundred Years of Mikhail Bakhtin* (Princeton: Princeton University Press 1997); Emerson and Gary Saul Morson, *Mikhail Bakhtin: Creation of a Prosaics* (Stanford: Stanford University Press, 1990) and Michael Holquist, *Dialogism: Bakhtin and His World* (London: Routledge, 1990). Finally, along with a parallel in intellectual legacy whose roots lie in the Neo-Kantianism of the Marburg School, I should note that like Leibowitz, Bakhtin spent his childhood in Russia, for a time living in Vilnius (Vilna), which is about as far from Riga (Leibowitz's birthplace), as is Kovno (Levinas's).

21. As much as was Bakhtin—though significantly, with far less ideological sophistication—Leibowitz was a beneficiary of the dominant Neo-Kantian paradigms that characterized much of Western European philosophy at the time (Leibowitz studied at the Universities of Berlin, Köln, Heidelberg, and later, Basel; Bakhtin absorbed Marburg school Neo-Kantianism under the tutealge of Matvei Isaevich Kagan, an émigré colleague of Hermann Cohen. And yet

Bakhtin's counterpart in synthetic and critical acumen here would have to be Levinas not Leibowitz, considering that it is the phenomenologist who applied to Husserlian theories of consciousness, and Heideggerian ontology the same powers of critique that Bakhtin directs at the looming, comparably idealist figure of Immanuel Kant. One can only wonder what a metahalakhic philosophy would have looked like had Leibowitz come across Bakhtin's critique of a Kantian "theoriticism" that exchanges lived possibilities of action for abstract categories. The interplay between *din* and *meshurat hadin* in the Halakhah as a movement between ad hoc and rule-bound judgment meshes much more meaningfully with the immanent conditions of answerability Bakhtin ties to concrete deeds in the world than with the laden structures of discursive reason in Kant he critiques in *Toward a Philosophy of the Act*. See Holquist's introduction to that book and *Dialogism: Bakhtin and His World* for the epistemological and metaphysical nuances here.

22. Rashi's commentary says that this signifies the giving of both a written and an Oral Torah. See also Nehama Leibowitz's discussion in *Studies in Devarim*, 321–326.

23. This "resonance of one language on several registers" (11) is the missing dimension in Jill Robbins's otherwise competent section on this essay in *Altered Readings* (136–143)

24. In *Thinking in Jewish* (Chicago: The University of Chicago Press, 1996), Jonathan Boyarin explains this usage, "peculiar to a certain intermediary generation, child immigrants and children of immigrants from Jewish Eastern Europe," [as] "a partial translation, a failed translation . . . to claim identity without being claimed by it" (1). Boyarin's book also contains an essay on a passionately argued monograph by Vassilis Lambropoulos, *The Rise of Eurocentrism: Anatomy of Interpretation* (Princeton: Princeton University Press, 1993), which intrepidly, polemically, and tendentiously rethinks the Hebraism/Hellenism antithesis so central to the Christian and European West, a dualism, however, that leaves no obvious room for third terms like *Yiddish* or *Yiddishkayt* (not to mention *Judeo-Persian*, *Ladino*, or *Maghrebi*). See Boyarin, "From Derrida to Fichte? The New Europe, The Same Europe, and the Place of the Jews," 108–139; the equally if not more incisive essay by Louis A. Ruprecht, Jr., "On Being Jewish or Greek in the Modern Moment," *Diaspora* 3.2 (1994): 199–220; as well as the important reminder of the paradoxically ambiguous position occupied by the Jewish (Levantine) East within Jewish studies itself, *Sephardi and Middle Eastern Jewries: History and Culture in the Modern Era*, ed. Harvey E. Goldberg (Bloomington: Indiana University Press, 1996). Finally, Susan Shapiro's "*Écriture Judaïque*: Where are the Jews in Western Discourse," in Angelika Bammer, ed., *Displacements* (Bloomington: Indiana University Press, 1994) explores a similar problem about how to place Jews in the discourse of Europe and the West that ties back to related issues I raise in my introduction.

25. Cohen fills out the Levinas biography in *Elevations*, 115–121. Given Levinas's role in the *AIU*, one should, however, consult the relevant articles in the Goldberg volume above, as well as Michael M. Laskier, *The Alliance Israélite Universelle and the Jewish Communities of Morocco, 1862–1962* (Albany: State University of New York Press, 1983).

26. A *Yizkor bukh* (memory book) for Strzegowo, containing an account of the Novogrodskys, was published by The Strzegower Relief Committee (New York, 1951). This final, elegiac, footnote is also the proper place to mention that on the eve of its destruction, Levinas's Lithuania saw the fullest flowering of Jewish culture: the Ponevezh and Telz *yeshivot*, the Hebrew literature of I. L. Gordon and Abraham Mapu, the founding of YIVO and the rise of the Bund, 160 Jewish organizations and six daily papers in Yiddish and Hebrew. Its capital—for Jews—was traditionally known as *Yerushalayim d'Lita*, the Lithuanian Jerusalem. Lastly, let this terminal fence-post of *The Fence and the Neighbor* gesture accordingly to the phenomenon of a *fin de siècle* Jewish diaspora that does not typically signify European contexts, despite a new and resurgent generation of post-Holocaust European Jewry. The journal *European Judaism* is an excellent resource for this "third possibility" (Robert Musil's phrase) outside the confines of Israel and the United States. See, for example, in issue no. 61 (Autumn 1998), Diana Pinto, "The New Jewish Europe—Challenges and Responsibilities" (3–15); fortuitously enough, this issue also includes a piece on Levinas. Accordingly, see Judith Friedlander's *Vilna on the Seine: Jewish Intellectuals in France since 1968* (New Haven: Yale University Press), 1990.

WORKS CONSULTED

Abrams, Judith Z. *The Women of the Talmud*. Northvale, N.J.: Jason Aronson, 1995.

Appiah, Anthony. *In My Father's House: Africa in the Philosophy of Culture*. New York: Oxford University Press, 1992.

Arendt, Hannah. *The Human Condition*. Chicago: University of Chicago Press, 1958.

Babich, Babette E. *From Phenomenology to Thought, Errancy, and Desire: Essays in the Honor of William S. Richardson, S.J.* Dordrecht: Kluwer Academic Publishers, 1995.

Bakhtin, Mikhail. *Toward a Philosophy of the Act*. Trans. Vadim Liapunov. Austin: University of Texas Press, 1993.

———. *Art and Answerability: Early Philosophical Essays by M. M. Bakhtin*. Trans. Vadim Liapunov. Austin: University of Texas Press, 1990.

———. *The Dialogic Imagination: Four Essays*. Trans. Caryl Emerson and Michael Holquist. Austin: University of Texas Press, 1981.

Bal, Mieke. *Lethal Love*. Bloomington: Indiana University Press, 1987.

———. *Murder and Difference: Gender, Genre, and Scholarship on Sisera's Death*. Bloomington: Indiana University Press, 1988.

Benhabib, Seyla. *Situating the Self: Gender, Community, and Postmodernism in Contemporary Ethics*. New York: Routledge, 1992.

Benjamin, Walter. *Illuminations: Essays and Reflections*. Trans. Harry Zohn. New York: Schocken Books, 1969.

Ben-Sasson, H. H. *A History of the Jewish People*. Cambridge: Harvard University Press, 1976.

Bergo, Bettina. *Levinas Between Ethics and Politics*. Dordrecht: Kluwer Publishers, 1999.

Berkovits, Eliezer. *Crisis and Faith*. New York: Sanhedrin Press, 1976.

———. *Major Themes in Modern Philosophies of Judaism: A Critical Evaluation*. New York: Ktav, 1974.

———. *Not in Heaven: The Nature and Function of Halakha*. New York: Ktav, 1983.

Berlin, Isaiah. *The Senses of Reality: Studies in Ideas and Their History*. London: Chatto and Windis, 1996.

Bernasconi, Robert and Simon Critchley. *Re-Reading Levinas*. Bloomington: Indiana University Press, 1991.

Besdin, Abraham R. *Reflections of the Rav: Lessons in Jewish Thought. Adapted from Lectures of Rabbi Joseph B. Soloveitchik*. Jerusalem: Dept. for Torah Education and Culture in the Diaspora of the World Zionist Organization, 1981.

Bhabha, Homi. *Nation and Narration*. London: Routledge, 1990.

Biale, Rachel. *Women and Jewish Law: An Exploration of Women's Issues in Halakhic Sources*. New York: Schocken Books, 1984.

Bialik, Chaim Nahman. *"Halachah and Aggadah."* Trans. L. Simon. London: Education Department of the Zionist Federation, 1944.

Bick, R. Ezra. "This Land Is My Land." *Yeshivat Har Etzion Virtual Beit Midrash*. Alon Shevut, Gush Etzion, Israel. February 9, 1999 <http://www.vbm-torah.org/>.

Birnbaum, Pierre. *Jewish Destinies: Citizenship, State and Community in Modern France*. Trans. Arthur Goldhammer. New York: Hill and Wang, 2000.

Boyarin, Daniel. *Carnal Israel: Reading Sex in Talmudic Culture*. Berkeley: University of California Press, 1993.

———. *Intertextuality and the Reading of Midrash*. Bloomington: Indiana University Press, 1990.

Boyarin, Jonathan. *Thinking in Jewish*. Chicago: The University of Chicago Press, 1996.

Bronner, Leila Leah. *From Eve to Esther: Rabbinic Reconstructions of Biblical Women*. Louisville: Westminster John Knox Press, 1994.

Bruns, Gerald. "The Hermeneutics of Midrash." In *The Book and the Text: The Bible and Literary Theory*. Ed. Regina Schwartz. Cambridge: Blackwell, 1990.

Canetti, Elias. *The Agony of Flies: Notes and Notations*. Trans. H. F. Broch de Rothermann. New York: Farrar, Straus, and Giroux, 1994.

Caron, Vicki. *Uneasy Asylum: France and the Jewish Refugee Crisis, 1933–1942*. Stanford: Stanford University Press, 1999.

Cavell, Stanley. *A Pitch of Philosophy: Autobiographical Exercises*. Cambridge: Harvard University Press, 1994.

———. *In Quest of the Ordinary: Lines of Skepticism and Romanticism*. Chicago: University of Chicago Press, 1998.

———. *The Claim of Reason: Wittgenstein, Skepticism, Morality, and Tragedy*. New York: Oxford University Press, 1982.

———. *This New Yet Unapproachable America: Lectures after Emerson after Wittgenstein*. Albuquerque: Living Batch Press, 1989.

———. *The Senses of Walden*. San Francisco: Northpoint Press, 1981.

Chajes, Zvi Hirsch. *Mebo ha-Talmud*. Trans. Jacob Shacter. New York: Feldheim, 1962.

Cohen, Arthur and Paul Mendes-Flohr. *Contemporary Jewish Religious Thought: Original Essays on Critical Concepts, Movements, and Beliefs*. New York: Charles Scribner's Sons, 1987.

Cohen, Richard. *Face to Face with Levinas*. Albany: State University of New York Press, 1986.

———. *Elevations: The Height of the Good in Rosenzweig and Levinas*. Chicago: University of Chicago Press, 1994.

Cohen, Hermann. *Religion of Reason Out of the Sources of Judaism*. Trans. Simon Kaplan. New York: Ungar, 1972.

Cohen, Nachman. *Master a Mesikhta Study Guides*. New York: Feldheim, 1989.

Cuddihy, John Murray. *The Ordeal of Civility: Freud, Marx, Lévi-Strauss, and the Jewish Struggle with Modernity*. Boston: Beacon Press, 1987.

Derrida, Jacques. "Interpretations at War: Kant, the Jew, the German." *New Literary History* 22.1 (1991): 39–96.

——. *The Gift of Death*. Trans. David Wills. Chicago: The University of Chicago Press, 1995.

——. *The Other Heading: Reflections on Today's Europe*. Trans. Pascale-Anne Brault and Michael B. Nass. Bloomington: Indiana University Press, 1992.

Dominguez, Virginia. *People as Subject/People as Object: Selfhood and Peoplehood in Contemporary Israel*. Madison: University of Wisconsin Press, 1986.

Eaglestone, Robert. *Ethical Criticism: Reading after Levinas*. Edinburgh: Edinburgh University Press, 1998.

Elshtain, Jean Bethke. *Public Man, Private Woman*. Princeton: Princeton University Press, 1981.

Emerson, Caryl. *The First Hundred Years of Mikhail Bakhtin*. Princeton: Princeton University Press, 1997.

Emerson, Caryl and Gary Saul Morson. *Mikhail Bakhtin: Creation of a Prosaics*. Stanford: Stanford University Press, 1990.

Fackenheim, Emil. *To Mend the World: Foundations of Jewish Thought*. New York: Schocken Books, 1982.

——. *Encounters between Judaism and Modern Philosophy: A Preface to Future Jewish Thought*. New York: Basic Books, 1973.

——. *Jewish Philosophers and Jewish Philosophy*. Bloomington: Indiana University Press, 1996.

Fackenheim, Emil and Raphael Jospe. *Jewish Philosophy and the Academy*. London: Associated University Presses, 1996.

Fenves, Peter. *Raising the Tone of Philosophy: Late Essays by Kant; Tranformative Critique by Derrida*. Baltimore: Johns Hopkins University Press, 1993.

Finkielkraut, Alain. *The Wisdom of Love*. Trans. Kevin O'Neill and David Suchoff. Lincoln: University of Nebraska Press, 1996.

Fox, Everett, trans. *The Five Books of Moses*. New York: Schocken Books, 1995.

Fox, Marvin. *Interpreting Maimonides: Studies in Methodology, Metaphysics and Moral Philosophy*. Chicago: The University of Chicago Press, 1990.

——. *Modern Jewish Ethics: Theory and Practice*. Columbus: Ohio State University Press, 1975.

——. *The Philosophical Foundation of Jewish Ethics: Some Initial Reflections*. Cincinnati, 1979.

Frank, Daniel. *A People Apart: Chosenness and Ritual in Jewish Philosophical Thought*. Albany: State University Press of New York, 1993.

Friedlander, Judith. *Vilna on the Seine: Jewish Intellectuals in France Since 1969*. New Haven: Yale University Press, 1990.

Frost, Robert. *Collected Poems, Prose, and Plays*. New York: Library of America, 1995.

Gauchet, Marcel. *The Disenchantment of the World: A Political History of Religion*. Trans. Oscar Burge. Princeton: Princeton University Press, 1997.

Gellman, Jerome. *The Fear, the Trembling, and the Fire: Kierkegaard and Hasidic Masters on the Binding of Isaac*. Lanham, Md.: University Press of America, 1994.

Gibbs, Robert. *Correlations in Rosenweig and Levinas*. Princeton: Princeton University Press, 1992.

Glazer, Nahum N. *Modern Jewish Thought: A Source Reader*. New York: Schocken Books, 1977.

Goldberg, David Theo and Michael Krausz. *Jewish Identity*. Philadelphia: Temple University Press, 1993.

Goldberg, Hillel. *Between Berlin and Slobodka: Jewish Transition Figures from Eastern Europe*. Hoboken, N.J.: Ktav, 1989.

Goldin, Judah. *Studies in Midrash and Related Literature*. Philadelphia: Jewish Publication Society, 1988.

Goldschmidt, Hermann Levin. *Das Vermächtis dutschen Judentums*. Vienna: Passagen Verlag, 1994.

Greenberg, Blu. *On Women & Judaism: A View from Tradition*. Philadelphia: Jewish Publication Society of America, 1981.

Greenberg, Irving. *The Jewish Way*. New York: Summit Press, 1981.

Habermas, Jürgen. *The Philosophical Discourse of Modernity: Twelve Lectures*. Trans. Frederick Lawrence. Cambridge: The MIT Press, 1987.

Halbertal, Moshe. Review of Yeshayahu Leibowitz, *Judaism, Human Values, and the Jewish State. The New Republic* 208.11 (March 15, 1993): 35–38.

Halevi, Judah. *Sefer ha-Kuzari*. Tel Aviv: Omanut, 1930.

Halkin, Hillel. "Israel against Itself: Yeshayahu Leibowitz and Israel's Trading of Land for Peace." *Commentary* 98.5 (November 1994): 33–39.

Handelman, Susan. *The Slayers of Moses: The Emergence of Rabbinic Interpretation in Modern Literary Theory*. Albany: State University of New York Press, 1982.

———. *fragments of Redemption: Jewish Thought and Literary Theory in Benjamin, Scholem, and Levinas*. Bloomington: Indiana University Press, 1991.

Hareven, Alouph. *Every Sixth Israeli: Relations between Jewish Majority and the Arab Minority in Israel*. Jerusalem: Van Leer Foundation, 1983.

Hartman, David. *A Living Covenant: The Innovative Spirit in Traditional Judaism*. New York: The Free Press, 1985.

———. *Conflicting Visions: Spiritual Possibilities of Modern Israel*. New York: Schocken Books, 1990.

———. *A Heart of Many Rooms: Celebrating the Many Voices within Judaism*. Woodstock, Vt.: Jewish Lights, 1999.

Hauptman, Judith. *Rereading the Rabbis: A Woman's Voice*. Boulder, Colo.: Westview Press, 1998.

R. Hayyim of Volozhin. *Nefesh ha-Hayyim*. Vilna, 1824.

———. *L'Ame de la vie*. Traduction par Benjamin Gross. Paris: Éditions Verdier, 1989.

Heinemann, Joseph. "The Nature of the Aggadah." In *Midrash and Literature*. Eds. Geoffrey Hartman and Sanford Budick. New Haven: Yale University Press, 1986.

Holquist, Michael. *Dialogism: Bakhtin and His World*. London: Routledge, 1990.

Hyman, Paula E. *The Jews of Modern France*. Berkeley: University of California Press, 1998.

Jospe, Raphael and Fishman, S. Z. *Go and Study—Essays in Honor of Alfred Jospe*. Washington, D.C.: Ktav, 1980.

Jospe, Raphael. *Paradigms in Jewish Philosophy*. London: Associated University Presses, 1997.

Kadushin, Max. *The Rabbinic Mind*. New York: Bloch & Co., 1972.

Kant, Immanuel. "Idea for a Universal History from a Cosmopolitan Point of View." *On History*. New York: Bobbs Merrill, 1963.

———. *Critique of Practical Reason*. Trans. Mary Gregor. Cambridge: Cambridge University Press, 1997.

———. *Religion within the Limits of Reason Alone*. Trans. Theodore M. Greene and Hoyt H. Hudson. New York: Harper, 1960.

———. *The Conflict of the Faculties*. Trans. Mary J. Gregor. New York: Abaris Books, 1979.

Kaplan, Lawrence. "Israel under the Mountain: Emmanuel Levinas on Freedom and Constraint in the Revelation of the Torah." *Modern Judaism* 18.1 (February 1998): 35–47.

Kasher, Menachem. *Hagadah Sh'lemah: The Complete Passover Hagadah*. Jerusalem: Torah Shelema Institute, 1967.

Katz, Jacob. *Exclusiveness and Tolerance: Studies in Jewish Gentile-Relations in Medieval & Modern Times*. New York: Oxford: 1961.

Kellner, Menachaem. *Maimonides on Judaism and the Jewish People*. Albany: State University of New York Press, 1986.

Kepnes, Steven, ed. *Reasoning after Revelation: Dialogues in Postmodern Jewish Philosophy*. Boulder, Colo.: Westview Press, 1998.

Kierkegaard, Soren. *Fear and Trembling and The Sickness unto Death*. Trans. Walter Lowrie. Princeton: Princeton University Press, 1974.

Kolbrener, William. "No 'Elsewhere': Fish, Sololveitchik, and the Unavoidability of Interpretation." *Literature and Theology* 10.2 (June 1996): 170–190.

Koppel, Moshe. *Meta-Halakhah: Logic, Intuition and the Unfolding of Jewish Law*. Northvale, N.J.: Jason Aronson, 1996.

Kraemer, David. *The Mind of the Talmud: An Intellectual History of the Bavli*. New York: Oxford University Press, 1990.

Kristeva, Julia. *Strangers to Ourselves*. Trans. Leon S. Roudiez. New York: Columbia University Press, 1991.

Krumbein, R. Elyakim. "On *Parashat Yitro*." *Yeshivat Har Etzion Virtual Beit Midrash*. February 2, 1999. Alon Shevut, Gush Etzion, Israel. June 18, 1998. <http://www.vbm-torah.org>.

Lambropoulos, Vassilis. *The Rise of Eurocentricism: Anatomy of Interpretation* (Princeton: Princeton University Press, 1993).

Lamm, Norman. *Torah Lishmah: Torah for Its Own Sake in the Work of Rabbi Hayyim of Volozhin and His Contemporaries*. Hoboken, N.J.: Ktav, 1989.

Landesman, Dovid. *A Practical Guide to Studying Torah*. Northvale, N.J.: Jason Aronson, 1995.

———. *As the Rabbis Taught: Studies in the Aggados of the Talmud*. Northvale, N.J.: Jason Aronson, 1996.

Leibowitz, Nehama. *Studies in Genesis, Exodus, Leviticus, Numbers, Deuteronomy*. Trans. Aryeh Newman. Jerusalem: Dept. for Torah Education and Culture in the Diaspora of the World Zionist Organization, 1982.

Leibowitz, Yeshayahu. "Commandments." *Contemporary Jewish Religious Thought*, ed. Arthur Cohen and Paul Mender-Flohr. New York: The Free Press, 1987.

———. *Judaism, Human Values, and the Jewish State*. Ed. and trans. Elizer Goldman. Cambridge: Harvard University Press, 1992.

———. *The Faith of Maimonides*. Trans. John Glucker. New York: Adam Books, 1987.

Levinas, Emmanuel. *Alterity and Transcendence (European Perspectives)*. Trans. Michael B. Smith. New York: Columbia University Press, 1999.

———. *Basic Philosophical Writings*. Ed. A. Peperzak, S. Critchley, and R. Bernasconi. Bloomington: Indiana University Press, 1996.

———. *Beyond the Verse: Talmudic Readings and Lectures*. Trans. Gary D. Mole. Bloomington: Indiana University Press, 1994.

———. *Collected Philosophical Papers*. Trans. Alphonso Lingis. Dordrecht: Martinus Nijhoff, 1987.

———. *Difficult Freedom: Essays on Judaism*. Trans. Seán Hand. Baltimore: The Johns Hopkins University Press, 1990.

———. *Entre Nous: On Thinking-of-the-Other (European Perspectives)*. Trans. Michael B. Smith and Barbara Harshav. New York: Columbia University Press, 1998.

———. *Ethics and Infinity*. Trans. Richard Cohen. Pitsburgh: Duquesne University Press, 1985.

———. *Nine Talmudic Readings by Emmanuel Levinas*. Bloomington: Indiana University Press, 1990.

———. *The Levinas Reader*. Ed., Seán Hand. Cambridge: Blackwell Publishing, 1990.

———. *New Talmudic Readings*. Trans. Richard Cohen. Pittsburgh: Duquesne University Press, 1999.

———. *Of God Who Comes to Mind*. Trans. Bettina Bergo. Stanford: Stanford University Press, 1998.

———. *Outside the Subject*. Trans. Michael B. Smith. London: Atlone Pres, 1993.

———. *Quatre lectures talmudique*. Paris: Ed. de Minuit, 1968.

———. *Otherwise Than Being; Or, Beyond Essence*. Trans. Alphonso Lingis. The Hague: Martinus Nijhoff, 1987.

———. *Proper Names*. Trans. Michael B. Smith. Stanford: Stanford University Press, 1996.

———. *Time and the Other*. Trans. Richard Cohen. Duquesne: Pittsburgh University Press, 1987.

———. *Totality and Infinity: An Essay on Exteriority*. Trans. Alphonso Lingis. Pittsburgh: Duquesne University Press, 1969.

Lichtenstein, R. Aharon. "Does Jewish Tradition Recognize an Ethic Independent of Halakha." *Modern Jewish Ethics*. Ed. Marvin Fox. Cleveland: Ohio State University Press, 1975.

———. "Prayer in the Teachings of Rav Soloveitchik." *Yeshivat Har Etzion Virtual Beit Midrash*, Alon Shveut, Gush Israel, 1997. <http://www.vbm-torah. org/>.

———. "R. Joseph Soloveitchik." *Great Jewish Thinkers of the Twentieth Century*. Ed. S. Noveck. Philadelphia: Jewish Publication Society, 1963.

———. "Study." *Contemporary Jewish Religious Thought: Original Essays on Critical Concepts, Movements, and Beliefs*. Ed. Arthur Cohen and Paul Mendes-Flohr. New York: Charles Scribner's Sons, 1987.

Llewelyn, John. *Emmanuel Levinas: The Genealogy of Ethics*. New York: Routledge, 1995.

Maimonides, Moses. *Hakdamah l'Perush haMishnayot*. Trans. Zvi Lampel. New York: Judiaca Press, 1975.

———. *Mishneh Torah*. New York: Moznaim, 1997.

———. *Moreh Nevukim*. Trans Shlomo Pines. Chicago: University of Chicago Press, 1963.

———. *Sefer Ha-Mitzvoth*. Trans. Charles B. Chavel. London: Soncino Press, 1967.

Mandelstam, Osip. *The Noise of Time: The Prose of Osip Mandelstam*. Trans. Clarence Brown. San Francisco: North Point Press, 1986.

Marantz, Haim. "Bearing Witness: Morality and Religion in the Thought of Yeshayahu Leibowitz." *Judaism: A Quarterly Journal of Jewish Life and Thought* 46.1 (Winter 1997): 35–45.

Margalit, Avishai. "Prophets with Honor: Israelis Martin Buber and Yeshayahu Leibowitz." *The New York Review of Books* 40.18 (November 4, 1993): 66–71.

McGuinness, Brian. *Wittgenstein, A Life: Young Ludwig, 1889–1921*. Berkeley: University of California Press, 1988.

Medan, R. Yaakov. "The Mission of the Spies: on *Parashat Shelach*." *Yeshivat Har Etzion Virtual Beit Midrash*. Alon Shevut, Gush Etzion, Israel. June 18, 1998. <http://www.vbm-torah.org/>.

———. "Redemption in *Megillat Ruth*." *Yeshivat Har Etzion Virtual Beit Midrash*. Alon Shevut, Gush Etzion, Israel. May 29, 1998. <http://www. vbm-torah.org/>.

Meir, R. Asher. "Lag Ba-Omer and the 'Sefrirat ha'Omer Jew." *Yeshivat Har Etzion Virtual Beit Midrash*. Alon Shevut, Gush Etzion, Israel. May 13, 1998. <http://www.-torah.org/>.

Mendes-Flohr, Paul and Jehuda Reinharz. *The Jew in the Modern World: A Documentary History*. Oxford: Oxford University Press, 1995.

Meskin, Jacob. "Critique, Tradition, and the Religious Imagination: An Essay on Levinas' Talmudic Readings." *Judaism* (Winter 1998): 91–106.

———. "The Other in Levinas and Derrida: Society, Philosophy, and Judaism." *The Other in Jewish Thought and History*. Eds. Laurence J. Silberstein and Robert L. Cohen. New York: New York University Press, 1994.

Meyerowitz, Rael. *Transferring to America, Jewish Interpretations of American Dreams*. Albany: State University Press of New York, 1995.

Mirsky, Yehuda. Review of Yeshayahu Leibowitz, *Judaism, Human Values, and the Jewish State*. *The New Leader* 75.11 (September 7, 1992): 18–20.

————. "The Rhapsodist." *The New Republic* (April 19, 1999): 36–42.

Nadler, Alan. "Soloveitchik's Halakhic Man: Not a Mithnagged." *Modern Judaism* 13 (1993): 119–147.

————. Review of Yeshayahu Leibowitz, *Judaism, Human Values, and the Jewish State. Commentary* 94.5 (November 1992): 57–59.

————. *The Faith of the Mithnagdim: Rabbinic Responses to Hasidic Rapture.* Baltimore: The Johns Hopkins University Press, 1997.

Neusner, Jacob. *Judaism and Story: The Evidence of the Fathers According to Rabbi Nathan.* Chicago: University of Chicago Press, 1992.

————. *Judaism as Philosophy: The Method and Message of the Mishna.* Columbia: University of South Carolina Press, 1991.

————. *Invitation to Midrash: The Workings of Rabbinic Bible Interpretation.* San Francisco: Harper & Row, 1989.

Newman, Louis E. *Past Imperatives: Studies in the History and Theory of Jewish Ethics.* Albany: State University of New York Press, 1998.

Newton, Adam Zachary. "At Play in the Piels (and Hiphils) of the Lord; Or, the Home of the Free and the Grave(n): A Passover Story of Freedom and Command." *Narrative* 4.3 (October 1996): 265–277.

————. *Facing Black and Jew: Literature as Public Space in 20th Century America.* Cambridge: Cambridge University Press, 1999.

————. *Narrative Ethics.* Cambridge: Harvard University Press, 1995.

Novak, David. *The Election of Israel: The Idea of the Chosen People.* Cambridge: Cambridge University Press, 1995.

————. *The Image of the Non-Jew in Judaism: An Historical and Constructive Study of the Noahide Laws.* Lewiston, N.Y.: Edwin Mellen Press, 1983.

————. "Maimonides on Judaism and Other Religions." *The Samuel H. Goldenson Lecture at Hebrew Union College.* Cinncinati, 1997.

————. *Law and Theology in Judaism.* New York: Ktav, 1974.

Nye, Andrea. *Philosophy & Feminism: At the Border.* New York: Twayne Publishers, 1995.

Oppenheim, Michael. *Speaking/Writing of God: Jewish Philosophical Reflections on the Life with Others.* Albany: State University of New York Press, 1997.

Ouaknin, Marc-Alain. *The Burnt Book: Reading the Talmud.* Trans. Llewellyn Brown. Princeton: Princeton University Press, 1998.

Pagels, Elaine. *Adam, Eve, and the Serpent.* New York: Random House, 1988.

Peperzak, Aadrian. *Ethics as First Philosophy: The Significance of Emmanuel Levinas for Philosophy, Literature, and Religion.* New York: Routledge, 1995.

————. *To the Other: An Introduction to the Philosophy of Emmanuel Levinas.* West Lafayette, Indiana: Purdue University, 1993.

Poirié, François. *E. Lévinas—Qui êtes vous?* Lyon: La Manufacture, 1987.

Poirier, Richard. *Robert Frost: The Work of Knowing.* New York: Oxford University Press, 197.

Ravitsky, Aviezer. *Messianism, Zionism, and Jewish Religious Radicalism.* Trans. Michael Swirsky and Jonathan Chipman. Chicago: The University of Chicago Press, 1996.

Richardson, William, S. J. *Heidegger: Through Phenomenology to Thought.* The Hague: Nijhoff, 1974.

———. "Heidegger and God—and Professor Jonas." *Thought* 40 (Spring 1965): 13–40.

Robbins, Jill. *Altered Readings: Levinas and Literature*. Chicago: The University of Chicago Press, 1999.

———. *Prodigal Son/Elder Brother: Alterity and Interpretation in Augustine, Petrarch, Kafka, Levinas*. Chicago: The University of Chicago Press, 1991.

Rose, Gillian. *The Broken Middle: Out of Our Ancient Past*. Oxford: Blackwell Publishers, 1992.

———. "Jewish Ethics and the Crisis of Philosophy." *Jewish Philosophy and the Academy*. Ed. Emil Fackenheim and Raphael Jospe. London: Associated University Presses, 1996, 167–173.

———. *Judaism and Modernity: Philosophical Essays*. Oxford: Blackwell, 1992.

Rosenak, Michael. *Commandments and Concerns*. Philadelphia: Jewish Publication Society, 1987.

Rosenzweig, Franz and Martin Buber. *Scripture and Translation*. Trans. Lawrence Rosenwald with Everett Fox. Bloomington: Indiana University Press, 1994.

Roth, Joel. *The Halakhic Process: A Systemic Approach*. New York: Jewish Theological Seminary of America, 1986.

Rubenstein, Jeffrey L. *Talmudic Stories: Narrative Art, Composition, and Culture*. Baltimore: Johns Hopkins University Press, 1999.

Ruprecht, Jr., Louis A. "On Being Jewish or Greek in the Modern Moment." *Diaspora* 3.2 (1994): 199–220.

Sacks, Jonathan. *Crisis and Covenant: Jewish Thought after the Holocaust*. Manchester: Manchester University Press 1992.

Safranski, Rüdiger. *Martin Heidegger: Between Good and Evil*. Cambridge: Harvard University Press, 1997.

Sagi, Avi. "Contending with Modernity: Scripture in the Thought of Yeshayahu Leibowitz and Joseph Soloveitchik." *Journal of Religion* 77.3 (July 1997): 421–441.

———. "Halakhic Praxis and the Word of God: A Study of Two Models." *Journal of Jewish Thought and Philosophy* 1 (1992): 305–329.

———. *Yeshayhu Leibowitz: Ha Ish, Olamo, VaHaguto*. Jerusalem: Keter, 1995.

Samuelson, Norbert M. *Studies in Jewish Philosophy: Collected Essays of the Academy for Jewish Philosophy, 1980–1985*. Lanham, Md.: University Press of America, 1987.

Scarry, Elaine. *The Body in Pain: The Making and Unmaking of the World*. Oxford: Oxford University Press, 1986.

Schroeder, Brian. *Altared Ground: Levinas, History, and Violence*. New York: Routledge, 1996.

Schwartzschild, Steven. "An Agenda for Jewish Philosophy in the 1980's." *Studies in Jewish Philosophy: Collected Essays of the Academy for Jewish Philosophy, 1980–1985*. Ed. Norbert M. Samuelson Lanham, Md.: University Press of America, 1987.

———. "The Lure of Immanence—The Crisis in Contemporary Religious Thought." *Tradition* (Spring 1997): 70–99.

Sebald, W. G. *The Emigrants*. Trans. Michael Hulse. London: Harvill Press, 1996.

Seeskin, Kenneth. *Jewish Philosophy in a Secular Age*. Albany: State University Press of New York, 1990.

Shapiro, Susan. "*Écriture Judaïque*: Where are the Jews in Western Discourse." In *Displacements*. Ed. Angelika Bammer. Bloomington: Indiana University Press, 1994.

Silberstein, Laurence J. and Robert L. Cohen. *The Other in Jewish Thought and History*. New York: New York University Press, 1994.

Sokol, Moshe and Walter S. Wurzburger, eds. *Engaging Modernity: Rabbinic Leaders and the Challenge of the Twentieth Century*. New York: Jason Aronson, 1997.

Soloveitchik, R. Joseph B. "Catharsis." "Majesty and Humility," "Redemption, Prayer, Talmud Torah." *Tradition* 7.2 (Spring 1978): 7–73.

———. *Halakhic Man*. Trans. Lawrence Kaplan. Philadelphia: Jewish Publication Society, 1983.

———. *The Halakhic Mind: An Essay on Tradition and Modern Thought*. New York: Seth Press, 1986.

———. *The Lonely Man of Faith*. New York: Doubleday, 1965.

———. *Shiurei HaRav: A Conspectus of the Public Lectures of Rabbi Joseph B. Soloveitchik*. Hoboken, N.J.: Ktav, 1994.

Sommer, Doris. "About-Face: The Talker Turns." *boundary 2* 23.1 (1996): 91:134.

Spero, Shubert and Yitzchak Pessin, eds. *Religious Zionism*. Jerusalem: World Zionist Organization, 1989.

Spiegel, Shalom. *The Last Trial*. New York: Pantheon, 1967.

Steinsalz, Adin. *Reference Guide to the Talmud, Steinsalz Edition*. New York: Random House, 1989.

Stern, David. *Parables in Midrash: Narrative and Exegesis in Rabbinic Literature*. Cambridge: Harvard University Press, 1991.

———. "Midrash and the Language of Exegesis." In *Midrash and Literature*. Ed. Geoffrey Hartman and Sanford Budick. New Haven: Yale University Press, 1986.

Sternell, Ze'ev. *The Founding Myths of Israel: Nationalism, Socialism and the Making of the Jewish State*. Trans. David Maisel. Princeton: Princeton University Press, 1996.

Stone, Ira F. *Reading Levinas/Reading Talmud: An Introduction*. Philadelphia: Jewish Publications Society, 1998.

Strauss, Leo. *Natural Right and History*. Chicago: University of Chicago Press, 1971.

Taylor, Charles. *Sources of the Self: The Making of the Modern Identity*. Cambridge: Harvard University Press, 1989.

Urbach, Ephraim. *The Halakhah: Its Sources and Development*. Trans. Raphael Posner. Israel: Massada (Yad le-Talmud), 1986.

———. *The Sages, their Concepts and Beliefs*. Trans. Israel Abrahams. Jerusalem: Magnes Press, Hebrew University, 1979.

———. *The Halakhah: Its Sources and Development*. Trans. Raphael Posner. Jerusalem: Yad le-Talmud, 1986.

Venclova, Tomas. Aleksander Wat: *Life and Art of an Iconoclast*. New Haven: Yale University Press, 1996.

Walzer, Michael, Menachem Lorberbauer, and Noam J. Zohar. *The Jewish Political Tradition: Vol. 1: Authority.* New Haven: Yale University Press, 2000.

Wat, Aleksandr. *My Century: The Odyssey of a Polish Intellectual.* Trans. Richard Lourie. Berkeley: University of California Press, 1988.

Waxman, Chaim. *Israel as a Religious Reality.* Northvale, N.J.: Jason Aronson, 1994.

Wegner, Judith. *Chattel or Person? The Status of Women in the Mishnah.* New York: Oxford University Press, 1988.

Wieseltier, Leon. *Kaddish.* New York: Alfred A. Knopf, 1998.

———. Afterword. *Yosl Rakover Talks to God.* By Zvi Kolitz. Trans. Carol Brown Janeway. New York: Pantheon Books, 1999.

Wright, Tamra. *The Twilight of Jewish Philosophy: Emmanuel Levinas' Ethical Hermeneutics.* Singapore: Harwood Academic Publishers, 1999.

Yehoshua, A. B. *Between Right and Right.* Trans. Arnold Schwartz. Garden City: Doubleday and Co., 1981.

Yerushalmi, Yosef Hayim. *Haggadah and History.* Philadelphia: Jewish Publication Society, 1976.

———. *Zakhor: Jewish History and Jewish Memory.* New York: Schocken Books, 1989.

Yovel, Yirmiyahu. *Dark Riddle: Hegel, Nietzsche, and the Jews.* University Park: Penn State University Press, 1998.

Zagajewski, Adam. *Tremors: Selected Poems.* Trans. Renata Gorczynski. New York: Farrar Straus Giroux, 1985.

Zeitlin, Hillel. "The Concept of Property and Acquisition in the Holy Scriptures." *Sifran Shel Tzadikkim.* Jerusalem: Mossad HaRav Kook, 1973.

Zornberg, Avivah Gottleib. *The Beginning of Desire: Reflections on Genesis.* New York: Doubleday, 1995.

GENERAL INDEX

SCRIPTUAL INDEX